Book of Kielce.
History of the Community of Kielce.
From Its Founding Until Its Destruction

(Kielce, Poland)

Translation of
Sefer Kielce. Toldot Kehilat Kielce. Miyom Hivasdah V'ad Churbanah

Original Book Edited by: Pinchas Cytron

Originally published in Tel Aviv 1957

A Publication of JewishGen
Edmond J. Safra Plaza, 36 Battery Place, New York, NY 10280
646.494.2972 | info@JewishGen.org | www.jewishgen.org

©JewishGen 2024. All Rights Reserved.
JewishGen is the Genealogical Research Division of the
Museum of Jewish Heritage – A Living Memorial to the Holocaust

Book of Kielce. History of the Community of Kielce. From Its Founding Until Its Destruction

Translation of *Sefer Kielce. Toldot Kehilat Kielce. Miyom Hivasdah V'ad Churbanah*

Copyright © 2024 by JewishGen. All rights reserved.
First Printing: August 2024, Av, 5784
Editor of Original Yizkor Book: Pinchas Cytron
Project Coordinator: Warren Blatt
Cover Design: Irv Osterer
Layout: Jonathan Wind
Name Indexing: Stefanie Holzman

This book may not be reproduced, in whole or in part, including illustrations in any form (beyond that copying permitted by Sections 107 and 108 of the U.S. Copyright Law and except by reviewers for public press), without written permission from the publisher.

JewishGen Press is not responsible for inaccuracies or omissions in the original work and makes no representations regarding the accuracy of this translation. Digital images of the original book's contents can be seen online at the New York Public Library website or the Yiddish Book Center website.

Library of Congress Control Number (LCCN): 2024942787

ISBN: 978-1-962054-04-1 (hard cover: 350 pages, alk. paper)

About JewishGen.org

JewishGen, is a Genealogical Research Division of the Museum of Jewish Heritage - A Living Memorial to the Holocaust, serves as the global home for Jewish genealogy.

Featuring unparalleled access to 30+ million records, it offers unique search tools, along with opportunities for researchers to connect with others who share similar interests. Award winning resources such as the Family Finder, Discussion Groups, and ViewMate, are relied upon by thousands each day.

In addition, JewishGen's extensive informational, educational and historical offerings, such as the Jewish Communities Database, Yizkor Book translations, InfoFiles, Family Tree of the Jewish People, and KehilaLinks, provide critical insights, first-hand accounts, and context about Jewish communal and familial life throughout the world.

Offered as a free resource, JewishGen.org has facilitated thousands of family connections and success stories, and is currently engaged in an intensive expansion effort that will bring many more records, tools, and resources to its collections.

Please visit https://www.jewishgen.org/ to learn more.

Vice President for JewishGen: Avraham Groll

About the JewishGen Yizkor Book Project

Yizkor Books (Memorial Books) were traditionally written to memorialize the names of departed family and martyrs during holiday services in the synagogue (a practice that still exists in many synagogues today).

Over the centuries, as a result of countless persecutions and horrific atrocities committed against the Jews, Yizkor Books (Sefer Zikaron in Hebrew) were expanded to include more historical information, such as biographical sketches of famous personalities and descriptions of daily town life.

Following the Holocaust, the idea of remembrance and learning took on an urgent and crucial importance. Survivors of the Holocaust sought out other surviving residents of their former towns to memorialize and document the names and way of life of those who were ruthlessly murdered by the Nazis. These remembrances were documented in Yizkor Books, hundreds of which were published in the first decades after the Holocaust.

Most of these books were published privately, or through *Landsmanshaftn* (social organizations comprised of members originating from the same European town or region) that still existed, and were often distributed free of charge. The languages used to document these crucial histories and links to our past were mostly Yiddish and Hebrew. JewishGen has undertaken the sacred responsibility of translating these books into English so that the culture and way of life of these communities will be preserved and transmitted to future generations.

In 1986, a group of farsighted JewishGenners started a project to pool their efforts together in groups based upon their ancestors' towns and donate funds to translate the Yizkor books of their ancestral towns into English. As the translated material became available, it was made accessible for free at https://www.JewishGen.org/Yizkor . Hardcover copies can be purchased by visiting https://www.jewishgen.org/Yizkor/ybip.html (see below).

It is our hope that the translation of these books into English (and other languages) will assist the countless Jewish family researchers who are so desperately seeking to forge a connection with their heritage.

Director of JewishGen Yizkor Book Project: Lance Ackerfeld

About JewishGen Press

JewishGen Press (formerly the Yizkor Books-in-Print Project) is the publishing division of JewishGen.org, and provides a venue for the publication of non-fiction books pertaining to Jewish genealogy, history, culture, and heritage.

In addition to the Yizkor Book category, publications in the Other Non-Fiction category include Shoah memoirs and research, genealogical research, collections of genealogical and historical materials, biographies, diaries and letters, studies of Jewish experience and cultural life in the past, academic theses, and other books of interest to the Jewish community.

Please visit https://www.jewishgen.org/Yizkor/ybip.html to learn more.

Director of JewishGen Press: Joel Alpert
Managing Editor - Jessica Feinstein
Publications Manager - Susan Rosin

Notes to the Reader

The images in the original book were reproduced from photographs from the time of the first edition. These reproductions were already of poor quality, being pre-war and at least 30 or more years old. As a result, the images in the book are the best achievable.

A reader can view the original scans of the book on the websites listed below.

The original book can be seen online at the Yiddish Book Center website:

https://www.yiddishbookcenter.org/collections/yizkor-books/yzk-nybc314204/sefer-kelts-toldot-kehilat-kelts-mi-yom-hivasdah-ve-ad

OR

at the New York Public Library Digital Collections website:

https://digitalcollections.nypl.org/items/92a45c30-79c4-0133-79df-00505686d14e

To obtain a list of Shoah victims from **Kielce, Poland,** the reader should access the Yad Vashem web site listed below; one can also search for specific family names using family name option. These lists are continually updated by Yad Vashem, so it is worthwhile to periodically search them.

There is more valuable information (including the Pages of Testimony, etc.) available on this website: https://yvng.yadvashem.org/

A list of all books available from JewishGen Press along with prices is available at: https://www.jewishgen.org/Yizkor/ybip.html

Additional resources for Kielce are:

https://www.kielce.org.il/
https://kieltzer.org/

Cover Photo Credits

Cover Design by: **Irv Osterer**

Front Cover:
The looted Kielce synagogue — [Page 1]
Rabbi Motele Twerski z"l – [Page 172]

Back Cover:
Left Column – from top:
    The Gaon Rabbi Mosze Nachum Jerusalimski — [Page 154]
    Kielce Jewish Community seal (Pieczec_Kielce)— http://swietokrzyskisztetl.pl/asp/pl_licznik.asp
    The Dramatic Circle of "HaZamir" — [Page 62]

Right Column:
    Memorial plaque at the house on Planty 7 in Kielce (Polish - Yiddish - English) where in 1946, forty two Jews were murdered in a pogrom – Wikimedia photo: https://commons.wikimedia.org/

Geopolitical Information

Map of Poland showing the location of **Kielce**

Kielce Geopolitical Information

Kielce, Poland is located at 50°50' N 20°40' E and 99 miles South of Warszawa

	Town	District	Province	Country
Before WWI (c. 1900):	Kielce	Kielce	Kielce	Russian Empire
Between the wars (c. 1930):	Kielce	Kielce	Kielce	Poland
After WWII (c. 1950):	Kielce			Poland
Today (c. 2000):	Kielce			Poland

Alternate Names for the Town:

Kielce [Pol], Keltz [Yid], Kel'tse [Rus], Kelts, Kilts, Kiltz, Kel'tsy

Nearby Jewish Communities:

Daleszyce 6 miles E
Krajno 9 miles ENE
Pierzchnica 10 miles SSE
Piotrkowice 12 miles S
Chęciny 12 miles SW
Sobków 13 miles SW
Chmielnik 14 miles SSE
Bodzentyn 15 miles ENE
Małogoszcz 17 miles W
Suchedniów 18 miles NNE
Łagów 19 miles E
Nowa Słupia 19 miles E
Raków 20 miles ESE
Łopuszno 20 miles WNW
Jędrzejów 21 miles SW
Pińczów 22 miles SSW
Szydłów 22 miles SE
Skarżysko-Kamienna 22 miles NNE
Wąchock 22 miles NE
Wierzbnik 24 miles NE
Waśniów 24 miles E
Busko-Zdrój 25 miles S
Radoszyce 26 miles NW
Kurozwęki 26 miles SE
Końskie 28 miles NNW
Iwaniska 28 miles ESE
Kunów 28 miles ENE
Bogoria 29 miles ESE
Szydłowiec 29 miles NNE
Wodzisław 29 miles SW
Staszów 29 miles SE
Stopnica 30 miles SSE

Jewish Population: 6,173 (in 1897), 18,083 (in 1931)

Table of Contents

Article	Page
Forward	2
Opening Remarks	5
Introduction	7
The Beginning of Jewish Kielce	9
The Development of the Kielce Community	13
The Economic Life of the Jews of Kielce	17
Relations Between the Jews and the Poles	39
Intellectual, Cultural and Social Life	49
Educational and other Learning Institutions	62
Social Welfare and Charitable Institutions	82
Political Parties, Movements and Organizations	92
Economic and Social Organizations	130
Rabbis, Religious Leaders and Scholars	144
Parnassim, Benefactors and Public Figures	177
Leaders of the Kielce Community	191
Authors and Scientists	203
Folk Artists	211
Portraits and Characters	215
The Story of the Ghetto and Liquidation	223
The Pogrom in 1946	235
Closing Words	239
Testimony of Mr. Jechiel Alpert	240
Kielce, from the Sketches of M. Tzanin (in Yiddish)	250
The Day of Mourning in 5666 [1906]	253
The Diary of Rabbi Jeruzalimski (in Yiddish)	254
Kielcer Organizations in Israel and the Diaspora	267
Appendix. A History of the "Poalei Tzion" Movement (Left)	276
Memorial to Natives of Kielce who Fell Defending the Land and the State	280
Index of Names	282
Name Index - English Edition	327
Appendix - Gershon Iskowitz	337

Book of Kielce. History of the Community of Kielce. From Its Founding Until Its Destruction (Kielce, Poland)

50°50' / 20°40'

Translation of *Sefer Kielce. Toldot Kehilat Kielce. Miyom Hivsuduh V'ad Churbanah*

Edited by: Pinchas Cytron

Published in Tel Aviv, 1957

Acknowledgments

Project Coordinator

Warren Blatt

Our sincere appreciation to Ron Peled, of the Kielce Landmanshaft in Israel, for permission to put this material on the JewishGen web site.

(Note the Kielce Landsmanshaft maintains a web site at: http://www.kielce.org.il/

This is a translation from: *Sefer Kielce. Toldot Kehilat Kielce. Miyom Hivsuduh V'ad Churbanah* (Book of Kielce. History of the Community of Kielce. From Its Founding Until Its Destruction) Edited by: Pinchas Cytron, published in Tel Aviv, 1957

Note: The original book can be seen online at the NY Public Library site: Kielce

---

This material is made available by JewishGen, Inc. and the Yizkor Book Project for the purpose of fulfilling our mission of disseminating information about the Holocaust and destroyed Jewish communities. This material may not be copied, sold or bartered without JewishGen, Inc.'s permission. Rights may be reserved by the copyright holder.

JewishGen, Inc. makes no representations regarding the accuracy of the translation. The reader may wish to refer to the original material for verification. JewishGen is not responsible for inaccuracies or omissions in the original work and cannot rewrite or edit the text to correct inaccuracies and/or omissions. Our mission is to produce a translation of the original work and we cannot verify the accuracy of statements or alter facts cited.

Forward

[Page-1]

Pinchas Cytron

Sefer Kielce

The history of the community of Kielce from its foundation to its destruction

Translated by Judy Montel

Edited by Warren Blatt

בית־הכנסת השדוד

The looted synagogue

Published by the Organization of Immigrants from Kielce in Israel / Tel-Aviv / 5717 [1957]

[Page-2]

All rights reserved
for the Organization of Immigrants from Kielce in Israel
Tel-Aviv P.O. Box 891

Copyright by
Irgun Olei Kieltz in Israel
Tel-Aviv P.O. Box 891

Printed by "Shem" Printers, Inc., Jaffa, 34 Street, No. 5, Tel. 82808

[Page-3]

פנחס ציטרון

Pinchas Cytron

[Page-5]

In memoriam:

My son Benjamin, Master of Mathematics, active in public affairs and Zionist.
My daughter Bluma Manela, certified in law and teacher.
My daughter Malka Cytron, paint and photography artist, and my granddaughter Guta Manela,
who were plucked in their youth and their ashes were scattered on the fields of Treblinka.
May this book serve as a memorial to their memory and the memory of all of my relatives and family
members, who perished along with all of the holy community of Kielce, may God avenge their blood.

P. C.

My thanks are given here
To the Committee of the Organization of Immigrants from Kielce in Israel, which published this book and the wise men Elazar Arten, Avraham Goldrat and Avraham Kirszenbaum, for the editing and phrasing of the book, improving its style and proof reading it.

P. C.

The chapters on the "Shomer Hatza'ir", "Po'alej Tzion" and the Revisionists were written by R. Nechustaj, A. Kirszenbaum and J. Kopf. The chapters about the banks and the Kielce organizations are by El. Arten.

[Page-7]

Opening Remarks

"The book and the sword, entwined, descended from the heavens".
(The Books of Ekev)

When the sword descended from the sky upon the six million Jews of Europe, the book did not descend with it. Six million Jews; Men, women and children were destroyed, murdered and slaughtered by the German tyrant and his assistants in cold blood and fully premeditated, exactly how and in what manners to carry out the liquidation in towns and villages, in ghettos and concentration camps, in gas chambers at Auschwitz, Treblinka and Maidanek, in all sorts of cruel and unusual deaths, the sword descended in the hands of devils upon the heads of the Jews in all of the holy congregations and they were killed, they and their wives, their sons and daughters and all that they had; And the defiled murderers not only killed and destroyed, but also pulled up from the root and erased from the face of the earth the memory of these congregations, their institutions and buildings, their houses of worship and study and also their cemeteries. Cemeteries were known as "Batei Olam" – Eternal Homes; The nation was sure that even if all of the private and public buildings in the communities were laid waste, the cemeteries would remain with their tombstones, serving as an eternal memorial for the communities that existed, flourished and blossomed for centuries.

However this calculation was in error – the tyrants poured their wrath also over the trees and the stones, and destroyed, together with the local populace – mainly in Poland – also the gravestones and the "tents" of the cemeteries and plowed up their soil, so that no name, remnant or memory would be left of the congregations of Israel after the death of all of the live Jews.

The Jews, who were murdered in the death camps, did not receive a Jewish burial and their names and memories were never engraved on a stone or a marker.

These martyrs were actually in good company. The father of prophets, [Moses] also "no one knew the place of his burial" and the prophet and messenger who rode the fiery whirlwind and who was separated from his student by horses of fire "went up to heaven in a storm", he too did not receive a Jewish burial. Our fathers and mothers, our brothers and sisters and all of hour holy relatives, fiery ovens separated them from life itself, and they went up to heaven in a holy and pure storm, even though they did not receive a Jewish burial.

Although, God agrees to the words of Moses, who wrote them himself, in tears "and no one knew the place of his burial" (although he carried the bones of Joseph around with him for forty years so that they could be buried in the land of Israel; he did not worry about his own bones and did not command that they be brought for burial in Israel), but to "erase me from your book" he did not agree with him.

The awakening that descended, as if from the heavens upon the survivors and refugees to establish memorials and testimonials to their communities by writing their histories in a book is therefore understandable.

This mission, to memorialize our community in a book, was taken on by the committee of the Organization of Immigrants from Kielce in Israel.

Our friend Mr. Pinchas Cytron, who had been a teacher and principal of a school in Kielce for many years until his immigration to Israel, as well as a member of the editorial board of the Kielcer weekly "Kielcer News" and one of the leaders of the Zionist and Mizrachi movements in our city, invested much labor and work collecting all of the details of the history of the Kielce community from the time of its founding up to its destruction and their transcription in the book.

This book, in which we have made several small additions and changes in style (in order not to alter the character imbued in it by the author) and to which we have added photographs and pictures from the public life and figures in our city, isn't perfect. We know this, yet we found it correct not to delay its printing for this reason, and thus delay this memorial to our community; For it has been already fifteen years since the destruction of the community, and we were burdened with the feeling that this time, it is up to finish the task, and if not now, when.

Tel Aviv, Chanuka, 5717 [1956]

Elazar Arten
(Chairman, Organization of Immigrants From Kielce in Israel)

[Page-9]

Introduction

Polish Jewry served as the cream and breadbasket of the entire people of Israel – the main artery of the nation. A tree whose roots put out branches in all of the Diasporas. This section of the nation was notable in its quantity and its quality. More than three million souls were numbered among the Jewish population of Poland. The inhabited cities and villages and made their mark everywhere both in their manner of living and with their economic endeavors. And because their habitations were concentrated and not spread out in small groups, they preserved the pure spirit of the nation and were not given to foreign influences. Trends of assimilation did not reach great proportions in Poland, as they did in other countries, especially the countries of the West.

Polish Jewry has a long history, covering centuries and even reaching a millenium. It contained ancient communities who counted their existence from the first kings of Poland. As time passed, new communities sprouted and grew in various places in the state. The community of Kielce is numbered among one of the youngest of these, whose existence began only about eighty years ago. And whoever had the opportunity to be in Kielce immediately recognized that the early morning dew still sparkled upon its markets and streets, its parks and buildings. But during the brief years of its existence, the Kielce community developed very rapidly, also spiritually, and also economically. In all areas of life, the great energies of the community were expressed, as well as its material and emotional strengths.

Every community in Israel was a cell in the national body tissue. In its procedures and institutions, it represented in miniature, the people of Israel in their entirety, but the Kielce community stood out especially among the other communities. Fresh energies pumped through it, and it grew and flourished, spread its wings wide, sent out roots in the ground and broadcast glory in every direction. The fruit that the Kielce community brought forth was a glorious and praiseworthy fruit. At its heart beautiful and encouraging orchards flourished; scholars, pious worthies, intellectuals and authors, merchants and industrialists, whose products found their way throughout Poland and Russia. Among them were notable national activists who did much to further the national renewal, whose names were known beyond the boundaries of their community. Wealthy benefactors dwelt there as well, who did much to improve the community: They established social welfare and charitable institutions and decorated it with public buildings.

The Kielce community excelled in its Zionist activities and its contribution to the national funds. Many of the youths of Kielce moved out and went to the land of Israel to participate in its reconstruction. Kielce was a training ground for hundreds of pioneers who found sustenance and support in the local community. The Jews of Kielce treated them fondly , those young people who left their parents' home, with all of their comforts, in order to train their muscles with hard labor and acclimate themselves to difficult living conditions, which awaited them as pioneers of the nation, who had taken on the burden of paving and straightening the path to the eventual rebirth of the nation in its homeland.

After the terrible Holocaust which came upon the European Diaspora, a Holocaust that had no precedent in the history of our people, we, the remnants of Polish Jewry, have a sense of being orphans; We have been orphaned of all those souls who were close to our hearts and souls. Together with the ancient communities of Israel, also the young community of Kielce was destroyed. Its Jewish inhabitants were liquidated in the gas chambers of Treblinka and Auschwitz. The city, in which we lived and worked, was emptied of its Jews. Its splendid synagogue stands orphaned, looted and defiled. The scrolls of the Torah, in which god-fearing scribes wrote each letter in holiness and purity were devoured by fire, and those which were saved from burning were trodden down as lining for Polish cobblers to line their shoes and their boots. Also in our cemetery, our enemies and their impure hands destroyed the wall; broke the tombstones used them to pave the sidewalks. Their cattle were sent to graze upon the graves that a Jew would have been careful of stepping upon out of respect for the dead. For our enemies – it was their highest desire, to erase every trace of Jewish settlement in this place.

Thus a Jewish community was erased from the face of the earth. Only a few, shadows, saved from the fire, who managed to escape while there was still time and chose to live a nomadic life in the Russian steppes, or those who retained strength to survive stubborn hunger, torture and the deprivations of the Nazi hell and the back breaking labor of the work camps, they constitute the remnant of the decorated community of Kielce.

With the strokes of sorrow and pain at the great destruction that came in our time upon large portions of the Jewish nation, our eyes tear in particular over the destruction of the community of Kielce, our childhood cradle and original home. We decided, therefore, to erect a monument to this community, in a memorial book of our people. It is a community worthy of being counted among the Jewish communities of Europe, which were laid waste in the Holocaust of 1940-1945.

The description of this community – its people, institutions and endeavors – is the goal of this book. This composition will be a partial relief for a sorrow that knows no limit, the sorrow of losing sons, relatives and friends, and above all, the sorrow at the loss of an entire community, of which we were an inseparable part, flesh and blood.

"In order that the last generation may know, children will be born, rise up and tell their sons."

[Page-11]

The Beginning of Jewish Kielce

Jewish settlement in Kielce was forbidden up until the second Polish insurrection, that is, 1863. Even during times that towns neighboring Kielce, such as Pinczow, Chmielnik and Checiny had glorious Jewish communities, Kielce was empty of Jews. Polish history mentions the fact that in 1535 King Sigmund I granted the inhabitants of Kielce a privilege, according to which they had permission to close the gates of the city to Jews. Afterwards, in 1761, the Bishop of Krakow renewed the ban, already in existence, of Jews settling in the town. In 1832, after the first Polish uprising, Jews petitioned the authorities to cancel the centuries-old ban of their living in Kielce. Their petitions bore fruit and they were promised habitation rights. The Jews of the area who lived in nearby villages began to settle in Kielce. However, in 1847 the Jews were expelled from the town, the petitions of the priesthood bore fruit and the earlier ban was reinstated.

In 1852, 101 Jews lived in Kielce and 3,639 Christians. These Jews were contractors of the Russian army and soldiers of Czar Nicolas I. This small number of Jews did not yet constitute an organized community; the births were registered in the birth registers of the community of Checiny, the dead were buried in the Checiny cemetery, and in general, in all religious matters, like marriage and divorce they were dependent upon the Checiny community, the village nearest to Kielce.

Kielce was obviously a city holy to the Poles. The Bishop had his seat there; many large churches towered over the north, west and east of the city, among them the cathedral with its beautiful buildings and towers. Close to the city limits, in Kadtzovka, a monastery was built up on a hill among the trees of the forest. Across from the cathedral was a seminary for the training of priests. In general, within its walls the city of Kielce contained a concentration of Catholic priesthood, whence it disseminated Catholic doctrine to the nobles of the area as well as the peasants. However, together with the love of Christianity, it also spread hatred of Jews, who had crucified their savior, and initiated despicable libels against the Jews. Anti-Semitism found deep roots in the hearts of the Poles who lived in Kielce and the area. Even later, when the Jews began settling in Kielce, hatred of them did not stop.

After the Polish insurrection of 1863 and after the liberation of the serfs of the estate owners, Jews were allowed to settle in Kielce. Earlier, Kielce had been a small town. Were it not for the splendid churches towering over the landscape and a few shops, whose owners were Germans, and several wine-drinking establishments, which lent it the flavor of a city, it could have been considered a large village. Its low houses with their thatched or shingled roofs, the many fruit orchards around the shacks, the fields of grain that stretched from the houses at the edge of the city to the nearby forests, the wells which were primitively dug in every yard, gave the place the air of a village.

When the Jews began settling in Kielce, its former atmosphere changed. Gradually, the trees, fruit trees and ornamental trees, disappeared, and in their place two and three story stone houses were built, in which shops were opened with display windows. The Jews came and saw the Kielce was surrounded by mountains which were as virgin soil, untouched by human hands, and immediately began to extract the treasures hidden in their midst; They set up great kilns for burning the limestone into whitewash, for firing bricks. The saw the thick forests that surrounded the city and established sawmills. Next to the forests several tanneries were set up to work leather. Industry developed, commerce developed, the population grew and Kielce, from a small town, wholly immersed in the holy waters of Catholicism, became a secular city, a commercial and industrial city, a central city for the whole district, which supplied not just the religious needs of the entire area, but also its daily needs, with textiles, leathers, colonial goods and drink.

Its wares reached places far away and out side of the state. The city grew wealthy, the Jews were the employers and the Polish residents were the employees. The concepts of exploiters and exploited were not known in those days at that place.

The Market Square in Kielce

The Jews who settled in Kielce remembered the days when they were outsiders in this city. Even sleeping there for one night was forbidden to them. During the great fairs, Jews flocked from the neighboring villages to sell their produce and wares. However, towards evening they were forced to gather their products, pack them up and take them out of the city to sleep in a nearby village located on the other side of the city. The next morning they returned to the city limits and again dealt with buying and selling until the fair was over and the nobles of the area returned to their estates. Their Polish neighbors regarded the Jews as lepers who contaminated the place with one night's sleep. The Polish author Adolph Dugszinski recounts in his memoirs how as a student at the Kielce Lyceum in the 1850s he saw no Jews in the entire city save two Jews: One called "Wilk" and another called "Lis", they would come to the Lyceum students to buy used clothing and books from them. They were also not permanent residents of the city at the time, but were nomadic tinkers and peddlers whose travels in search of a livelihood led them to step upon the "holy" soil of Kielce as well where they negotiated with the Lyceum students, sons of nobles who needed pocket money for their games and entertainments. They sold the clothing off their backs and their schoolbooks. The same two Jews can be found later on in the city when they were older and respected homeowners. They raised large families, children and grandchildren, some of them merchants, some artisans, some pious Hassidim, Torah scholars, and in later days, also Zionists.

Hanna Kochen – who died at age 106 – one of the first to settle in Kielce

After the second Polish uprising in 1863 conditions changed in the land of "Polin"; the limited local powers the Poles had had until then was taken away entirely; The local authorities also passed into the hands of the Russians. The estates of the nobles, who had participated in the uprising, were confiscated and handed over to Russian Generals and these leased them to Jews. From this time, the Jews began to settle in Kielce without hindrance. And after a time the Jewish community was organized.

In 1868 the names of Jewish births began to be registered in the birth lists in Kielce. That year fifteen births were registered, and they were:

Name	Birth Date	Father's Name	Father's Occupation	Mother's Name	Mother's Maiden
Kalman Bunem Moszkowski	January 16, 1868	Izrael	merchant	Szarceh	Grynbaum
Abram Mosze Goldberg	February 8, 1868	Michl	owner of a tavern	Pesil	Marmont
Josef Lis	February 16, 1868	Anszel	merchant	Hanna	Kwekzylber
Szejndl-Ita Lapa	April 7, 1868	Hersz	tailor	Perel	Pomeranc
Hynda Goldszajder	April 17, 1868	Abram Dawid	glazier	Sora	Kuperberg

Mosze Haim Kaufman	May 3, 1868	Awraham-Icak	tailor	Ester	Haus.
Josef–Lajb Zylbersztajn	15 June 1868	Jakob	butcher	Frajda	Blacharowicz
Bajla Giser	August 1, 1868	Dawid	clerk	Duba Rajzel	Dziadek
Izrael Cwajgel	September 11, 1868	Nachum	glazier	Frajdl	Zilberszac
Szlomo Wajs	September 12, 1868	Mosze	merchant	Malka	Szapiro
Awigdor Mendl Klajnsztajn	September 18, 1868	Josef	teacher (melamed)	Myrjam	Wajsbrot
Jakob-Lewek Moszenberg	October 7, 1868	Josef	teacher (melamed)	Rywka	Berkowicz
Hersz Wasserman	October 21, 1868	Icak	bartender	Chawa	Igelberg
Frajda Hajt	November 9, 1868	Hersz	merchant	Fajga	Zalcer
Hinda-Fajga Moszkowski	December 7, 1868	Josef	merchant	Anna	Klajnsztajn

The same year the Kielce Jewish cemetery opened. On the tombstones there are no engravings from before the year 5630[1870]

Izrael Cwajgel, one of the first Jews to be born in Kielce.

The Development of the Kielce Community

The community of Kielce did not come into being in one day. Gradually, Jews began settling there. After the Polish revolt [of the early 1860s] against the mighty Russian Czar and the failure of that revolt, Poland was overrun with Russian military forces. In every city and town a permanent force of the Russian army was stationed in the barracks. Two infantry battalions established themselves in Kielce as well. Along with the Russian army came Jewish contractors, who provided the army with its supplies and were also construction entrepreneurs, who built their barracks and military hospitals for them, and they too settled in Kielce.

After them came the Jews with special privileges, such as soldiers of Czar Nicolai I who had franchises for selling salt, kerosene, cigarettes, and similar good, and they too joined the pioneers, and thus the nucleus of a Jewish community was created in Kielce.

Jews from the surrounding villages began to gather around the early settlers, and the Jewish settlement in Kielce continued to grow.

The number of Jews in the city grew markedly after the Warsaw-Vienna railway line was built. Jews participated in the endeavor as labor contractors and suppliers of construction materials and wealthy people appeared who built themselves beautiful homes in the city.

The authorities also transferred their offices to the city. Kielce became the district and provincial capital [in 1867]. The district governor and minister of the province settled there with all of their clerks and secretaries. A branch of the national bank opened in the city. The district court made Kielce its seat. The city was full of officials, and for their children, who needed schools; two Gymnasia (high schools) were opened for boys and for girls. The Jews played an important role here; they were the construction contractors, the suppliers of furniture to government offices.

Energetic Jews were attracted to this city, for they saw it was doing well, and that there was a wide field for their activities there. If a fire broke out in a neighboring village and its homes went up in flames, then instead of rebuilding the ruins where they stood, the townsfolk moved to Kielce. In Checiny a fire broke out in 1905, and most of the homes of the Jews became mountains of ash. The crowds of Jews with their wives and children flocked to Kielce and remained there permanently. The Kielce community expanded at the expense of the Checiny community. The inhabitants of Kielce had a saying: "Kielce was built on the ruins of Checiny."

The community of Kielce became wealthy physically and spiritually. People of intellect arrived along with people of economic prowess: teachers, educators and other holy vessels.

Members of the free professions, doctors, lawyers, clerks and accountants also found many opportunities for advancement in Kielce. Bankers also appeared in this continually growing city. Large banks opened branches in Kielce. Their managers were mainly Jewish, for the banks' customers were Jewish merchants and industrialists. The Jewish community developed rapidly alongside the development of the industry and commerce in the city, whose primary movers were Jews. As the community grew, it established charity organizations, educational institutions, and economic institutions as was customary in well-regulated communities of old.

The time came when the Jewish population became varied: Hassidim, followers of the enlightenment and educated people, artisans and simple laborers made up the assembly.

The lack of a central synagogue in which this variegated population could gather in prayer was sorely felt. And then, such a benefactor was found in the community, Rabbi Mosze Fefer, a man of great donations; the community's affairs were close to his heart and he built a splendid synagogue, built in the accepted synagogue style; a house of study in one wing and in the other a large hall for the charitable institution "Achi'ezer". On the upper floor was the women's section, supported by pillars. A magnificent Holy Ark stood at the eastern wall, which was approached by marble steps and was decorated with a gilded Torah crown. At its side was a loft for the singing choir. The raised "Bima" in the middle of the synagogue, also approached by steps, was a work of art. The walls and ceiling of it painted by an artist-painter; figures of the zodiac, the Seven Species of Fruit with which the Land of Israel was blessed, holy animals and verses selected from the prophets adorned the walls and the ceiling. The stained-glass windows that stretched from floor to ceiling gave all those who arrived to pray an uplifted spirit and a holy feeling would conquer their being and direct their hearts towards the heavens.

A cantor known for his talent and ability to conduct a choir was invited to this synagogue. His prayers and tunes attracted great numbers of worshippers to the synagogue. The synagogue would be full to the brim, people standing crowded together without feeling pressed, all eyes raised to the heavens, instilled with lofty feelings, the feeling of spiritual delight, which attended them at the sound of the melodies of the cantor accompanied by his choir. This synagogue served not only as a place of prayer, but also for public gatherings, in this large building the words of the rabbi, the lecturer and great speakers of the time were heard.

Such a splendid community needed a worthy rabbi to serve it. After the death of its first rabbi, Rabbi Tuwia Gutman HaKohen, Z"L [may his memory be a blessing], the Gaon Rabbi Mosze Nachum Jeruzalimski, Z"L, who had become famous in his own circles, in which he demonstrated his great knowledge in rabbinical literature, his sharpness and the depth of his intellect, was summoned to serve in Kielce.

When the Zionist movement came into being in the Jewish world, the Jewish inhabitants of Kielce did not stand idly by, but participated in activities in support of the rebirth of the nation in its homeland as a living organ of the national body. A Zionist Association was founded in Kielce that contained all of the activist energies that yearned to uncover cultural, educational, social and national activities and which consisted of the cream of the community.

View of the Synagogue – in all of its glory.

The community was young and fresh and easily impressed by everything going on in the wider world. This is why it did not remain unaffected even by the revolutionary workers movement, cells of workers' groups were set up there who operated underground against the existing political regime and against the regime of exploiter and exploited.

Every movement in the world in general and in the Jewish world in particular found a place in the hearts of the Jews of Kielce, and they responded to them in different ways.

Eventually, Kielce also attracted Hassidic leaders – "Admorim" – pious men. The community grew and there were no pious men to defend it. From near and far, religious people came and settled there. The community was blessed and made holy by the courts of the "Admorim", to which Hassidim flowed from near and far to crowd close to the images of their leader, bask in their glory and receive their blessings.

At the start of the twentieth century, a Jew who found himself in Kielce and didn't know its history might think at first glance that he was in one of the ancient communities of Poland, a community of settled procedures with sophisticated embellishments, with all of the adjustments necessary to the normal development of a public entity. It would not occur to him that the years of this community's existence numbered only a few decades and that it did not yet have any ancient traditions, ties with well-born families, customs and behaviors that had become sacred with the passage of time. But Jews in the Diaspora, in general, and the Jews of Poland in particular, had a special virtue: that places in which they set foot – flourished. The Jews of Poland excelled in their well-developed national recognition, whether they knew this or not, and this feeling functioned as a sort of glue to unify and cohere the individuals into a homogenous public body. The creative powers with which they were endowed acted to create the organs needed for their existence.

Here is a table that shows the growth of the Jewish population in Kielce.

Year	Jewish Population
1873	974
1882	2,659
1897	6,399
1909	11,206
1921	15,530

In 1939, which was the year the World War II broke out, the number of Jews in Kielce was estimated to be 25,000. According to the local statistics, in 1921 Jews had 633 industrial plants.

These numbers prove that the growth of the Jewish population in Kielce accelerated from year to year. In spite of the great migrations of Jews to other countries, their numbers not only didn't shrink, but conversely, held to a steady growth. Kielce was the center and it attracted Jews on the periphery. The Jewish settlement in Kielce was an entire economic unit, and it was not easy to dislodge it from its economic position.

Kielce could have been a notable example of the fact that has been repeated so often in our long history: wherever the Jews went, economic life developed; industry, commerce and various skilled crafts began to grow and flourish. A Jew creates sources of livelihood wherever he finds himself, not only for himself but also for his neighbors. If he is granted some flexibility and freedom of movement, he doesn't sit idly by but begins the task of development with great energy, which brings blessings to the place and its inhabitants. The results of the development projects are the plenty and wealth that are bestowed on the entire area. The population grows, life in general is enriched, not only economically, but also in other ways. Cultural and social life are improved. According to the old adage: If there is flour – there is Torah. The multitudes of landless laborers flock to the city from the villages and find work, the farmers have a market for their agricultural produce, therefore they have an interest in increasing the quantity of their produce since they are getting a decent price for their work.

Kielce was a living example of the power of the Jews to cause life and work to grow wherever they set foot.

Up to 1863 Kielce was a hamlet, despite being called a city. It had only a few homes, a few inhabitants numbering less than three thousand souls. There was no trace of a respectable industry except for small cottage industry. It had a few shops, whose owners were of German extraction, and most of their trade was beverages and various sweets. Their customers were the estate owners in the area, who would gather there from time to time for entertainment, pleasure and religious assemblies, for Kielce was a religious center for the Christians. In those days, it occurred to no one that Kielce would become the district capital, to an industrial city, a populated city whose inhabitants would eventually number sixty thousand souls.

[Page 21]

The Economic Life of the Jews of Kielce

The Jews: Industrial Pioneers

Translated by Judy Montel

Edited by Warren Blatt

Kielce began developing from the day Jews received permission to live there.

The Kielce area is full of natural resources. Mountain slopes, full of limestone and marble. The mountains were covered with thick forests. None of the Poles had the initiative to utilize the wealth hidden in the ground. The landowners would sit on their estates, spending their time in drinking parties and games, hunting animals and other such activities. The farmers were enslaved to the "Portzim", the landowners, with no will or initiative of their own. The middle classes, concentrated in artisan guilds called "Cachim", did not venture out of their areas of expertise and had nothing to do with industry. There were also Germans, who had settled in Poland in the days of the Tartar invasion; but they founded agricultural colonies and worked the land; some of them, who settled in the cities, were shopkeepers or managed the wine and liquor stills for the landowners. The Jews were the first to develop the various industries in Kielce, whitewash and brick factories, marble stones and gravel for paving roads; wood industries, planks for building and furniture making; the leather industry: tanners and shoemaking factories; enamel ware and the like, the soap and candle-making industries, and dozens of other sorts of small industrial factories.

The first pioneer who began utilizing the limestone around Kielce was a Jew from Dzialoszyce, Jehuda Ehrlich. He bought a mountain to the south of Kielce from a landowner and built himself a kiln for firing the limestone into whitewash. At first this work was done in a primitive manner; even so, the Kielce whitewash soon had a good reputation and was known throughout Poland for its quality. The owners became wealthy. They developed their business, new buildings were added to it, and they built a spur of the railroad from the main line. Cases of whitewash rode upon it, and from them the whitewash was loaded onto the boxcars of freight trains which delivered this building material to every corner of the state. The "Kadzilna" whitewash (the name of the factory) was in great demand. This factory employed hundreds of workers, clerks, technicians and artisans.

[Page 22]

The factory founder was a devoted Jew; on Sabbaths and holidays he prayed in the study house and wore silk clothing like one of the Chassidim, however his ever-growing wealth gradually distracted his attention from religious matters. His sons, who received higher education, distanced themselves from Jewish affairs. The current of assimilation, which attacked well-known circles among the wealthy in this period, carried them along as well. To their credit, let it be said here, that they kept the traditions of their late father, and the management of their large factory was in the hands of Jews. Jews were the bookkeepers, the clerks, and the technicians. Only the laborers in the quarry and by the kilns were Poles.

The "Kadzilna" factory enriched not only its owners; it brought affluence to the Jewish community of the city as well, since many of the Jewish residents of Kielce found their livelihood there. This was the first factory, which did much to aid the development and growth of the Jewish community. Smoke rising from kilns was, for the Jews of the city, like the holy smoke of incense.

The Jewish managers of the factory were Wolman; the first husband of Mrs. Stefanja Wolman, who founded the girls high school, and later the brothers Jankielewski, from the family of Rabbi Gold, the leader of the "Mizrachi" movement. Among the technicians and artisans were Rzok, a nationalist Jew and Ch. Kochen, who were regular employees of "Kadzilna" and others.

A mountain like this fell into the hands of the Zagajski family as well. Anyone who knew this place formerly would not have imagined that a simple mountain, that the herders used to pasture the animals of the city, contained such treasures, which sufficed to keep three generations of this family in wealth and prosperity. A person would not jump upon this mountain, made up of boulders that stuck out of it and above it. Barren mountains like this were plentiful around Kielce. Awraham Zagajski acquired this mountain for almost nothing. A short time after the purchase, limestone was discovered there. Zagajski began to utilize it, built ovens as whitewash kilns, paved a road from the kiln to the railroad, to ease the transfer of the whitewash to the train and to send it out by box car all over the state. The factory began to develop very quickly. The number of laborers who were employed there kept on growing until there were six hundred of them, not counting overseers, clerks, and bookkeepers necessary, as usual, to such a large industrial factory. Awraham Zagajski, the family elder, transferred the company to his two sons, Jakob and Cwi, in his old age. With their initiative and energies as well as an open eye to the future enlarged and broadened the factory. Their wealth grew; they built themselves splendid homes in Kielce. Cwi's son, Elimelech (Miczislaw) opened a branch of the company in Warsaw as well, in order to distribute their product from there to more distant places. The house of Zagajski rose to glory and honor in the Kielce community.

In the business of stones and whitewash, bricks and tiles the following families took part: Rozenholc, Goldfarb, Lifszycz and Chelmner, Krystal, Josef Orbajtl and Lemel Kahana.

This business enriched its owners and was one of the economic foundations of the Jews of Kielce.

[Page-23]

A second important economic branch for the local Jews were the wood factories that the Jews set up around the city. Thick forests covered the mountains of Kielce. Forests of pine, oak, cypress and beech surrounded the settlements of the area and waited for the arrival of the Jews, who began to utilize this natural wealth. Traders with capital would buy parcels of forested land from the landowners, set up sawmills for hundreds of workers and would turn the raw logs into planks, sills, beams, and pillars and would send them by train to other countries, near and far. Jews handled the export of this raw wood and the wood factories employed hundreds and thousands of workers. Rows and rows of farmers' wagons flowed on the road that led to the train station and brought worked and unworked logs there to be loaded on the freight cars. The train delivered these goods to the shores of the Baltic Sea, and there they were loaded onto boats that sailed with the export goods to England and France. In the wood industry the following were employed: the brothers Herszl and Eliezer Rajzman, the brothers Joel and Icak Klajnman, the Golembiowski family, the Machtynger family, Ajzenberg, Bugajer and many others. A great bounty flowed to the city and to the Jewish community from the wood industry. The inhabitants of the Polish village and the Jewish settlement were nourished by this plenty, and noticeable poverty was not common either in Kielce or its surroundings.

Another part of this branch of the economy was the furniture business, which developed in Kielce and its environs. This business employed the carpenters. Mosze Dawid Ajzenberg worked in the Kielce suburb of Bialogon [about 4 miles southwest of Kielce], as well as Herman Lewi and A.B. Ajzenberg. The furniture of Kielce was well known for its praiseworthy quality and beauty. Orders for this furniture arrived from distant places as well. The factory owners grew wealthy and filled an important role in the development of the city.

Jews also wholly owned the leather industry. Jewish tanners had been processing animal skins for a long time in a primitive fashion; to work the leather they used the bark of oak and pine trees that were plentiful in the thickly forested area. However, this industry had progressed in leaps and bounds in the past several decades. Several large factories for processing leather were founded, they were equipped with the latest machinery, and they began using chemical substances in extracts for processing the leather. This industry employed hundreds of families. Laborers found in it work and livelihood. In this industry the following families were famous: the Orbajtl family, whose patriarch, Awraham Orbajtl, one of the first to settle in the city, was called by his profession Awraham Gerber (tanner), his son Szmul Orbajtl in partnership with Mosze Dawid Ajzenberg, the Kaminer family, Mosze Chaim and his sons, the Waksberg family headed by Jeszaja Waksberg, and other tanners who continued to work the leather in the traditional fashion. In Bialogon, which was considered a suburb of Kielce, the Tenenbaum family members processed leather as well. The Kielce tanners' products were distributed through the entire country.

In connection with the tanners, another related industry developed, and this was the shoemaking trade. Kielce shoes were famous throughout Poland for their excellent quality. Before World War I Kielce shoes reached Siberia, to the edge of the Far East. The owners of these factories grew wealthy, built themselves big stone houses, and brought plenty and abundance to the city and its inhabitants, employing thousands of cobblers, Poles and Jews, residents of the city and of the surrounding villages. Every Saturday night there was much activity in the city streets. The cobblers were hurrying with their packages, containing dozens of pairs of shoes of all sorts, the fruit of their labor for the week, and bringing them to the managers who handed out work to receive their wages and materials for the coming week.

[Page-24]

At the same time there was activity in the shops and pubs. The Polish artisan, who received his wages from his employer, would hurry to the shop to purchase his wants for his day of rest. On the following day, on Sunday, the activity did not cease in the streets of the city; this was the activity of the shoe salesmen, great and small, who came from cities far a near to place their orders and shop. The goods, as usual, were bought on credit, with bills, whose terms of payment were generally six months from the date of purchase. The local banks saw increased custom on Mondays. The holders of the bills gave them to the banks for clearance and received cash for them, with which they paid their own bills that had come due. This repeated itself every week. The businesses were dependent upon one another like gears and cogs in a machine, where one propels another, and that one yet another, and so on, and altogether a general motion is generated directed towards the desired goal.

The shoemaking industry had a tremendous effect upon Kielce, and the name of the city became known throughout the country as a shoemaking center. "City of Shoes" was another name for the city of Kielce. When a stranger came to town and passed down Szinkibicza Street – Train Street – which led from the station to the town, the shoe industry caught his eye immediately. Nearly all of the large shops along the street, which was the main street of the city, displayed all sorts of shoes in their windows, sewn according to the newest fashion. Next to the shops were the factories, where the upper parts of the shoes were prepared, which were then distributed to cobblers, who did the finishing work on the shoe.

The odor of leather that had just left the factory and that of the shoe polishes tickled the nose of the stranger, who stepped onto the soil of Kielce for the first time. Here were the artisans, who specialized in their craft and produced fancy shoes both beautiful and nicely finished; here were the designers, who cut the leather according to the pattern they themselves had invented. They raised the craft of cobbling from its lowly status and turned it into a delicate craft that demanded expertise and a feeling for taste and beauty.

This branch of industry was handled by the Jews who developed it to a very high level and brought plenty and wealth to all the inhabitants of Kielce and its surroundings.

The first, shoemaking industry pioneers in the city were as follows: Simcha Bunem Izraelski, the brothers Ch. B. Rotman and Szlomo Rotman, D. Rembiszewski and his sons. After them came a longer list, B. Szmulewicz, the brothers Lewensztajn, the brothers Piasecki and Herszkowicz, L. Rozenberg and his son Cwi, Wajcman, Mendelewicz, Szapiro and many others who were a part of this business on a smaller scale. During the economic crises that affected the country from time to time, many of them were not able to survive, collapsed and did not rise again. The small businessmen in this branch were most numerous when the luck was with them. However, any tremor in the economic life of the country bankrupted them and many never recovered. They had to pull up their stakes and emigrate over the ocean with the remnants of their possessions.

[Page-25]

The ironmongers Sztarke & Bruner dealt in the business of casting iron and enamel; their factory also employed hundreds of workers. Their product was very much in demand all over the country.

Among the various crafts and factories there were also those for manufacturing candles and soap. Several families produced candles and soap in a primitive fashion. They did not have steam vats for cooking the materials for production, but used regular vats, the handiwork of their ancestors, and they introduced no innovations to the production of these commodities; even so, they were successful at their handiwork and grew wealthy and built themselves homes. The brothers Szmelke and Hirszel Ajzenberg and the Rubinek brothers took part in the soap and candle industry. Their products were for local consumption and local markets.

Aside from the important industries mentioned, which filled an important role in the development of the city, there were also small factories that employed Jews, and among them were factories that not only maintained their owners, but also brought them wealth and abundance. I will mention here, for example, one of these factories which demonstrates that the Jewish initiative and creative spirit which were embedded in the blood of the Jews could create very real results even in a field that had hitherto been abandoned by all, and their creativity brought a blessing to more than a few families.

In the early years of the twentieth century a young man came to Kielce and opened a photography shop. This was the first photography shop whose owners were Jewish. A Christian Pole named Szwianski had a photography shop in the town, but he was set in his ways, clung to old-fashioned methods and didn't introduce any progress in the art of photography. The young man quickly became known in the city, where he was known as a photographer who understands his art. The number of his customers grew from day to day and he wasn't set in his ways and he didn't cling to old-fashioned methods, but introduced numerous improvements and changes to his profession. His name was Kopel Gringras and his photography shop was called "Moderne". The name was evidence of the photographer's direction, and his efforts to acquire the tools of his trade and improvements in it. He came to Kielce from Switzerland, where he learned his trade from experts. He also knew the art of sketching, married and was blessed with many sons, who, when they grew up, helped their father in his trade.

However, he invented a new profession in this craft, which spread and grew later and gave work to many of the younger generations, and brought wealth to several youngsters of energy and initiative. He organized a laboratory for enlarging photographs. A small photograph, given to him, would be returned enlarged according to the wishes of the customer. Agents went out to all corners of the state carrying bags with examples of enlarged photographs. They would take orders to enlarge photographs of people living and dead. The enterprise grew so large that dozens of young men and women were engaged in the occupation as well as dozens of agents taking orders.

[Page-26]

Several of his students left his shop and opened their own laboratories, running their businesses on their own. Some of them were successful in this business, acquired capital and built themselves glorious stone houses. The more famous of the owners of such businesses were Cytryn, the grandson of Mejer Cytryn, and Oberzanski. They developed this type of business to the pinnacle of its potential, and provided employment for many families in the city.

This photographer, Gringras, also founded a factory for photographic negatives in Kielce, which had hitherto been imported from Germany. In his unrelenting energies, and especially with the help of his son Leopold, who specialized in this production, he created a new industry that had not been dreamt of previously in Poland. This factory also employed dozens of men and women laborers. This source of income saved the many young men and women who wished to become productive and they devoted themselves to this work and became expert at it.

Thanks to the industry that the Jews developed in Kielce, its population, of both Jews and Christians, grew. In 1918, when Poland became an independent state, Kielce became the capital of the district, an area whose population numbered close to three million souls, and the industry of the city supplied their wares.

However, the Jewish population of Kielce did not live by industry alone. Trade and crafts were in the hands of the Jews and from these sources thousands of families drew their livelihood, and a number of them did very well, became wealthy and famous among the Jews of Poland.

About them and their activities in the following sections.

The Status of the Traders in Kielce and it Representatives

On the first line of the traders of Kielce stood the textile traders. This business found its best outlet and development only in the hands of Jews. The owners of the textile mills in Lodz knew that when they entrusted their wares to Jews it would get a wide distribution, reaching even the most remote places. The Jewish trader alone was capable of dealing with this branch of trade. The Jew, being quick and speedy, knew how to stock his store at every moment and every time with the goods that were appropriate to that or another season. The Jew, who made do with little, would sell his wares cheaply, with a marginal profit. Most of the efforts of the Jewish traders were in enlarging the turnover of his wares, so that it would not collect on the shelves of his shop and sit there like a stone no one could move; therefore he sold goods on credit as well and would trust even the poorest of the poor. His motto was: "There is no person who does not have their hour; if they don't pay today, they will pay tomorrow." The Jewish trader would give credit to everyone, and would spread his wares out on every side. He was careful of only one thing; that the goods not get old in his store. Two good things came out of this tactic of the trader, who mediated between the producer and consumer. A good thing for the producer – his wares were distributed among all of the inhabitants of the land; a good thing for the consumer – if they were available, he could find clothes with which to cover himself, whether he had money or not.

[Page-27]

When anti-Semitism grew stronger in the country and the anti-Semites were very eager to remove the Jews from their economic status, they took as a motto: "Swoj do swego", "Your countrymen before strangers", and would preach from the pulpits of their churches and in their houses of legislature that the Jew should be boycotted, not to buy or sell anything to or from him until he will be forced, from lack of a livelihood, to remove himself from the land and then the main inhabitants would inherit his economic standing.

The anti-Semites then saw, to their great sorrow, that the important branch of trade, the clothing trade, was entirely in the hands of Jews. They began to hatch plots to get the textile trade out of the hands of the Jews. First they opened shops in the large Polish cities for the sale of various types of cloth. Using credit they received from the government they were able to supply their shops with a great variety of textiles, woolens, material, cotton and silk. The shops had luxurious furnishings. The display windows were large and lit up with electric lights in the evenings to attract customers. A troop of managers, clerks and assistants conducted the entire business.

In Kielce as well, on the main street, Szinkibicza Street, such a shop opened, above the entrance a large sign proclaimed in gold and gaudy letters: "Polish Textile Shop". And in the large display windows pieces of various materials were spread out.

However, not the sign, not the new and glittering furniture, not the lighted display windows and not even the troop of clerks and assistants attracted customers to their store. The goods rested quietly on the shelves, the clerks and assistants sat with folded arms, yawning from lack of what to do. Soon after, the founders found it necessary to shut down this economic venture upon which so many of their hopes had depended. The government grants did no good, nor did the great oral and written propaganda that supported the Christian economic status. It gave up the ghost after existing for two years. The expenses were great, and the income – nil. They, the gentiles, did not penetrate the secrets of the Jewish traders, and did not adopt the attributes that these had acquired over generations, thanks to which they were able to run their businesses in times of ebb and flow. This branch of trade had been in Jewish hands for generations, and it was difficult to remove it from their hands. Both the manufacturer and the consumer preferred the Jew to the Christian, who entered into foreign territory and was more likely to ruin things than to fix them.

There were such textile traders in Kielce as well; who inherited the profession from one generation to the next, from father to son or daughter. The most well-known traders in the field were: The Ajzenberg family, whose original founder, Rabbi Josel Ajzenberg, or, as he was known Josel Kaczka, came originally from a family of respected lineage from Checiny, next to Kielce. Rabbi Josel son of Rabbi Mosze Dawid Ajzenberg was one of the well-known Chassidim of Kock [Kotsk]. Their opponents called members of this family "Kaczka" – a corruption of the name "Kotsker". Rabbi Josel was an iron trader in Checiny. According to the advice of the Admo"r of Kock, Rabbi Mendel, Z"L, Rabbi Josel moved to the city of Kielce. There was a local legend that this Admo"r advised him to buy the house that was underneath the pillars, and there he would find plenty. And, when the latter complained to him that there were no Jews and Torah scholars in Kielce, he promised him that this city would become a place of Chassidism and Torah. He bought that house and in its cellar found a treasure: a barrel filled with gold coins. If there is any truth to this tale, one cannot know, but Rabbi Josel was very successful in his business.

Rabbi Elija Naftali Ajzenberg

His son, Elija Naftali, opened a textile shop, and he also was successful in his business. He was known among he traders as an honest man, who kept his word under any and every circumstance, and besides this, became known in the city for his piety and generosity. Mostly his wife, Sara Frajda, who was known as an excellent and wise businesswoman, ran the business. After he died in excellent repute, the shop passed to his son-in-law, Eliezer Tauman, who continued the family tradition. They became linked by marriage to some families of highly respected lineage in Israel. Many members of this family are presently in Israel, since they left in time and came to settle here.

The Blicki family was also prominent among the textile traders. The shop of the family head, Szmul Abesz Blicki, was the largest of the shops for woolen weaves. Anyone who was marrying off a son or daughter and wanted to make them wedding clothes would go first to Blicki's shop, there one found their heart's desire and could buy the cloth at reasonable prices and conditions. After his death, his sons Jakob and M.B. Blicki continued their father's business, and were very successful. Of this family only one woman was saved, the daughter of Sz. A. Blicki, and she and her two daughters are in Israel.

Dawid Zylberszpic, a man of considerable importance, one of the leaders of the city, was also a textile trader. He had a large shop for cloth in his home in the market. However, after World War I this family moved to Lodz, the industrial city of Poland, and there, together with another Kielce resident, also a textile trader, they founded a textile factory called Zylberszpic and Tenenbaum. However, his cloth shop in Kielce was not closed. It was transferred to another owner, to Mordechai Fiszel Kaminer.

The Rozenberg family, one of the older families in Kielce, whose father, Josel, was called by his mother's name, Josel Sara Chana's, was also among those trading in this area. Josel Rozenberg also left his shop to his sons. However, over time his sons left the field. Several of them immigrated to the United States and several found other professions.

Rabbi Josel Sara Chana's

Echezkel Bimka, one of the followers of Alexander [the Chassidic Rabbi of Aleksandrow Lodzki], inherited his textile shop from his father-in-law, Kalman Lemels. This family had also made this area of trade a tradition, Efrajm Wlodwer, the son-in-law of Elija Naftali Ajzenberg, founded himself a branch of his father-in-law's store and managed it quite successfully. After them, came a long line of textile traders who did not inherit their trade or get it from family tradition, but served first in textile shops as assistants, or married women who had served in such a capacity before their marriage, and after gaining much experience in the field, opened their own shops. In this category are the brothers Awraham and Zecharja Gertler, Beril Piotrowski, Ben-Cion Sztern, Gerszon Rembiszewski, Dawid Garfinkel and others.

Among these traders were also some who entered the trade because of World War I. During the war years there were people among the inhabitants of Kielce who had ready cash, and when they saw that the value of the money was growing less and less, they exchanged their money for trade goods, especially for textiles. Several of them were successful in this business, acquired capital and remained in the business even after the war was over. Among those were M.P. Kaminer, R. Ziunczkowski and others.

Aside from these traders who were independent, there were also merchants who functioned as representatives of others or managed branches which Lodz factory owners opened in Kielce, like Szajbler, Gajer and Poznanski. Among these were Jechiel Szajnfeld, Icak Majer Rapaport, Mosze Kalichsztajn, Nechemja Kajzer and others.

[Page-30]

I will not mention the names of the minor tradesmen here, who were employed in this business, for they were numerous and the space doesn't allow. These latter had small shops. On market days and at the great fairs, they brought their wares to the market to sell to the farm men and women. This small trade supported dozens of families; several of them were successful and later opened up large shops. I will mention the names of only a few of this type of textile tradesmen: Dawid Kochen, Morgensztern, Wajntraub, A. Rotenberg.

This area of trade, which was entirely in the hands of Jews, was a source of income for dozens of families and brought several of them great wealth. A textile merchant was respected in the community, and people gave him honor. This merchant did not need to necessarily be busy in his shop; many of them left the business in the hands of their wives, and they themselves were busy with the affairs of Chassidism; they would spend hours in the "sztiblach" – small study and prayer houses – learning a page of Gemara, grabbing a word about the activities of the Admo"rs; also celebratory meals, the anniversary of the death of some righteous man, took up much of their spare time. The Chassidic merchant could devote himself to spiritual affairs with a quiet mind, in the secure knowledge that his wife, a woman of valor, was keeping an eagle eye on his material affairs and arranging them in the way best suited to the success of the business. From time to time he would travel to Lodz and arrange his accounts with the manufacturer, and at the same time pay a visit to his Admo"r in Gur [Gora Kalwaria] or Alexander [Aleksandrow Lodzki], ask his advice and learn from him ways of serving the Lord.

And if the textile merchant ran into a crisis and could not pay his debts and pay off his bills, that is, if he became bankrupt; even then there was not a lot of noise or fuss over this occurrence in the city. The shock passed in silence; the sides came to some kind of agreement "The Valley of Equality" in the language of the merchants. The merchant continued to receive "packages", and in the city, nothing was known of this occurrence. The textile traders were a world unto themselves, and no foreign eye could penetrate to know its secrets.

The leather trade was also in the hands of the Jews. Chmielarz, Rotman, Markowicz and Jura, Tenenbaum were the main suppliers of this raw product to the cobblers and shoe manufacturers. Kielce, which was the city of shoes, imported thick leather and soft leather for shoemaking also from Radom and from Warsaw, where there were large factories, which processed great quantities of leather.

We will not spend too much time on this branch of trade, since we have already discussed the leather industry at great length. We move on to the commerce in iron, which was also in the hands of Jews. The largest iron shop in Kielce belonged to the brothers Ajzenberg, Mejer and Mendel, who inherited it from their father Josel Ajzenberg, who was mentioned above. Natan Mordkowicz and his sons, as well, were honest merchants, who became wealthy and respected. Also the brothers Lajbel and Zew Goldberg and Bornsztajn worked in this business and their sons after them. There were other smaller tradesmen whose main business was with junk iron.

This area of commerce that was held by the Jews was also a thorn in the side of the anti-Semites. They did not rest until they had opened a large shop in the market with ironware. They wanted to try their hands at this business; perhaps they would be able to wrest it from the Jews. They began using all sorts of incentives, running a broad campaign in favor of their shop, attempting to attract the farmer, the blacksmith and the locksmith to their store. They promised buyers heaven and earth, high quality goods and low prices. However, they did not succeed with this shop.

[Page-31]

The Polish farmer or artisan, when he entered the shop of a Jew, could feel free in his speech, his behavior, he dared to disturb the shopkeeper and demanded to see all sorts of nails, all sorts of iron tools, which were in the shop, to choose the one best suited to his purposes. And if he happened not to have any cash in his pocket, the Jew would not send him away but would sell it to him on credit.

However, when he entered the Christian shop it was as if he were standing before his teacher, constrained and bridled in his speech and movements, he didn't find what he needed and had to pay for the goods that he bought, and pay in cash.

This shop continued to exist; but it was a paltry existence, which needed occasional "injections" in the form of financial grants from their organizations and banks, in order to cover the deficit. Here too, it was difficult to take this area of commerce from the hands of the Jew, an area from which many families in the city drew their sustenance.

The commercial area of haberdashery, which then divided into two parts: haberdashery goods and confectionery goods, was also entirely in the hands of the Jews. Only the Jews were capable of developing this area of commerce and reach such a pinnacle. In this area the Jews were both the manufacturers and also the merchants who served as brokers between the manufacturer and the consumer. In Warsaw and in Lodz they manufactured things in a cottage industry: gloves, parasols, umbrellas, pockets, purses, handbags, wallets, buttons, women's dresses and sweaters and dozens of other objects. These products were then sent all over the country. The Jewish merchants would distribute them among all levels of the population. The shopkeeper did not even have to travel to the merchandising city to purchase his wares. In every city there were "Szpilters", sort of agents or messengers of merchants and shopkeepers. Such a "Szpilter" would travel to Warsaw or Lodz on Saturday night with a list of goods that he needed to buy there, and to deliver to their destination as quickly as possible. These messengers would stay in Warsaw or Lodz all week and would return to their homes from Sabbath to Sabbath. You would always find them at the train stations, heavily laden with suitcases and packages of goods. When they saw someone from their city whom they knew they would immediately request him to: "Keep your eye on the suitcase or on the package which I am going to put in the train carriage on the shelf above or underneath the seat." And from those who came from his city he would receive bundles of money and letters with lists of goods that he needed to buy and to send along on the next train. And when the train reached the shopkeepers' city, they were already waiting there, they themselves or their wives, to receive the goods their emissary had sent them.

There were two benefits that the merchants got from this in the purchasing of their wares. First of all, because of the speediness of their messengers, they always had the goods they needed for their customers. Second of all, they were relieved of the travel expenses themselves, which would have raised the price of the goods. The "Szpilter" made do with a small percentage of the cost of the goods as his commission, which barely effected the price. In addition, the merchants were saved the price of delivery. The quantity of haberdashery goods was not large and the train deliveries traveled as light baggage, which a passenger took with him on his journey. No passenger would refrain from taking a suitcase or small package under his care.

Only the Jew was capable of inventing these sorts of ways and means in commerce. The intention of the Jewish merchant was to reduce the costs of brokerage and to remove the burden of extra costs from the goods. The owner of the optical instrument shop, a Christian Pole, used the Jewish "Szpilters", when he saw the tremendous benefit to trade that they brought with their great agility.

Among the haberdashery and confectionery merchants in Kielce several notable ones were Icak Kopel, Wolf Kopel, Pinchas Rudel, Chanoch Fajgenblat, Mosze Ajlbirt, the brothers Sztrosberg and many others.

In the area of Colonial merchandise, the Jewish merchants took the lead. In this area there were also Christian merchants, mostly of German descent, who, together with tea, coffee, cocoa, nuts and raisins, sold fine wines. However, most of them were Jews. The most important of these were the Zylbersztajn family, Szymszon Sztrosberg, Dawid Manela and others.

B. Lewi, Federman, Jakob Hilel Paserman and his sons, Szajnfeld, Mejer Zloto, Szlomo Manela, Nachman Diamend, Rechcman and many others sold wine, beer and other drinks.

Awraham Kohen, Grynberg, Joske Fiszman, Jegier, Ehrlichman, dealt in kitchenware. The Cwajgel family took over the trade in glass.

Those who traded in tobacco and its products were Hassenbajn and P. Zauerman and others. The coal merchants were Todros Herszkowicz, Bukowski, Lewinzon, Wikinski, Jurkowski.

The first flour merchants were the Moszkowicz family, Chaim Judel Ajzenberg. The Kochen family took over the egg trade. After these come a long list of grain and fodder merchants, fish and poultry merchants, traders in horses and other animals, feather merchants, soap and candle merchants, fuel merchants, in which the Rotenberg and Szajnfeld families were chiefly occupied, construction materiel and automobiles and their parts, and a long line of grocery merchants – all of these were a special class, the merchant class.

This class was a major artery through which the abundance of the economic life flowed to all parts of the public. The government also received an important part of its income from the merchant class. The merchant, the grocer, had to equip himself with a merchant's license at the start of every civil year, called "Patent" in Polish. The Patents had various degrees. After that, each merchant had to pay income tax, property tax, and war-profits tax. The local municipality also had its communal taxes which it levied mainly on the merchant, he had to pay sign tax, apartment tax and other temporary taxes. This tax burden weighed heavily on the merchant class. There were many that collapsed under the affliction of the taxes, and fell unable to rise again. The government's aim was to suppress the Jewish merchants, which were the most vital core in the economic field of the Jewish population. This most useful tool that had been used against the Jews for untold ages was levying heavy taxes on them, that would be unbearable and make them unable to be fruitful and multiply in the land. When the Jews lost their source of income, the various anti-Semites thought, they would be forced to emigrate or would be subject to a slow atrophy and extinction by a natural process.

But most of the Jewish merchants held on despite all of the afflictions and persecutions, which passed over their heads in the period between the two World Wars. The Jew with his intelligence, his life experience, his energy and his stubbornness fought against all of the plots of his enemies, who wished to deprive him of his economic status. Even the harsh measures, which the anti-Semites began to use against the Jews, such as: smashing display windows, throwing stink bombs into their shops, setting up guards by their shops that didn't allow Christian customers to enter – such acts of hooliganism were also not sufficient to confuse Jewish commerce.

The Jewish merchant, like the rest of the Jews of the Diaspora, was used to insults, beatings and damages – and continued with his life. Among the Jews of the Diaspora a philosophy of life was created that told him "No phenomenon is forever; it appears, continues for a while – and in the end it disappears over the horizon of experience." The Jew needed, therefore, to be stubbornly patient and to wait for better times, to cleave to the words of the prophet: "Wait almost a moment until the fury is past." The Jewish merchants were more than usually optimistic. Even in bad times, their spirits didn't fall; they did not despair, but held fast. Their instinct for life was very strong, and it gave them tools, that enabled their existence in all circumstances and conditions. The solidarity between them was amazing. The degree of mutual aid was especially developed in the merchant populations. A merchant, who had to pay significant amounts the following day at the bank in order to redeem his notes that had come due didn't worry at all, he slept well. Even though his pocket was still empty, his spirit was quiet. He was sure that in the morning he would easily collect the sums he needed; the merchants who were free from redeeming notes on that day would offer him the necessary funds. A merchant would not turn away his fellow who asked him such a favor. The latter knew that if he were to request a favor the day following such a refusal, he would meet with sealed ears. This benefaction brought much blessing to the honest merchants, who did not consider bankruptcy and didn't want to pay interest to the banks for either a large or small loan. The interest, they knew, upsets the situation of both large and small merchants. A merchant who is paying interest has a continual additional expense over and above his many expenses, and he is destined to go bankrupt.

Although there were some among the merchants who went into trade to begin with in order to go bankrupt; among these fellows the loan sharks went around who gave them loans at a reduced rate of interest. These loan sharks were called "Alokos" (Leeches) in our place, since like leeches, they sucked the blood of their customers, who became entangled in their net. But the honest merchants, who were careful of their souls and their good names, kept away from such creatures.

[Page-34]

Artisans

The artisans of Jewish Poland have a long history. Many authors dismissed them and described their lowly status in the Jewish community, both spiritually and materially. In spite of the praise expressed in the Talmud and the Midrash for those who learn a craft and for those who earn their living from the product of their handiwork, the Jews of Poland despised craft for many generations. Families of lineage avoided marrying craftsmen. A tailor or cobbler in the family was a defect. But over time, opinions changed; the attitude towards the man of labor, who lives from the fruit of his hands, became one of tolerance, and also one of respect.

In the Kielce community artisans had a position of honor to begin with. The Jewish community was without a long tradition. Until the twentieth century it was still in a formative period and took on a specific shape only with the onset of the twentieth century and onwards. In this period, there were already tremendous changes taking place in the attitudes of the Jewish public. The great movements which arose from within the Jewish community and also from without, elevated the productive element in general, and the Jewish artisan in particular, from his lowly material and spiritual status. The laborer and artisan were no longer like doorsteps, trampled by the aggressors; they began to demand their rights from society openly and to express opinions regarding various communal affairs. The Zionist movement on the one hand and the Socialist movement on the other were the main causes of the higher respect accorded to artisans by the Jewish public. The artisans participated in all the affairs of the congregation, and they helped give it its shape.

Several of the craft professions were, without exception, in the hands of the Jews. The clothing professions, tailoring and hat-making were held tightly in Jewish hands, and no propaganda on the part of the anti-Semites helped the Poles penetrate the ranks of this profession. During the years before World War II the Poles founded a cooperative of Christian tailors. They brought a group of tailors from other places, provided them with woolen cloth and sewing machines, rented them a spacious workshop and distributed announcements, that a cooperative had been opened in Kielce by expert Christian tailors with diplomas, and it was receiving orders for men's suits. At first Christians went to them with their orders, mainly government clerks. But as time went on, their customers dwindled. Even the clerks were not satisfied with their work and began leaving them and returning each to his Jewish tailor, who knew his customers' tastes. The cooperative didn't last.

The Poles also sought strategies for entering the hat makers' profession. They opened a hat shop. But what a problem, there were no hat makers among them who could provide them with goods. They went and found a Jew who agreed to work for them and teach the craft to their apprentices. Their intention was to remove in this manner the profession of hat making from the hands of the Jews, but in this they were not successful; buyers could not be found for their wares. People did not enter their shop, and those who did – left empty-handed, for they could not find what they were looking for there. And these professions remained in the hands of Jews.

Among the tailors who excelled in their profession were Wloszczowski, Borkowski, Granek, Pukacz, Micnmacher and many other young people, who learned their profession from experts and knew how to sew a suit in the latest fashion. Among these tailors were some who had their own workshops and clothing shops; like Moszenberg and his sons, Blicki and his sons, Emberg, Ajzenberg, Rondberg and others. Some of them were wealthy, owners of stone houses and respected in the city. Ickowicz was a furrier by profession and successful in his work.

Among the hat makers, the following were especially notable: Mosze Kinigsberg was a Zionist, devoted to the movement of the rebirth of the nation in its homeland from the very beginning of its growth; Hirsz Lejb Abramowicz and his sons, Izrael Icza and Abisz, Jews who feared the Lord and kept his commandments; Dawid Zylberspic and his son, the respected home-owner; Pesach Cukerman, a pious man. They produced many students, who held to the profession and did not leave it, even when they left the city of their birth and immigrated to other countries.

There was another profession, which began entirely in Jewish hands, but later, under the influence of the anti-Semites, Poles began infiltrating and displacing the Jews. This profession was that of the tinsmith. Covering the roofs of the houses with galvanized steel. Jews were agile in this work. Jews were accepted even to the covering the roofs of churches and their domes. Both Jews and Christians trusted them and gave them important jobs in the building of houses. Many members of this profession were enriched by their work; built themselves stone houses and acquired a good reputation among their co-religionists. The foremost representatives of this profession were the members of the Kochen family. The first in this family, Izrael Kochen, a respected householder in his community, head of a large family, reached a ripe old age and continued his trade even when he was an elderly man, over 80 years of age. When he was older, his acquaintances asked him: "Why are you working? Why climb on roofs? Poverty cannot force you to work, for you are well-to-do and the income of your household keeps your family honorably?" He would answer jokingly: "I don't want the Angel of Death to find me easily at home; let him trouble himself a bit to search for me on the sloping roofs, at my place of work." After the death of his wife, when he was seventy-five years of age, his neighbors and friends asked him: "Why don't you marry a woman, a housekeeper, to look after you and your house?" And he would joke and say: "What kind of a woman would agree to marry such a mischievous fellow as I who climbs on the rooftops?" He was an old man with a healthy sense of humor, who loved his work and kept to the traditions, holding to the deeds of his ancestors.

Also his son, Chaim Kochen, continued in his father's path, keeping to his profession and acquiring trust and respect from all the inhabitants of the city, Jews and Christians alike.

[Page-36]

The brothers, Barukh and Yek'l Kuperberg, tinsmiths and plumbers, who knew their trade and were expert at it, were also important homeowners in Kielce. They were also government sub-contractors. They acquired capital and built themselves homes in their city and enriched the city, and gave their children a higher education. Members of the Cyna family were tinsmiths for generations. The writer of these words still knew Josef Cyna, or Josef Blacharz, as his fellow townsmen called him because of his profession. This Josef was a pious man, learned in the Torah, who would hold a "Tikun" every night at midnight and was one of the "Old Ones" who rose early to come before dawn to the Beit Midrash to worship God. On Sabbath and holidays he would collect the apprentices of the various tradesmen and read to them and explain the portion of the week with the commentary of Rash"i.

His son, Lemel Cyna, also a pious Jew, an artist at his craft, when he heard that Jews were moving to the Land of Israel and settling the wilderness and rebuilding its ruins, decided to aid in this holy task – and moved to the Land of Israel and worked at his trade here as well. He built the dome on the roof of the great synagogue in Tel-Aviv. On his Sabbaths in Tel-Aviv, he did much charity and many good deeds. Like his father, he lived a long life and went to his eternal rest at the age of over ninety. His brother, Chaim Jeszaja Cyna, worked at his trade and was also known as an honest man who knew his work. There were other Jewish tinsmiths in Kielce, but the Christian tinsmiths began to push them out of the field. From the time that anti-Semitism began increasing in Poland, and especially in Kielce, no Christian, not even the best of them, dared to give work to a Jew. The tinsmith's work, which was carried out on the rooftops in full view of everyone, was different from other types of work in which the Christian could contact the Jew without the anti-Semites knowing anything about it. But to publicly give work to a Jew was uncomfortable for a Pole, even one who was not infected by anti-Semitism. The Jewish tinsmiths began immigrating to other countries and their numbers dwindled in Kielce.

Jews played a small part in the profession of shoemaking. In Checiny, the town close to Kielce, there were many Jewish shoemakers; they specialized in stitching boots from thick leather for the farmers of the surrounding villages. They used to travel with their wares to nearby cities and towns on market days to sell them there. However, in Kielce itself, the Jewish cobblers served the Jewish population as menders of old shoes. New shoes were bought in shops. There were also shoemakers who worked for the shoe salesmen; however, there were only a few of them. The shoe salesmen employed mainly Polish shoemakers. But within the profession of shoemakers, the Jews developed the art of stitching – a more important level than shoemaking. A stitcher doesn't sit on a stool, pierce with his awl and hit with the hammer. His craft is by the sewing machine, stitching the upper parts of the shoe. Other workers, experts at the craft of cutting, would cut the leather into its parts. Among them, the "Modelists" excelled especially; they would invent different kinds of patterns. They had highly developed taste and were blessed with a sense of the aesthetic. A "Modelist" would earn twice as much as a simple stitcher. The stitching was a Jewish profession, and Poles had no part of it. Usually, a stitcher would go out on his own after a while and set up a factory for leather goods. Many of the owners in this type of industry started out as simple stitchers, working as laborers for others, and over the years became independent. The profession of stitching had a higher status than shoemaking. The Jewish mother would threaten her lazy son, if he did not progress in his studies and would say: "I will give you to the shoemaker!" But stitching – this was delicate work, and even respectable parents who had never had a craftsman in the family would send their sons to learn the craft. This was a new branch of work, and it carried no stigmas, for good or for ill, from the past. Whoever was looking for a "vocation" for his son chose this type of work, which had opportunity for the future.

[Page-37]

There were two types of Jewish carpenters: Building carpenters and furniture carpenters. Carpentry was in a state of decline among the Jews of Kielce, especially during Polish independence. Building was slow due to the economic crises, which was a chronic phenomenon in the new Poland, and also due to the anti-Semitic method that all the various governments of Poland clung to. It was hard for a Jewish carpenter to find work at the government buildings or with Poles. In this area the Christian artisans were the deciding factor. Furniture factories were also established, which the carpenter who worked with his hands could not compete with. The younger carpenters left the country and emigrated overseas, to America or the Land of Israel. And the older ones continued their miserable lives in want and poverty, in expectation of financial support from their sons who had emigrated overseas.

In contrast to this, the professions of painter and glazier were in Jewish hands, and there was not even one attempt by the anti-Semites to remove these professions from them. The first painters were enriched by their work and built themselves houses. The Lewi brothers, Simcha and Sender Goldfarb started off as painters; afterwards, when they were wealthy and had collected some capital, they left their profession, the ladder and the brush – and became contractors. The latter, Sender, did not leave his profession entirely, and together with painting he also worked in photography. Aside from the Goldfarb family, the Goldszajder and Gutman families were also well known in the city. Among them: Josef Goldszajder and Judel Gutman who were famous not only in their professions but also for their public activism.

Among the glaziers I will mention here Anszel Zalcberg and the Cwajgel family, of whom one, Izrael Cwajgel, also had a large warehouse for glass; two of his sons came to Israel, and one of them follows his ancestors' profession here as well.

Jewish tradesmen were very active in the food industry. Jewish bakers and butchers sold bread and meat not only to Jews, but also to a large portion of the Christians. The Jewish butchers in particular supplied beef to the entire Kielce population, Jewish and Christian. In the local slaughter house it was customary to have the Jewish butchers in one wing slaughtering large and small grazing animals, and in the other wing, the Christian butchers slaughtering pigs. No one entered the realm of his fellow. The Jews were forbidden to deal in the unclean animal, and it was not worthwhile for the Christians to attempt the business of selling beef. This kind of business was for them close to a loss and far from profitable. The Jews would sell the Christian the hindquarters of the animals at a low price. On the other hand, the other parts of the animal were sold to Jews at a high price. In Poland, the Jews did not customarily puncture the hindquarter meat [necessary to make it kosher]. The "Gentile" gained from the Jewish laws, because he got good meat at a low price. Also "trajf" meat [meat that had been found not kosher for any reason] were sold cheaply to Christians. These conditions did not allow the Christians to work in the business of slaughtering beef; they couldn't withstand the competition with the Jews. Things had been like this for many years. However, in the years before World War II, when racist anti-Semitism was growing in all levels of the Polish population, the Hitlerian methods found fertile ground in Poland. Both the parliament and the government lent a hand to remove the Jews from their economic standing – their first step in this area was – forbidding "szechita" [ritual slaughter]. A proposal for a law was entered into the Polish Sejm [parliament], according to which the Jewish ritual slaughter would be forbidden. With this proposal the Poles meant to kill two birds with one stone, to wrest an important source of livelihood from Jewish control and to force the religious sections of the Jews, those who clung to their traditions, to emigrate.

During this short period the Poles succeeded in taking trade in meat away from the Jewish butchers. They were forced to close their shops and seek other sources of employment. But, up until that time, this area of livelihood was in Jewish hands. Many families were supported by this work. Several butchers amassed wealth and built themselves houses. Of these homeowners were M.L. Szmulewicz, Zylbersztajn, B. Goldberg, Bialobroda and others.

Many families were likewise supported by the work of baking. The Jewish bakers in our city were mainly wealthy. The Goldblum, Diamend and Grosman families were wealthier than the other bakers and they were considered respectable homeowners in the city.

In all of the professions mentioned hitherto, Jews had some control and they also were passed from father to son. However, there were also professions from which Jews were barred. The blacksmith's trade, plastering, building, and locksmiths were generally in the hands of the Christians. If a Jew appeared in one of these professions, he was the only one in his city, and it wouldn't be one of the prominent inhabitants of the city. On the other hand, if a new profession should turn up, like that of an electrician, for instance, the Jews were usually the first to take them on, and develop it to perfection. A Jew, Mendel Elencwajg, was the first to open a cinema in Kielce. Jews brought radio and other electrical devices to the city. Minc and Zylberman were the first to distribute these to the inhabitants of the city. Watchmakers, jewelers, brass and coppersmiths – were Jews with no exceptions. The Rechcman family worked at the art of copper and brass. The Kaner family was occupied in watchmaking. Members of this family, together with those of the jewelers, owned shops that sold silver and gold utensils and various jewels and were of the most respected in the community. There were other areas of work that Jews controlled, such as lithography, engraving, brush-making, knitting, cloth dyeing, raisin-wine making; but only a few did these and they were not popular occupations.

There were several printing presses in Kielce, which were owned by Jews. They served mainly tradesmen and banks. The owners of the print shops would either do the typesetting themselves or hire workers for wages. Icak Kaminer owned the first press in town, and after him came the brothers Rzendowski and Jechiel Mitelman, who also set up presses. The youngest of the press owners, who inherited the machines from their owners, were Eliezer Skura, the Moszenberg brothers and Baruch Wajnryb, at whose press the weekly Jewish "Kielcer Zeitung" was printed.

[Page-39]

These workmen were the essential healthy kernel in the fabric of the Jewish community of Kielce. Among them were important homeowners, who did much to aid the development of the city as a whole and the Jewish community in particular, they carried the main burden of the community's responsibilities. Among them were Chassidim, pious men of action, from whom national and socialist activists came forth, who aroused the masses from their apathy and directed them towards light and progress. The Jewish artisan was the backbone that the entire public body leaned and depended upon. With his faith, devotion to his profession and precision he earned respect and honor not only among his brothers and co-religionists, but also among those who were not his co-religionists. In periods when anti-Semitism had not taken hold of the Polish public, the Christian also preferred the Jew to his fellow Pole, his co-religionist. The Polish employer regarded the Jew as being expert in his field and honest in the commission of work that was given to him. And especially, for an additional reason, drunkenness was not common among the Jewish workmen, in the way that it was among the Christian workmen. The workmen of Kielce as professionals contributed their own thread to the formation of the character and nature of the community, a bold thread that caught the eye.

The Status of Jewish Laborers

The Jewish laborers in Kielce did not join up from the factories of heavy industry nor from quarry laborers, since Jews were not employed in these places; Jewish laborers were mainly workers in light industry, with Jewish artisans or as apprentices and assistants, and also as clerks in the shops and banks. Therefore, they did not have the same attributes of a proletariat as in the large cities, Warsaw, Lodz – they were temporary workers. Every laborer became independent after a while. Therefore, there were not any professional associations in Kielce; and the worker's movement was limited merely to a political framework. Strikes of Jewish workers were rare; generally, the employer and employee came to an agreement without it coming to a strike. They were divided according to profession, the sewing workers, the leather workers, the wood workers, and the food workers. From the start of the "Chalutz" [Pioneer] movement, Kielce became a training center for pioneers, to which many young men and women came, even from distant places, to undergo the training period; they started to spread into work places that had never held a Jew before. We saw them working in the quarries, the sawmills, and also at heavy labor, as porters, woodcutters, and others.

In the years before World War I, the local Jewish laborers were bubbling over and activists in the revolutionary activities against the government of the Czar; however, during the period of Polish independence things quieted down; and the Jewish laborers used their energies to work towards the rebirth of the nation in its homeland.

[Page-40]

Members of the Free Professions

On the front line of the free professions stood the Jewish doctors. The Jews had a predilection for medicine. Jewish doctors are to be found in the courts of kings and dukes; even the Christian clergy, the Popes, were healed by Jewish doctors. And there is not nation in the world who needs a doctor's advice in the least bit of illness like the Jews do. You haven't the smallest Jewish settlement, even the tiniest of the tiny, which does not have its own doctor. To the Jew, life and health are precious gifts that were given to humanity, and must be safeguarded at all costs.

In Kielce as well, as the Jewish community developed, there was no lack of doctors to be found there. The first Jewish doctor in Kielce was Dr. Werman, a gynecologist and internist. His wife was from the Epsztajn family of Warsaw, a radical and assimilated family. He himself still felt the need for tradition. When he had a son, they entered him into the covenant of Abraham [i.e. a circumcision ceremony] and held a festive meal, as is customary in the Diaspora. For the Passover holiday he would send his wife to her parents and hire himself a Jewish housekeeper, who cleaned his house, burned the "chametz" [leavening], bought new kitchenware for the holiday and prepared the holiday necessities for him in accordance with Jewish law. Indeed, he gave her permission to act totally at home. The traditions of his ancestors were still a part of him. But his wife couldn't stand Jewish customs, and she left her husband during the days of the holiday. After him, Dr. Perelman came to town. He was a nationalist Jew and the founder of the local Zionist Association. However, because of his Zionism, the Chassidim, who were opposed to Zionism, boycotted him, and in cases of illness they would go to Christian doctors. Perelman left the city and moved to Sosnowiec, there he found a broad scope for his both his Zionist activity and his medical activity.

Dr. Lewinzon, another gynecologist and internist, kept away from any national or social movement; although he contributed to the Zionist funds and the charity institutions, he did not participate actively in any movement or institution. He acquired the trust of broad swathes of the Jewish and Christian population, succeeded in his medical practice and became wealthy, built himself a splendid stone house on Tadeusza Street, the street of the Polish intelligentsia.

Dr. Zylberszlag, a popular doctor, was famous among the poor as an expert physician. He headed the Jewish hospital in the city, after Dr. Lewinzon resigned from this position.

When Poland regained its independence and all of its various parts were reunited, young Jewish doctors from Galicia began flocking to Kielce where they settled, some of them Zionists and some of them public activists. The most noticeable of them was Dr. Felc, a community activist, who introduced exemplary order to the Jewish community. He was the community representative to several public institutions and protected Jewish interests in the outside world. With his energy and initiative, he strove unceasingly to improve the lives of Jews from within and to return battle to the anti-Semites without.

Dr. Szac, the son-in-law of Maurberger, was a Zionist and was the leader of the Revisionist movement.

These doctors belonged to the second generation of Jewish doctors. The Kielcer homeowners also established a generation of energetic doctors from their children, who were set up with modern equipment in the field of medicine. The young doctors were nearly all nationalists and Zionists. These graduates of the Hebrew High School [Gymnasia], who carried with them facts from our national-spiritual treasures, were lively with a yearning for their national origins, and the hopes of the people of Israel beat in their hearts. Assimilation was already regarded, in their day, as a counterfeit coin, and it was no longer popular in the Jewish street.

Dr. Polak, despite having gone to the Russian High School, was also swept up in the national current, and participated in the Zionist youth group. Dr. Krauze was not a Zionist in public, but did not refrain from contributing to the funds. Dr. Firstenberg, son of the white-washer of Alexander [Aleksandrow Lodzki], who was dressed in Chassidic clothing himself until the age of sixteen, began later to learn the curriculum of the High School on his own, took the exam and received a matriculation certificate. He studied medicine at the university in Warsaw. After he finished his studies, he received his medical doctorate. Kielce, his birthplace, received him as its doctor, and its Jewish inhabitants put their faith in him. He was successful in his profession and immediately made a name for himself as an excellent physician. Several of the young doctors who had been raised in Kielce left the city of their birth and moved to the Land of Israel. Here, they served the Jewish settlement. The brothers Awraham and Jakob Herman, Icak Kajzer, Cel-Cion – are all originally from Kielce.

I will mention the Jewish medics ("feldszer", in their tongue). They were a type of popular physician. The Jewish and Christian population preferred the medic to the expert doctor. In cases of mild illness they would go to the medic and he would write them prescriptions with the permission (and also without permission) of the doctor, legally and illegally. The pharmacist would prepare the medications according to the medic's prescription. The doctors overlooked the medic's actions, since every doctor had his own medic, who, in cases of more serious illness would recommend him and refer his patients to him. There was a mutual agreement between the doctors and the medics; neither entered the other's area. Medics never went into the homes of the wealthy; the medics had contacts chiefly among the less well to do people. They received a meager wage for their work, and despite this, were nearly all of them rich. Every one of them had a stone house in the city.

Among them, the medic Rotman amassed a considerable fortune. He had many houses in the city. He was the most famous man in the city. He was especially well known among the women. He never rested; everyday he roamed the city visiting his patients. His sons gave him no satisfaction, one even left Judaism, and his father disowned him.

[Page-42]

The first medic in Kielce was Kiper, a man dressed in long clothes, with a white beard, early and late to the house of prayer. After him Zyngerman came, who was an expert at every discomfort and illness, extracted aching teeth, attached the surgeon's horn, let blood, put leeches on affected places and in general – would use all the various types of medicine that were customary in those days.

The medic Judel Praszowski gained the greatest fame, especially among the poor and the farmers in the villages around Kielce. He was the son of a Jewish villager, educated in the strict Jewish tradition. He was more knowledgeable about the various farming tasks than about anatomy. In his youth, it never occurred to him that fate would choose him to be a medic to his people. When he was twenty-one years old, the army accepted him for employment. At the time, an epidemic of cholera broke out in the western provinces of the Russian Empire. The epidemic spread through the army as well. Due to the lack of doctors, students from the medical academies were also sent out to fight the epidemic, which was killing hundreds and thousands. Even ordinary soldiers were appointed as assistants in caring for the ill. At that time, the army medical people looked to the Jewish soldier, who was modest and could concentrate, who observed everything and seeks to understand and know things. One day, his superior approached him and said: "You will be a medic", and sent him to the hospital. There he had the opportunity to observe the different diseases and phenomena. While attending surgery, he learned to recognize human anatomy. As a medic he was given classes in elementary anatomy and therapy and absorbed all of this information and remembered it as if his heart had foreknowledge that he would need it one day. And so it was. When he finished his service in the army and returned home, he began using the knowledge he had acquired in the military hospital to cure sick farmers in the area. In the morning he would leave home with a leather bag in his hand containing various medical instruments, pliers for extracting teeth, dishes of leeches, a surgeon's horn for drawing blood, and various other signifiers. Equipped with these instruments he would return to the nearby villages and visit the sick farmers and extend medical treatment. He soon had a reputation among the village inhabitants, and when someone was ill they would go only to him. The farmers believed of him that he could cure every disease and would say, "if Judel can't help, no one can help."

When he saw that he was succeeding in his work, he married and moved to the city. From that time he ceased to return to the villages; the patients were brought to him or a cart was sent to bring the doctor to the patient. The Jews of Kielce did not have much faith in him to begin with. They said: " a simple Jew, dressed like an ordinary person, who prays morning and evening, will be our doctor" – thus they mocked him. And in addition, they knew his past, that he had been a milkman in the past, he would bring milk jugs on a farmer's cart from the village to sell in the city. Suddenly he changed into – a doctor. But little by little he succeeded in gaining the trust even of his fellow Jews. He also became wealthy over time; bought himself a house and his reputation as an expert physician grew in the city as well. But he did not live long. During World War I, carrying out his duties curing patients ill with typhoid, he caught this dangerous disease, fell ill and did not recover. He died aged forty-nine. His son Welwel inherited his profession from him and with the aid of the doctors of the city he was allowed to work at curing patients.

I will mention the names of several other medics, such as Krauze and his two sons-in-law, Szeftel and Fiszer, and Mitelman, who served the inhabitants of Kielce in the last years before World War II.

With this we conclude the section of the doctors, who were an inseparable part of the Jewish public in Kielce. The doctor was at home in every Jewish family. The secrets of each and every person were revealed to him. Everyone complained of all the troubles that weighed on their hearts to him, as well as the joys that expanded their lives. The spirit of life that beats so strongly in the heart of every Jew led him to care for his body. In the case of a slight ache, of indigestion, of a slight cold, and others, the Jew turned to the doctor immediately. The medical expenses in a Jewish home were an important part of the annual budget. Wealthy and poor alike called the doctor, if their child coughed or had a bit of fever. The doctor was never out of work, was busy with visits until the evening. Sometimes his sleep was interrupted at night as well. It is no wonder; therefore, that nearly all of them made a small fortune, built themselves houses and enlarged their holdings. Some of them were community activists, and some national activists, and they had an effect on the formation of the special character of the community.

Jewish Dentists

To the list of Jewish doctors in the city I will add the Jewish dentists as well.

Many years passed without there being a Jewish dentist in Kielce. If one had a toothache, the Jew went to the doctor, and he would extract the sore tooth and that was that. They didn't know to use medications against toothache. Fillings for cavities, crowns, false teeth were still in the realm of fairy tales that people who had lived in the big city for a long time talked about. When people like that came home they told everyone about the amazing things they saw there.

One day a young man came to town, rented himself an apartment, on the door hung a sign upon which it said in gold lettering: "Dentist with diploma, J. Auerbach". Everyone, who walked by stopped for a moment, read the sign and walked on. No one went in to him even if he had a terrible toothache. Everyone knew his doctor who cared for his teeth, he would kill the root of the tooth with iodine, and if the pain didn't stop, would extract the tooth. To go to a special tooth doctor was unnatural to him. He was afraid that instead of easing his pain, he would damage his health. The Jew naturally holds to old-fashioned things, he has no faith in things that are too recent. The young dentist saw that he would starve to death if he did not find some trick to combat the public apathy to his important profession.

[Page-44]

Finally, he invited a matchmaker to his home. He revealed his desires to him that he was looking for a wife; but that she needs to be the daughter of a wealthy man who would bring him a decent dowry. He had arrived – the dentist said, to explain this request of his – in a place where no one knew him, he had few patients, and many expenses, and in order to establish his standing in the Kielce community, he needed money. The matchmakers fell upon this opportunity, like a hawk on its prey. They knew, that several of the wealthy daughters cherished hopes of marrying only a doctor. And how many doctors could there be in one market? If they had no choice they would settle for a dentist as well. The matchmaker said to him: "Rest quietly, sir, trust me and I will do as you wish, and everything will work out well." This matchmaker, when he left the dentist, went to the house of one of the wealthy men in town, whose daughter was waiting for a doctor to come and take her under his wing. The matchmaker offered his "wares" to the wealthy man, and after all of the praises and compliments that he scattered generously regarding the potential son-in-law doctor as his profession demanded, he added: "this is not an ordinary doctor, such as the ones you can find anywhere, but a tooth doctor, called "dentist" in their tongue, the only one in the city, who is earning the treasures of "Korach" in his profession." The wealthy man was not foolish enough to believe the words of the matchmaker. He knew that matchmakers were prone to exaggeration. He replied: "I will go and investigate and see if your words are true." Meanwhile, the matchmaker and the dentist put their heads together how to fool the wealthy man, in order to convince him that the dentist's income is really great, and that his daughter will be entering a king's palace. This matchmaker had many tricks. What did he do? He went to several of his acquaintances and relatives and requested them that on such-and-such a day, at such-and-such a time they should come to the dentist, and pretend that they had come for him to heal their aching teeth, and afterwards should give the doctor his honorarium, payment for healing them, most generously, with gold coins. And, of course, the money would be returned to them in full. At the same hour he would arrive with the wealthy potential father-in-law at the dentist's house, and everything would work out well. Everything worked according to the plan. The potential father-in-law, when he saw that there were many people seeking out the dentist, and his income was so great, agreed to the match, his daughter entered the chupah in good time with a young man of her own age, the dentist. She had, indeed, the privilege of being called "Mrs. Doctor," but she did not find happiness with him. This was the history of the first dentist who was willing to come to Kielce.

But in the meantime, Christian dentists had settled in Kielce, and they prepared the ground for the Jewish dentists as well, who came along later and were successful in their work. Anszer, the son of the lawyer, who was famous in the city, was an outstanding dentist. Many of the Jews of the city had him cure their toothaches. At the same time, a second dentist arrived in Kielce, named Serwetnik. He was close to the Zionists at first; however, later he left them and moved to the people's party "Folkisten". However, the greatest success in dentistry was that of the brothers Grojsem. They opened themselves a clinic in a large hall filled with all the latest equipment. Anyone with a slight toothache among the Jews or Christians began flocking to them in droves. Their waiting room was always full of patients who were waiting for their appointments. They became wealthy, built themselves an elegant house. They were not active in community affairs; all of their energies were invested in their profession and they strove to improve, correct and bring the profession of dentistry to perfection. Their hearts were not free to deal with community activity. They made generous donations to local community causes as well as the national funds. In general, they viewed the movement of the rebirth in the land of Israel with favor. Other than these, Dr. Feuer, the wife of the principal of the Jewish High School, excelled in her specialty. After them came the young dentists; but they settled in Kielce only a few years before World War II and were active their for only a short time, and did not have time to influence the Jewish population of the city in great or small measure.

Jewish Lawyers

In Czarist Russia there were two kinds of lawyers: avowed and private, that is, accredited and amateurs. Jewish lawyers fell into these two categories as well. It must be noted that the avowed Jewish lawyers were radically assimilated even to converting their religion. There were those in Kielce: the avowed lawyer Majzel and his brother-in-law Kowalski. Majzel was Fejwel Blachatowski's brother-in-law, who owned a press and published books in Piotrkow. They both converted. The first converted to Christianity shortly before his death and the second in his youth. The Poles rewarded him for switching into their camp and appointed him head of the district court in the city. They left the camp of Israel. In contrast, Anszer, a lawyer in Kielce, was very connected to tradition and came to synagogue; he was something of a scholar, and very knowledgeable in civil law. The traders would go to him with their arguments and disagreements. The judges also respected his knowledge and mastery of the codices and would take seriously the reasoning and evidence he brought when he stood before them to defend his clients' affairs.

Frajzynger was a private lawyer. When he came to town he began involving himself in community affairs as well, but was quickly silenced. He was of a weak spirit, and the fear of the anti-Semites fell upon him, lest they accuse him of belonging to the national Jewish camp. Another radically assimilated person was the lawyer Hassenbajn, he was a trial expert; in any difficult question even Polish lawyers would turn to him. He was faithful to his profession and everyone trusted him, but he was a stranger to the Jewish community, and had no interest in its needs and affairs. Also the young lawyers, J. Manela, Majfeld, Szrogroder were apathetic to Judaism and its needs. They stood with one foot still in the Jewish camp, and with the other they had stepped over the abyss that separated the two camps. None of the local Jewish lawyers became community or national activists. They held to the slogans of assimilated Jews in spite of the fact that they had become out of date and no longer appropriate for the living conditions. Several young people, who received their early education in Kielce and moved to Israel, completed their education here and serve as lawyers to the Jewish settlement of Israel to the best of their abilities. Elimelech Kirszenbaum (El-Roi), Jechiel Herman, famous lawyers in Israel, are originally from Kielce. Similarly, the lawyer Kaspi, son of Izrael Zylbersztajn is also a native of Kielce, but he received his training in Israel.

[Page-46]

Lawyers from Galicia also came to Kielce; but they were all equally apathetic to and alienated from the various streams that were running through the Jewish community at the time. They did not influence the community nor were they influenced by it. They were snobbish, closed into their narrow fields and participated in neither the community's troubles nor its celebrations. While in Warsaw, in Lodz, in Wilna, in Lwow, famous lawyers arose who devoted their energies to the affairs of their people as well, the lawyers in the peripheral cities still held to the old tradition according to which the intelligentsia must distance itself from its people and their affairs. Out of consideration for their Jewish clients, they didn't dare to take the last step, to tear the last thread that tied them to the body of Israel. For the trunk of the national tree, these were like withered leaves, that even a breeze could cause to fall from the branches.

Doctors and lawyers were the only members of the free professions that were common among the Jews of Kielce. In contrast to these, there were no engineers, architects, and agronomists. A Jew who completed his studies in these fields had no livelihood. The Russian government and later also the Polish government would boycott the educated Jews and did not allow them access to any government positions, and the Polish citizens avoided hiring Jews in their companies. A young Jewish engineer would be finally forced to change to another area of work that had no connection to his profession. Therefore, there remained before the Jewish students two professions: medicine and law. In later years, when Jewish educational institutions were opened, elementary and high schools, Jewish youth began to go over also to the study of mathematics, physics and pedagogy. They could find work in the Jewish educational institutions. But, about these latter, the teachers in the schools, I will speak in a special chapter.

[Page-47]

Relations Between the Jews and the Poles

Translated by Judy Montel

Edited by Warren Blatt

As I am writing the history of the Jews in Kielce it is also worth knowing about the relations that existed between the Jews who lived in the town and their Polish neighbors, from the beginning of Jewish habitation until their total extermination in 1942.

The Poles looked unfavorably upon the economic status that the Jews acquired in the city of Kielce, which was their city, and on whose soil Jews had been forbidden to step [until 1863]. In the relations that grew between the Jewish inhabitants of Kielce and its Polish inhabitants, one must differentiate between two periods: the first period includes the days of Poland the yoke of Czarist Russia, and the second, shorter than the first, the days of Polish independence [after 1918]. The aspect they have in common is that in both periods there was very strong anti-Semitic feeling in the hearts of the Poles with regard to the Jews of the city. Feelings of hatred and jealousy simmered in the hearts of the anti-Semites as they watched the Jews succeed in their endeavors.

However, during the first period, the hands of the Poles were shackled, and their anti-Semitism was only expressed openly in their Kielce newspaper "Gazeta Kielecka". In this newspaper poisonous articles against the Jews would appear from time to time; for instance, that the Jews were turning the cities of Poland into Jewish cities, the Jews were exploiting the farmer and the laborer. The Jews are parasites, live off of others; such headlines decorated their articles, which were filled with words of hatred and poison. These hateful words did not reach the broad masses of the Polish population, who were mostly still illiterate, peasants, who could not read or write. At the time, anti-Semitism was the heritage of the Polish intelligentsia and did not translate into tangible actions. The hatred radiated from the eyes of the Polish lawyer and clerk, who would gaze upon the Jew with disdain and sneers and to an extent dismiss him. They would call Jews "Gospaciarza" – businessmen – who are always chasing after business affairs, and have no concern for anything beyond their own narrow world of business rules. But they, the Poles, were noble. They had lofty ideals. They had a developed aesthetic sense, dealt with art, with literature, with philosophy and science. The Jews were not like this – they are materialistic. Business and Mammon – these were their goals in life.

However, because things did not turn into actions, the Jews were not excited by these disgraceful words. "Let the dogs bark, don't provoke them, they will quiet down on their own." Thus did the Jews calm their spirits and continue with their affairs, which brought plenty and wealth not only to themselves but to the Polish population as well.

[Page-48]

The N.D. party, "Narodowa Demokracia" – the National Democracy, the chauvinist Polish party, which was ready to put up with the Czarist subjugation in return for a mess of pottage, the internal rule in the cities and villages, and included in its plans and goals the topic of the war against the Jews. The Andeks distributed poison and hatred of Jews among the populace, saying that the Jewish influence was growing in the state; especially by their infiltrating Lithuanian and Russian Jews into the country who were mostly nationalists. Speaking in their jargon or in Russian and thus helping the Russians in their system of "Russification".

In Kielce, the influence of the N.D. was quite strong, here its propaganda found no opponents. The P.P.S. party, socialist Poles, was weak. Aside from several intelligent people they couldn't rally masses of workers to their banner. Kielce was a nest of anti-Semitism. Roman Damowski, the founder of the N.D. and its head would visit from time to time and attract new souls to his party. The outstanding Andeks were well known in Kielce: the Polish lawyers Donin, Jeronski, Dobrzanski and the chemist Saski. Jeronski the lawyer gained fame among the Jews of Poland with his anti-Semitic declaration in the second Russian Duma. The Russian government, at the demand of the Poles for political autonomy, agreed to grant them independent internal self-government in the cities and villages. The Andeks agreed to this gift, that the Czarist government was willing to bestow upon them in its great generosity. They always tended to compromise, they were those who grabbed the small portion, in contrast to the P.P.S., the Polish Socialist Party, which demanded full independence and invested its hopes in the general war for freedom going on in Russia itself.

At this time, when the proposed law regarding self-rule in the cities of Poland was being debated in the Duma (the Russian house of Representatives), Jeronski, the delegate from Kielce, arose and read a declaration in the name of the Polish "Kolo" (faction) in which they announced to the government that they were willing to make do with mere autonomy only if the Jews were denied the right to vote in elections of local government. He explained this demand with the fact that in most of the cities, the Jews constituted a majority of the inhabitants, and if they are given an active and passive right to vote, these cities will lose their Polish character.

Such a declaration on the part of the Polish faction infuriated not only the Jewish delegates, but also the Kadets (the Russian Liberal Democratic Party), who advocated the slogan of equal rights for all nations without discrimination of religion or race.

But in this period, even the confirmed anti-Semites in Poland did not use the methods of "The Black Century" in Russia. They did not unleash pogroms against the Jews, as was common then in Russian cities. Such a radical method, even if it were something they approved of and desired, would have brought them political damage in their aspirations for independence. They did not want to disgrace their people in the eyes of the civilized world, which had an enthusiastic attitude to the Polish nation which was groaning under the yoke of bondage, and therefore they were satisfied with anti-Semitic propaganda on paper, which didn't make an impression or noise in the world.

[Page-49]

Polish anti-Semitism took a totally different form after the First World War. In this period, the Polish anti-Semites in general, and those of Kielce with them, showed their true face. From inciting hatred against Jews verbally and in print, they now moved to action. With the entrance of major army divisions of the Russian camp to Poland, a difficult and bitter period began for the Jews. The Poles informed on the Jews, saying that they were spying for the enemy. The results of the informing and the false libels were very bitter for the Jews of Kielce, who were close to the front lines of the war. They suffered also from the Russians and also from the Polish legions. The former suspected the Jews of being in favor of the enemy and spying on his behalf. The commanders blamed the Jews for their defeats; and the latter said the reverse, that the Jews were agents of the Russians and spying on their behalf. The Jews were stuck between the hammer and the anvil. Innocent Jews were executed. On orders from the Poles, the Cossacks looted the shops and homes of Jews.

But all these oppressions were null and void compared to the ruthless and wild deeds of the Poles against the Jews from the day that Poland achieved its independence. They wished to show the Jews that a new period was now beginning, that from now on they were rulers, and that they, the Jews, were like potters clay in their hands. They made great efforts to prove to them in a real and crude fashion that they were the lords of the land. They began abusing Jews in various ways, they would shave off the beards of the Jews who were riding on trains, would beat them freely, would throw them out of the train carriages when the train was travelling at its fastest speed. Riding the train in those days became full of danger for a Jews. A Jew who had to travel to another city for his business preferred to travel by cart and lose the time than to risk his life taking the train.

The Jews of Kielce then felt on their flesh an actual pogrom in all of its exact details. Let us give a full description here of the events in Kielce in the year 1918. [1]

The Jews of the city had gathered in the local theatre to discuss the founding of a national local council. Participating in this meeting were representatives of all of the parties and factions, from the "Bund" to the "Aguda". The meeting was being conducted in quiet and order without any disruption. Everyone felt the seriousness of the hour, that Polish Jewry was standing before many dangers, and it was essential to organize and create a representation of Polish Jews, to stand on guard and protect them from having their rights injured. Meanwhile, a large gang of Polish thugs organized, all of them equipped with thick sticks and iron gloves, and among them also Polish soldiers. They gathered on Szinkiwica Street and filled the sidewalks on both sides of the street, next to the theatre. The Jews gathered in the hall and balconies of the theatre were listening to the speeches of the representatives of the various parties and factions, and from time to time, the theatre hall thundered with the sound of applause and cheers that burst out after each and every speech, and it never occurred to them that a pogrom was being plotted against them outside.

Suddenly those gathered awakened to movement, horrifying rumors reached the ears of the audience. A voice passed through the boxes of the theatre: "They are beating the Jews! Pogrom!" A commotion arose. A mass of men and women burst out in the direction of the doors; but in the corridor and on the steps stood "Szkejcim" [Gentiles] and showered those bursting out with heavy blows, heavy sticks came down upon the head, the face and the back. And also, whoever succeeded in bursting out into the street did not escape the hands of the rioters in one piece, as new punches awaited him there, which were generously bestowed by the thugs, who lined the two sides of the street. The crowd was shoved back into the halls of the theatre.

Footnote:

1. For more information on the 1918 pogrom, see the article "Opinie o Wystapienach Antizydowskich w Kielceach w dniah 11 I 12 listopada 1918 roku", by Adam Penkalla, in *Builetyn Zydowskiego Instytutu Historycznego w Polsce* , 1993 #3 (#191), pages 55-69.

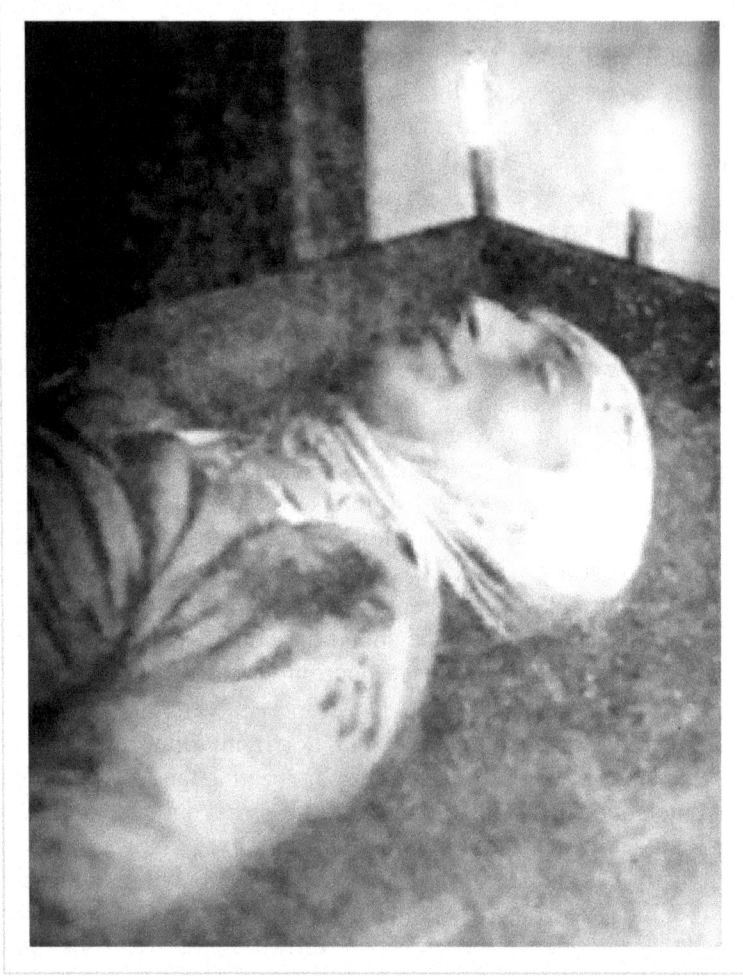

Ubszani, an inhabitant of the city – one of the victims of the pogrom

Self-defense on the part of the Jews was not possible: first of all, the assault was sudden and there was also no time for orientation and to understand what was going on. Secondly, the crowd gathered there was made up of men, women and the elderly as well, who were not in a state for defense without any tools, objects with which to defend themselves. The confusion that arose at the start of the assault had its effect. Everyone searched for an escape from the trap, and fell into the pit.

The rioters meanwhile spread out through all of the boxes of the theatre, to all of the balconies; its entrances and exits and were beating and abusing every Jew who fell into their hands. Members of the leadership, who were sitting up on stage by the table, were not injured in the riots, since the police arrived and arrested them. They led them to the jail where they sat until daylight without knowing anything of what was going on in the streets of the city.

Meanwhile, the rioters ran wild and were beating and injuring any Jews they found. After they finished their deeds in the theatre, they went out into the streets of the city, and there they laid waste without any interference, within the gaze of the city guards, they exploded the glass panes in the windows of Jewish homes. The Jews closed the gates of the houses to keep the destroyer from entering their courtyards. The rioters set off for the station house. The Jewish passengers who arrived on the night train had no idea of what was going on in the city and when they entered the station, fell victim to the blows of the rioters. Once the destruction was given license, it did not discriminate between the Jews of Kielce and the merchants who came from other cities for purposes of business. Every Jew, who fell into their hands, came out broken, shattered, injured and bleeding. It was a fearful night for the Jews of Kielce. The Jews did not suffer from theft and looting on that night. In this sense, this pogrom was different from the rest of the pogroms in the cities of Ukraine and Russia. The Poles meant only to teach the Jews a lesson, that they should understand and recognize that from now on they were the masters, and the Jews would not be allowed to stand tall and demand rights. From now on the Jews were slaves who lived in hopes of charity from the masters of the land.

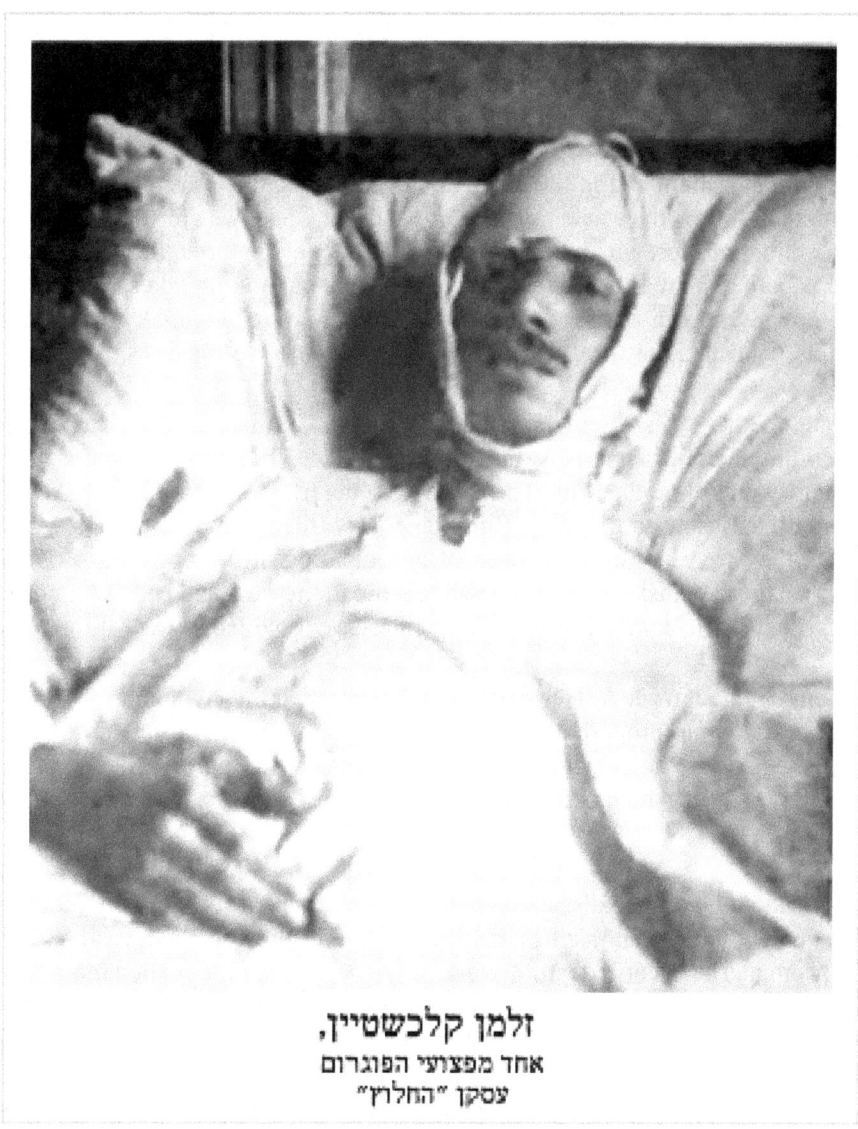

Zalman Kalichsztajn, one of those injured in the pogrom, a "HeChalutz" activist

The next day, when the news reached the farmers of the area of the license given to Poles to assault the Jews and beat them, they arrived in masses equipped with sticks and clubs to beat and take their part of the loot and property of the Jews. However, apparently, the local authorities received certain instructions from the central government regarding the scope of activities that they were permitted, and to exceed its boundaries was forbidden. In the morning, shifts of guards and soldiers were stationed in the market and on the streets who dispersed the gathering crowds and order was restored.

[Page-52]

The serving of the pogrom that the Jews of Kielce received from the independent Poland was four Jewish deaths and about four hundred injured, many of who remained disabled for the rest of their lives.

The local Polish press described the events in the theatre and the city streets as a mild scuffle, which broke out between Jewish and Polish youths, due to some incitement, provocation, and whose results were injured on both sides. The police were investigating this sad matter, and would certainly find the guilty parties, and those who would arouse argument and fights between the two ethnicities – would receive their punishment. Democratic Poland – the Polish press continued hypocritically – which had been reborn after hundreds of years of bondage, needed peace and quiet, and such events brought shame upon the Polish republic. In this announcement and in the distortion of the facts, this press wanted to absolve the Poles of blame, and attempted to show the world its pig's foot and say: "See, we are entirely kosher, we are civilized people and such actions are foreign and mysterious to us." They distorted the course of events and blurred their true nature, labeling them as the kind of altercation that commonly takes place in any large gathering. The Poles were already known as hypocrites, doing any abomination and showing their hooves to show how kosher and unblemished they are.

The delegate to the Polish Sejm [parliament], Icak Grynbaum, filed a motion with the Polish government regarding the pogrom against the Jews of Kielce. The local procurator was formally required to conduct an inquiry regarding the riots. They also staged a trial against a few "Szkejcim" [Gentiles] who had participated in the assault on the Jews. Simultaneously, the main perpetrators who had conducted the riots walked free; they were not even accused of participating in the riots. To satisfy the appearance of justice, a trial was staged against several thugs whose role in the riots had been secondary. Eventually, they too were acquitted, since there were not sufficient witnesses or evidence against them.

The arguments of the lawyer A. Hertglas - who represented the demand to sort out the matter that the indictment was not drawn up properly, that the main perpetrators, among them also police officers, were strolling through the halls of justice with smiles on their lips – were to no avail, and the trial was conducted against a few thugs, against whom there was not even clear evidence of their direct participation in the assault on the Jews.

Finally, the trial at the Kielce district court regarding the pogrom was concluded the way such trials were concluded in the rest of Poland's cities. Kielce was not the only one in those days among whose Jewish inhabitants a pogrom had been carried out. A wave of pogroms (the Poles called them "Ekscesen" – clashes) swept over several Jewish settlements. The intent of the Poles was the stifle, by terror and fear, by means of terror, any aspiration in the hearts of the Jews to full civil life, to equality and the rights of a citizen in the country. Although, according to the Versailles Treaty, they were bound to recognize the rights of the minorities, including the Jews, the Poles wanted this recognition to be "Halacha [Rule of Law] – upon which we do not act"; that the rights would remain on paper, and in reality, the minorities would be oppressed in the state. They wanted to demonstrate that they were the masters and the government was in their hands.

After this pogrom, the Jews of Kielce learned as their heralds had foreseen, that with the establishment of Polish independence they were not entering a period of liberty and peace; but true lives of exile were ahead of them, lives of bondage and humiliation. Several young people of upright posture, lovers of liberty, rejected Diaspora life and moved to the Land of Israel; some of them immigrated to the United States. However, most of them thought otherwise: "Since Poland is a democracy, equal rights for Jews are promised in its constitution, and over time, relations between the Poles and the Jews will settle down." Thus were the thoughts of most of the shortsighted Jews, whose horizons were narrow and who could not see what was brewing. The bitter reality disappointed these hopes.

A farewell ball for the first pioneers moving to the Land of Israel in 1918

The twenty years of Polish independence, until the invasion of the Nazis, were one long chain of trouble and tragedy for the Jews of Poland in general, and those of Kielce in particular. As long as [Prime Minister Józef] Pilsudski was alive, the Polish anti-Semites did not dare to attack the Jews openly. He controlled the base impulses of the anti-Semites, whose greatest desire was to return to the period of bondage of the "Poritzim", and their goal – to enslave the Jew materially and spiritually.

However, after Pilsudki's death [in 1935] the hatred of the Jews flared up in all of its strength and attacked across wide circles of the Polish nation. And, the lot of the Jews of Kielce was, as usual, a double portion of the anti-Semitic outbursts.

After the first pogrom, the soldiers of the Polish General Haler ran wild in Kielce for a period, known as "Halerczikes" by the Jews. From the day these soldiers arrived in Kielce the Jews knew much trouble and suffering. They would abuse the Jews, torture them and humiliate them in public. Their favorite targets were the pious orthodox Jews, with their long beards and traditional costume, as these hooligan soldiers demonstrated their "bravery" with an old and weak Jew…

After the death of Pilsudski, and after Hitler's rise to power in Germany, all the various types of anti-Semites raised their heads proudly and declared a free-for-all of the wild spirits of the men of the netherworld criminal element against the Jews. A period of great suffering began then for the Jews of Kielce as well: physical beatings and injury and damage to property. The shattering of the glass display windows, throwing stink bombs into the shops of Jews – these were everyday events. The Jews grew used to these actions and would no longer respond to them. On Sabbaths and holidays the Jews of the city were careful not to go stroll in the city park, because there too beatings awaited them. In the summer, they avoided settling in certain summer camps in places where the inhabitants hated the Jews and would stone them. On market days, the merchants were terrified of being set upon and of having their wares destroyed. The Jew saw himself in a bad position, which worsened from day to day. At that time, even optimistic Jews began to recalculate their plans. The future they saw was painted in dark colors, and whoever had the opportunity, packed his possessions, left his home and moved to the Land of Israel or immigrated overseas.

From the time that the Nazis began preparing for war and organizing a fifth column in each and every country, the divisive propaganda against the Jews began in full force. Simultaneously, many journals appeared whose task was to incite the masses against the Jews, and to accuse them of despicable conspiracies. In the legislature and government offices as well there were crude assaults on the Jews. Demands were heard to remove the Jews from their economic standing, to exclude the Jewish students from institutes of higher education, to increase their burden and embitter their lives until they would be forced to leave the country. Morning and night new laws were created that discriminated against the Jews and which reached a peak with the ban against ritual slaughter, which served the purpose of removing an important area of livelihood from the hands of the Jews. It seemed that the Poles had no other concerns, only one single, unique concern – how to be rid of the Jews. Instead of focussing all their thoughts on one point; increasing their defensive abilities, which was faulty in every way, they concentrated on the propaganda of the fifth column and cried out "Jews are on you, Poland". With their exaggerated arrogance, the Poles imagined that they were strong enough to stand before the enemy threatening them from the west, as well as their enemy to the east. The Polish foreign minister, Beck, conducted Poland's policy according to Hitler's instructions until it brought about a crisis, and then all of its weakness was revealed. Only in one area, in the area of hatred of the Jews, did the propaganda of the fifth column do much productive work. And during this period of time, the anti-Semites of Kielce and the area were the most active, and the Jews of the city suffered a double portion of the troubles that descended upon the Jews of Poland. The pogrom in Przytyk, a town in the Kielce district, was a natural result of the incitement against the Jews, which was conducted methodically and with a special stubbornness by the anti-Semites of Kielce.

[Page-55]

The anti-Semitic propaganda, which was being conducted in Poland before the outbreak of the Second World War, trained the hearts and prepared the ground for the deeds so horrifying in their cruelty and ruthlessness during the war. When Hitler's minions invaded Poland they found Poles who already agreed with them, for regarding the destruction of the Jews there were Poles who were of one mind with the Nazis. The Poles were well trained by the fifth column, Hitler's agents, who spread hatred of the Jews. The Nazis found in the Poles not opponents, but loyal assistants in the act of destruction. All circles of Poles participated in this project of mass-murder, from the laborer to the priest.

One young woman, who survived the death pit, told the writer of these lines that because of her work in the underground she also visited their churches, so that she would not be suspected of being Jewish. Once she heard the priest who stood at the pulpit and preached to his flock say, among other things: "Although the war has brought a Holocaust upon us, but the silver lining we have is that we are rid of the Jews this way, who suck our blood."

This was the Christian ethic that the priests of the church preached to their congregants, a uniquely exalted ethic…

Due to this attitude of the Poles regarding the Jews, can it be surprising that Poland was chosen by the Devil and his demons of destruction to be the arena for the destruction of European Jewry. The ground here had been worked and prepared enough for the task. The Nazi monster was certain that its satanic enterprise would have a one hundred percent success rate here. And also in this time of horror, the Jews of Kielce drank and sucked the cup of poison until its last drop. If in the rest of the cities of Poland a certain percent of the Jewish inhabitants survived, the number of survivors from among the Jews of Kielce reached only a few dozen, that even a child could list. From a community that numbered twenty-five thousand souls, a few dozen young men and women remained, and they too were not saved by any help from their neighbors, but by a miracle. Not only that there was not a single Pole in Kielce who could be a member of the Righteous Gentiles and give shelter and a hiding place to a Jew being pursued for his life, but they also helped actively in the planning of the blueprints for destruction and would reveal the Jews' hiding places, in order to take over their property. According to the few reports which arrived from this killing field, it becomes clear that also after the liberation of Kielce by the Russian army, the Polish murderers continued to murder the few remnants who came out of their hiding places, thinking that succor had arrived. The murderers are even mentioned by name. In the destruction of the survivors, Kielce stands in the front row. The city of Kielce was discolored with an unremovable stain by the last pogrom, that the Poles conducted against several dozen survivors who returned from Russia to visit their homes, which had now fallen into the hands of strangers, in the hopes that the Poles would receive them in friendship. However, the neighbors met them with pistols and daggers, killed and murdered those who hoped to go forth from darkness into the light. Forty-eight Jewish victims were killed, the remnant of a great and splendid community.

[Page-56]

This is the Christian ethic, which aspired to be the most exalted ethic for all of humanity. With regard to the Jews, Christianity – of which the Poles were considered its most devoted practitioners – was revealed in all of its despicableness and lowliness. Christianity did not purify their souls: they remained wild, blood thirsty, just as they had been a thousand years before when they were still sunk in the ignorance of paganism. The moral and humane imperative of our prophets: "My refugees shall live among you, hide the refugees and do not reveal the wanderer!" [Isaiah 16/3] – such an imperative was strange and foreign to our Polish neighbors. It is not surprising, therefore, that the Jews, survivors of the death camps in Germany, did not want to return to Poland, their birthplace; didn't want to step upon soil soaked in blood, on a land saturated with the blood of Jews, the blood of the elderly, the young, the blood of mothers and their children, didn't want to look in the faces of those who had murdered their parents, brothers and sisters.

The prayer: "Pour forth your wrath upon the Nations…" [Jeremiah 10/25 & Psalms 79/6] which in a period of equal rights we had begun to think of as an anachronism, something whose time had passed, here, in our own times became relevant, became lively and fresh. The "Gentileness" ["of the Nations" Hebrew: "goyut"] was and will always be the supreme forefather of impurity, the impulse for bloodletting rules it with unrestrained authority. And, from time to time, it bursts forth with insolent rage poured out over the weakest of the nations, upon the Jews, who cannot expect help from others. The Jew would lift his eyes to the heavens and cry out "My succor is from God, creator of the heavens and the earth" [Psalms 121/2] for the rabble of the nations there is never any corrective. "Pursue them with fury and destroy them from under the heavens of God!" [Lamentations 3/66] is a prayer better understood now than in any other time or era.

I now understand one event that at first I didn't notice. The day that I left for the Land of Israel, my friends held a party or farewell ball, and to me the jealousy was very noticeable, that I was able to move to the land that is the focus of every Jew's yearnings, and they were forced by fate to remain in the Diaspora among the wolves of the steppes. A silent prayer was on the lips of everyone present: "Would that God would give me also the opportunity to get out of this Vale of Tears and go up to the Land of Israel, to breathe her air and aid in her construction." In this serious mood that surrounded the gathering, a veteran Zionist got up, his name was Berel Moszenberg, and burst into hysterical tears, and called out in a choked voice: "Pinchas, to whom are you leaving us?!" and could speak no more. But this spontaneous cry had a depressing effect on those present; it felt like a prophecy had been thrown from the mouth of this veteran Zionist, for who sensed the dangers approaching the Jews more than the Zionist? For the founder of the Zionist movement saw this danger decades earlier. The Zionists, who had a broader outlook and their field of vision encompassed greater territory in time and place were always announcing the danger that was growing and approaching.

I now understand this event: even if Moszenberg's eye did not foresee the Holocaust that would break upon the heads of the Jews, his heart foresaw it.

[Page 57]

Intellectual, Cultural and Social Life

Translated by Judy Montel

Edited by Warren Blatt

During the (long) period that lasted up to the beginning of the twentieth century, the Jews of Kielce had a monochromatic form: traditional Judaism with a Chassidic flavor. The Jews were noticeable in their garments, their speech, their faces. The holidays, celebrations of Mitzvah [commandments], and the visit of the Admo"r [the Chassidic rabbi/leader] to the city were attractions that changed the gray pace of Jewish life somewhat. Education of the children was in the hands of the "melamdim", teachers. When they finished the "cheder" [primary school], the young boys would continue their studies in the study halls or in the "shtiblach" [small houses of worship]. Early marriages, eating at the table of the father-in-law, the blessing of sons – these were the foundations upon which the community was based.

Aside from individuals who were called "Daitchen" -- who broke the barriers and wore short clothing, or, in the words of the wits of those days: "who wore long underclothing and short overclothing", and spoke in the language of the Gentiles -- the members of the community were in the main one unit. No foreign current had penetrated their lives; no strong wind blew through their homes. They had frozen in place, and lived their lives without changes or alterations. This life also had a special name: "Yiddishkeit". This life was very clear and obvious to the eyes of everyone, and whoever went outside of its boundaries was a "criminal of Israel", someone to pursue and whose life it was a good deed to embitter. A solitary rebel like this, whose spirit yearned for some space, for freedom, someone for whom the air of the study hall had become narrow and stifling, was forced to leave his birthplace, his parents, and to wander for great distances, or at the very least to the big city, to Warsaw or Lodz. That was the reality until the Zionist movement arose, which brought movement and changes of values to the Jews of Poland, and new cultural foundations arose instead of the ancient and old-fashioned foundations.

The First Zionist Association in Kielce

The Zionist Association that was founded in Kielce in 1900 concentrated within itself all those who were filled with one idea, one aspiration: to raise up the masses of Jews from their low material and spiritual level. Most of them, filled with the national idea, aspired to the renewal of the nation in its ancient homeland, in the land of Israel. They made up the core of the association. But there were those among them who aspired to renew the lives of the masses by a socialist revolution; some outstanding assimilated Jews, members of the P.P.S. [Polska Partia Socjalistyczna, the Polish Socialist Party] joined the Zionist Association in the fist days of its foundation. Without having a field of activity in any other place, they hoped to gain access to the masses of the Jews and to influence them with their opinions and views. The association therefore had quite a varied composition; next to members of the intelligentsia, doctors, bank managers and their clerks, the veterans of the study hall, who peeked in and were caught, found a place; artisans sat next to merchants, the distinctions between one rank and another were blurred. Goodwill and friendship existed between the members.

This was the romantic period of the Zionist movement. The youth were particularly engulfed by a great enthusiasm; the vigor and fresh energies that beat in their hearts pushed them to activities. The Yiddish press, which then began to appear, spread the concepts of renewal among the boulevards where the Hebrew word was like a sealed book.

The Zionist Association also had several young women members. For the first time the daughter of Israel began to appear in public also, she, who up until then had remained at home. The verse: "All of her glory is a king's daughter within" [Psalms 45/14], ruled until then with extreme strictness in the houses of Israel. Songs of Zion which were sung in a chorus of men and women, lectures about various topics, lessons in the Hebrew language, in scripture and in Jewish history – all of these attracted the young heart to the Associations hall. There he found interest in life, beauty, education, a field of activity, there he acquired polite manners along modern lines, a feeling of self-respect, and the daring and courage to express his opinions. The debates awakened the intellect, gave opportunities for speech also to the shy, who suffered from stage fright whenever they had to express their opinions.

I remember, at the first meetings of the members of the Association, while the chairman read aloud the agenda to those gathered and turned to them with the question: Does anyone have something to add to the agenda or want to change it, there was silence in the hall. No one was willing to open their mouths, fearing their words would become subject to scorn and mockery. The chairman, who spoke Polish, spoke to their spirits and called to their hearts, that they should speak as they wished, express their opinions, not be ashamed, not be too humble, speak in the language they knew. Every one of those gathered had the right to speak and must use that right. Here there would be no regime of demagoguery. Matters would be settled by majority vote. Every question needs to be clarified and analyzed from all angles and everyone must participate in this clarification and express his opinion. With much effort, the chairman succeeded in extracting some words from one or two people, and encouraging them, and even they spoke with a stammer, with illogical connection and incomplete sentences.

However, when they began making the first steps in debating the issues, in the battle of ideas that arises of its own accord in any gathering of comrades who come together for any purpose, activity or endeavor, people slowly got used to participating in negotiating and arguments. From meeting to meeting, the number of those raising their hands to request the right to speak grew. Before a short time had passed the members had adopted the form of speech openly, everyone tried to appear in public and make an impression in his manner of speech, his knowledge, in his victory over his rival. Everyone already knew the parliamentary rules and would verbally demand his right to express an opinion. Sometimes, the chairman had to cut off the list of speakers since the meeting had gone on for too long.

At the meetings and sessions, over time, people also learned to listen patiently to the views of their opponent, not to stop a rival and not to interrupt his words. In the beginning it was hard for many of the members to unlearn their habit of speaking when others were talking. In the study hall, when a gabbai [synagogue manager] was being chosen, those who spoke in public would gather; no one could stop his spirit and not speak, when his friend was expressing himself. The words would cross, get confused. In the mixture of voices it was impossible to understand the opinion of everyone. However here, in the Zionist Association, the members adopted polite manners. From this point of view the Zionists were very active in the area of adult cultural education.

The founding of the Association was accomplished after a difficult battle against inner and outer obstacles. The rule of suppressing human liberty and free speech, which existed in those days in the country of the Czar, in the days of the Russian hangman, the Minister of Interior Pelwa, took on a most terrible form. Founding organizations and associations was considered a most heinous crime. It was impossible to legally found any sort of association, whether political, social or cultural. This left only one avenue, which would allow people to get around the police, and this was – to found the association under the camouflage of religion; that is to say, to rent a hall which would formally function as a house of worship. The authorities did not get involved in the area of religion and would allow the opening of synagogues and "cheders" [primary schools] for the children of Israel with no limitations. And indeed, in every small town, synagogues appeared and grew like truffles and mushrooms. Every Admo"r had a "shtibl" where he and his disciples and admirers prayed. They were opened without any unusual difficulties. The authorities did not intervene in religious matters. Once in a long while a sanitary committee was sent to oversee the sanitary conditions, which were required of every building in which people gathered; but they paid no mind to their internal affairs.

However, because of this particular point, it was difficult to obtain a hall for the Zionist Association. The Chassidim were frightened of the new movement, the Zionist movement, whose goal was, in their opinion, to destroy their marsh, and they did everything they could and used every means to sully their reputation in the eyes of the religious masses. And they announced: "The Zionists are rebels, irresponsible delayers of redemption, "Shabtai-Tzvi-niks" [i.e. adherents of the 17th century false messiah who later converted to Islam, Shabtai Tzvi] of a new sort, corrupters of youth, distracting from the study of Torah, and other negative remarks. They had one goal – to suppress the movement at the start of its growth, to cut its wings, not to allow it to develop and flourish. Their first act was to decree excommunication upon any landlord who would be willing to rent out space to the Zionist Association. However, this excommunication had no effect. A landlord was found in the city, Chaim Kochen, a tinsmith by trade, who was not influenced by the fear of the Chassidim, did not depend upon them and who leaned towards Zionism in his heart; he arose and rented them an apartment. As I mentioned above, the apartment was rented as a synagogue, and thus it was registered with the police.

The head of the Zionist Association and its founder was Dr. Perelman, a community activist and a man of tremendous energies. His secretaries were his brother-in-law Paradystal, a bookkeeper at the branch of the Commercial Lodzer Bank, Wolman, manager of the whitewash kilns "Kadzilna" of the Ehrlich brothers. Among the most active members I will mention Mendel Elencwajg, a delegate to the third Zionist Congress, Ajzik Zylbersztajn, Berel Moszenberg, Dawid Dyzenhaus, Mosze Kinigsberg, and the banking brothers Nowak.

From the day that they acquired the apartment the Zionists began working intensively. Besides the direct Zionist work: selling shekels, shares of the Colonial Bank, collecting money for the land of Israel, they began developing a wide sphere of public relations: holding lectures balls for entertainment. They arranged a reading room and small library in their apartment.

ועד אגודת הציונים בשנת 1917

Zionist association committee in 1917

Sitting from the right: N. Kajzer, Ch. Waksberg, D. Rozenberg, C. Piekarski , Sz. Kajzer.
Standing: Dajbuch , D. Goldblum, P. Kalichsztajn, M. Zajde and N. Rotenberg.
Second Row: M. Krakauer, Fridman , Z. Kalichsztajn, C. Waksberg, N. Finkelsztajn , Sz. Kajzer

During the meetings they would set watches in order to avoid danger to those gathered. In the hall there was a Holy Ark, a table for reading the Torah. On Sabbaths and holidays the members would worship there as a community. Some of them would leave their prayer shawls there from week to week.

And then, one evening, during a members' meeting, the watchman alerted those who were gathered that the Pristew (police officer) with several policemen was standing in front of the courtyard and speaking with the landlord about a society of revolutionaries which had found a place in his house, and he had come to see what they were up to. As soon as the members heard this they stood up and wrapped themselves in their prayer shawls, which were stacked on top of the ark, and picked up their prayerbooks. One of them stood in front of the ark and sang the Czarist anthem: "Borza Caria Charany" – "God, Keep the Czar, etc.". Those present sang it in chorus. All this was done in a flash. When the Pristew entered accompanied by the policemen and heard the anthem, they all stood at attention and saluted, in honor of the Czarist anthem. And thus they stood at attention, not moving a muscle, until the singing of the anthem was over and the cantor continued reading Psalms, and the assembly after him with out paying any attention to the police representatives, who were standing by the door puzzled and amazed: "Kremoloniki" (revolutionaries) singing the Czarist anthem and wrapped in prayer shawls are standing there and praying. Their minds could not comprehend such things. Finally the Pristew turned to one of those praying and asked: "Today is not a Sabbath and not a holiday; what are you holding here?" Then the chairman approached him and explained that in honor of the death of one of the famous rabbis, who had lived in the middle ages, a memorial service was being held here, as was customary, and at this opportunity they pray for the welfare of the monarchy. The Pristew looked suspiciously at those present to begin with; but when he saw the ark and the other implements of worship and nothing suspicious appeared to his eyes, and besides that, he had heard all of those gathered singing the anthem in chorus, he was totally convinced that the informers had misled him. The Pristew was satisfied with the demand that they show him the permit for the synagogue. And when his demand was met, he left with his escorts to the heartfelt joy of the Zionists.

The Zionist movement conquered the hearts of those who frequented the study halls, artisans and intelligentsia, who had an affinity for Judaism and its hopes in their hearts. However, over time there began to be changes in the make-up of the Zionist Association in Kielce. The unified body began to split and divide. At first, the various streams acted in concord; the contrasts between them were not so great that they prevented cooperative efforts.

In the breadth of Russia, in the meantime, new winds began blowing; winds of liberty began penetrating every corner, even to those places cut off from others. After the assassination of Interior Minister Pelwa, who had organized the riots against the Jews of Kishinev, and after the outbreak of war with Japan in the Far East, in 1905, there arose throughout Russia a strong liberation movement. Various parties arose at that time, each with its own "Credo" and program. Each party built its own platform. Then it was time for things to come apart in Kielce as well. Paradystal and Wolman and all those who followed them were swept up into the P.P.S. and battled for the cause of Polish national liberation. They and their wives founded a Polish school for Jewish Girls, which introduced the ideas of the assimilated Jews into the homes of Israel. Young artisans, influenced by the doctrine of Socialism that began spreading in the Jewish street, couldn't sit together with the bourgeoisie. Some of them cut off their contact entirely with the Zionists and became Bundists, Social Democrats, and they conducted a war against Zionism. Some of them did not distance themselves entirely from Zionism. However, their ties with Zionism were weakened to the same extent that the liberation movement progressed across Russia. There were others who joined the "Poalei Zion" movement, S.S., and others. Some of them were later prominent labor activists and active artisans, like Judel Gutman, Josef Goldszajder, Szmuel Lajchter, the Strawczinski brothers and others. They did much in their energetic work to raise the level of the artisan from its lowly economic and social status.

[Page-62]

In these days of the disintegration of the Zionist Association, many remained in it who were committed to the idea of national renewal in the land of Israel, whom the general current of the liberation movement did not succeed in sweeping away in its waves. Dr. Perelman moved to Sosnowiec. In his place, Mosze Piekarski came to live in the city, an outstanding Zionist, who did not leave his position as the chairman of the Zionists of Kielce until he moved to the land of Israel after the First World War. The Zionists then concentrated in their new apartment. The bankers, the Nowak brothers, gave them an entire house, in which there was a synagogue called "Sha'arei Zion" whose gabbais [managers] were Szmuel Lewartowski and Nachemja Ostrowicz (may God avenge their deaths), and a committee house for the Zionists. There was also a charity organization that was sympathetic to Zionism and among whose membership were several outstanding Zionists, which found a home there for a synagogue and an office for its work. The "shamash" (beadle), Zelig Grosfeld, who was known among the people of Kielce as "Zelig Paczke", was the caretaker of the house, and he had an apartment there for his family. This beadle was a fanatic Zionist. He fought fiercely against those opposed to Zionism. When the awful rumor arrived regarding the death of Dr. Herzl, Z"L, a great sorrow spread among the Zionists. With a lowered head and depressed spirit, they would walk through the streets, as if the wreath had been snatched from their heads. Those on the other side, who opposed Zionism, showed their joy in public. One of the assimilated Jews, his name was Littauer, went out to the market place and announced in a joyful tone in a group of people: "Herzl is dead! There is no more Zionism!" Zelig the beadle, who was among the listeners, could not listen with a quiet spirit to the blasphemy coming out of the mouth of this man, went over to him in a fury and treated him to two slaps on the face. This event was a subject of discussion by everyone for a long time.

This action by a simple beadle, who so drastically and obviously, in the public eye, was zealous over the honor of the Zionist leader, raised his stature in the eyes of the Zionists who remained in that camp and they kept him in his office until the end of his days.

This was the beginning of the Zionist movement among the Jews of Kielce, as it was etched in my memory. Over time, young forces came up and they kept the flame of Zionism from being extinguished. After the First World War the movement grew and flourished until it was nearly part of the common culture.

The "Ivriya" Association

Together with the political Zionism of Herzl Z"L, there was also a movement that arose in Zionist circles to restore the Hebrew language to popular usage, and to turn it into a living language that would be used not only for writing but also for speech.

For this purpose an association was also founded in our city in 1906 called "Ivriya". The regulations of the association required its members to use the Hebrew language in conversation, in buying and selling, in debates, and in general to make an effort to adopt the language to the extent that the members of the association would become fluent in it in such a manner that they could express their opinions, their thoughts and ideas freely without difficulty or stammering. To achieve this goal, the association needed to hold lectures from time to time, conversations of the members in Hebrew, to organize trips to public places and speak Hebrew out loud, in order to demonstrate the renewal of the language to the outer world as well, to do public relations for it, to attract new members to the ranks of the association.

The enlivening spirit of the "Ivriya" Association was Kino, Z"L, Anszer's brother-in-law. He later moved to settle in Israel and acquired a stone house on Yavne Street. He held to the philosophy of the "Poalei Zion" movement, was a talented speaker and author, and defended his views vigorously. He published a number of articles in Polish in the local newspaper, "Eko Kielcke", "The Kielce Echo", the journal of the progressive Poles, in which the author attempted to base his Zionist outlook from the viewpoint of socialism. These articles of his started a debate with the Polish-Jewish author Balmont. He reacted to Kino's articles with a string of articles entitled: "Zionist Dwarves in Marx's Clothing", in which he attempted to contradict the ideology of the "Poalei Zion". This author, an obvious assimilationist, determined that the moment that socialism was realized, and the reins of government would be in the loyal hands of the people's elected representatives and exploiters and exploited no longer exist in the social sphere, there will no longer be any place for anti-Semitism, the question of the Jews will cancel itself out, since social equality will reign in the world. Anti-Semitism is the fruit of competition; the dark forces of an acquisitive society, who want to continue the old system of government encourage it, in order to distract the hatred of the exploited for their exploiters in a different direction.

Kino was active in the "Ivriya" Association. He was fluent in Hebrew and would lecture in it regarding all matters which were of interest in those days and about which people wanted to hear. Another who stood at his side in the dissemination of the Hebrew language among the youth of Kielce was a young man named Frydland, Kligman's brother-in-law. He was from a family of Chassidim and rabbis, and he had a chassidic enthusiasm and also great devotion to the matter of restoring the Hebrew language to popular usage.

Every Sabbath afternoon all of the members would go out to the city park for a stroll. They would walk in couples. Every couple chose a topic for conversation. If a difficulty in expressing a concept arose in mid-conversation, they would turn to the couple passing them with a question – and immediately the difficulty would be resolved, and the conversation would continue as it had earlier. The conversations, the questions and answers were conducted in a slightly raised voice, so that others would also hear, and become interested in learning and knowing Hebrew in writing and speech. The Hebrew speech of the strollers indeed made a positive impression upon elders and youngsters, men and women, who had made a habit of strolling in the city park on Sabbath afternoons. Christian walkers also stopped when they heard the sounds of a language they were not used to hearing and asked what it might be. They received a comprehensive explanation about Zionism, its purpose and aspirations and about the training of the generation to be ready for the lofty role standing before it: the renewal of the people in its homeland, in the holy land, and restoring the Hebrew language to fluency among the youth, the language of our prophets, a language holy also to Christians.

Among the members of this association, the most active ones besides those mentioned above were also Mosze Kalichsztajn, Fiszel Lewi, Dawid Rozenberg, Mendel Elencwajg, and others, who participated in the meetings, but did not take an active part in the debates, the discussions. They were, to an extent, acted upon and not actors.

Culturally, the "Ivriya" did much to broaden the horizons of the veterans of the study hall; it introduced new ideas in the hearts of the young people and stirred many of the older generation from their apathy. Aside from their chief goal: restoring the popular use of the Hebrew language, they also had another educational goal – including youth in the sphere of activities that refine the soul, which chase away boredom and foreign tendencies. These activities were, to be sure, not complete; they were only an introduction to broader activities that came later as the circumstances and times changed. They created a foundation upon which later the establishment of the Hebrew school was based, which will be mentioned in later chapters. The "Ivriya" took the Hebrew language out of its holy place and made it a tool for every day use, for ordinary matters. Not "the holy tongue", as it was called earlier, but simply "Hebrew". The Hebrew newspapers began the process of secularization of the language: "HaMelitz", "HaTzefira", "HaShachar" and others; however, they did not have the power to make it a living language the way the "Ivriya" did. Associations like "Ivriya" did much to make Hebrew a spoken language like any other.

The Zamir Society

The renewal movement among the Jews of Poland was not limited to narrow areas, its aspirations were rather far-reaching, its goal was to instill new content in the lives of the masses, to broaden their horizons, to take them out of the spiritual ghetto that fettered both their bodies and souls. Among the authors there were also those who demanded a change of values. Instead of the tendency that existed among Diaspora Jewry to develop only the spirit and moral values, there needed to be an opposite directive, developing the body and aesthetic values. There was a demand to weed out the view that the main point was the world to come from peoples' hearts, the view that this world is secondary and should not be given too much attention. They believed that the renewal of the nation could only occur if it covered all areas of human culture, literature, art, social and economic sciences; all of these would inject new currents of blood into the frozen limbs of Polish Jews, straighten their bent posture, their circle of vision would broaden – and then they would be worthy of redemption.

There arose, therefore, a movement among the Jews of Poland to further aesthetic values in the masses and to improve their taste in this way and arouse a sense of beauty in them. This movement did not pass over the Jews of Kielce. While societies were being founded in the large cities for this purpose called "HaZamir" [The Lark], many of the youth in Kielce also desired to found such a society in our city. The

Zionist Youth was especially active in this area. Dr. Gerszon Lewin was invited to Kielce, a well-known personality in Warsaw as an author, lecturer and a doctor. He lectured on Hebrew literature in general and about art in particular at the local theatre. He brought quotes from the works of Jewish authors and demonstrated that their content shows the eye of an artist, and determined that there are artistic works also in the spoken language. If in the plastic arts -- in painting, sculpture and carving -- the Jews do not have a firm place, on the other hand, in the art of the voice, in song, music, also literature, the Jews have superior talents. And we must develop these arts and they will infuse a spirit of ecstasy and joie de vivre in our gloomy worlds and improve our reputation also in the eyes of other nations. His lecture was fruitful. Several days later the inaugural meeting was set up to which men and women from all circles were invited, from those who aspired to introduce light and life to the Jewish street. At that meeting, the "Zamir" society was founded.

In its regulation book it stated that its goal was to develop an aesthetic sense and taste among the masses of the Jews by developing the various branches of art among them: song and poetry, plays, lectures about artistic subjects, reading literary works. Because the task of the society was educational and cultural, it declared itself to be unaffiliated with any party. A committee of twelve people was elected, among them Zionists, regular intellectuals, laborers. In general, anyone who had a spark of talent for singing and playing was later added to this committee. The committee members immediately began to work in the areas they had chosen.

החוג הדרמטי של "הזמיר"

The Dramatic Circle of "HaZamir"

Two battalions from the Russian army were stationed in Kielce, and they had a military band. The conductor was a nationalist Jew. The officer's uniform that he wore gave him a special importance. This conductor volunteered to organize a Jewish choir and orchestra from among the members of "HaZamir" which would be able to appear in public concerts. The talented members of the local youth found a place and opportunity to develop their talents more fully. In a large and roomy hall, which was called "The Viennese Hall", which was rented for "HaZamir", young men and women rehearsed the art of playing and singing. From time to time they held concerts, in which the musicians performed playing wind and string instruments; soloists appeared who were received enthusiastically by the audience; young men and women singers were immediately noticeable singing folk songs to the audience. The audience learned to distinguish between the different vocal parts and to recognize the "soprano", the "alto", the "tenor", the "baritone" and the "bass". They became understanding and expressed opinions about the vocal arts and singing.

The Committee of "HaZamir" Association at a farewell ball for Mrs. Elbaum who was moving to the land of Israel.

Among those present: Chairman C. Piekarski, Asst. A.J. Wilner, M. Elencwajg, A. Wargon, G. Rembiszewski, Jakob Jakubowicz, H. Herszowicz, the "Zamir" conductor, J. Rozen and Mrs. Elbaum

Immediately, actors and actresses turned up and founded a section of amateur theatrical enthusiasts. They prepared to present new plays, the fruit of the new authors, and also plays from the life of the nation in olden times. Of course, this was all done without a teacher or coach. Because of the lack of trained forces in dramatic acting, it was all done from their own intuition or by imitating what they had once seen in Jewish or Polish theatre, which visited Kielce occasionally. In spite of the flaws that could be discerned in their acting, the audience, whose demands were also not excessive, greeted them with great applause. They also knew that they were watching novices taking their first dramatic steps. Every Friday night there were lectures, readings and recitations accompanied by poetry and song. The audience's favorite narrator was Josele Badchan (Josef Rajzler). When he would read to the audience from the works of Shalom Aleichem, the hall echoed with thunderous laughter. It was not just the humorous elements of this excellent author, but also the tones of voice, the look in his eyes, the facial expression and bodily movements of the narrator. He knew to suit himself to the material, to merge his own soul with the soul of the hero of the work and to create a harmony between the work and its expression out loud. The audience left the hall happy, satisfied and entertained.

אגודת הספורט "מכבי"

The Sport Association "Maccabi"

"HaZamir" introduced interest and life to the youth of Kielce. Far from the traditional study hall, without the opportunity of continuing their studies, the youth found in "HaZamir" a place to make their own. "HaZamir" chased away the boredom from a gray life.

In the period between the two World Wars, new movements began which encompassed nearly all of the youth of Kielce. First the Scouting movement started up, which had an educational and cultural character, after that the sports movement grew wider. The organizers of this movement had two goals: the development of the muscles of the body, to straighten the backs bent under the yoke of exile and also to give the youth an interest that would challenge them – contests in physical exercises, in football, sharpened the physical prowess of the youth, their limbs became strong and flexible.

The sports societies of "Maccabi" and "Bar-Kochba", who played tennis, were formed then. Every society had patrons, coaches, chairmen, secretaries and treasurers, as was customary. The organizers were mainly from the intelligentsia of Kielce, which attracted the youth. Thus, for example, Fajga Arten, Hela Rotenberg, the teacher Tula Kopel and others were members in the women's committee of the "Maccabi" tennis section.

The tennis club committee in Kielce

A branch of the Geographical Society also organized in Kielce: RZ.T.K., whose chairman was H. Elazar Arten, and among whose committee members were: Stefanja Wolman, I. Edelsztajn and others. This society organized trips and hikes all over the country, to historical places located between the two seas, from the Black Sea to the Baltic, to the coal and salt mines and in general to all the places that are worth knowing and seeing. These trips broadened the horizons of those who participated in them.

In all areas movement and ferment could be felt, and those who continued still in their former ways also organized into a society. The society "Tiferet Bachurim" [Glory of the Young Men], whose members were drawn mainly from those who worked as artisans or in trade. They had a special minyan [quorum] for prayer on Sabbaths and holidays, and besides community worship, devoted hours to studying Bible, Sayings of the Fathers and Midrash.

During this period a secular club was born, in which its members spent the evening hours reading newspapers, talking to friends and various activities, and lectures were also held there on various topics. At the head of the club stood Mosze Kaufman, Dr. Feuer, Rzymnowoda and others.

The Popular Jewish Library

The Jews carry the additional name "People of the Book." There is not nation in the world that loved the book as well as the Nation of Israel. In all of his wanderings, the Jew carried the book with him. It was a source of consolation and soothing in the days of his humiliation and poverty. When he had no material goods, he found sufficient satisfaction in his spiritual assets. There was not a town in Poland, even the poorest, that did not treasure in its study halls rabbinical and Chassidic literature, Mussar books; also sometimes books on inquiry and science sometimes found their way into the study hall library.

However, each generation has its own books. The content of the books changes; but the affection for the book remains. The Jew, a man of thought, would reread the book and endeavor to acquire a many books as possible. The favorite presents that were given to bridegrooms were the books of the Talmud and later rabbinical arbiters. In every study hall a "Book Buying" society was organized whose purpose was to acquire books.

Also when the socialist, nationalist and social movements removed the Jewish youth from the study hall and showed them other directions in life, they did not stop liking books. Even in he remote corners where the echoes of these movements had not penetrated, pioneers arose who were active in founding libraries for the youth who were thirsty for books.

At that period, "The Popular Jewish Library" was founded in the city, which existed for some twenty-five years. This library was considered a valuable cultural asset; education and knowledge went out from it to broad avenues of the people. The moving spirit behind the library was Mosze Lewensztajn, the pharmacist, who was devoted to it with his entire heart and soul. The library was housed in a two-room apartment, a book room and a reading room. The library was created almost from nothing. From several dozen volumes that were collected from the members, it grew and expanded and became a large library with three thousand volumes. The group of young men and women did not spare themselves labor and effort and concentrated themselves on the sole purpose of enriching the library with new books that were hot off the presses. An amazing order ruled there. All of the books were listed in two catalogs, one alphabetical by title and the other alphabetical by author. The books were arranged on the shelves in order of their contents. Belles-lettres in one section and science books in another. The newspapers and periodicals were organized on tables, ready for reading. The books were nicely bound. The affection and devotion of these young people was everywhere evident, who all worked as volunteers and devoted many hours to this cultural institution.

This library, which was like an independent organism, without allotments from other sources, and which contained the best of Jewish creativity and thought in various languages, was a blessing for the Jews of Kielce, especially the working youth.

The community of Kielce grew and expanded. During the First World War many Jews from nearby villages flocked to the city and settled there. During the democratic regime that arose in the country after Poland regained its independence, political, social and economic parties were established among the Jews, sporting associations were organized, educational and charitable institutions were founded. In the community council and the municipal council there were occasionally meetings of their members where speeches and arguments were heard. All of these changes and alterations which occurred in the lives of the Jews who lived in Kielce required that they create a newsletter, a periodical, which would express all the things that were happening in their sphere and give explanations and clarifications regarding all the decisions that were being taken in the municipal offices and in the various institutions and in general, serve as a mirror of the lives of the Jews

Mosze Lewensztajn

Several young people with energy who felt they had journalistic talent got up and founded the weekly "Kielcer Zeitung" [Kielce Newspaper], which would appear on Fridays and was eagerly accepted by the Jews of Kielce. The editors of the newspaper changed for various reasons. The first editor was Cwi Nibilski, after him came Chaim Rzylony, Szymon Strawczinski and finally – Lajbl Rudel. Each one of them was blessed with different personality and attitude; but the side they all shared was that they were all outstanding Zionists, devoted to the idea of the renewal of the people in their homeland, involved in the life of the nation and drawing their inspiration from its eternal sources.

This local weekly appeared for twenty years, and its publication ceased together with the loss of the community that it served so faithfully.

[Page-71]

Educational and other Learning Institutions

Translated by Judy Montel

Edited by Warren Blatt

Until the twentieth century, there were only traditional "cheders" [primary schools] in Kielce, in which the Jewish children of the city received their education. There was no demand on anyone's part to change the nature of the educational experience. Like the other forms of Jewish life, which were set and crystallized, so too the paths that led to the education of boys and girls were paved, and no alterations were made to them. The "melameds" [teachers] taught Torah to the children of Israel in the time-honored technique that was accepted in all of the Diaspora of Israel.

Over time, there were some new faces among the "melameds", and they brought the learning of the Hebrew language and its grammar within the "cheder" walls.

Wawe Fuks, who immigrated to the United States towards the end of his life, was a pioneer in the city of Kielce in the area of teaching our ancient language to the children of the Jews of the city; for this purpose he invited a Litvak to his "cheder" who came from Lithuanian Brisk [Brest-Litovsk, now Brest, Belarus], named Jakob Dajbuch, and he taught the children of the "cheder" Hebrew. Of course, the instruction was primitive, without plan or method, as in: he commanded, I commanded, you commanded, etc.

But to begin with, the first push to learn our national language came from that "melamed" and his name is worth mentioning with praise and glory.

Rabbi Nachman Dawid Kaszanski, Z"L [may his memory be a blessing], a speaker and poet, did much to spread the knowledge of the Hebrew language among our young people. Also in the "Talmud Torah" school, of which he was principal, and also in his private lessons, he taught the Hebrew bible and the Hebrew language with good taste, intelligence and a nice erudition. Many acquired biblical sayings with the greatest pleasure and began to have a sense of their beauty, and thus later also came to read the books of the new Hebrew literature, which began developing at the same time, and also to read the Hebrew periodicals, "HaMelitz" and "HaTzefira". And through this, secular education began to infiltrate the study hall and find a place in the hearts of the youths that studied there.

Another speaker of the Hebrew language who lived and was active in Kielce was Szaul Eliezer Fridenzon, Z"L. He also wrote articles and composed a commentary on the Scroll of Esther. He was a rival of N.D. Kaszanski. They would compete with one another in the area of private lessons and in writing inscriptions upon monuments and gravestones. And they would dismiss one another; each one would point to his fellow's faults. However, the envy of scholars promotes wisdom. Their efforts started the "melameds" inclusion of some fresh air within the mildewed walls of their "cheders". Study of Hebrew bible, to which the "melameds" formerly devoted just one hour, which is neither a day nor a night, began to have a more prominent place in the curriculum, and they paved the way for the Hebrew schools which arose later. One "melamed" called "Kozowski" opened a "cheder" in which besides Jewish studies the children also learned Russian, mathematics, the Hebrew language and its grammar. This was a kind of "enlightened cheder", which served as a transition to the schools in which there were no longer "melameds", but men and women teachers, and the curriculum in them was the same as the curriculum in the general government schools.

[Page-72]

The fundamental change in Jewish education did not occur in one month and not in one year; a long war was conducted between the "cheder" and the modern school, a war that in the city of Kielce took twenty years. Even afterwards, when the school had finally won a decisive victory on the Jewish street and reigned supreme in children's education, the "cheder" did not disappear completely from the world; it continued to exist alongside the school in a slightly different form, in accordance with the demands of the time. The "cheder" was removed from the private sector and into the public sector. The private "cheder" which was limited to several dozen students in a narrow room, turned into a public "cheder" with hundreds of students which was housed in large rooms equipped with educational instruments and more or less appropriate to hygienic and sanitary demands.

The "Yavne" society founded a type of "Mizrachi" "cheder", and "Aguda" founded the "Yesodei HaTorah" [Foundations of the Torah] "cheder". And in order to survive, these "cheders" also had to include the subjects studied in the public schools into their curriculum.

I will briefly go over the process by which education developed in the city of Kielce, the wrestling between the new and the old until it was finally necessary to remove the old to make way for the new.

In 1904, a school was founded in the city, directed by H. Szrajber, a man of broad knowledge, much energy and eager for adventure. (He later held an important position in Russia in the Krenski government). He school was in spacious rooms and in accordance with sanitary demands; the curriculum was suited to that of a public school. The students were divided by grade. Every subject had a special hour devoted to it. Between lessons there were breaks. The ringing bell would announce the beginning and end of the classes. The students wore a uniform. Such a uniform blurred the distinctions between the poor and wealthy children and also gave the students a special look that elevated them above the "cheder" children. In those days, uniforms reminded people of authority and aroused proper behavior in the hearts of the masses towards the person who wore one. Aside from this, they attracted the children, who loved anything new. And in addition to all of these reasons, the uniform contained another sort of educational principle. The children were recognized in the street, and the teachers could distinguish between their students and the other children, and they could keep a sharp eye on them, that they not leave the school's strictures when they were outside the school walls.

This first school in Kielce ran into difficulties and obstacles from its inception that held back its development. And despite all of the efforts by the principal and the Zionists who supported it, it ceased to exist. Two years from the day of its establishment it was forced to close, to the joy of the "melameds", for whom this school was a thorn in their sides.

[Page-73]

The main reason for the closing of the school was the lack of a qualified teaching faculty who were able to direct such an education institution. The teachers who were invited to teach at the school were mainly dilettantes in the teaching profession. They were students, or advanced "melameds"; but neither the former nor the latter knew a single chapter in pedagogy and didactics. The students made no progress in their studies; the parents were forced to send their sons to "cheder" in the afternoon hours so that they would not remain ignoramuses for the rest of their lives. The "melameds" found its weak point which they used to undermine its existence. In this school, Hebrew bible studies were an important part of the curriculum. One "melamed", when he wanted to show the child's father that his son who studied at the school didn't know a verse from the bible, asked the student in front of his father: "Son, who were "Gidalti and Romamti?"" The child shrugged his shoulders and said in embarrassment that he had never heard such names. The "melamed" cried out in triumph: "You see what I told you, they don't even know the bible, their main subject at the school". And without hesitation the "melamed" takes the book of Chronicles from the bookshelves and shows, black on white that in chapter 25 it says that "Gidalti and Romamti" were sons of Asaf who served with musical instruments before the Ark of the Lord.

The student apologizes and says that in his school, they are not learning Chronicles, but the "melamed" does not release his prey and continues to test the student saying: Yes, Chronicles you aren't learning; but the Pentateuch, of course, you are learning. And without a doubt in the book of Genesis, which is the first book in the Torah, the students are as expert as they are in "Ashrei Yoshvei" [Happy are those… Psalm 84/5, an introductory verse, in addition to Psalm 144/15 to Psalm 145 all of which are recited numerous times in the daily prayers.] If so, tell me who said: "One [am] I and he [is a] man"?

The "melamed", knowing before whom he stands, that the student's father is ignorant of the Torah, purposely says the words out of context in order to cause the student to fail and to prove the righteousness of his words when he claims that the parents are, with their very own hands turning their sons into ignoramuses, into "Goyim", as it were, when they send them to the schools. And that these are not a "cheder" or a Yeshiva, but a sort of factory for turning young innocent children into heretics, freethinkers, without Torah and without manners or common sense. "For your eyes are those that see," continues the "melamed", triumphantly, "that the child, a pupil of the school, doesn't know the Pentateuch." And he takes down the Book of Genesis and shows the child who is standing ashamed, the words in the Torah portion of Miketz: "And we dreamed a dream in *one* night, *I and he* [each] *man* his own dream etc." [In the Hebrew text the italicized words are consecutive].

With such strategies the "melameds" attempted to give a bad odor to the school in the eyes of the masses, who were mostly observant of the commandments and kept the tradition of their ancestors.

The Zionists who conducted propaganda in favor of the school were considered: "Fine to speak of it, not so fine to fulfill it". They themselves sent their sons to the Russian Governmental Gymnasium [high school]; those whose sons did not get in to the Gymnasium sent them to the Polish trade school or to private Polish schools which were being set up in those days with a government license.

The masses began to pull their children out of the school and to send them back to the "cheders", when they saw that the school had disappointed them and that their sons were not succeeding in their studies.

The progressive wealthy members of the community turned their backs on the Hebrew school. They preferred the educational institutions of the Gentiles to a Jewish school, which to them was a sort of "cheder". And the first Jewish school in Kielce was left abandoned on all fronts, struggled for its existence for two years until it passed on.

[Page-74]

A few years passed without a Hebrew school in the city. And then two brothers named Joskowicz arose to renew the Jewish school in Kielce. These were years of revolution throughout Russia, the Jewish press, which was born and developed in those days and gained wide distribution among the masses of the Jews, propelled Jewish life forward. Among the masses a movement began to create a modern school in which their children would receive the knowledge they needed for a life that was changing and making giant strides forward. Many of them looked to the brothers Joskowicz, who were meagerly educated, who worked at private education, that they should be the initiators in this matter, and they received promises from many artisans that they would give financial and moral support – if they would just open a school.

After they had overcome obstacles and difficulties they finally opened a Hebrew school. Much emphasis was placed in the curriculum on the Hebrew language and Jewish history; public school subjects were also given an important place.

But this school as well did not get through the year. The constant undermining of its existence by the "melameds" on the one had and a lack of administrative abilities on the other caused it to close only six months after it opened. The "melameds" spread libel about Izrael Joskowicz, who was known in the city as Izrael Jekil's and who had secular education and was a Zionist, saying that he was a heretic who didn't believe in the existence of the soul. They repeated a tale about him that when his child died, he didn't sit "shiva" – the seven days of mourning. In response to the questions of his neighbors, who spoke to him about the matter, why he was changing the traditions that were set down by wise men? He responded dismissively: "Ah, nonsense! The electricity was turned off, why are the mourning customs necessary?"

With such fictional deficiencies they besmirched his name, so that parents would not send their children to him.

In those days there was a Jewish school in Kielce; but this was a girls' school, and according to the curriculum, it wasn't a Jewish school at all, since no Jewish studies were taught there; it was modeled upon the curriculum of the Polish school. Even the most orthodox sent their daughters to this school; they thought innocently that girls might acquire knowledge and education. An educated daughter was a glory in the house; her education also improved her chances of a good match afterwards. It was not necessary for her to learn Torah. "Whoever teaches his daughter Torah, it is as if he is teaching her foolishness." Running a household according to the rules of the "Shulchan Aruch" [book of Jewish law] is something she can learn from her mother. And Judaism was losing nothing from the education of their daughters.

Some of the most religious and the Chassidim, when they later saw their error and tried to repair the damage, were too late – the defect had already spread through their homes, and it was not possible to cure it even by founding the special "Beit Ya'akov" schools for their daughters. "Beit Ya'akov" was attended mainly by the daughters of the poor, and the daughters of the wealthy Chassidim continued to be educated in regulated schools which were supervised by the government.

[Page-75]

Mrs. Stefanja Wolman was the one who founded the girls' school in Kielce. It is worth expanding our description of this woman. Even if she was a member of the assimilated circle, she had some precious qualities that gave her a special value and raised her honor even in the eyes of her opponents. Her first husband, by whose name she was known even after his death and her marriage to another man, was outwardly crippled: a short hunchbacked man, but his spiritual gifts, his broad knowledge impressed the young Stefanja, who was charming and beautiful. She did not reject him, a spiritual closeness grew between them and they married.

After the death of her husband, she and a friend, Mrs. Paradystal, decided to open a school for girls. It began as an elementary school, like all the pubic Polish schools that existed at the time, but over time it developed and became a high school, a Gymnasium for Girls.

Her school was run as an exemplary educational institution with its excellent regulations. The principal influenced her pupils with the quality of her spirit, her energy and her strong will. Her students held her in affection, respect and admiration. She would teach them manners and good values: to speak the truth, to speak briefly, to speak to the point, to keep their word. "Try to have your wishes come true," she would say, "if you are convinced that your cause is just, don't be soft as a reed or melting like wax under the influence of others' desires."

המנהלת סט. וולמן וכיתת הגימנסיה שלה

The principal Stefania Wolman and her Gymnasium class

She would devote an hour a week to teach her pupils the ways of life. She mainly emphasized the importance of character in a person. She would say: "Try to emphasize your personality and focus your character, so that it will be as solid as iron, because only those who are graced with an aggressive will and who have a strong and crystallized character can walk securely on their life's path with confident steps, and gain respect for themselves."

[Page -76]

And because she did what she said, for she herself had these characteristics, her influence upon her students was very great.

Although at the beginning of her activities in the field of education she was far from matters pertaining to Judaism and kept Judaic studies out of her curriculum; she did not offer even the religious study that was required in government schools in either Hebrew or Polish. But over time, under pressure, the demands of the parents, who were infused with nationalistic feeling, she also included the study of the Hebrew language within the walls of her school, in order to satisfy the wishes of her students' parents. But the students did not succeed in this subject. The principal introduced the study of the Hebrew language to her school not of her own desires but as a side issue; therefore, she considered the subject as a foreign implant that did not "take" in the soil of her school. This attitude to our national language was noticeable also in the selection of a Hebrew teacher. In all the other subjects, she endeavored to acquire outstanding pedagogical forces, and for the study of the Hebrew language she took whatever came to hand, even from the detritus. The students, who sensed the derogatory attitude to Hebrew on the part of the principal, began to also hold the teacher and the Hebrew language in contempt. The teaching of Hebrew served as an advertisement for the school without any positive results.

Towards the end of her life there was a change in her attitude and she began to grow closer to the Jewish masses. She was active in the orphanage, which was established at her initiative in Kielce after World War I. Also the "HeChalutz" movement that began then among the youth, whose goal was to move to the Land of Israel in order to bring its wilderness to life, struck a chord in her heart and she treated it enthusiastically. During the last years of her life she would also contribute to the Zionist funds.

At her death she was accorded great honor by the Jews of Kielce, who accompanied her to her eternal rest with aching hearts; they knew that they had lost and active woman of initiative and her death left an empty space in the field of community activism. Her loss was felt in many circles of the Jews of Kielce.

I will mention here the name of another woman who was active in the field of girls' education in Kielce. Mrs. Sloma Rajzman, the wife of Icza Mejer Rajzman, opened a girls' school as well at the same time. Mrs. Rajzman, an educated woman, knew something of pedagogy, industrious and active, she knew how to administer her school and establish it, so that it could stand up to unexpected winds of change or opposition. This woman was full of a positive attitude towards Jewish values and included the study of the Hebrew language within the walls of her school and dealt with this subject with no less attention than that she bestowed upon any other subject matter. A young man of energy, talented and with pedagogical abilities was invited to teach the Hebrew language; the students succeeded, therefore, in their studies. Some of them left this school knowing Hebrew quite well.

המנהלת גב' רייזמן ותלמידותיה

The principal Mrs. Rajzman and her students

Mrs. Rajzman's school, from its inception, was meant for girls from the popular social strata. Daughters of artisans, grocers, laborers; in contrast, Mrs. Wolman's school was the educational institution of the wealthier social classes. For a long time these two schools existed alongside one another without either interfering in the other's territory. There was a place for each and they did not compete.

However, after World War I, independent Poland began developing a chain of public government sponsored schools and instituted compulsory general education. The sons and daughters of the Jews began attending the government schools, whose doors were open to them, and where they could receive their first education for free. And in addition to the schools for girls that were already in existence, the Minc sisters opened a private school for girls in Kielce.

The principal of this school, Mrs. Myrjam Minc, a well known Zionist activist, invested of her spirit and soul in the education of the pupils, and in infusing their hearts with nationalistic values. The Minc sisters were active in Jewish public life and supported Zionist slogans. One of them moved to the Land of Israel afterwards. In their school they devoted lessons not only to the study of Hebrew, but to the study of the Hebrew bible and Jewish history as well.

[Page-78]

During this period there also began to be competition between the girls' schools in the city; they became less respected and discipline suffered.

In this kind of a situation every educational institution was forced to use means that had a whiff of commerce about them: advertising and public relations, and whoever succeeded more than his fellow would gain a larger number of students.

A month before the beginning of the school year the public relations and advertising mechanisms were already active. The homes of the Jews were filled with announcements and flyers in which the administrations of the schools promised the parents mountains and proclaimed the innovations that would be introduced to their school. A Jew who picked up the morning newspaper would find among its pages various types and styles of announcements from the schools.

בית הספר של האחיות מינץ

The Minc sisters' school

In those days there were several private and public schools for boys, and each school would do a lot of public relations and advertising on its own behalf. The innocent parents stood at a loss and did not know how to use their judgement amid the wave of advertising. This one pulled them in one direction, and this one in another. Soon the times of needing to visit the parents in their home in order to win their son or daughter had returned, just as the "melameds" had done in their era. The state of the Jewish schools had reached such a low level during the period before World War II. The result of this degraded level was the diminishing of the image of the Hebrew school.

[Page-79]

I will return to the history of the development of the schools for boys in Kielce. As we already mentioned, the first attempts to establish a school for boys were not successful. The first schools, which were founded with great effort, were not able to stand on their own. Their time had not yet arrived. They were like wild flowers that blossom early and wither quickly. The first frost defies them and freezes them entirely. Thus the schools of the early founders did not succeed. The old "cheders" continued to exist. The parents would send their sons to "melameds", and fed them Torah according to the old method.

Meanwhile several young men from Lithuania came to Kielce and they gave private lessons in Hebrew and Russian. Children who learned at the "cheder" would take private lessons in the evening hours from teachers whose income came from teaching "what the hour demanded". These young men prepared the ground upon which the Jewish schools were later established. They worked underground, they did the work of secular education in secret; their activity was not noticeable. And despite this they prepared the hearts for the enormous change that was about to take place in the education of boys. But not everyone could afford to pay tuition to both a "melamed" and a private teacher. For this reason, a strong demand for a school was created, which would include in its curriculum Judaic studies and also secular studies, which a person needed in life.

About two years before World War I, a man called Chwat arrived in Kielce, with very little education but with initiative. He got up and founded a school for boys. He found teachers and assistants among the young men who were giving private lessons, and who were already known to the parents of the teachers as being qualified for their positions. This school found students easily. Chwat, in order to insure his own material existence and not be entirely dependent upon his school, which had many expenses in the first several years, attempted to convince the authorities to accept him at the Russian government Gymnasium as a teacher of religion. His request was accepted. He was became a teacher of religion at the Gymnasium for the Jewish students who, at the time, numbered several dozen. A position in a government educational institution given to a Jew was an unusual phenomenon in our city. This position elevated Chwat's reputation in people's eyes. Especially, on holidays, when prayers were held in the synagogue for the welfare of the monarchy, and he would come leading his Jewish students from the Russian Gymnasium, wearing the hat of a Russian clerk, with a two-headed eagle attached to it and a small sword clasped to his hips, he made an impression with this appearance of a man who was close to the monarchy. In those days, one did not scorn the reputation of such a man.

Indeed, his students at the Gymnasium mocked him, when they heard the Russian language that came out of his mouth, distorted and ridiculous; but what happens between the walls of the Gymnasium does not leave them. This position of his in society was a big help to him also in his private school.

However, even this school did not exist for many years. World War I broke out. During the early years of the war Kielce was nearly a battlefield. Battalions would travel through and also be stationed in the city. All of the educational institutions were closed. Only in the third year of the war, when the front lines moved farther away from Kielce and the Austrians made themselves a permanent encampment in the city did the schools reopen as well as the high-schools. In this period Jewish Gymnasiums began appearing in Polish cities. Galicia supplied great numbers of teachers.

Chwat was invited as a Hebrew teacher to Szefer's Gymnasium in Lublin. He did not remain in service there, teaching in a Jewish Gymnasium was not his strength; he was lacking the necessary pedagogical information a teacher needs; he suffered greatly also from the students and also from the Gymnasium administration. And in addition to that, his family affairs were defective. Life became difficult for him. All these things sent him to an early grave – and he was only forty-five years old.

Meanwhile a young Litvak named Prybulski opened a Hebrew school in the city. He gained experience in teaching from his private lessons as well as from his work in Chwat's school. He found teachers from the students of the Wolman Gymnasium. He was the first who introduced female teachers to boys' school. His school succeeded and continued to exist up to the outbreak of World War II. Its owners became wealthy. Before World War II broke out the owner of the school acquired a large stone house. Prybulski was physically weak but fierce in spirit. He had pedagogical talents; he knew how to handle children and also how to run a school. He arranged his school in such a manner that its expenses would be small and its income great. And since in the first years he was the owner of the only school in the city that was known to be well run, he succeeded in his endeavor. Also afterwards, when dangerous rivals arose who knew how to teach according the new methods, his school continued to exist through the force of inertia and the power of the advertising he had acquired in previous years.

Prybulski's school

At the same time in 1917, the "Mizrachi" association was founded in the city. Among the other tasks it took upon itself -- political, national and community-wide -- it devoted much energy also to cultural activity, especially to educating the boys and girls in the spirit of Torah and tradition, to plant love and affection for our national holy emblems, for the Land of Israel, for the Hebrew language and for Jewish history. As soon as the "Mizrachi" association was founded it opened a schools called: "Torah VaDa'at"

[Torah and Knowledge]. In its early years the "Mizrachi" ran into many difficulties in realizing its goal of its educational institution. The main difficulty was the lack of national-religious teachers. There was not yet a college for such teachers in Poland. The teachers' seminaries in Vilna and Grodno did not produce religious teachers. The "Mizrachi" did not want to bring secular teachers into its school, to prevent them from influencing their students with their opinions and views. The school committee preferred to introduce "melameds" of the old type to its educational institution for religious subjects, and local teachers for the secular subjects.

The Jews of Kielce received the first announcement regarding the opening of a school in which the students would receive national-religious education with great joy and enthusiasm. This was the school they had been waiting for.

In the very first days after the publication of the announcement regarding the school founded by the "Mizrachi", parents crowded in dozens in the small "Mizrachi" apartment where they came to register their children at the new school. A total of over two hundred children of various ages were registered at that time.

The "Mizrachi" had a serious problem – for two hundred children they needed large rooms and an apartment like that was unobtainable at any price. During the war construction ceased in all the cities of Poland and apartment rentals were scarce everywhere. This was true in Kielce, especially, which was close to the front, since the inhabitants of all the neighboring villages found a safe haven in the district capital. The houses were very crowded. Even a private individual had trouble getting a room, and a large apartment for a school was out of the question. Finally the problem of the apartment was solved as well. The Kozowski brothers inherited a "cheder" from their father, who died around that time, with all of the furnishings in it. For a short while they continued to run the "cheder" but the school of the "Mizrachi" saw them as a serious rival to their "cheder". And indeed many of their students came to register at the "Mizrachi" school.

In one day they found themselves without a livelihood. Therefore, when they heard that the "Mizrachi" was looking for an apartment for their school, they came to the "Mizrachi" committee and offered them their apartment which had four rooms with a long and broad corridor, which could also be used as a classroom if the need arose. The apartment was found suitable for the school, because it could contain about two hundred children. But the condition they set was that they be accepted as "melameds" at this school.

[Page-82]

With no choice, the "Mizrachi" committee accepted this proposal. The national-religious school opened, the first public school in the city. The best of the "melameds" in the city were invited, Hillel Oberman, of the "Mizrachi" founders from Kielce, a famous Torah scholar in the city, Bunem Wirzewa, a gifted man with a talent for exposition, and even if he had not read many pedagogy texts, he knew intuitively how to approach a child, how to analyze a difficult matter and explain it so the child would understand it. Adults also enjoyed listening to the way he would explain a difficult topic in the Gemara. He also knew how to catch the children's interest.

However the parents' enthusiasm waned when they saw over a period of time, that this school was not fulfilling the hopes they had of it either. Although the two "melameds" mentioned above did their jobs in the best possible way, after a few hours of study the children were left on their own. The Kozowski brothers, "melameds" of infants, were not wholly suitable to classroom instruction, they didn't know how to teach a class of forty children, how to maintain order in the class. They were used to teaching children individually.

But the main disadvantage was the lack of a principal. No educational, commercial or public institution can exist without appropriate direction. The "Mizrachi" committee, which had no experience in this matter, opened a school and left it to its fate. True, a special committee had been selected whose function was to deal with the school; but its activities were limited to administrative matters alone, in managing the financial matters, income and expenditure, taking in the tuition fees and paying out salaries to the "melameds" and teachers. A public school needs a principal who will devote his attention to the internal affairs of the educational institution that has been put in his care, to oversee the course of studies, make sure that they are conducted according to schedule, correct defects, fill in faults, seal the cracks and holes that turn up from time to time. The principal must stand on guard and enforce the internal discipline with the teachers as well as the students; he must ensure that the curriculum is carried out, that one "melamed" complements another, that there is not confusion in the manner of learning, that one teacher does not pull in one direction and a second one in another, that no one is left working on their own. The principal must organize the work in such a way that a unifying spirit hovers over them that joins the various actions to a unified general movement that meets the goal that was set up by the founders and initiators, who came to create a public educational enterprise.

And without appropriate direction the structure began to fall apart. At the end of the school year the number of students fell. Meanwhile, the "Aguda" also opened a public "cheder" and the "melameds" who had not found work at the "Mizrachi" school gathered there, and competition between the "Mizrachi" and the "Aguda" began in earnest. In this situation the school committee felt it necessary to take vigorous action so that their tender creation continue its existence and not expire in its infancy.

The first action was the severing of the ties between the school and the brothers Kozowski. To do this it was necessary to make the effort to acquire appropriate quarters for the school, in order to be rid of "melameds" who were not worthy of their diplomas. The school had made it an aim to raise the education of the boys in accordance with the spirit of the time and the nationalist demands that were awakening then with greater urgency, with the advances of the Zionist movement among the masses of the people in connection with the Balfour Declaration.

[Page-83]

The committee searched tirelessly and succeeded. The Gertler brothers bought an old building from a Pole and rented it to the "Mizrachi". The building was prepared and adapted to a school building; an additional advantage was that it also had a big yard that the children needed during recess.

For the second academic year the school was moved to new quarters. New "melameds" were taken on as well as teachers for secular studies. The direction was put in the hands of the writer of these paragraphs, and the "Mizrachi" school stood fast against all the competition from the right side, as well as against private competition.

The same year, 1918, a Jewish Gymnasium opened in Kielce as well. During the third academic year, the number of students at the "Mizrachi" school shrank again, as some of them transferred to the Gymnasium.

The Gymnasium, the high school, had a powerful magnetic force still from the days of the "Haskala" movement [which was in favor of secular education]. The "Mizrachi" school was forced also to interrupt its functioning for a time because the military authorities took over the school building for those conscripted to fight against the Bolsheviks, who were approaching the capital city of Warsaw. The principal himself was conscripted. The students scattered and it was difficult to assemble them again when the war was over.

However, a short time later a young man appeared, the son of holy people, with lots of energy, Icak Finkler was his name, about whom we will have more to say in the coming chapters. He infused a new spirit into the "Mizrachi" association and also was very active and did much to revive the "Mizrachi" school. He reorganized the school, introduced new local forces as well as from other places; Women also began to serve as teachers for secular subjects. The school took on the sophisticated appearance of an educational institution, religious and nationalist, and finally joined a chain of schools that were sponsored by the National "Mizrachi" Union called "Yavne".

During the days of the [First World] war, life went on in Jewish settlements. The east and the west had mutual contact. There was a constant stream from west to east and from east to west. The borders were opened and the Jews of the east came into contact with the Jews of the west and they influenced one another. Those from the west found in the eastern Jews a strong and vital Jewish life, both religious and national life. The small villages in which the Jews constituted a majority of the population were a new discovery in their eyes, remnants of the Middle Ages; they were charmed by their romanticism. Many things that the western emancipation had made them forget were aroused again, all unnoticed and they began to pay attention to these things. The authors described the atmosphere of eastern Jews in their works; the artists began describing in the plastic arts, whether with paintbrush or gouge, to their brothers in the west, types of eastern Jews.

And on the other hand, the external manners of their western brothers had great influence on eastern Jews, their ironed European clothing which removed the barrier and external difference between Jew and Christian, their fluent foreign speech which had no accent that marked it as Jewish; the politeness with which they treated one another, particularly men and women – all these had a great influence on the Jews of the east, in particular on the younger generation, which began imitating the manners of their western brothers. First of all, they exchanged their traditional Jewish costume for European clothing. Yesterday he wore a long "kapota" [coat] and a soft hat with a brim, and the next day you saw him newly incarnated, dressed according to the latest fashion in a short jacket, long ironed trousers, wearing a molded derby like one of the aristocracy. Those who were unable to part from their traditional clothing all at once, separated between the sacred and profane, saved their traditional garb for Sabbaths and holidays and wore the European clothing on weekdays, days when they came into contact with the outer world.

[Page-84]

Secondly, they began learning the national language. These changes and alterations entered the lives of the Jews not from a tendency to assimilate; on the contrary, at the same time nationalist feelings were growing among the Jewish masses as was quite well known, as a result of the events that were occurring during the same period in the wider world and in our Jewish world. The resurrection of small nations to new life, the hopes that filled hearts as a result of the Balfour Declaration, caused a great awakening of national emotion among the younger generation, to infuse the concepts of the rebirth that Zionism had fostered for the past twenty five years. Also in circles that up until now had regarded the Zionist movement with apathy or scorn, the idea of the renewal of Israel in its ancient homeland found a place. Also the very religious, who fought against the Zionists, even they began to express an interest in the land of Israel. Many of them joined the "Mizrachi" which was very active at the time. Young rabbis with energy spread out then in all of the cities and villages to spread the word about the Zionist idea.

Thus the Jews also wanted to straighten their posture, to emphasize their essential qualities, their independence from their neighbors. Therefore they were rapidly influenced by their western brothers, because they saw this as a means of being liberated from the bonds of exile that were so burdensome to them. In various areas the Jews began to show their activity: in the fields of education, politics and the economy.

During this period Jews established elementary and high schools for themselves. A national council was organized which administered the policy of the Jewish population; financial institutions in the form of popular banks, savings and loan banks, commercial and industrial banks.

In this general state of the Jews, the Kielce community could not remain backward and failing. It too opened a Jewish high school in a building that it rented for this purpose from the Sztrozberg brothers. The opening of a Jewish Gymnasium in the city was the kind of surprise for many of our brethren that refreshed their hearts. Every father who sent his son to the Gymnasium saw him in his imagination as a doctor, engineer, lawyer. They began registering their sons to the Gymnasium with enthusiasm. Willingly they paid the sums that were levied upon them. The question of teachers didn't exist. Horizons opened and from Galicia, which was a overflowing with intelligentsia, academics with their doctorates, lawyers, doctors and teachers began flowing into Congress Poland [the former Russian "Kingdom of Poland" (1815-1918), which included Kielce], people who did not find a field of activity in their places of residence while here there was still a wide open field in this area, and the newcomers conquered the vacancies. In Congress Poland the [degree of doctorate and the] title "Doctor" was an honorable title, an important title, a title of studiousness and inspiration. A "Doctor" was respected wherever he turned up. In the synagogue he was seated in a place of honor, at meetings he was elected to be the chairman. But from the time the "Doctors" of Galicia began to arrive in the cities of Congress Poland, their honor was diminished somewhat; the masses ceased to respect them.

[Page-85]

Not everyone, in spite of his or her honorary title, was truly successful at higher education. There were some among them who were uneducated, and it was impossible to know how they had achieved the title of "Doctor". There were some whose level of morality was not in line with their respectable degree.

Galicians of all levels of education began flowing to the city of Kielce as well. And when the announcement was publicized that a Jewish Gymnasium was opening in the city, and teachers were sought, an entire flotilla of male and female teachers, all of them bearing the title of "Dr." and offering their willingness to accept a position at the new institution.

After investigating and checking into every single candidate, and many debates and evaluations, the faculty was finally selected. Dr. Noach Braun, a man of academic education, qualified in various eastern studies, a religious and nationalist Jew who sympathized with "Mizrachi" was accepted as the principal of the Gymnasium. There were many among the teaching faculty who were outstanding in their fields. There were poets and authors among them, who occasionally would publish their works. The most well known among these were Dr. Rotman, who today is an educator in Israel, the Cantor and Dr. Baruch, who also later moved to the land of Israel.

ועד הגימנסיה היהודית בקילץ

The teachers and a class from the Jewish Gymnasium in Kielce

A special committee was organized by the teachers' parents to support the Gymnasium. Several of the committee members devoted themselves heart and soul to improving and updating this educational institution. The Gymnasium officially belonged to the community authorities, but found no help there; the community council members from the "Aguda" faction did not permit the community authorities to allow the Gymnasium to function under its auspices, nor to take in interest in it and supply its needs. Among those who were active in the Gymnasium's favor, Chaim Wajnryb stood out, a public activist without compare; from the day the Gymnasium was founded he stood at its side and guarded this educational institution like the apple of his eye. In good days and bad, he did not remove his attention from this hobbyhorse of his. He dealt with it always with affection and devotion. There were times when the Gymnasium would be going through a serious crisis; danger that this entire edifice, which had cost so much money, energy and strength would crumble and dissolve entirely; but in these critical moments Wajnryb stood like a fortress, gathered his friends and with joined forces they succeeded in extricating the Gymnasium from the breaking waves and to bring it to a safe harbor. Among the committee members who stood at his side it is worth mentioning and remembering Aharon Josef Moszkowicz, Elazar Arten, who was the chairman of the committee until he immigrated to the land of Israel in 1932 (currently the chairman of the Organization of Kielce Natives in Israel), Grynberg, Mosze Kaufman and others.

Elazar Arten
Chairman of the Gymnasium committee
(currently the chairman of the Organization of
Kielce Natives in Israel)

The first principal, Dr. Noach Braun, in spite of his education and pedagogical talents and his abilities in all respects to stand at the head of this sort of educational institution, did not serve in his position for long. Although during his stay in Kielce the inhabitants were fond of him, everyone regarded him as a man elevated above the average person. Immediately in the first year after his arrival he began to be active outside the walls of the Gymnasium as well. He would give speeches at public meetings and give educational lectures to advanced youths. His speeches and lectures were full of content.

In spite of this, he did not feel solid ground under his feet. Within the Gymnasium as well, disagreements broke out, arguments and squabbles between the teachers; not everyone wanted to accept the principal's authority. The disagreements between the teachers affected the course of studies badly. The principal saw himself as too weak to enforce discipline among the teachers, and was forced to leave his position at the Gymnasium, to the disappointment of many who had experienced his company and enjoyed the fruits of his mind. He later settled in Israel.

After him the engineer Rusek came to direct the Gymnasium. He was a Zionist activist, a man of energy. He understood how to direct an educational institution with great success. However, he also didn't live in Kielce very long. During his tenure the Gymnasium committee was wrestling with financial difficulties. The principal was never sure whether his salary would be paid on time and in full, and therefore, when a principal's position in another city was offered to him in more congenial conditions, he left the post.

[Page-87]

The third principal was the engineer Icak Rzelinski, who now lives in Israel and has an important position with the manufacturer's association. He was a Zionist activist well known in the cities of Poland, and settled in Kielce for a long time and held the post for many years. He developed broad and varied Zionist activities in the city; he participated in every Zionist endeavor with his strength and energies. Without flagging energy, he did his national, education and cultural work. Afterwards as well, after he left the position, he would visit his former workplace from time to time; he was unable to leave it completely. There were many emotional ties between him and the city's inhabitants. Rightly, Rzelinski was considered a "Kielcer", even here in Israel, he does not go far from the natives of Kielce, participates in their meetings, their celebrations and also their sorrows. The Kielce residents are used to saying, when they mention the name of the Gymnasium principal "our Rzelinski", because he justly earned with his activities a citizen's rights among the Jews of Kielce.

After him, until World War II broke out, Dr. Feuer held the position of principal at the Gymnasium, a personality in the national sense, not too warm and not too cool. Our national tongue was foreign to him as well. He began, therefore, to study Hebrew with the writer of these lines; but his free hours were taken with other matters, and the rules of the language, which had been strange to him from the days of his childhood, did not take root. After several months, when he saw no success from his study, he said a final farewell to the Hebrew language.

This principal served only as a front for the authorities; and he had only a small influence on the course of studies and its direction; the spirit was given and created by a few teachers, who were gifted with inspiration, and Dr. Pelc, who at the time was made head of the committee that dealt with the affairs of the Gymnasium.

Among the Gymnasium teachers one young man, called Grojbrad, was particularly impressive, a Hebrew and Jewish history teacher. He had the gift of speech; his public speeches made a deep impression upon his listeners. He had a particularly large influence upon the youth who were drawn to him, and he served as a counselor, a lighthouse, and was well liked by the younger generation.

The relations between the Gymnasium and the private and public elementary schools were decent in the first years of its existence; there was no competition between them. The elementary schools prepared the students for the Gymnasium, and the latter would make application materials available at the start of the academic year. However, in the last few years before the Shoah that overtook European Jewry, the Gymnasium administration decided to open lower grades as well, in order to improve the state of its budget by adding students. But by then wild competition was out of hand also in the education of boys, and the results were bad for education in general in the city.

I will mention here also the "Tushia" [resourcefulness] school, which was not really a special school with any unusual direction, but was a sort of continuation of the school founded by the "Mizrachi". The change here was not in the essence of the curriculum and also not in the make-up of the faculty, but a change of ownership is what occurred here. The members of the "Yavne" school committee of the "Mizrachi" were mostly businessmen, sunken head and shoulders into their private businesses, and their minds were not free to deal with school affairs. As long as Reb Icak Finkler stood at the head of the committee, all was well; he did not take his eye off the school; if he felt any lack there, he did not rest until he removed it, and order returned. But his father, the Admo"r of Pinchev [Pinczow] moved to Sosnowiec with the members of his family. The "Yavne" school was left with barely any responsible stewardship. No one was in charge of its internal procedures, or of its budget. Months went by and the teachers did not receive their salaries.

In this situation, the teachers decided to take the school into their own hands. The "Mizrachi" committee did not agree to turn its educational institution over to private individuals of its own free will, not even the teachers who were members of the "Mizrachi". However, the parents of the students were on the side of the teachers. They were convinced that the course of studies would improve and be run in better order in a situation where the teachers themselves had an interest in the schools existence and when its responsibility was on their shoulders.

The faculty finally opened the "Tushia" school. Appointed as principals were the writer of these lines and Mr. J.L. Micnmacher, a young man with much energy who understood pedagogical ways in all their various methods. Many improvements were made to this cooperative school, new and appropriate furniture; a radio, that in Kielce at the time was something of a rarity, was introduced to the school, in order to give the child an opportunity to enjoy the special children's programs that were broadcast at specific hours during the day.

ביה"ס "תושיה", חבר המורים והמנהל פנחס ציטרון

"Tushia" school, the teaching faculty and the principal, Pinchas Cytron

The "Tushia" school developed rapidly and its importance and value grew from year to year, not just in the eyes of the parents, but also in the opinion of the authorities. The government inspectors were always expressing their satisfaction from the order that ruled there.

The "Mizrachi" however, didn't give up its school, and it continued to exist under the direction of Fiszel Guthart, an activist in the "Torah VaAvoda" [Torah and Work] faction. Teachers were brought in from other places; however it continued for only one more year, for the members of the "Mizrachi" soon learned that they were keeping it going for naught. They could see with their own eyes that the children were leaving their "Yavne" school and transferring to "Tushia". Eventually, the "Tushia" school remained the sole heir of the "Yavne" school, which also continued its tradition, did not leave the path that the "Mizrachi" had laid down for it in the matter of educating boys by even a hairsbreadth and only occasionally introduced internal and external changes depending on the pace of its development. Alongside the school, a library of scientific and pedagogical books was established. The school made significant contributions to the "Keren Kayemet" and the "Keren Hayesod" Funds [Jewish National Funds]. The school had a "Keren Kayemet" committee whose members were students. This committee collected respectable sums from the students for this national financial institution, and the teachers did not prevent themselves from making an effort to promote it to the students.

The "Aguda" also ran a line of "cheders" called "Yesodei HaTorah" [Foundations of the Torah], in which the city's "melameds" taught the children the Pentateuch and the commentary of Rash"i, Gemara and the commentary of the Tosafists according to the time-honored fashion. And several hours a day were devoted to secular studies, which were entrusted to the graduates of the Gymnasiums. I will mention here the names of the outstanding "melameds" who taught Torah to the children of Kielce: Rabbi Mendel Paczanower or Bornsztajn, a Chassid of Alexander, a great Torah scholar, his son Rabbi Motel served as the rabbi of Checiny. Rabbi Judel Rotszild, a Chassid of Gur – great in Torah and in personal qualities, Rabbi Mejer'l Bajrzeciner, a Chassid of Checiny, Rabbi Heszel Zalcer, Rabbi Aba Charendorf and Rabbi Mosze Jakubowicz, Chassidim of Alexander, and of the "melameds" of the younger children I will mention Wolf Horwicz, one of the first "melameds" in Kielce, Dawid Chroberski (Belfer) and others.

הנחת אבן היסוד לביה"ס "יסודי התורה"

Laying of the cornerstone for the "Yesodei HaTorah" school

Before World War II broke out, the "Aguda" in Kielce was about to build a large building on a lot that Rabbi Fiszel Kohen had dedicated to this purpose, in which all of the "cheders" of "Yesodei HaTorah" were supposed to be concentrated as well as a trade school, from which religious artisans who observed the commandments and earned their livelihood from the work of their hands were meant to eventually go forth. The cities leading citizens participated in the laying of the cornerstone and at that very spot respectable sums were raised to carry out this essential endeavor, which was supposed to reflect glory on the community of Kielce. However, in the midst of the construction work the war broke out and together with other plans, this plan was also cancelled, eternally.

In Kielce there was also an educational institution for poor children, abandoned children, called "Talmud Torah". This institution began its existence at the beginning of the twentieth century, as soon as the community developed and those that stood at its head had to also worry about the education of the children whose parents could not care for them, because of their poverty, or who were orphans. The children received a basic education there as well as clothing from time to time. At the head of the Talmud Torah stood a principal who himself taught the children. Aside from him there were also an infant's "melamed" and a teacher who taught the children to read and write in the language of the country. Among the principals, Nachman Dawid Kaszanski, Bunem Wirzewa and Elazar Manela particularly excelled.

With this we conclude the portion of the education and cultural institutions in Kielce, and its development from the old fashioned "cheder" to a modern nationalist school. We saw the long process of the struggle of the old with the new until the crystallization of the later in a synthetic manner in the sense of old wine in new vessels.

But all the efforts and all the energies that were invested in the institutions were, unfortunately, wasted and for naught. No edifice in the Diaspora can continue, it hasn't a solid foundation. A storm came and uprooted the tree from its roots to its branches and fruits.

I have written in this book the manner in which the development in the field of education was conducted in our city and the names of the people who were active in the field of Jewish culture in our community so that they will remain in the memory of the descendants of Kielce natives, and that the names of the people will not be erased from our hearts, for their activities deserve to be engraved on the memorial monument of the martyrs of our people. The tree was uprooted, but it sent its seeds to great distances, and thanks to them we have been fortunate enough to become an independent nation in our ancient homeland, in the State of Israel.

[Page-91]

Social Welfare and Charitable Institutions

Translated by Judy Montel

Edited by Warren Blatt

I now turn to another field, to devote myself to the charity and social welfare institutions that existed in the Kielce community and their activists as well, who devoted their energies and strength to establish and improve the community with all sorts of improvements and reforms so that it would be worthy of taking its place among the veteran communities of Poland.

As I have already mentioned, there was a charitable organization in Kielce called "Achiezer", in Polish – "Bratnia Pomoc" – the masses knew it by the name of Dobroczynnosc and it was the oldest charitable institution in the Kielce community. It was established at the beginning of the twentieth century by a group of wealthy people from the city who volunteered to do charitable activities to benefit the poor of the city. Among the founders were Chassidim and assimilated Jews as well. The good deed of charity blurred the outlines and differences of opinion between the Chassid and the assimilated Jew.

The tasks of this charitable institution were: A) maintaining the "Talmud Torah", where the poor children received their early education and, before holidays, also clothing and shoes. B) Maintaining the Jewish Hospital. C) Maintaining the Chevra Kadisha [Burial Society]. D) Maintaining the social welfare fund for giving small loans to the poor in exchange for a pledge or the guarantee of one of the members. E) Distributing food to the poor before holidays and coal and potatoes in the winter.

Its main income consisted of the members' contributions, the synagogue income, which was earmarked for its use, the income of the Chevra Kadisha, legacies and so forth.

All of the affairs of the organization were run by a committee, which was elected at a general meeting of the members. Its most active members were Rabbi Mosze Fefer, Firster, Hassenbajn, the Zagajski brothers, Awigdor Rajzman, Rabbi Eli' Naftali Ajzenberg and his son Rabbi Mosze, Lemel Kahana and others.

Over time, some changes occurred in the circle of activities of the "Achiezer" society. Some of its jobs were taken from it.

When Poland achieved its political independence [in 1918], the cities received independent local authority and the sphere of action of the Jewish communities broadened; at that time the maintenance of the Jewish Hospital was transferred to the local municipality. The cemetery and Chevra Kadisha moved to the auspices of the Jewish community. The activities of the "Achiezer" society were then limited to minor philanthropy and maintaining the "Talmud Torah". Its income also shrank in those days. Its "shamash", Mr. Sukenik, had to bestir himself to collect the members' monthly donations.

[Pag- 92]

"Linat Hatzedek"

"Linat HaTzedek" was a charity organization whose task was caring for the sick, ensuring that medical supplies reached impoverished sick people, arranging round the clock care for patients who needed constant medical attention, sending patients who needed it to medical spas and convalescent homes and similar activities that brought great relief to the lower classes who for various reasons needed the public's aid, especially in days of illness, when the head of the household was on his deathbed and the members of his family were looking at starvation, "Linat HaTzedek" came to their aid. This society was a popular institution; its members were mostly artisans and small shopkeepers. Their goal was to found an institution for mutual aid. To further this goal, they made an agreement with a group of doctors to receive patients and make house calls at the expense of the society.

The activities of the society expanded greatly, especially when Dr. Pelc, who was a well-known activist of great energy and solid character, headed it. He also established a clinic alongside "Linat HaTzedek" where during several hours each day patients could receive an examination at a nominal fee and treatment to prevent their disease developing further.

The "Linat HaTzedek" committee in Kielce
Among those present: Zew Kluska , Daniel Szalit , Awraham Piotrkowski ,
Mosze ozenblum, Szmuel Kligman, Chaim Wajnryb and Sz. Z. Chmielnicki

The "Linat HaTzedek" institution was very popular with many of the city's inhabitants and its membership grew from year to year.

[Pag- 93]

From among its active members I will mention here only a few names, of those who were most noticeable in their activities to develop the society: Mendel Lifszycz, who stood at its head from the day it was founded and whose attention, without wavering, hovered over it at all times and in all circumstances. Lajbel Goldberg, a simple householder, was always ready at the first request to come and visit the patient, to see to his needs and care for him; even though he himself was familiar with illness – he was plagued by asthma to the end of his life – even so, he did not prevent himself from sleeping at the patient's side. Josef Gertler, a peddler, childless, was devoted to the society with his entire soul. He would care for the patient with warmth and love and spared no effort in his attempts to ease the patient's pain and suffering. Aszer Kazlowski who also stood at head of the society and did much to balance its budget. Szmuel Lajchter, an artisan with a large family of his own to worry about, a public activist, also found the time to act, work, and do things for "Linat HaTzedek. In his speeches he would arouse the audience and show them the benefit and advantage in this charity endeavor.

With sincere and simple words that penetrated the heart he would describe the physical and emotional sufferings of the patient to the audience; how much a person needs the help of others and their words of encouragement when he is lying helpless on his bed, and his family are worn out taking care of him. How the patient especially needs other's help during the hours of the night, when everyone else in the house is asleep and he needs care and has no one to turn to; and then the person who comes to his house appears before him like a redeeming angel. The value of the good deed of visiting a patient when they are alone with themselves is immeasurable.

Lajchter was attached to "Linat HaTzedek" with his whole heart and soul, and even his own illness did not sever this bond to the institution. There were cases in which he himself was ill when he was called to an urgent meeting at "Linat HaTzedek" and he would find the strength and get up to participate in it. And the protests and yells of his wife, that he was endangering his own life by going out to participate in the meeting when he ought to be in bed, did no good.

All of these I mentioned here by name and many others who were not mentioned here were worthy of being remembered for a blessing among those who worked for the benefit of their brethren and did not remain within the four "amot" [cubits] of their own personal lives.

Supporters of the Poor

This society was founded during World War I and continued its existence for many years afterwards as well.

During the war, many of the Jews of the city lost their livelihood; in addition to the local unemployed, many more refugees arrived from the surrounding villages who had been expelled from their places of residence and found shelter in Kielce. Both groups were facing hunger and disease.

[Page-94]

Several activists therefore sat down and founded the "Tomchei Aniyim" [Supporters of the Poor] society, whose goal was to give support and aid to the poor in an organized fashion. First of all they opened an inexpensive kitchen where anyone who was hungry could receive a delicious and satisfying meal for a nominal fee. They announced a project of collecting clothing, underwear and shoes for the refugees, who came from their places of residence with only the clothes on their backs. After that they also opened a shop that supplied the needy with basic necessities at very low prices. In general the society then devoted itself to a broad variety of activities that extended aid to the needy affected by the war. The means for these activities were gathered from the contributions of members, from one time donations, from community allocations and various other sources, such as the income of the prayer house that the members of "Tomchei Aniyim" founded for themselves and that was dedicated to the needs of the endeavor. The most active members of this charitable society during the days of the war and the years afterwards were: Dr. Krauze, who participated in the society when he was still a student, Josel Kohen, Josel Marynka, Sztrozberg, Jona Rotman, Zilberberg and others.

First Row: Dr. Fleszler, Rabbi Horberg, Rabbi Rapaport, I.M. Rajzman,
J. Kohen and B. Sokolowski.
Second Row: J. Gutman, J. Klajnman, M. Horberg, Ch. Sz. Lichtensztajn,
Zew Kluska, Rabbi I. Finkler, A.B. Ajzenberg, S. Kaminer, and others

After the war, the society continued with its activities and adapted them to the conditions of the times and its needs. The main activities of the "Tomchei Aniyim" society were restricted afterwards to supporting people from the middle class who had fallen upon hard times. Its activity was mainly constructive. A peddler, a small shopkeeper, who needed a certain some of money to survive, and not become indigent and no longer be able to climb back – the society arrived and extended the necessary support and set him up on his feet. In the same way there was a tradition in this society to arrange a kosher kitchen and prepare all of the requirements of the Passover holiday for the Jewish soldiers who were stationed in the city.

החיילים היהודיים ועסקני הכשר לפסח

The Jewish soldiers and the kosher for Passover kitchen activists

A. Goldberg, S. Kligman, M. Zloto, A.B. Ajzenberg, Z. Kluska,
Ch. Sz. Lichtensztajn, Rabbi I. Finkler, E.I. Rozenblum and R. Rafalowicz.

[Page-96]

"Moshav Zekeinim"

The "Moshav Zekeinim" (Seat of the Aged) was founded by the brothers Jakob and Cwi Zagajski and was a blessing to the elderly of Kielce and the area. Elderly people who had been abandoned, who needed to rest when they reached the days in which they were not wanted, found shelter, care and rest in spacious and clean rooms. The residents of the city showered blessings upon the heads of the founders, whose generosity prompted them to open this institution for the benefit and comfort of the elderly. Dark and lonely old age did not burden them, the elderly, for the care and comfort that they found there distracted them from tragic thoughts, they knew and sensed that they were not superfluous in the world as long as there is still an eye looking over them.

משפחת זאגאיסקי וראשה ר' צבי ז"ל

The Zagajski Family and its patriarch, Reb' Cwi Z"L

Even after the building was erected and the institution created, the benefactors kept a careful eye on it, were always trying to improve it, reform it and bring it up to date. If they found some lacking in the institution they didn't rest nor have peace until it was corrected, all of their desires and efforts were focussed on making the elderly's last days more pleasant. Here too the activist who knew no rest, Dr. Pelc, was very busy with his advice and knowledge that included this beneficial institution. He endeavored to improve the state of the elderly men and women as much as he could. He strictly oversaw the sanitary and hygienic conditions at the institution. The kitchen was also under his supervision. He took care that the nutrition was appropriate to the weakened digestions of the elderly. He was particular about absolute cleanliness in the rooms, which is the precaution for the health of the individual and the community.

רעד "מושב זקנים", העסקנים והזקנים

The "Moshav Zekeinim" committee, the activists and the elderly

Sitting: D. Herszkowicz, Heszel Goldberg, D. Szalit, Dr. M. Pelc, S. Kligman, C. Zagajski, M.P. Kaminer, Mejer Ajzenberg and Benjamin Lew.
Among those standing in the second row: Josef Enach, M. Ajzenberg, Ch. and J. Zagajski

[Page-98]

Orphanage

An important and beneficial institution existed in Kielce, and this was the "Beit Yetomim" [Orphanage]. This institution was brought to life by a group of men and women who were active in public life during the days of World War I.

In those days, there were many orphans in the city. The epidemics, the infectious diseases that accompanied the war, wrought devastation among the population. There were orphans left without father or mother. There was an urgent need for shelter for these abandoned and miserable children. Then the Orphanage was founded which sheltered dozens of orphans under its roof, supplied their needs, care, food, clothing and shoes, basic education. For this purpose the Orphanage hired a childcare worker, a woman with experience. Tender looks and affection surrounded the orphans, and they continued to grow without sensing their being orphaned or lonely. Many of them later became excellent and useful artisans; the most talented among them were accepted at the Jewish Gymnasiums, where they received a high school education.

With the help of this institution, the sad orphans, as a group, became people who contributed to society and to the nation. The Jewish inhabitants were also very fond of the institution and many contributed aid and helped when they saw the excellent results of this charitable endeavor. Without appropriate care these children would have become street children, abandoned children, wild without education and they would have atrophied. This institution saved them from both poverty and abandonment and acted as both father and mother to them.

Mrs. Wolman, the principal of the girls Gymnasium, was the patroness of the Orphanage. She and the members of the committee, whose members included Zagajski, Rajzman, Dr. Pelc, Nechemja Ostrowicz, Mrs. Fajga Arten, were devoted heart and sole to this important institution. The orphans, graduates of the institutions, would recall their names with gratitude. The Zagajski brothers, with the help of city benefactors, erected a beautiful building for the Orphanage in 1930 that was gloriously furnished and improved to the great comfort of the orphans.

In Kielce there were other smaller charitable societies: "Hachnasat Orchim" [Hospitality], "Hachnasat Kallah" [Aid to Brides], an aid society for impoverished women who had just given birth, and a "Chesed Shel Emet" society [burial].

The task of the hospitality society was arranging places to sleep for poor guests who could not afford a hotel. Such citizens were used to sleeping in study halls and places of worship putting their heads on the benches and the tables which they used as a "made bed", cloths and towels, old prayer shawls and whatever they found there, and thus they would sleep through the night.

Of course, such an arrangement was not good for the public health. Poor guests sleeping in public places were likely to transfer disease bacteria from place to place. To close the houses of worship in their faces was also not possible: to Jews known as merciful, such an act would be considered ruthless, and no Jewish mind would tolerate it.

The public workers at the Orphanage and the children

From top to bottom: Mrs. Diament, Sara Erlich, Zagajski, Frajman , Chawa Kajzer, C. Kaufman, M. Kaufman, Dr. Krauze, Finkelsztajn, S. Maurberger, Merber, Engineer Piekarski, H. Mincberg, C. Wilner, B. Rotenberg, F. Arten, A. Edelsztajn, F. Zajde, A. Rotenberg and others

To correct this problem, a small house was rented at the initiative of the sons of the Admo"r of Chmielnik, beds were set up there with soft, clean bedding. For a minimal fee a guest found shelter and a place to sleep there.

The supervisor of this institution was Josef Szymon Chmielnicki, the beadle of the synagogue.

The bridal society took care of poor brides, ushering them under the "chupah" and supplying them with their wedding needs. In this society as well as that for poor women who had given birth, mostly righteous women of he older generation took part, who hewed to their mothers' tradition.

Close to the outbreak of World War II a "Chesed Shel Emet" society was founded in the city. The energy behind this society belonged to Dawid Rozenwald. The Jewish settlement in Kielce had expanded and it happened sometimes that the deceased had no relatives and there was no one to look after his burial – several inhabitants of Kielce felt the need to establish a society to observe this commandment of kindness with the dead who had no one to care for them.

All of the above-mentioned charitable institutions brought tremendous benefit to the Kielce community. Nearly every Jewish resident was a member in one of them, participated in their meetings, contributed from his money and strength to maintain them. The Jew did not feel himself isolated even in the most critical situation. He knew that he was a limb in a living, developing body, he was not detached from the community; thousands of tiny blood vessels connected him to the ancient trunk, that no force of wind that one might find in the world – and that one might not find in the world – could uproot.

The charitable impulse that is implanted in the heart of every Jew in the world, that is a basic element of the essence of his soul, is what allowed the Israelite nation to survive even in the worst periods in its history.

A Jew, who was forced to leave his place of residence and take the travelers' staff in his hand, did not get lost on his wanderings. Wherever he came, he found his brothers who were organized into a community who would receive him, care for him and welcome him into their homes not as a stranger, who came to disturb their rest, but as a brother, a friend and a companion. A wanderer like this was not discouraged, did not despair on his wandering path; on the contrary, he found encouragement wherever he went; he knew that everywhere he went he would find brothers, co-religionists, whose homes would be open to him, and in which he would find a resting place after the effort of the road and the weariness of travel.

Ever community in the Diaspora had its own charitable institutions; even the smallest of them represented, in miniature, the entire assembly of Israel. At the head of every community stood the public leader, the "Parnas", a rabbi and his rabbinical court. It had "melameds" and teachers, who disseminated Torah and knowledge, study halls and synagogues, in which there was a Ner Tamid lit, an eternal light of the soul of the nation, and the charitable institutions cared for the weaker ones, those who had come down in the world, and the sick and supported them so they could stand on their feet. The community members ensured that even one soul of Israel was not lost.

Only Israel had the command – a very important one morally and nationally: "Whosoever saves one soul of the nation of Israel, it is considered as if he had saved an entire world". Only we, the children of Israel, knew how to cherish and respect the image of God that is in human beings and made the effort to preserve this image in its purity and wholeness. We made the greatest efforts to ensure that this image did not atrophy in the hardship of bondage and the bitterness of the exile.

Thanks to these attributes of every community, we survived the most difficult conditions of the exile. The expulsions, the persecutions, the riots, the despicable murders and conspiracies, which our persecutors invented against us, did not have the strength to erase the image of God from our faces, to blunt the exalted feelings in which the Jewish nations excelled in us, from the time we were a nation on the earth.

The communities were the cells, the fibers in which the national strengths accumulated and were preserved.

[Page-102]

Political Parties, Movements and Organizations

Translated by Judy Montel

Edited by Warren Blatt

The Kielce community, even if it was young and had only recently outgrown its diapers, still managed to develop its institutions like one of the most ancient communities. It excelled not only in its charitable institutions, whose purpose was local philanthropy, extending a helping hand to the local poor; it was outstanding not only in the educational institutions it established to grant knowledge and information to the children of the city; but national institutions were also established there, political parties that had the future of the nation at heart and for whose sake they developed extensive groundwork.

Every party acted according to its outlook and views. However, all of their activities had one side that was equal, in that they didn't limit themselves to the four cubits of private benefit, or local benefit, but their ultimate goal was the good of the entire nation.

The most active party in the city was the Zionist party, and we have devoted earlier pages of this book to describing the founding of the Zionist association and its early activities. I mentioned there the names of several of its founders and their endeavors.

However, over time the first group came apart; some of them passed away, some of them left Kielce, some of them, one by one, abandoned the camp and became indifferent to the national project. Many left Zionism and joined other groups.

But in their place new members arrived, most of them from the seats of the study hall. They stood with the Zionist camp as a solid rock. Even during the most difficult days of the Zionist movement they stood at their posts and did not abandon camp.

Zionism encountered crises after the death of Herzl, Z"L, the initial enthusiasm faded. Also during the period of the Russian liberation movement, many left the national movement and the vision of the rebirth of the nation in its homeland. Impatient spirits found themselves disappointed when they saw that the redemption was tarrying and began to believe that the political and social revolution would bring salvation and redemption to the nation of Israel as well. They deluded themselves that the source of anti-Semitism lay in the policies of an autocratic government that was backwards in its reforms for the benefit of the masses, and in order to divert people's anger in a different direction, purposely inflamed the hearts of the masses to hatred against the Jews, by pointing to them as exploiters of the populace, as the only ones responsible for the decrepit state of the nation. But when the revolution succeeded and the people will take the reins of government in their own hands and establish democratic rule, then the situation of the masses would be improved by social reforms. In the new conditions, the country would turn into a Garden of Eden, peace and goodwill would exist between the nations and there would no longer be any place for anti-Semitism.

Collective photograph of the Zionists activists in Kielce on the twenty fifth anniversary of the movement, 1909-1934

Thus argued many of those who turned their backs on the Zionist movement. Also later, when the revolution did not succeed, and the reactionary force returned to its former rule and demonstrated its power in riots that it held in dozens of cities and towns, in spilling Jewish blood and in despicable plots that they conspired against them – Zionism did not succeed in those difficult days in acquiring new adherents in Kielce or in penetrating the masses, on the contrary, many of its earlier disciples left it.

Bitter disappointment attacked the masses of Jewish people at that time, they saw no salvation or redemption in any of the movements, despair overcame them, and to escape their distress they left their places of residence, took up the staff of the wanderer and immigrated to the countries of the Americas and to other parts of the world. The Zionist movement at the time was quieted; its impress was no longer noted on the Jewish streets. Besides selling a few "Shekels" and gathering money for the Odessa committee, there was no real Zionist activity on the Jewish street.

However, even in days of crisis like these there were a few for whom Zionism was a part of their spiritual essence, their faith in it was strong and no force could uproot it from their hearts. They stood on guard and kept the flame burning so that it didn't go out. They endeavored to keep an eternal flame burning on the altar of the Zionist idea.

I will mention here mention the names of the active Zionists who were most distinguished in the field of Zionist action in Kielce.

In the front row stood the Kajzer brothers. They were the priests of the Zionist idea in Kielce, they lived the life of Zionism, did not let the Zionist flag out of their hands in all conditions and circumstances. While still on the benches of the study hall they began to spread the Zionist idea among their comrades in scholarship.

Later as well, when they left the study hall and began to work in negotiation and trade, the Zionist idea continued to glow and shine in front of their eyes. They arranged their homes, educated their children in the spirit of the Zionism they had been instilled with in the days of their youth. In Kielce, the name "Kajzer" was a synonym for the concept of Zionism. The elder of them, Szymon Kajzer, Z"L, who owned an emporium for books and writing implements, made his home a center for the Zionists. In his shop and also in his home, those friendly to the idea and to action would gather to consult about Zionist matters. When a young man happened to arrive in the city and was thinking of joining the Zionist circle, his first path was to the home of Szymon Kajzer. He was the address for the pads of "Shekels" for sale, flyers and brochures with a Zionist content to be distributed.

Even during times when Zionist activities were forbidden by the Czar's government, Kajzer continued his activities for Zion in spite of the ban and in spite of the searches of the police, who would visit his home from time to time. Once, the police arrested him, when they found pads of "Shekels" in his possession. When he was released he continued with his work.

Meetings of the local members were held in his house. In order to throw off the police, the members didn't enter or leave all together, but one at a time from different directions. They would take short cuts, walk a round about way to show that they had another goal in mind until, quite innocently, they found themselves at Kajzer's house.

[Page-105]

When a Zionist speaker came to Kielce, or a national preacher or activist – their first stop was the home of Sz. Kajzer.

Towards the end of his life he traveled to the land of Israel as a tourist. He wanted to first see the conditions there and later also to settle there with his family. He toured the country up and down and returned to his home to liquidate his business and his assets and realize the dream of his soul; however, death caught him first, and his bones did not get to lie in the soil of the holy land, object of his heart's desire his entire life, whose rebirth and reconstruction he had so yearned to see.

His brother Nechemja was also devoted to the Zionist idea his whole life. He was the agent of the Zionist Organization in Kielce, all the affairs of the Zionists were in his hands: the affairs of the national funds, matters pertaining to immigration to the land of Israel. His wife, Ester Kajzer, a woman of valor, and activist in WIZO [Women of the International Zionist Organization], also participated in every Zionist and national enterprise. They sent their son Icak to the land of Israel; he is now a doctor in the Israel Defense Forces. Their commercial ties did not allow them to leave their dwelling place and to move to the land of their inspiration themselves. Their younger brother settled in the land of Israel when he was still young and as a construction worker he worked towards the rebirth of the country. The flesh-pot of the Diaspora did not have the power to draw him back to his parents and his brother, who lived a life of wealth and lacked nothing.

At the side of the Kajzer brothers stood the Zionist Mosze Piekarski. A man of noble spirit, instilled with Jewish values, well read in its ancient and modern literature, he devoted his physical and spiritual strengths to the Zionist idea and the rebirth of the nation in its homeland. His home was also filled with a Zionist atmosphere; his children were educated in the national-Zionist spirit. He was a model and exemplar of the Jew who was complete in his attributes, his opinions and his manners. Attached to the tradition of his forefathers, he did not regard the new currents in Jewish life negatively. His opinion was that whatever a Jewish mind conceived and thought, whatever Jewish energies created and activated – was dedicated to the nation, and entered its treasury of assets. Having common sense of his own, he knew how to appreciate the common sense of others too.

As the head of the Zionists in Kielce he did much to infuse the Zionist idea in the hearts of the Jewish masses, and to this end he gave popular lectures on subjects and problems of current interest and also in the field of Hebrew literature. He was one who did what he said. After the publication of the Balfour Declaration, when the vision of generations began to be realized, he liquidated his assets and moved to the land of Israel with his family, to the land his heart desired.

When he arrived in this country he did not take up trade as he had in the Diaspora; he knew that the land needed active hands to be renewed from its desolation – and he became a farmer. Even though he was approaching old age, he approached the difficult agricultural work in an unaccustomed climate with youthful heat and enthusiasm. The idea that he had been able to be one of the builders of the homeland and among those making its wasteland fruitful, made all the work pleasant to him, including the most difficult. This is the figure of a Jew complete in all aspects!

[Page-106]

Here is another elevated figure of one of the Kielce Zionists: Alter Ehrlich, the son-in-law of Rabbi Cwi Zagajski. Alter Ehrlich – this is a delicate figure, an undramatic sort of generous character. The son of a wealthy family – he chose in his life not a life of pleasure and private happiness, as his situation warranted and allowed, but devoted himself with every fiber of his being to the national task, the Zionist task, in which he found satisfaction for his soul and ease for his spirit. He did not seek out other pleasures. True pleasure he found only in the opportunity to do something for the good of the nation. Every piece of information that contained a hint about some Zionist success, he brought to me in excitement, and his face glowed with inner joy. It was as if a private life did not exist for him. He lived the life of the nation. He rejoiced in its joys and was saddened by its sorrows.

As the son of Chassidim, he did not initially leave their community even when he was a Zionist. However, he was not able to remain in their company for long. He could not tolerate the mockery, the scorn and the pointed remarks at the expense of the Zionists on the part of the zealous Chassidim. His sensitive soul was full of love and affection for every single individual of the people of Israel, and jealousy and hatred were foreign to his spirit and he was unable to calmly tolerate the arrogance of certain Chassidim who felt that they themselves were the *creme de la creme* of the nation; and that those who were not members of their community were like garlic skins in their eyes, and they would annul them like dirt [a phrase from the Passover rituals].

He separated himself from them not out of hatred, heaven forbid, but because he was unable to remain in their narrow confines. His soul yearned for spaciousness and wished to include all segments of the people – all were important in his eyes.

According to his views, every single limb of the national body had an essential role. Although there were weaker limbs, limbs which would eventually detach themselves from the body. But as long as the limb is part of the body, and is supported by it – it was not superfluous, it has value for the entire body. There is a mutual influence between the body's limbs.

This was the opinion of Ehrlich the Zionist, at which he arrived not as the result of thought, but which flowed directly from his heart's values, from the warm affection that burned in him like a holy flame for his people who were enslaved and bound by the bonds of the exile. Zionism was an exalted vision of his heart, upon whose realization the redemption of the nation depended, as well as its internal and external liberation, and he devoted himself to the movement and worked and acted in its favor until his last breath.

Even during the days of his long illness, he did not abandon his national work. He was also a delegate to the Zionist Congress in Vienna. With the aid of his wife, who was a loyal partner in his Zionist endeavors as well, he continued to weave in his spirit's dream the long thread of the redemption of Israel, so that its tip would reach a rebuilt and liberated Jerusalem.

I will mention here also Mosze Kalichsztajn, Z"L. He was also one of the outstanding Zionists in Kielce. He also came to Zionism from the benches of the study hall. The Zionist idea took him hostage and did not let him go until the day of his death. He was devoted to it not only with abstract love, with him Zionism took a concrete form. First of all, he gave his sons and daughters a Zionist education. And when they grew up, most of them moved to the land of Israel and settled there. He himself also moved to the land of Israel and lived there for a number of years. Here in Israel he did difficult labor and did not get upset; for the land of Israel he accepted everything with love and satisfaction.

[Page-107]

However, he was not buried in the soil of the land of Israel, of which he was so fond all of his life. He returned to visit his old birthplace for family reasons and remained there for several years. When he was preparing to return to the land of his aspirations, whose praises and glories he had never ceased to sing, he took ill with a terminal illness which cast him upon his deathbed, from which he did not arise again.

This enthusiastic Zionist did not have time to pack his belongings and to return to the renewed homeland, to his offspring, who had meanwhile become involved with the land that was being reborn.

The inhabitants of Kielce gave him great honor at his death, eulogized him properly and as befits a man who devoted his life not only to selfish goals, to establish a standard of life for himself, but for the national task, its culture and the rebirth of its homeland.

Among the outstanding Zionists a leading position was given to Mosze Rotenberg, Z"L. The son of a family of lineage, the grandson of the Rabbi of Witoslaw in the Kielce district, he entered the Zionist circle when still a young man, there he found his place. He lived the task of the nation body and soul. He worked for his brother and the members of his community in the city of his birth in public institutions, and in gratitude the inhabitants of Kielce elected him to be a member of the municipal council; in the council he was elected to the municipal authority. There he stood, firm as a rock among the Polish members of the city authority who were mostly anti-Semites and struggled with them and did not allow the municipality discriminate against the Jewish inhabitants of the city.

Mosze Rotenberg Z"L

However, he could see in his soul that there was no future for Jews in Poland, in which anti-Semitism was growing stronger. He moved to the land of Israel with his family and settled there. Here he also did not disdain any work; every job, even the most difficult, was attractive to him, for he knew that working here was national work; the homeland would be built only by much hard and exhausting labor. In the land of Israel he devoted the entire warmth of his heart to the work of "Kofer HaYeshuv" [Ransom of the Yishuv – tax owed to Turkish authorities] and organized the payments of "Kofer HaYeshuv" from [fees from] transportation and margarine. He was also very active in the "Conscription Appeal" which was founded during World War II as the financial project of the "Hagana".

One of the most popular and favorite figures among the Zionists of Kielce was Szmuel Lewartowski, Z"L.

From his youth an enthusiastic Zionist, public activist and devoted to the common weal.

He was one of the founders of the Zionist Association in Kielce. During the pogrom in 1918 he was seriously injured during the Zionist meeting, when he defended the national honor. He was active in the Zionist institutions and a generous contributor to the national funds, was known as the "gabbai" of the Zionist study hall and synagogue of the Zionists, "Sha'arei Zion" [Gates of Zion] for many years.

[Page-108]

Not only Zion captured his heart, but also the fate of the disadvantaged and those suffering in society was another area of his broad public activity.

With all the warmth of his heart and his energy he was devoted to the Orphanage, and was also one of the activists on the committee of the new old age home, "Moshav Zekeinim".

Concerns for education were also not foreign to his mind – he was among the first to be a patron of the Jewish Gymnasium and one of its loyal friends and supporters.

In 1937 he visited the land of Israel to investigate the possibility of settling here with the members of his family; he remained in the land for three months and was enthusiastic about every thing large and small that was being done in our land.

Szmuel Lewartowski

Upon his return he fell victim to the Fascist and anti-Semitic regime in Poland. He was jailed in the infamous camp "Bereza Kartuska" on suspicion of transferring funds to the land of Israel.

When Hitler's minions entered Kielce he was taken along with the forty respected Jews of the city as a hostage. During the days of the Nazi occupation he was known as an indomitable spirit which did not give in to the suffering that existed in the alleyways of the ghetto, and perished together with his wife, Rachel Lewartowski, nee Szofman, who was an exemplary Jewish mother, and their two daughters, Guta and Cwia.

His third daughter and two sons survived who, thanks to the Zionist education they received from their parents, moved to the land of Israel in time and still live here.

There were other active personalities in the Zionist party; but these were also well known in other spheres of action and I will yet have an opportunity to mention their names and discuss their activities.

In general, the Zionists of Kielce were very aware of everything that was going on in the Jewish world and the outer world and reacted according to the principles of Zionism.

The "Mizrachi" Association

The "Mizrachi" Association was also active in Kielce. It was founded in Kielce in 1917, during the third year of World War I. This does not mean that it didn't have adherents in Kielce beforehand; earlier there were many members among the Zionists whose worldview was that of the "Mizrachi"; however, until that year the "Mizrachi" types were mixed in among the general Zionists. And only when the news of establishing the national homeland began to make waves among the Jewish population and faith in the dream grew stronger among the Jewish masses, that the redemption of Israel would arrive with the end of the war, did the "Mizrachi" form an association and begin diverse activities in a big way in all areas, in education, in the local community, in the national and Zionist areas. Their contribution was noticeable in every public, cultural and political activity.

[Page 109]

Its early founders were Chassidim who clustered in the shadows of various Admo"rs, whose attitude to the land of Israel was a positive one. The Chassidim of Radomsk, Piaseczno, Checiny and a portion of the Alexander Chassidim joined the "Mizrachi" movement in Kielce. Only the Gur Chassidim stood apart and did not allow anyone of their number to move into the "Mizrachi". The married students [avrechs] whose hearts were devoted to laboring for the nation were forced to leave the "sztibl" [small synagogues attached to specific Chassidic rabbis] and the Admo"r as well, in whose shadow they had clustered until now. The Zionist idea, which penetrated deep into the hearts of the masses of the nation of Israel, also in circles which had been, up to this time, its chief opponents – overcame the courts of the Admo"rs as well, whose field of vision had until now been limited to the four cubits of the members of their courts and their adherents and had not strayed from their narrow framework.

The young rabbis who came to Kielce to preach religious Zionism caused a revolution among the various ranks of the Chassidim. The Chassidim and very orthodox were surprised by the appearance of rabbis propagandizing Zionism, a role that until now only members of the free intelligentsia had filled, who were far from traditional Judaism.

First a young rabbi named Rapaport visited Kielce, the rabbi of the small town of Andrzejewo in Lodz province. With fiery words he preached the Zionist concepts. His words awakened voices and strong yearnings for Zion deep within the hearts of his listeners. This was an unimaginable sight – that a rabbi with a rabbinical cloak should stand on the platform and speak in praise of Zionism and shower praises and compliments on those who stood at the head of the movement and on its leaders, and the name of Herzl would be mentioned by his lips with awe and honor. Words of mockery, protests and smears about Zionism and its words had been heard from the mouths of rabbis up until now, and suddenly, here was a revolution in the spirits of the rabbis. One after another they come up and join the "Mizrachi", join the wing of the religious Zionist, and begin widespread public relations on the Jewish street.

The words of these rabbis found listening ears and a wide field of activities opened up before the lovers of Zion. The echoes of redemption were in the air. On one side were the horrors of the war, which had especially injured Jewish habitations, false libels, expulsions, riots, murders, which poured down upon the heads of the Jews during the war years. In spite of the full participation of the Jews in the war, at the side of all of the other soldiers, they were still not exempt from the disasters; their homes were destroyed, their families moved from place to place. It was not enough that they spilled their own blood on the battlefields, the additional blood of their fathers, brothers and sisters who remained behind the front lines was spilled as well. Jewish blood was spilled for no reason and no purpose. The tragedy of the Jews in all of its terror was revealed to all eyes.

On the other side, rumors of a Jewish legion fighting in the land of Israel to release its homeland from the yoke of the Turks. They heard about a second Cyrus in the form of Balfour, the British Foreign Minister, who publicly declared before the nations that the land of Israel would be given to the Jews, and that they would establish there a national home for their brothers who were scattered in all the countries of the world. All these rumors excited the minds and prepared the hearts to receive the consolatory words of the Zionist propagandists and to join their ranks.

[Page-110]

The zealous opponents of Zionism in the city wanted to weaken the tremendous impression that the rabbi of Andrzejewo made upon his Chassidic listeners, especially upon the younger ones, therefore they put out a story that some Zionist propagandist had dressed up like a rabbi and was traveling around the cities of Poland in order to steal souls from the Torah of God and obtain them for the camp of the free-thinkers and those who had overthrown the yoke [of religious observance]. However, these scornful words had the opposite effect. People were no longer innocent and gullible enough to believe everything, as they had been at the start of the Zionist movement. The war, and mainly the press, which was mainly pro-Zionist, had done its work, eyes were opened, hearts were prepared to understand how things truly stood. The Zionist movement became dominant on the Jewish street and became a grass-roots movement.

This mood allowed the founding of the "Mizrachi Association" in Kielce, which had illustrious people among its founders: Hilel Oberman of the Piaseczno Chassidim, Zew Kluska, of the Alexander Chassidim, Icak Kirszenbaum of the Kozienice Chassidim, Jakob Szlomo Zylbersztajn, of the Radomsk Chassidim, Izrael Zylbersztajn and Zyskind Herman, of the Sokolow Chassidim, Awraham Ber Ajzenberg of the Checiny Chassidim, and aside from them, a large group of young people and "avrechs" [married yeshiva scholars], who had left the "sztiblach" because they couldn't bear the atmosphere that reined there.

After the first rabbi, a second rabbi came to Kielce, Rabbi J.L. Zlotnik from Gombin [Gabin], a great speaker; with his words, spoken with enthusiastic pathos; he took many souls hostage. Women threw their jewels at his feet; men committed themselves to donate large sums to redeem the land. The youth were charmed by his speeches and were ready to get right up and move to the land of Israel, and even to sacrifice their lives for the homeland. I have never seen such enthusiasm envelope the masses as that which was revealed when this rabbi spoke about Zion and Jerusalem. Those gathered carried the speaker on their shoulders. Cheers and applause were deafening. The tremendous impression that this rabbi made in his speeches was not erased from the hearts of his audience.

After these two rabbis other rabbis of repute would visit Kielce from time to time. Especially Rabbi Amiel of Grajewo, who was later the chief rabbi of Tel Aviv, made many souls for the "Mizrachi" idea. This rabbi was a speaker of a different sort, he spoke from the mind and not from the heart. In his style the brain was stronger than the emotion. His words were logical. He would convince not with his pathos, not with his enthusiasm, not with his flowery words or empty phraseology – his strength was not in these. He was moderate in his speech; emotionally calm, he would analyze the matter about which he was speaking. With his logic, his great knowledge of our ancient and modern literature, and that of other nations as well, with his literary style which would have placed him among the first rank of modern speakers – with these qualities of spirit he triumphed over his opponents and gathered souls to his opinions and views, which were all devoted to the nation, to Israel, to its teachings and its land.

[Page-111]

Faced with this rabbi, who had a reputation also as a Gaon [religious prodigy] in his own generation, even the zealots lowered their heads, the fiercest opponents of Zionism did not dare to assault him crudely and mockingly. Their opposition to his opinions was expressed by proof texts from scripture and Jewish law that forbade connection with evildoers, who have thrown off the yoke of the Torah.

At a debating party which was held in the "Kostarski" hall, in which members of the "Aguda" participated, and at which their best speakers gave speeches, with the goal of weakening the great influence of Rabbi Amiel upon his listeners, his opponents didn't dare to attack him with crude epithets as was their wont; they referred to him politely and with manners, with quotes taken from Jewish law and lore with which they attempted to prove that the path of the rabbis who were joining the Zionist camp was not the correct one and is opposed to the Torah and also to the decisions of later arbiters.

The rabbi, of course, gave them satisfying answers; the national emotion that beat in his heart, together with his healthy logic gave him what to say in response and he contradicted their words with ease. According to the verse: "answer the fool with his nonsense", the rabbi gave proofs with the generosity of his great knowledge, that according to Jewish law and the arbiters there is no ban on joining even with free-thinker, when the good of the entire nation is their goal; the reverse is true, when they reveal a love of Israel and give their lives for the nation, they are kosher Jews and cannot be considered with those who sin against the nation, whose actions cause catastrophe for the entire people.

The explanation of one of the maxims of the sages that I heard from this rabbi at that party remains etched in my memory. He quoted the sayings that are brought in the Talmud about the reasons that led to the destruction of the second Temple. In one place it says: "Jerusalem was destroyed only because people based their words upon the law." and in another place it says: "Jerusalem was destroyed because of baseless hatred." These two reasons are the same in their essence, there were people who wished to sow hatred between the various parts of the people, they would search and find a law, and based upon it they would justify their acts of separation.

After Rabbi Amiel's visit to Kielce the "Mizrachi" grew stronger and many members joined its ranks.

Kielce was also fortunate enough to greet Rabbi Kowalski of Wloclawek. This enlightened rabbi had become famous among the Jews of Poland from the time he was elected as a Senator in the Polish Senate. It was a time when the election of the president was supposed to take place, the head of the Polish state. The president, according to the country's constitution, was elected by a majority of the votes of the delegates of the Sejm [parliament] and the Senate. The candidate for the head of the state was Professor Narotowicz, a well-known democrat, and he had a good chance of winning an absolute majority of the votes. This progressive and popular candidate was a thorn in the sides of the Endeks [National Democrats], who objected to his election. In order to reduce the number of democratic voters, the Endeks used acts of terror against the delegates of the Senate and the Sejm. They enlisted student thugs to stand in long rows along the streets that led to the Sejm who would stop the democratic delegates and especially the Jewish delegates and force them to retrace their steps, and if anyone refused to do the bidding of the thugs, he would be savagely beaten.

[Page-112]

Rabbi Kowalski was not afraid of this terror, and with unusual courage traveled to the Siem by carriage, together with Deuczer, the delegate from "Agudat Yisra'el", in order to fulfill his civic and Jewish duty. The thugs, of course, had no respect for the aged and "honored" him with a hail of blows. The rabbi and Rabbi Deuczer, beaten and injured, entered the gates of the Sejm to cheers of encouragement and respect. The democratic delegates shook their hands in appreciation of their coming to fulfill their responsibility without regard for the dangers involved.

When this rabbi came to Kielce on Zionist business, his reputation preceded him and the city's inhabitants showered him with honor. The synagogue was opened for him and there he preached to the audience sermons that attracted the heart of whoever heard them, in their content and in their beautiful style. Every time the rabbi appeared to give his speeches the synagogue was filled to the brim.

This rabbi did not avoid bringing quotes and opinions of Jewish and non-Jewish scholars to bolster his opinions. Rana"k [Rabbi Nachman Krochmal], Achad Ha'am [Asher Ginsburg], also Hegel and Kant were people he frequently mentioned, not to argue with them, but to demonstrate how the words of our sages in ancient times also contained opinions and views that were expressed by wise men who lived many years after them. He used simple and popular language, which came from the heart, full of love for the nation and all it held holy. He was not used to bringing a verse and introducing the many problems it contained, like the other preachers, and afterwards by sophistry "solving" them with clever thoughts; instead he approached a verse directly, in order to reveal its true meaning. Maxims of the sages he approached without short cuts and revealed their inner meaning. He based his words on his knowledge of the ancient and modern literature of Israel and Jewish history. His speech, which usually lasted for two hours, did not bore; the gathered stood as if nailed to their places, their ears pricked up to listen and not to lose even one of his words. He opened new horizons before them. Things they had never heard, their ears told them – and all of it in simple language understandable even by someone who had not read and learned much.

Those gathered would leave the synagogue full of pleasure and relaxation; their eyes had seen and their ears had heard, that in their own generation there were rabbis who were worthy of the rabbinical cloak and who were graced with a heart full of the love of Israel, and who had an eye that could see – to great distances, encompassing times and places far removed from their narrow field. Everyone saw it as a sign of the times when a group of rabbis appeared who were patient and who were willing to work for the good of the entire nation and did not limit themselves to the four cubits of their own communities. The rebirth of the nation's hopes for redemption is what, finally, awakened its words, its propagators, those who aroused it and its heralds.

The "Mizrachi" at that time gained esteem in the camp of its opponents as well. They learned that the movement included famous Torah leaders of the day, whose qualifications, purity of spirit and depth of thought should not be ignored. The "Mizrachi" became a major carrier of all Jewish values: Torah and commandments, national goals and rebirth.

[Page-113]

Among the nationalist rabbis who visited Kielce the figure of Rabbi Zew Gold, president of the International Mizrachi Association, especially was engraved on the hearts of its inhabitants. This was the type of rabbi they had in the western countries. The rabbis of the west attempted to influence their listeners not only with depth of thought and precision of mind; but also with their outer look, with the harmonious movements of their limbs, the expression on their faces, and mostly the way their voices went up and down. They had something of the art of an actor. Rabbi Gold was expert in these attributes to a very great degree. When he was speaking, he passed pictures and figures before his listeners, and with his gestures, his facial expressions and the colors of his voice he gave them a three-dimensional shape. It seemed to you as if they were standing, live, in front of you.

When he first spoke in Kielce he reminded the audience of the popular legend that in the days of the Messiah, the Jews would walk upon a bridge of paper and would not fall into the water, and their enemies would walk upon a bridge of iron and would perish in the depths. The way he told this legend charmed his listeners; with his graphic speech and his gestures he awakened the imagination of the audience until it seemed to every one that the bridge was in front of us, the Jews were walking securely and their enemies faced the yawning abyss.

He had the power to transport his listeners from the real world to the imaginary world. When he described the life in the land of Israel he gave it colors, light and glow; the shadows faded in the light that he was able to grant them with his gifts of speech. He did not deny things or change the facts, he did not want to win hearts to the movement by altering the situation; but it seemed as if the deep love that dwelled in the heart of this speaker for the homeland that was renewing its youthfulness, this forced us to see all the forms of its development as positive phenomena which warmed the heart, until even the shadows within them shone with the light of rebirth.

An argument between the sellers in the Tel-Aviv market was in itself a negative social event. The fight of poor women over a meager penny – this was certainly not a pleasant vision for sophisticated minds. But with an artist-speaker like Rabbi Gold, who saw sparks of rebirth and development even in the ugliness of life, the insults of "She-donkey!" "Despicable one!" "Stupid!" become pleasant to the ear, showing the distinct signs of the rebirth of the Hebrew language, which had penetrated even to the lower classes of the Jewish settlement there.

The pathos that did not leave him for even a moment did its work; the listeners were charmed by his manner of speech and were hypnotized by him when he stood on the platform and described to them, like a movie, scene after scene of life in the Jewish settlements in the land of Israel as it was being reborn.

The Jews of Kielce yearned for Rabbi Gold. An announcement of his arrival would fill their hearts with joy. The last time he visited the city he lectured in the hall of the local theatre. Great masses of people came then to hear his words. The hall was crammed with people, because Rabbi Gold was a great favorite of the Jews of Kielce.

Also Rabbi Sz. Brot, head of the rabbinical court of the holy congregation of Lipno, a delegate to the Polish Siem, visited Kielce once.

"Mizrachi" celebrated the completion of the writing of a Torah scroll. In honor of this important event this rabbi was invited to glorify the celebration of a commandment with his presence. This gave the Jews of the city an opportunity to meet this important rabbi and to hear his wonderful sermon from his mouth, which demonstrated the depth of this sharp mind and also his amazing knowledge in all areas of Judaism.

[Page-114]

I will also mention here the visit of Rabbi Bronrot of Ciechanow in Kielce, who later became head of the rabbinical court in the Tel-Aviv community. He was a type of Chassidic rabbi. Even after he joined the Mizrachi camp he did not cease from remaining close to the Admo"r of Alexander. When he arrived in Kielce, the Alexander Chassidim received him with great respect as a most important one of their number.

This rabbi clung to the habits of the rabbis of the older generation who generally approached the verses with questions and afterwards, in their efforts to answer them, inserted intentions and ideas into them, which suited the purpose of sermon. According to their final conclusion, all difficulties were removed, all questions were cancelled, the verses emerged from their veil, clear in every way.

Rabbi Bronrot did not like fancy speech; his style was straightforward, popular. He used simple means when he came to influence his listeners, and his words made an impression. The listener saw before him a rabbi, speaking words that came naturally from the heart, without pretensions before those gathered of brilliant, artificial words; therefore his words entered the heart and his influence was no less than that of the greatest of speakers for whom speaking was a profession.

After every visit of a rabbi, the "Mizrachi" received a new infusion of blood and continued its national labor with renewed energy. Young forces were added to it that were alert and always prepared for work. The "Mizrachi" acquired a lovely, spacious apartment with many rooms, and there installed the prayer room for the "Mizrachi" members, a room for the secretariat, a reading room. Evening classes in Hebrew and Jewish history were arranged; with classes in Talmud on Sabbaths and holidays as well as on "The Kuzari" [philosophical text by medieval Sephardic Rabbi Yehuda HaLevi], "Chovat Halevavot" [Requirement of the Hearts, a moral treatise from 19th century central Europe], etc. Young and old were especially drawn to the "Mizrachi" hall for the "Oneg Shabbat" [Sabbath Pleasure] parties, at which participants found physical and spiritual pleasure; singing, poetry, dancing and interesting lectures, and after them a glass of wine or beer which warmed the hearts and raised them above the lowliness of life, spreading a sublime holiness among the members.

The classes in scientific texts were given in a new method, with historical and philosophical interpretation, and they were something of a surprise to their listeners, sort of a revelation of new worlds and the participants grew in number from Sabbath to Sabbath.

The Culture Committee, which was composed of the members Cwi Nibilski, Josef Kaszanski, Elijahu Iser Rozenblum, Fiszel Guthart and the writer of these lines, worked without cease and with great enthusiasm in order to strengthen the light of the Torah in the hearts of the young people and to keep them in the "Mizrachi" camp, so that they would not leave and go off to other camps and follow foreign slogans.

It is worth writing a few lines about every one of these members just mentioned.

[Page-115]

Cwi Nibilski, the son-in-law of the Rabbi of Wloszczowa, was a married scholar filled to the brim with knowledge about Judaism, expert in ancient and modern Hebrew literature, fluent in foreign languages and well-read in their literature. However, he was shy by nature, humble, modest in his intercourse with others.

He never wanted to stand out or to brag about his knowledge; only in a narrow circle of friends did he come to reveal his soul, among them he found the appropriate atmosphere for his soul and spirit, and among them he would freely express his opinions and ideas, which came out of his mouth like an unending river current. It was pleasant to sit in his company or to walk with him during the summer days, on a Saturday afternoon, after learning in a class at the "Mizrachi", between the fields of grain. He would explain every difficult saying in the Talmud or the Midrash, in Rash"i and other commentaries in an easy manner by adding a word, or setting it in its proper place. Sometimes he would explain an enormous question by changing a letter. He would easily settle contradictions and straighten out misunderstandings, for this man was expert in the pearls of the Talmud and in various literatures, ancient and modern. By nature he was a literal thinker, and casuistry was hateful to him; he would attempt to banish the difficulty with understanding by studying the different versions [of text].

His powers of observation were highly developed. On walks along the paths in the fields, he would identify every bird and insect by name, and he would describe at great length the attributes and nature of every tree and grass; and it seemed to you as if some professor of science was standing before you and giving a lesson in zoology or botany.

His profession was bookkeeping. And in this too he injected much of his talent. For a long time he worked as a clerk at the Hebrew Gymnasium, afterwards at banks and private commercial concerns, and in every place he excelled in his precision and devotion to his profession.

Josef Kaszanski was a rival of Nibilski. Neither wanted to recognize the advantages of the other. Mr. Kaszanski had ambitions to be a poet. He would compose poems and send them to the newspaper editors; but they were never printed. His habit was to complain to his friends about the newspaper editors. He worked as a teacher of religion at the S. Wolman's Gymnasium for girls.

His faith in his own strengths and knowledge was so strong that he had successes in life because of it. First of all, he got the job as a teacher in the Gymnasium without any complication. Secondly, he became the official translator at the district court. Others, whose knowledge of languages and general education were much greater than the knowledge and education of this professor, didn't dare to vie for official posts, and he with his mediocre knowledge attained what others in their wisdom did not.

His post as official translator in the district court intensified the hatred between him and Nibilski. How? And why? I will tell things here as they happened, because they reflect the relations between the Jews and the Poles, which worsened drastically in the years before World War II. This detail comes to describe the generality.

[Page-116]

Hitlerism, which was rampant in Germany with its point aimed at the Jews, penetrated Poland also. Anti-Semitism, which lurked in the hearts of the Poles, raised its head and increased seven-fold. The Nazis were their exemplars and they imitated their actions. Wild anti-Semitic incitement began to take place. On the pages of the newspapers, from the platform of the Sejm and the municipal councils the anti-Semites dripped poison and venom upon the Jews. Assaults on Jewish students in the institutions of higher learning, riots against the peddlers on market days, were regular occurrences, to which no one paid any attention. This got to a point where Polish thugs dared to assault Jewish passersby in the streets of the city, or those walking in the city's parks with iron gloves and sticks in broad daylight and in full view of the police.

These things also happened to the Jews of Kielce.

One Saturday afternoon, when the Jews of the city went out, as was their habit, to walk in the city park and along "Karczowka" Boulevard, thugs assaulted them with bloody blows. When they went to the police for help and protection, they received the response that "as long as no one had been killed in the fight between the two groups, they would not get involved. Fights like this can always break out, and one doesn't need to call the police for such ordinary matters."

The local paper, "Kielcer Zeitung", published a detailed description of the events in the city park and together with this pointed out that the attitude of the police and its behavior were unjust: not only did it not respond to the events, but even after being turned to for help, it insolently [with chutzpah] evaded helping and protecting the victims.

The police considered itself insulted by the word "chutzpah" and sued the newspaper's editor, Cwi Nibilski, for insulting the police in print, when it [the police] was guarding the country and keeping the peace.

During the proceedings at court, Nibilski announced that the newspaper delivered the facts as they had actually occurred and that he had had no intention whatsoever of insulting the police. In his opinion, the term "chutzpah", has a specific meaning that is: having a stubborn and brave position and does not contain any hint of insult. As evidence and proof of his words he brought the Talmudic sentence "Chutzpah even towards the heavens is pleasing". And there it is impossible to put any other intent into the word "chutzpah, except the definition appropriate to the sayings meaning, that is, a brave and stubborn attitude is successful even towards God.

The prosecutor, on the other hand, argued that according to the translation of the description it appears that the meaning of the word "chutzpah" was effrontery that knows no shame, and that is an insult to the police, which must defend its honor. The police are a public institution, and whoever injures it injures the political authorities. Finally, the accuser demanded that the court give the editor a severe sentence.

The court could not make a decision about this philological question and decided to postpone the proceedings until they could hear the opinion of a philologist, someone who was expert in linguistic questions.

As an expert, Professor Kaszanski was summoned, the official translator, this expert found it convenient to side with the police and testified that also in the Polish-Hebrew dictionary the word "chutzpah" was translated as "bezczelnosc" – effrontery.

[Page-117]

At this time, a lawyer represented for the newspaper who discredited Kaszanski entirely from being an expert in this question, but establishing that the person posing as an expert knew neither Polish nor Hebrew. As an aid to his words, he pointed out mistakes in his speech, and that he didn't know how to follow the stylistic rules of the Polish language, and that the court must not rely on the opinion of a man who doesn't have any familiarity with scientific questions.

During the speech of the lawyer, Kaszanski attempted to apply to the head of the court and demand that the latter protect him from the attacks of the lawyer, but with no result. The head of the court declared that the accused had the right to discredit the expert who is testifying against him with arguments that he, the accused finds to be correct.

The court postponed the proceedings once again in order to hear the opinion of Professor Szor in this matter.

The expert left the courthouse with his head hung low. He was humiliated in full public view before the judges and the people in the courtroom who had come to follow the proceedings.

This trial continued for a long time. Professor Szor did not respond to the summons of the court. He was out of the country at the time, participating in some scholarly convention. Meanwhile, World War II broke out and the order of the world was changed.

From then, from the beginning of the trial and its continuance, the hatred between Nibilski and Kaszanski grew stronger and each one of them would attempt to publicly demonstrate the ignorance of the other.

Despite the flaw of pride and the desire to be superior, which Kaszanski had, to a great extent, he also had positive characteristics as part of his make up. First of all, he was a national religious Zionist. And to a certain extent he knew the Torah, was well read in the Scriptures, in the Hebrew language and its grammar. Thanks to these characteristics he found a place in the ranks of the "Mizrachi". He participated in classes for youth, gave speeches at various opportunities and worked on public relations for the land of Israel and its funds.

Since he was a member of the cultural committee of the "Mizrachi", the other members with whom he came in contact influenced him quite a bit. Slowly, he grew to respect other peoples' opinions and to change his own opinion regarding his own importance.

Elijahu Iser Rozenblum – he was a very special type of both public and national activist. It is worth spending some more time, therefore, and to reveal the hidden paths along which the spirit of this man developed.

If a person has a sensitive spirit and an inner ability to be impressed, no security measures will suffice. Even if he is hidden in darkness, even if he is kept from contact with other people, he will still extend his limits and absorb the opinions and the yearnings that are borne and reveal themselves in the space of the world.

[Page-118]

Such a spirit was the kind that E.I. Rozenblum had. His father, a simple householder, cared for his son like the apple of his eye. In his childhood, he handed him over to outstanding "melameds", and in his youth he sat him in the study hall. There he studied the Gemara, the commentaries and the arbiters in the company of the other students. His father did not take his eyes off of him, watched over him that he not stray from the path that tradition laid out for him, that new ideas, that had begun to circulate among the youth, not penetrate his mind. When he was eighteen years of age, his father attached a millstone around his neck in the form of a wife, and he began to work on the commandments of daily life and the business of a livelihood. He wrote in a language his father did not teach him. "Keep your sons from logic" – this saying remained in front of his father's eyes as he directed the education of his son. After the marriage, his father-in-law and his father handed him over the Gur Chassidim, and were certain that they had given him into trusted hands. The Gur Chassidim would knead the dough they had been given and give it a nice shape according to their spirits and the spirits of his ancestors. In general, his parents had done all that they could that the twig be bent as it was meant to grow.

However, as I have said, the soul of Elijahu Iser was made of such delicate stuff, that it could not be struck and not be impressed by the movement of the rebirth that was making waves on the Jewish street. With unending enthusiasm he joined this movement. He left Chassidism, neglected his business and devoted himself heart and soul to the new currents. From the Chassidim he inherited enthusiasm, devotion and zealousness. He was a zealous Zionist, after also a zealous and even extreme "Mizrachi" member. The idea and the action that he found appropriate and correct conquered his essence and he fought for them stubbornly, with exaggerated extremism, that sometimes made him shocking to his listeners.

In his youth he did not study writing and grammar. Some of his knowledge about the world came to him from reading the Yiddish newspapers. In spite of these disadvantages in his education he did not avoid appearing as a speaker at every meeting and every convention. The idea that crept into his mind dominated him and pushed him to get up and express it with his primitive dialect. However, since his entire soul was concentrated in his words, all the elements of his being participated in it, and the words were expressed in an ecstasy, from a divine enthusiasm – this had an influence and impressed his listeners.

Although in the eyes of some of his listeners, he was out of the ordinary, they saw in his enthusiasm a sign of an empty spirit. A superficial idea, words of minor value would enthuse him to such a great extent, as if they were really things of great import.

Sometimes, when he came to express an insignificant idea he would insert dross elements that would counterfeit it, and on such things he would expend lots of energy and tension of forces more than was necessary.

Thus were the most active members in the "Mizrachi" movement in the city, with all of their virtues and faults, attributes and talents. They gave the "Mizrachi" a special color, a local and original color.

In 1924 a scholar called Fiszel Guthart arrived in the city of Kielce, and he also did much in the "Mizrachi" arena, and especially in the "Torah vaAvoda" movement [Torah and Labor].

This scholar grew up among Chassidim, and absorbed their enthusiasm and devotion; his entire being expressed Chassidic characteristics. He was in constant motion, he soul knew no rest; he was entirely like quicksilver, sensitive to everything that fell into our camp. He was only at home during the late hours of the night, meant for sleeping. All the other hours of the day we would find him in meetings, gatherings, among the youth, among the city activists. In society, in public, that was his place, there he lived like a fish in water. He too, like his friend Rozenblum, didn't distinguish between important work and unimportant work, in things great and small he invested his maximum strength.

[Page-119]

His jobs were varied and many. He taught at the "Yavne" school of the "Mizrachi", gave private lessons at the homes of the wealthy, in order to cover the deficit in his budget, the youth organization, evening classes and lectures. He hadn't a single free hour to go home to eat lunch with his family, and would grab a hasty meal wherever he was and continue with his work. He was entirely given over to working for the general good, working for the people. Educating the youth was his chief occupation. He also had some of the attributes of the persevering scholars of the study hall, where they would continue to live like monks, separated and removed from the tumult of the world, from the delicacies of life, finding pleasure and reward in a page of Gemara spiced with the innovations of the "Maharsh"a" – thus Fiszel Guthart found the satisfaction of his spirit and the life of his soul in his public and national work, and his care for the youth and its organizations. Dancing in a circle together with the young boys, members of the "Torah vaAvoda" organization, would fill him with such enthusiasm that he forgot the world and its flaws. His soul floated in the upper spheres, like the soul of one of the early Chassidim, divine holiness. There were times when there was not bread in his home; but the spiritual joy did not leave him even then, and with constant stubbornness he continued to follow his path, a path of working for the nation. The qualities of his spirit and his talents made him a favorite of the youth. The were all close to him and willing at any minute to do his bidding.

Icak Kirszenbaum

One of the notable activists of the "Mizrachi" was Icak Kirszenbaum. He was the "gabbai" of the main synagogue for many years, one of the earliest proponents of Hebrew, the "Mizrachi" representative on the community committee, a member of the National Jewish Council, and others.

Born in Radom, one of the descendants of the Kabbalist, Rabbi Szymszon, the rabbi of Ostropoli; a great grandson and grandson of Rabbi Jechezkel Landau (The "Noda Beyehuda"); a yeshiva graduate; one of the outstanding Chassidim of Grodzisko and Kozienice; he moved to Kielce after his marriage. Here he married Cipa'le, the daughter of Rabbi Dawid Lewartowski; one of the first merchants of Kielce.

[Page-120]

Rabbi Icak earned himself a reputation as an honest tradesman (first in wholesale trade in kerosene; pickles and salt and later in groceries), and his wife contributed to this to a large extent. Generally, though they were occupied with matters of earning a living, they also knew how to lay the foundations for an outstanding Zionist and Hebrew home. When Menachem Prybulski Z"L arrived in Kielce, they entrusted him with the Hebrew education of their children. They had a sign in their house "Jew, Speak Hebrew!", and indeed, this was the first Hebrew-speaking home in the city. Not only did the local people find a Zionist-Hebrew atmosphere in their home, but so did the emissaries of the pioneer movement from the land of Israel. Their daughter, Sima, Z"L, who later perished in the Warsaw Ghetto uprising, was the first Hebrew speaker in the city.

It was interesting to see how the first journalist from the land of Israel who visited Kielce viewed the life of the family.

"Thirty years ago I had a mission to the holy congregations of Poland, and among other places I arrived in Kielce. I met there the sons and daughters of one family, enthusiastic and devoted members of the "Poalei Zion", who knew Hebrew, were preparing to move to the land of Israel (one member of the family was already living there at the time). I was invited to their home on Sabbath evening. I found a glorious patriarchal Jewish family. The father, respected, the mother, beautiful, the sons and daughters, warm and charming (the entire family moved some time later to the land of Israel, and only the daughter remained in Warsaw – her fate was that of all of our brethren there). The father was a religious man, blessed the wine, sang Sabbath songs, the sons, zealous members of "Poalei Zion" – sat with their heads covered and contributed to the atmosphere of the Sabbath Queen." (Excerpt from the sketch of the editor of "Davar", Mr. Chaim Szorer, "Davar", 26.3.56).

In 1933 Rabbi Icak and his family moved to the land of Israel. The same year he appeared in public as the representative of the Kielce community at the celebrations of the jubilee of Tel-Aviv. During the period he lived in Tel-Aviv, Rabbi Icak devoted his time to learning the Torah. A modest and humble man of a good temper, widely read and an excellent prayer leader, he lived to a ripe old age and died on the eve of the first of the month of Nisan, 5713, [May 15, 1953]. His widow, who did much for the Home for the Aged and the Orphanage in Tel-Aviv, died on the 4th of Av, 5714 [September 2, 1954]. They left four sons after them (E.J. El-roi, lawyer, Awraham, Arje and Mosze Kirszenbaum) and two daughters (Ada Zakaj and Cila Zylbersztajn), all of them in Tel-Aviv.

All of these that I mentioned here, by name, and all of those who were not mentioned and their names were not published, also in other places -- all of them were diligent workers in their narrow circle. And who knows, if we had weighed, on a scale, the activities of these modest workers with those of other activists whose names ring out in the world -- whose side would be heavier?

These humble people of the world, who are modest in their actions, who work diligently and devote their souls without tiring and with great stubbornness, each in his own small area, they are the ones who have brought us to this point, to realize the dream of the return to Zion and the establishment of the State of Israel, in the land of Israel.

[Page-121]

"Hashomer Hatza'ir" in Kielce

"Hashomer Hatza'ir" is undoubtedly numbered among the first Zionist youth movements which were established and organized in Kielce.

Towards the end of World War I – when the armies of Austria and German conquered Congress Poland – the "Shomer Hatza'ir" movement, then called the Hebrew Scouts, penetrated from Galicia into the main Polish cities and into Kielce as well.

In 1916, the "Hashomer" nest (as it was then called) was founded in Kielce, which collected within it the Jewish youth who were studying at the Polish schools (during that time the Hebrew Gymnasium had not yet been founded). At the head of the organizers and counselors were the students of the upper classes at the Polish Gymnasium named for Sznidski, among them Ignasz Edelsztajn, Ludwig, Polak, Elencwajg, Birencwajg, Henik Rembiszewski, Merber; Szymon Frajman; Pola and Guta Kaufman, Lubliner, and others. Very quickly students from the few elementary schools still left in the city joined the movement. The students from the Polish school for girls and Mrs. Stefanja Wolman's also joined.

In a short while, from the ranks of the "Shomer Hatza'ir" they organized the youth that was not learning in school – "No'ar Stam" ['Merely' Youth].

The main club and the administration of the 'nest' were at 54 Staro-Warszawska Street for the boys, and the second club for the girls was on Bodzentynska Street.

[Page-122]

The 'nest' organized three "battalions" in the city and counted hundreds of young people of both sexes in its ranks. The organizers and counselors of the youth not studying in school included the Zajfman brothers, Krystal, Szaul and Awraham Kalichsztajn, Herszel Zysman, Mordechai Garfinkel, Fajvel Dajbuch, Goldblum, Ben Cion Goldfarb, Szlomo Kajzer, Szlomo Szpilman and others. That same year, there was the first regional convention in Kielce of the 'nests' of the "Shomer Hatza'ir" from Kielce and the cities of the district. At the initiative of the regional administration and the group in our city, 'nests' were established in most of the cities of the district and the surrounding area and they stayed in close contact with them in the area of the counseling, the organizing and the work.

The first public trip and sailing activity on Lag BaOmer 5677 (1917) was memorable as was the tremendous impression that this procession made upon both the Jewish and non-Jewish inhabitants, as an organized and amazingly orderly appearance of the national Jewish youth in Kielce.

The 'nest' included both youth from assimilated or partially assimilated families, and youth from the most outstanding householding families. All of these found a place to meet and to cooperate in the framework of the 'nest' in the instilling the spirit of Zionism, scouting, and the youthful spirit amid the ranks of the members.

This was a period of awakening and national recognition on the Jewish street after the removal of the rule of the Czar over Congress Poland [in 1918], and of intensive activities and organization of political, Zionist, religious and workers' associations, as well as anti-Zionist ones of various kinds. But the crowning achievement was the organization of the Jewish youth in our city into the "Shomer Hatza'ir" which collected into itself the best of Jewish youth.

In 1918, on November 11, when the anti-Jewish riots broke out in Kielce – the well known pogrom in the Polaski Theatre – most of the members of the "Shomer Hatza'ir" who participated in that meeting were injured and severely beaten. This event as well as the severe limitations of the local Polish authorities especially towards the youth organizations – brought about the disbanding of the 'nest' and the ceasing of its activities.

In response to the despair and low spirits that then overtook Jewish public life, the first group of the counselors and graduates of the 'nest' who were planning on moving to the land of Israel got together at this point. The severe blows of the pogrom and the pain that surrounded everyone, and the echoes of the calls to move to the land of Israel (the Third Aliya) that arrived with the end of World War I – found willing ears and a desire for fulfillment amidst the 'elderly' members of the 'nest' in Kielce. The first group organized and moved to the land of Israel, and immediately afterwards additional groups traveled on harrowing journeys until they had also gotten there. The first people who made aliya from our city from the veteran members of the 'nest' were the Kalichsztajn brothers, Szlomo Szpilman, Szlomo Kajzer, Jechiel Zloto, Icak Goldberg; Kohen; Glikman; Baruch Grynberg and many others.

As I have said, the "Shomer Hatza'ir" movement was paralyzed and scattered after the pogrom of 1918; and only about two years later was the movement reorganized by Pinek Rozenkranc and Artek Friszman (now in Israel) who founded the 'nest' anew.

[Page-123]

Meanwhile, there had been changes in public Jewish life during the few years of Polish independence. The severe persecutions of the Jews in the economic as well as social-political arenas led to a firmer stance towards their oppressors and the drawing of Zionist and pioneering conclusions.

The renewed 'nest' led by Artek Friszman included at first only a few students from the Hebrew Gymnasium, who constituted the first founding group. Female counselors and members of the earlier nest who accompanied them were Sela Fridman, Jegier, Lea Kajzer, Pnina Potasznik and others, who organized the students from the Jewish schools for girls in the city within the new 'nest'.

Starting with slow steps, and later growing in the scope of their operations, the movement organized again and once again was the glory of the Jewish youth in Kielce. It was the most popular and favorite movement among the Zionist youth in the city. The best and most energetic of the youth, the most creative teens with national consciousness gathered there. For the first time, scouting summer camps were arranged in Kielce, plays and various cultural endeavors; and above all, active and lively participation of all its members on the work of the national funds.

During 1925-6 the first graduates of the 'nest' began moving to the land of Israel – Rafael (Polo) Kuperberg (Nechusztai) and after him Cwi Potasznik, Manja Ajzenberg, Pnina Potasznik and others. This time too, they were the first in our city to "break the ice" of renewed aliya to the country, and others flowed in their footsteps and came after them.

In 1929 after the riots in the land of Israel, another wave of members of the "Shomer Hatza'ir" came, among them Dolek Skorecki, Dawid Rembiszewski, Jakusz Zajfman, Mosze Kligman, Lula Bornsztajn and others. After a few years, once again the graduates of the 'nest' flowed to the country, and they are now located on kibbutzim, moshavs, cities and various settlements and live a life of toil and creation, each in his place in the country.

Here I must mention those from Kielce who fell in battle – Izrael Korngold Z"L in the battle that conquered the lands of "Ramat HaShofet" and Szaul Korman Z"L who died defending Jerusalem.

From the mouths of surviving embers, members of the "Shomer Hatza'ir" in Kielce, who arrived in Israel after the terrible slaughter in the countries of Europe during World War II, we learned of the existence of the 'nest' of "Hashomer Hatza'ir" during the horrific days of the ghetto in Kielce, about their underground work to gather youth and children, Zionist activities and the publication of an illegal Hebrew broadsheet in conditions too difficult to bear. The members of "Hashomer Hatza'ir" acted and worked up to the last days of the ghetto's existence and were liquidated by Hitler's minions.

The "Poalei Zion" Party – Socialist Zionists in Kielce

The beginning of the "Poalei Zion" socialist Zionist party in Kielce goes back to the period before the Russian revolution of 1905.

[Page-124]

A young man from Wloclawek, Izrael Kino, who had married Najcze Elbaum, from one of the first families in Kielce, was the founder of the "Poalei Zion" group, and under the code name "Felix" stayed in touch with the center in Warsaw. This was at the time that Dov Borochov and his friends Itzchak Ben-Tzvi, Zerubavel, Rafelkes, Itzchak Tabenkin and even David Ben-Gurion were in a difficult battle with the Bundists, the Siemists and others, and out of the tempest of the disagreements the ideological lines of practical and principled Palestinism were drawn, and their synthesis – prognostic Palestinism, Borochovism. Incidentally, I. and N. Kino moved to the land of Israel in 1908, he died in 1954 and his widow, may she have a long life, remained in her home in Tel-Aviv.

With the granting of the Czarist manifest in October of 1905, it seemed that a time of momentum and tremendous development for all of the liberation movements in Russia and the countries that were under its rule. However, the rude awakening came immediately and the disciples of liberty, both nationalist and socialist, learned that the oppressive regime had tricked them. Then came a period of reaction that continued with interruptions until the end of World War I. Only then, when Russia was overtaken by the great storm of freedom, did the Jewish street also begin to arouse itself. A stream of people began to arrive at the gates of the homeland in unimaginable ways, the Zionist movement received a tremendous push towards activity (also thanks to the Balfour Declaration), and Jewish socialism took the worker's classes by storm. The drive to adjust to the new conditions of political life in Russia, and the hope that Bolshevism would storm to victory over the world, caused a split in the international movement of "Poalei Zion", and thus the faction "Independent Poalei Zion" was formed (its opponents called it, to discredit it "Right Poalei Zion").

The founders and leaders of "Poalei Zion" in Kielce

[Page-125]

In its early days this party was very weak in Poland. The professional unions of the workers were mainly held by the Bund, and a few of them were overseen by "Poalei Zion Left". The flirtation with Soviet Russia and the left wing phraseology dominated the Jewish street, and methodical, in-depth public relations work was necessary in order for this party to acquire any professional organizations – at least locally – in order to give the new party a minimal base for class activity.

There were several young men wandering around Kielce at the time, dreamers and fighters, whose souls had given up on general Zionism and its methods of work, which were based upon a superficial household approach, without any Zionist-pioneer public education, without going to the working classes which were the human reservoir which was likely to build the country.

These young men, headed by Awraham Kirszenbaum, who had always been attracted by the "Poalei Zion" movement in America which was devoted to building the land of Israel, felt that now, with the split, their hour had arrived. Together with several fellows (notably Josef Zinger), who left the "Poalei Zion Left" because it was turning away from practical Zionism; they founded the party branch in Kielce.

"Chalutz" in Poland, Gordon Group, Kielce Branch

[Page-126]

Not many days passed and the party got the meat workers union on its side, as well as various groups of members of other professional unions which were in the hands of "Poalei Zion Left" (the Bund, the Siemists and various haters of Zion had no base in our city). A study group named for Borochov was founded whose members studied there regularly, as well as evening classes in Yiddish, Polish, scientific subjects and others that gained a reputation in the city. They conducted methodical professional activity on the one hand, and on the other hand, work devoted to the Zionist Funds.

Eventually they joined up with the Socialist Zionists (after the split in "Tzi'irei Zion" [Youth for Zion]) and this gave them renewed impetus for intensive activity, especially in the area of preparing youth for moving to the land of Israel, founding the "Chalutz" branch and more.

There are many names of members who were notable in their efforts. I will attempt to mention several of them here (in alphabetical order); with a description of their profession when they arrived in Israel.

Borkowski, Szmuel, Tel-Aviv, member of the Executive Committee of the General Labor Union in Israel. Borsztajn, Aharon, Haifa, a clerk in one of the General Union institutions. Ginzburg, Dow, Tel Aviv, Driver. Ginzburg, sisters: Jochewed, married to Sz. Borkowski; Towa, married to M. Dzjura; Jehudit, married to J. Rozenwald; Chana, married to A. Lerer, Tel-Aviv. Dzjura, Menachem, Tel-Aviv, shoe manufacturer. Zinger Josef, party founder, Tel-Aviv, stone mason and manufacturer of artificial stone. Tenenwurcel, Aleksander, kibbutz member. Tencer, Lajb, mosaic manufacturer, died in Tel-Aviv, Sivan, 5716 (June 1956). Lewensztajn, Josef, Bnei Brak, construction carpentry contractor. Mordokowicz, Kalman, Tel-Aviv, works at the Executive Committee of the General Labor Union. Machtynger, member of Moshav Tzofit. Strawczinski, Szymon, perished in the Nazi Shoah. Pachel, Ester, coordinator of the female workers group in Petach Tikva. Piwko, Awraham, Tel-Aviv, mosaic manufacturer. Kirszenbaum, Awraham, party founder in Kielce, Tel-Aviv, agricultural manufacturer. Rozenwald, Josef, Tel-Aviv, shoe manufacturer.

If we wanted to note what made the "Poalei Zion" – Socialist Zionists unique compared to other parties in our nation, then we must say: realizing the goal of Aliya. There were hardly any active members in this party who did not move to the land of Israel and did not take their place among those "doing the work and holding the weapon".

The Revisionist Movement in Kielce
(Massada, Beitar, "Brit Hachayal" and the "Tzohar")

… When we return, at least in imagination, to our youth – we find everything wrapped in a halo of romanticism – for from the distance of time, we can encompass an entire scene at one glance. The past appears before us as an entire series of static pictures of colorful events with the nostalgia and dreams, as if they had been painted and decorated for us by a wondrous artist. Our memory – nostalgia plus the feeling that indeed, there is no possibility to actually return to our youth – gives all these pictures a glow and a light that is not from this world. The emotions of a man from the exile of Poland, when he remembers the quarry from which he was hewn, is soaked in a special sadness, for it is diluted in a special emotion, since it all stopped suddenly – everything, as if it had been suddenly extinguished. There was no continuation – the memories are memories, as if of an ephemeral dream…

[Page-127]

Kielce, a relatively young city, did not have deep historical roots. Neither did Jewish Kielce. The Jewish settlement in Kielce was young, the community was young, its social life and cultural life were still young. A special sadness surrounds us when we recall the past; memories from this city, while we were a part of its life, with all of our being and with the fire of our youth – when we remember that all that was has suddenly gone with the wind – gone never to return…

The city had a special charm. Truly, nature had granted it an abundance of color, surrounded by forests and hills, groves and a wonderful park. The lack of industry saved it from noise, soot and ugliness – and added a slower pace to life, dreamy and romantic. The Christian population, religiously Catholic and nationalistic, was noted for its anti-Semitism. The break between the groups was very deep, and this tightened the communal and cultural relations within the Jewish group.

The city was young. The young Jewish community grew from the unending stream of Jewish arrivals from nearby towns, bridegrooms who were leaving their father-in-law's tables arrived at the growing and developing city. Young men who felt hemmed in in the villages and whose souls yearned for culture and experience, to fulfill ambitions and desires. It was no surprise that such bubbling material created a varied Jewish life in cultural and social terms, a specific life, though closed within the ghetto walls, since the national Catholicism of the Poles did not allow normal contact and relations. The Polish culture penetrated Jewish life indirectly, via osmosis; strained and distilled – it penetrated in the form of romantic adventures from Polish heroism via the literature of Mickiewicz, Sienkiewicz, Rymont and Zyromski…

Revisionism – which caused a revolution in the international Zionist movement and pushed it into the political arena, was the cause of a revolution in the life of the nationalist youth in Kielce. It activated them, gave them a goal in life, made the Zionist movement in Kielce the lot of the masses of all ages and all classes.

Jewish youth in Kielce read and absorbed a lot, were influenced by Hebrew and Jewish literature, and also by romantic and heroic Polish literature, whose heroes suffer the pain of the nation defeated and humiliated under the Russian boot, which is a recurring motif, in several variants; the internal battle between Gustaw the romantic and Konrad the active warrior for his people's liberty and independence…

Until Jabotinsky appeared in Kielce and founded the first Revisionist cells in this city – the nationalist Jewish youth was like Gustaw – romantic, Byronic, full of energy – Revisionism took the heroism of the youth from the realm of potential to the realm of action.

Jabotinsky and his teachings charmed – the doctrine of political Zionism acted also upon the youth of Kielce, the wave of enthusiasm that attacked the youth with the appearance of a leader – did not die down – it became fruitful. The activation of the nationalist youth began and with it came increased activity of the other classes of Jewish Kielce.

[Page-128]

The beginning was modest: founding the "Massada". It was natural that Jabotinsky's doctrine found its first expression in the hearts and souls of the school children, who felt that indeed ideals and heroism were not just for other nations, that courage beat in our hearts as well, that our liberation depended upon the liberation of the homeland – and that a Hebrew state was not just a Messianic dream, but an ideal we were commanded to realize in our own generation. This idea was like a spark in the hearts of the youth that carried the torch.

Around the writer of these lines (Y. Kopf [Yiddishe Kopf]) a small group of youth who were students in Kielce formed. The students: Jakob Zloto, Szmuel Jura, Chaim Haller HY"D, Izrael Dzialowski, E. Lewartowska, Dora Herszkowicz and Jechiel Alpert - may they live a long life - were the very ones who established the foundation for the Revisionist youth movement. Wide concentric circles formed, which included nearly all classes of nationalist youth in Kielce.

"Massada" was the union of students, the younger generation organized into its ranks, students, boys and girls, who dreamed about a Zionist state, great Zionism, which would instill in youth the consciousness that they were descendants of the Maccabees, and that it was incumbent upon them, with new acts of bravery to reconnect the past to the future. The first "Massada" members in our city began to think in new concepts, these concepts infused them with an ideal that they had to turn into a reality. A Hebrew state, a Hebrew army, a national discipline, festive ceremonies and the willingness to make sacrifices.

"Massada" attracted the student intelligentsia, felt itself a pioneer in paving the political road for masses of others.

The student youth, which had the capacity for intellectual thought, knew how to absorb the political romanticism of the historical past of the Jewish nation that had lived upon its own land – the echo of the struggle of the judges of Israel who saved it in times of trouble – the honor and glory of the kingdom of Solomon and Alexander Yannai. – Felt the courage and sacrifice of the zealots of Jerusalem and the heroes of Bar-Kochba. – They were also impressed by the heroism and romanticism of small nations in Europe, who had known to fight for their own independence. The members of "Massada", even after they had finished their Gymnasium studies – when they traveled to universities, became loyal emissaries spreading, at the universities, the nationalist doctrine they had forged among their schoolmates.

… We now see standing in front of us dreamlike figures – like Cwi Leszec, Z"L, who had a spiritual fluid streaming from his eyes – Mosze Klingbajl, noble and pleasant, Lajb Rudel, HY"D, talented journalist, hero and martyr, one of the commanders of the Warsaw Ghetto, the tender young women – Luba Aharonowicz, Rozszka Tenenbaum and Dora Kopf; the gifted teacher Master M. Witlin and the idealists, the brothers Wajnsztok, HY"D. – This was a society that fired many hearts – and due to its influence, the political Zionist camp in Kielce grew.

"Beitar" was established after "Massada", and its establishment was due to "Massada", which prepared the ground for founding a popular legion of pioneer youth.

[Page-129]

The Jewish youth of Kielce, intelligent, blessed with a fondness for culture and esthetic values, was in an emotional and economic crisis. Outwardly, life appeared to be going on as usual. The fathers pulled the yoke of livelihood, and the sons who grew up were helped by them or made efforts in the existing circumstances to build themselves an economic base and family nest, something that became more difficult from year to year. The economic sensation of Jewish youth in Kielce was – the younger generation was going to have to look after its own future, and this should not be on Polish soil. They needed to emigrate – but to where?

Jabotinsky gave the solution, "Avocation". – At first glance the plan seemed cruel and aroused a wave of protest from the overt and covert assimilation, and also from the Zionist circles of little faith – to uproot tens of thousands of Jews from their apparently peaceful existence. It seemed absurd then – and the bitter reality proved the reverse…

The "Beitar" was organized according to the needs of the time. It was organized and lived its organizational life in accordance with the needs of the time. "Beitar" consisted of young people who had made Herzlian Zionism their life's purpose. Here in Kielce, they needed to receive their national political training. They learned marching drill, military discipline, the ideal of sacrifice as was appropriate for future members of the IZL [Irgun Zva'i Leumi – National Military Organization]. The young people of "Beitar" saw what was coming and prepared for the future and many of them were able to move to the land of Israel in time. The life in Polonia appeared to be quiet and calm, aside from hooligan's riots and the movement to restrict Jewish economic life. Life was quiet, but the nationalist youth felt that the earth beneath their feet was starting to tremble. The quiet before the storm, which wound up sweeping away the Jews of Kielce entirely, as it swept away all of Polish Jewry… Those fellows who were commanders of "Beitar" are remembered: J. Gros, Sz. Mengel, B. Zalcman, Ch. Opatowski, Master M. Witlin, Mendel Wajnsztok, HY"D and Dawid Lewartowski. They are remembered in their fevered activity, filled with energy and vision, who prepared themselves and others for the great goal – redeeming Jewish honor in the ghettos – or battle with the British enslaver in the land of Israel.

מייסדי וראשי "מסדה" בעירנו

Founders and leaders of "Massada" in our city

[Page-130]

The revisionist movement in Kielce was a movement of circles whose center was "Massada" since it had established the intellectual cadres and grounded the ideology and inspired the youth with enthusiasm. "Beitar" made up the second concentric ring – the *creme de la creme* of the petit bourgeois youth. The third concentric ring was "Brit Hachayal" [Soldier's Covenant].

"Brit Hachayal" had a special influence. Anyone who has read "Men of Shklov" by Shneiur and "Well-Built Aryeh" by Bialik, can understand and appreciate these fellows. Physically strong, released soldiers, from the "Horopsznik" classes – wagon owners and porters, who were ready at any moment to take on anyone who injured the body or honor of a Jews. The Revisionist movement, which was making waves in Kielce, penetrated these classes as well. They were especially taken with Ze'ev Jabotinsky, founder of the Jewish Legion, and the doctrine of physical strength that together with the eternal spiritual strength of the people of Israel, paved the way to its national and political liberation. We remember fondly the devoted commanders: Adolf Lewi, Szlomo Zelinger, Alter Renkoszynski HY"D, and Icak Albirt, may he live a long life.

The fourth circle was the "Tzohar" – it could be said that the "Tzohar" covered the entire Revisionist movement in Kielce in its many hues and personalities such as: Dawid Rozenberg, Dr. Jakob Szac, L.

Rudel, Master M. Witlin, Mejer Zloto and Josef Rachum. The "Tzohar" was a combination of people of middle age, intellectuals from all classes, who dreamed the dream of redemption, devoted some of their, spirit, culture and capital to the movement.

Once upon a time, there was a glorious and varied Revisionist movement in Kielce. It was active, and prepared hearts for redemption and struggle – it was and it is no more. It passed, the way glorious Polish Jewry passed with its entire spiritual and cultural splendor. It is impossible to forget all of the noble spirits who so enriched our lives in exile. They created values – which still nourish us. Those who passed, the dreamers and pure fighters like a dream – and they live in our souls like the heroes of legends, and thus will remain in our memories forever…

"WIZO"

Among the Zionist organizations in Kielce, the "WIZO" organization (Women's International Zionist Organization) was the most popular. This organization, which was actually a branch of the international one, demonstrated great activity in every area of social, political and especially Zionist life. At the head of the organization stood Sara Ehrlich, Ester Kajzer, Chana Finkelsztajn, Fajga Arten, Mina Alter, Fajga Fajngold, Bela Rotenberg, Hela Rozenberg, Lea Orbajtl-Rozenberg and others.

There was no Zionist activity in which the women of "WIZO" did not take a notable part. Distributing the Zionist shekel, collecting commitments to the 'Keren HaYesod', collecting subscriptions to the golden book of the 'Keren Kayemet', collecting funds for 'Keren Ezra' [Aid Fund] for the victims of the riots in the land of Israel in 1929, and collecting equipment and traveling expenses for pioneers who were moving to the land of Israel; in all these activities the "WIZO" women took a prominent role.

[Page 131]

When the poet Bistricki visited Kielce on behalf of the 'Keren Keyamet' it was these "WIZO" women who went through the city like a storm, held wonderful receptions for him, public meetings and helped him in his work to collect many more donations and subscriptions for the golden book in Kielce than in other cities he visited.

Aside from political and Zionist activities, the "WIZO" women also developed social activity among their membership. Every Friday evening they arranged tea parties for members (who were allowed to bring their husbands with them). Every week a party like this took place at the home of one or another of the members.

Various lecturers were invited to these parties to speak about matters that were then at the top of the Zionist and political agenda of Polish Jewry, and after the lectures arguments took place regarding the subject, as well as ordinary conversation of friends.

The "WIZO" organization was actually the vibrant center of the women of Kielce, which acted in all areas of public and social life in the city.

Agudat Yisra'el (Peace and Faith of Israel)

The association "Peace and Faith of Israel" [Shlomei Emunei Yisra'el] which was also a political party, collected under its wing Chassidim of all shades. Especially the Chassidim of Gur, Ostrowiec, Sokolow and Sochaczew. The association learned what the other political parties were doing in a very short time. They held meetings, gatherings, invited speakers for propaganda; it published its own newspaper as well, so that its members and supporters would not need to resort to the free press. It founded a public "cheder" as well, called "Yesodei HaTorah" [Foundations of the Torah] and introduced secular studies to its curriculum as well as Gemara, the legal arbiters and commentaries. It also established a school for girls called "Beit Ya'akov". It also opened a bank for association members, which was essentially a private bank, but since it was under the supervision of the Center for "Aguda" Cooperatives in Warsaw, it was called the "Aguda" bank.

In general, the "Aguda" [Association] developed widespread activity in all areas of public life. They tried to gain an important place on the community committee, in the municipal authority and council. In the elections to the Siem and the Senate the "Aguda" people appeared on their own special lists. The "Aguda" in all of its activities tried to curry favor with the government; the government, on its part, would glance sideways towards the "Aguda". Among the "Aguda" members were also active public workers who knew a chapter of the ways of politics.

In order to strengthen the ideology of the "Aguda" they would bring in outstanding speakers from other places. Natan Birnbaum, the philosophical author who became orthodox, came to Kielce, and in his two-hour speech he proved that according to logic and according to the history of our nation the main principle of our existence in the world was observing the values of the Torah and the commandments, the minor with the major.

[Page-132]

After him the Admo"r of Sokolow came to Kielce and spoke in the Viennese Hall. An excellent speaker, with warm emotion, he influenced a sizeable portion of the Jews of Kielce; after them other activists and speakers came and did not allow the "Aguda" people to drowse in their four cubits. Later their tendency to participate in the building of the land of Israel as well became noticeable; according to the instructions and opinion of the head of the "Aguda" the Admo"r of Gur; but they had time to spread this idea only a little bit among their supporters, until the ax came and cut off the tree with its branches.

At the head of the "Aguda" in Kielce stood Rabbi Mordechai Fiszel Kaminer. The Kaminer family was famous all over Poland. The court of the "Gur" Chassidim and the Kaminer family were connected by marriage. The Admo"r of Gur, author of the "Sfat Emet" was the son-in-law of Rabbi Judel Kaminer, who leased a large estate near the town of Checiny from a Russian general. This estate, called "Podzamcza" was in the hands of the Kaminer family until after World War I. Independent Poland appropriated all of the properties and assets that had belonged to the Russians for itself. In accordance with the law of the state, the Kaminer family was dispossessed of the estate that had been in their hands for over five decades.

This Rabbi Judel had seven sons and three daughters. Among his sons, Mosze Chaim Kaminer was notable in his public work, and for many years he was the head of the Kielce community, also Mordechai Fiszel Kaminer, the chairman of the "Aguda". In Warsaw, Rabbi Judel's grandson, Meszulam Kaminer, was known when he became head of the "Aguda" there, which published an "Aguda" newspaper that fought for the viewpoints of its party.

M.P. Kaminer came to Kielce in 1906. He was the son-in-law of Bels, one of the heads of the Jews of Warsaw and the brother-in-law of Daniel Sirkis, later the head of the community committee of Tel-Aviv. As a capitalist, M.P. Kaminer lived off the income from his capital. Over time, when his family grew larger and his expenses grew, he was forced to try his hand and commerce. During the days of World War I he brought textiles from Lodz. The textile trade stayed with him after the war as well. He opened a large shop in the city market for all sorts of textiles and, apparently, succeeded at this trade, for his store was open up to the outbreak of World War II.

His oldest son, Judel Kaminer, married the daughter of a wealthy man from Opatow. During the period that cooperative banks were being set up, which were basically private banks, and public on the basis of cooperatives only in the eyes of the authorities, the father and son, Mordechai Fiszel and Judel, founded such a bank which existed up to the outbreak of the war. This bank was called the "Loan Bank" and functioned as an "Aguda" bank.

M.P. Kaminer aroused respect in his appearance and his personality. His home was the home of a leader in Israel. His wife Brajndl was a delicate and polite woman. His daughters were educated at Mrs. Wolman's Gymnasium for Girls, and his sons were entrusted to "melameds" to teach them Torah and commandments.

[Page-133]

However, of all his sons, the only one to follow in the footsteps of his ancestors was his eldest, Judel, whom we just mentioned. He hewed to his father's path and was one of the pillars of the "Aguda" in Kielce.

He learned Hebrew, Russian and Polish from private teachers. He was especially interested in medical texts. He would acquire popular medical books for himself and would read and study them very diligently. During World War I, when there were many injured and sick people crowded in the city with no place to put them, and every single hour they were bringing additional wounded from the front, and caregivers were needed from among the local inhabitants, Judel Kaminer volunteered to care for the war wounded in the local hospitals. This interest of his in medicine and the experience he gained caring for the sick and wounded gave him a certain degree of knowledge in anatomy and also in therapy and from then he began giving advice to sick people, first in the circle of his family, and afterwards also in his circle of friends and acquaintances.

Not long had gone by before Rabbi Judel Kaminer became known and an outstanding doctor, and even other inhabitants of the city came to ask his advice; and he, as a specializing doctor would write them prescriptions according to which the pharmacists would concoct the medicines for those who requested them. His fame as a doctor reached such a point that many preferred to go to him in emergency cases than to an official doctor. In truth, it must be said that he didn't take any money for his advice, and didn't do his medical tasks for any reward. In many cases he was doing a favor to the ill. Poor people who were sick, for instance, who could not afford to pay a doctor's fee, would turn to J. Kaminer, and he would visit the home of the poor sick person and appear like a redeeming angel, care for the patient, give advice and medicines and infuse a spirit of hope in despairing hearts.

The women, in particular, would shower him with amazing blessings. First of all, it was considered a great honor that the son of Kaminer from a family with such lineage was willing to step over their doorstep and grace the patient with his presence, and secondly, it was all done for free.

In this manner, he became a great favorite. In the elections for the municipal council, Judel Kaminer stood for the "Aguda" at the top of its list. Although he wasn't elected, his non-election was not the fault of the Jews, but of the anti-Semitism that was growing in those days in all the Polish circles. The Jews came out in their masses to the ballot box; however, the Poles, who looked upon the Jews with disfavor, attempted with all the means at their disposal, kosher and not kosher, to keep them away from the municipal councils. They removed the names of many Jews from the voting lists; they purposely distorted the names of Jews, so that they could disqualify them at election time. In places where the majority of voters were Jewish, they stood their own thugs in line who would push and hit the Jews to discourage them from standing in line in the heat and receiving even more blows. The Jew who insisted, and in spite of all the persecutions arrived at the ballot, left in despair. His name was not found on the voting lists or his was disqualified because his address was wrong or because his name had been misspelled.

Such a Jew who left the ballot waved his hand in despair towards the Jewish voters waiting in line, as if to say: "It is not worth it, my brothers, to crowd here and receive kicks and blows, for in any event you will not vote, these evil ones will no doubt find something wrong with each and every one of you."

[Page-134]

In the face of such persecutions that even the government looked upon favorably, it is no wonder that the number of those elected from the Jewish population went down to nil.

In the "Aguda" Benjamin Lew, a well-known public worker from the Gur Chassidim was very active. He was an egg merchant. Outwardly, he appeared to be a regular type of Jew. But a holy flame burned in his heart, the fire of religious zeal, and it propelled him towards the "Aguda" camp, where he became its spokesman, its representative and its proxy at all of the municipal and public institutions. In his heart also dwelled a love for the land of Israel. When the "Mizrachi" was founded in Kielce, he also participated in its early meetings. However, apparently, his soul did not find enough satisfaction in the "Mizrachi" and he joined the "Aguda" camp. Yet his love for the land of Israel did not change, it continued to grow, to deepen and broaden in his soul until it forced him to leave his dwelling place in the Polish exile, leave the honorable roles he had in his city and to set out on a journey, to move to the land of Israel with his family. In Kielce he was a member of the council of the Jewish community, a member of the municipal authority, a representative of the merchants of the city of Kielce at the government chamber of commerce, and many, many more – all of these respectable positions were not enough to keep him in his place.

His secular education was meager, but in spite of this he influenced his audience when he spoke and not with his speaking abilities, but with his Jewish intelligence. He would instantly grasp the matter that was up for debate in its full breadth and knew how to discuss it with his considerable logical strength. His reasoning and evidence, which he brought to bolster his ideas and viewpoint, were solid enough to convince not only those who shared his opinions, but also his rivals and opponents, not only the Jews, but also the Gentiles. And many of them came to consult him regarding important city affairs.

When he arrived in the land of Israel, the travails of absorption and acclimatization were his lot. During the riots, it was difficult for a person to manage. He didn't have time to look around and find himself in the local conditions and to make commercial ties, before a dangerous disease, appendicitis, attached him. He was taken for treatment to "Hadassah" hospital and after an unsuccessful operation he died.

People from the city, who knew him and his deeds, his activities and his public work, mourned the loss very much. Lew was a public worker who knew how to respect his opponents. When he was in a debate, he would argue with great fury and contradict his rival's and opponent's words with force and didn't want to give up as much as a smidgen of his opinion; but afterwards, when the debate was over, and spirits calmed – he was once again the friend of his opponents and would walk with them as a friend and a brother, as if nothing had occurred between them.

In the "Aguda" camp another very active public worker who was famous among the Jews of Kielce was Mosze Dawid Ajzenberg, Mosze Eli' Naftali's, as his fellow citizens of the city called him. He was also from the Gur Chassidim; he was a public worker from birth and before. He spent more time on public needs than on his own. Even before the "Aguda" was founded, he was the "gabbai" of the "Chevra Kadisha" [Burial Society] for many years. In spite of his many businesses – he owned a furniture factory and a leather factory – he also found time to deal with public matters. He was the "Aguda" representative to the community's executive committee, was as expert in community matters as he was in his own affairs. He spent more time sitting in the community office than at home. He found a special pleasure in his activism; this was truly activism for the sake of heaven. A person could not suspect that he had a vested interest in things, or that he was involved in public work for his own benefit; everyone saw that he neglected his own businesses for the community's needs. And indeed he did not acquire wealth, and was not overly ambitious to be wealthy like others, whose main goal was acquiring assets and property. For him, movement and activity were more important than wealth.

**Mosze Dawid Ajzenberg
(Mosze Eli' Naftali's)**

The land of Israel was his heart's desire. When he saw that his sons were beginning to leave him and move to the land of Israel, he too wished to follow them. He had a certificate, and was already prepared for the journey, but fate intervened to delay him, obstacles stood in his path, external ones and family ones, and his travel was delayed. Afterwards riots broke out in the land of Israel and he said: "I will wait until the fury passes." Meanwhile, World War II broke out and the borders were closed.

I will bring here the content of a conversation I once had with him on a summer evening while we were walking in the market "among the pillars."

This conversation took place before I left for the land of Israel, it was a farewell conversation, and for this reason it was serious and things were said very openly. Therefore, it is worthy of being remembered.

We began to discuss something regarding the state of the Jews in Poland, about the anti-Semitism that was spreading all over the country, about the dispossession of the Jews of their economic positions, about the assaults upon solitary Jews, about the stink bombs that were being thrown into Jewish shops, about the smashing of display windows, and finally we also arrived at the matter of the riots in the village of Przytyk, which had taken all Jewish circles by storm at the time. And we both came to be of the opinion that the Jews had no future in Poland; the ground was slipping out from under their feet. Hitler's methods and his faction were being transferred to Poland. The riots that had occurred in Przytyk, were not an isolated phenomenon, but the result of the oppression and the libelous words of the anti-Semitic press, which filled its pages, day after day, with slander and false libels against the Jews.

We finally reached the conclusion that a Jew who wishes to exist, who wants to be secure of his life and property – has no other path before him but to leave his birthplace, which had become a step-mother to him, and to head for the ancient homeland, the land of the patriarchs, which was our only hope, and the ambition of every Jewish soul, towards which all eyes were gazing.

Handwritten caption:
"Agudat-Yisra'el" Kielce, on the occasion of the trip of our comrade,
Mr. Benjamin Lew to the land of Israel.

**Sitting (right to left): M. Horberg, I. Rapaport, Mejer Ajzenberg, B. Lew, M.P. Kaminer,
Mosze Ajzenberg, R. Rafalowicz, and J. Prajs
Standing (in the second row): Jakob Kaminer, L. Lew, J.M. Giefilhauz , B. Kaminer,
Judel Kaminer, J. Szajnfeld, Eli' Justman
(in the third row): Mosze Lew, Josef Enach, J. Kaminer
and others**

[Page-137]

"I," I said to him, "have decided already to execute this thing, that I have been carrying around in my heart for a long time; I am leaving 'Tushia' and moving to the land of Israel."

And he then revealed to me all that was in his heart and said: "Know, my friend, that the matter of the land of Israel was always close to my heart, even if I am a member of the "Aguda" camp, and I can't join together with the free-thinkers, the land of Israel is very close to my heart. And here is your proof, that I didn't prevent my sons from executing their plans; on the contrary, I gave them my blessing on their new path and in my heart I am glad that they have reached their goal. According to the news I hear from them they are managing there and are satisfied in their new homeland, but my hour has not yet arrived to leave the dwelling place of my ancestors. I am still tied to my place with strong cables and I can not detach them at this moment. A day will come and we will meet again face to face over there in the land of Israel."

We parted from one another with a great deal of friendship.

After I moved to the land of Israel I awaited his arrival from day to day. From time to time I would ask his son Baruch and his son-in-law Elazar Arten: "When is Father coming?". But, apparently, he was still busy with public needs, he was sunk head and shoulders in the concerns of the community until he forgot himself. Even during the days of the war, when the Jews of Kielce were locked in the ghetto, he did not leave his post as a public worker, as refugees from the Kielce ghetto told me, he took care of the ill in the Jewish hospital during these difficult days, and supplied them with milk and other foodstuffs.

And he certainly did not cease his activism even on the death train, on which the Jews of Kielce were sent to Treblinka, to the gas chambers, and as the "gabbai" of the "Chevra Kadisha" prepared them to die the death of martyrs. May his memory be for a blessing.

Alongside the "Aguda" there were youth movements and labor unions such as: "Poalei Agudat Yisra'el", at whose head were R.B. Wajsbrot, R. Ejdels, S. Rzetelny and J. Strozberg. The youth organization "Tzi'irei Agudat Yisra'el" from whom, in the first period, the following excelled: I.P. Holc, M.Ch. Waksman, J. Staszewski (an excellent speaker who "slipped" and became a Bundist) and later M. Gotfrajd, Michl Gertler, A. Goldrat, Baruch Rapaport and others. They also had a women's organization called "Bnot Agudat Yisra'el" which developed cultural activities which was headed by the teachers from "Beit Ya'akov".

קבוצת עסקני "צעירי אגודת ישראל" בקילץ

A group of "Tzi'irei Agudat Yisra'el" {Agudat Israel Youth} in Kielce

Sitting: (from right to left) Alter Minc, Awraham Goldrat, J. Kaminer, Baruch Rapaport.
Standing: Alter Albert, B. Rzetelni , Menasze Minc and A. Ajlenberg

קבוצת "בנות אגודת ישראל" בקילץ

A group of "Bnot Agudat Yisra'el"
{Daughters of Agudat Israel} in Kielce

[Page-139]

Economic and Social Organizations

Translated by Judy Montel

Edited by Warren Blatt

The Artisans Union in Kielce

There was an Artisans Union in Kielce; which as it developed influenced various areas of public life, including cultural, economic and political areas. The Artisans Union was founded in 1918 after the end of World War I.

In democratic Poland, which came to life after a century of bondage, the Jews too, received equal rights, even though it was just on paper: active and passive voting rights to the municipal councils and the houses of legislature, and the right of self determination as a national minority. The Jewish community also took on a democratic form; its leaders were chosen in general elections in which all segments of the public participated.

At that period monies were arriving from America for reconstruction, to provide work-tools for those who had, during the wanderings and upsets of the war, become impoverished and lost their work-tools, and also to create new sources of livelihood for the Jewish inhabitants who had been deprived of their economic positions. Food and clothing arrived from there for distribution to the classes who had suffered the most from the events of the war.

All of these changes in the social and state political structure allowed individuals with energy and inspiration to stand out and rise up; they were given the opportunity to arrive at the level of respectable activists of some union or organization; and from there they could expect a higher level – to be elected as a "Parnas" on the community council, as a member of the municipal council, in favorable conditions there was a chance, though distant, of being elected as a delegate to the houses of legislature.

Due to these opportunities, would-be guardians attacked the flock with no shepherd, the masses of the Jewish population living in the lowest conditions, from all directions. These guardians would gather the masses and with long speeches full of demagoguery would prove to them that the reason for their low state was lack of organization. Should they organize they would have a hand in the aid that was arriving from America, a representative in all of the public institutions. To the artisans they said that as long as they didn't organize and unite for a general purpose, to elevate their cultural and material state, their social status would also continue to remain low and disrespected and they would be destined for exploitation with no hope of improving the conditions of their lives.

[Page-140]

At the founding meeting of the artisans, assimilated representatives from the PPS [Polska Partia Socjalistyczna, the Polish Socialist Party] participated who wished to increase their influence upon the Jewish masses; Zionists arrived who wished to acquire the artisan masses for the camp that stood for national rebirth; representatives of "Shlomei Emunei Yisra'el" appeared in order to ensure that the "flock" remain with the "shepherd" [i.e., remain religiously observant]; people took part in it, also, who had not yet had time to chose themselves a direction in life, and who were always willing to follow the direction of the spirit that attempted total rule over the Jewish street, and meanwhile, they vacillated, not revealing their opinions openly, but showing a span and covering up two, leaving themselves an opening to leave this camp and move to another one – everything according to the direction of the winds and the conditions which change from time to time.

From the assimilated camp, Messrs. Paradystal and Rawicki participated in this meeting. We will draw a brief caricature of these two men, who were active and who worked among the Jews of Kielce.

The first, Paradystal, was a bookkeeper at the Kielce branch of a Lodz commercial bank. He had an honest character, learned and knowledgeable in various branches of science, of a high cultural level; a man who aspired to advance, hated the old, the tradition of the ancestors, the "moldy scrolls", as he once said openly. He had freed himself long ago from the suffering inflicted by the inheritance, tradition, the language of his nation, its hopes and hearts' desire – all these did not find resonance in his soul. He was far from sentimental towards his nation.

His brother-in-law, Dr. Perelman, tried once to introduce him into the Zionist camp; but he could not remain there for long. Cut off from the tradition, a stranger to Hebrew culture and to its ancient and modern literature, a graduate of the progressive Polish school – for him the atmosphere in the Zionist camp, was stifling and depressing. He went out and found his proper place in the camp of the progressive Poles, who concentrated, in Kielce, in the PPS party.

But he did not want to give up on the Jewish street entirely; from time to time he appeared at meetings of Jews. He sought to bring a bit of light, so to speak, into their darkness, and also on the chance of perhaps succeeding in catching some fish in the dirty waters and pulling someone into his own camp, that of the Polish socialists.

Paradystal did not hide his intentions. He came to the masses of Jews and told them openly, that his purpose was to spread Polish culture among the Jews, to draw the hearts of the two nations sitting upon one land closer together. He wanted to destroy the barriers of ancient laws that separated between them.

The Jews, in his opinion, could exist in independent Poland only if they removed their external symbols – their strange costume and their jargon, for these were the main obstacles hindering greater closeness between Jews and Poles. The Jews must be Polish citizens. The chief way to acquire Polish citizenship was to absorb the values of Polish culture into the Jewish heart, then the gates of Polish society would open before them and they would be welcomed there with open arms, and the Jewish question would solve itself. He continued the ideology of the assimilated people from the previous generation, with his own additions. The earlier assimilated Jews ruled out only Jewish nationalism, but they treated religion positively. Their version was: "Poles of the Mosaic Faith", but Paradystal and his friends took another step forward, they freed themselves completely from the burden of their inheritance, in their eyes religion was something that belonged to the past, a matter for old men and women; and the young generation, which sought freedom must first of all cut the ropes with which the capitalists had bound them. This generation must gather its strengths and fight with twice as much energy for the establishment of new social and economic rules, in which there would be no place for exploitation and parasitism. There was no battle of nations here, but a battle of classes.

[Page-141]

This kind of assimilation was worse and more damaging to the national cause than the method of earlier assimilated Jews. The earlier ones remained in the Jewish camp, they would come to the synagogue to pray, would be active in charitable matters, and some of them were quite religiously devoted.

However those later assimilated Jews cut all ties with the Jewish. The path to mixed marriages and merging with the Gentiles was the logical consequence of their ideology.

However, this ideology was counterfeit on all sides, even from the point of view of the assimilated Jews themselves. The Poles were full of anti-Semitism and did not want to accept the Jews into their society. Both the bourgeoisie and the proletariat viewed the Jews as dangerous competitors who threatened their very lives with their energy and hardworking habits, and they wanted to get rid of them somehow. And even conversion ["shmad"] was not welcomed by the anti-Semites because it did not eliminate the danger of the competition.

The nationalist Jews, on their part, were already so full of the idea of rebirth, that even this unusual wing did not move them from their attitude.

And indeed, Paradystal was not active in the Artisans Union for very long. After a few weeks he saw and understood that Jewish artisans are not raw material that one can knead into whatever shape one wants. The elder artisans were wholesome and God-fearing Jews, and some intellectual who speaks a foreign language wasn't going to change their minds; the young people there were influenced by the nationalist spirit and were not convinced by his lectures and reasoning.

The national movement put down deep roots in their hearts. The Jewish newspapers supplied them with spiritual food and broad knowledge about everything that was going on in our own world and in the outer world.

A cultured man like Paradystal didn't bring some new idea with him, some new method, which was not known to them in its every aspect. Jewish society at the time was well formed in all of its parts and rejected any foreign graft, which had not grown up from within itself. Finally, Paradystal left his position as the chairman of the Artisans Union; he felt himself alienated and isolated in an environment steeped in Judaism and nationalism without any foreign ingredients.

[Page-142]

Also the second of these, Rawicki, who was also from the assimilated ranks, quickly left the company of the artisans, when he saw that these Jews, who up until now had respected him and would refer to him respectfully and admiringly, scorned him and did not elect him, not to the council and not to the executive committee.

Earlier, these members of the intelligentsia had acquired a certain importance among the Jews of Kielce. Their education, their clear Polish speech, their expertise at bookkeeping and business management made them efficient in Jewish society. Owners of large concerns even in Chassidic circles entrusted them with the management of their businesses because they found them worthy. They also functioned as mediators between the authorities and the Jews, and all of this added to their honor. They Jews of the previous generation treated them with great respect. At meetings, they were given a place at the head, and they were the speakers, the consultants, those in the know and the clever ones.

Over time, these members of the intelligentsia got used to this kind of treatment by "the darkened masses" (that is how they used to call the Jewish masses) – in whose eyes this was a totally natural way to treat them, treatment that was their due according to tradition. The Jew was always groveling before the "Poretz" [estate owner], and whoever spoke Polish and wore Gentile clothing was considered a "Poretz" by the Jews, this is how it was and, they hoped, thus it would always be.

However, times change. A new generation arose, new winds began blowing. On the one hand, the workers' movement arose, which put out its own leaders, and they were scornful of members of the intelligentsia who served the bourgeoisie. On the other hand, the movement for national rebirth was felt among the bourgeoisie as well, nationalist feelings began beating in their hearts; they too began to demand respect for themselves, their language and all they held holy. These members of the intelligentsia were left high and dry on all sides.

The clever ones among them, when they saw that their time had past, and in order not to lose the ground beneath their feet, moved rightward or leftward. And those who were frozen in their places, those who were slow moving physically or spiritually were suddenly disappointed when they saw that they had lost their charm in the eyes of the masses. At first they grew angry, left the meetings, distanced themselves from people; they still hoped, in their hearts, that their respect would somehow be restored. Eventually, they gave up on it, cast down their eyes and grew continually more atrophied.

This is what happened to Merber, the treasurer at the Lodzer Bank, and to Rawicki, who for many years was the manager of Icak Kaminer's press and book outlet. At the end of their days they were shrunken and humiliated without any influence. Whoever had known them during their days of greatness was astonished at the sight.

I have digressed somewhat, but I wanted to describe, in a few clear lines, the types who wished to infiltrate the "Artisans' Union" and who did not succeed.

In the committee that was elected at the founding meeting, the Zionists prevailed. Although Paradystal was elected as chairman, Icza Mejer Rajzman, who favored the Zionists and was the exact opposite of Paradystal, was elected as his assistant. The writer of these lines was elected as secretary, with Alter Ehrlich as his assistant. The committee members were also mostly either Zionists or people who tended towards Zionism, like Judel Gutman, Herszel Waksberg, Dawid Rozenberg, Szmuel Lajchter, Josef Goldszajder, who at the time also tended towards Zionism. There was just one "Bundist".

[Page-143]

In this group Paradystal found himself isolated; and it was no wonder that he was unable to stand it there; in addition, Rajzman began to undermine the position of his opponent, trying to take his place. After a short time, Paradystal handed in his resignation and Rajzman inherited the position.

The committee began first of all, to develop cultural, economic and community projects among the artisans. Lectures were held every Saturday. On weekdays the artisans would gather in their spacious apartment, which also functioned as a club, a reading room and a venue for lectures. They would spend the evening hours there in conversation with friends, settling disagreements, organizing projects to aid their less fortunate comrades. Some of them would read newspapers; some of them would play dominos or chess.

Instead of going to pubs, which was where the artisans were used to spending their free time, drinking a glass of beer, they would now choose to go to their club, in which they met with their friends and would hear the news and occasionally also an interesting lecture.

From the circles of the artisans themselves, young forces sprouted and grew who acted to raise the social and cultural level of the artisan class for the better. Outside forces, which they needed when they first founded the Artisans Union, became superfluous. They began to find lecturers, counselors and organizers from their own ranks. Two activists in particular excelled in their activity and cultural level – Judel Gutman and Josef Goldszajder.

Judel Gutman was a painter by trade. He began his involvement in community matters while still a youth. He was one of the first "Poalei Zion" in the city of Kielce. But his Zionism overcame his socialism. Especially after he turned from a proletarian to a member of the bourgeoisie. His activism did not stop him from taking care of his own needs. Over time, he acquired property and became more distant from the affairs of the laborers. He had lots of energy and definite ideas and always knew how to find supporters in order to triumph in a clash with his rivals. Thanks to these qualities of his he established a permanent position for himself in the Artisans Union, and was the artisans' representative at all the community institutions, the municipality of Kielce, the community committee, the directors of the "Popular Bank", the government "Czechim" institution, where the artisans received their licenses. At every opportunity he would appear as the representative of the Artisans Union. He participated in conventions, in parades and delegations. His desire was to emphasize himself at every opportunity, to publicize himself and to give the impression of a "Tribune" who protects the interests of his lowly class. At literary balls he was one of the lecturers and spoke even about matters that were far from his expertise; to participate in a meeting and not have his voice heard – this to him was like participating in a feast and not tasting a thing.

This next episode will describe Gutman's personality. At a meeting, which was called by the old community authority, in order to discuss the composition of the new community committee, which was supposed to be elected according to the democratic rules of the government, representatives of the synagogues and houses of worship participated, among them Judel Gutman as the representative of the small synagogue alongside the Artisans Union. The goal of the organizers of the meeting was to seek the possibility of a mutual agreement and arrange the composition of the community committee with out the battle of an election campaign.

[Page-144]

The outgoing "Parnas" invited M.P. Kaminer to chair the meeting. Then Gutman, still a young man, got up and demanded aggressively that the chairman of the meeting be elected by a show of hands of the participants. At the meeting, every matter must be decided by majority vote. "There is not room here for 'honorable ones'" he added, in the synagogue you may honor Mr. Kaminer with the first "Hakafa" [circuit with the Torah scroll] or a "Fat Aliya", in a popular meeting there are no procedures like these, but everything, large and small, is decided by vote.

Joske Fiszman got up to respond to Gutman's words and said, that even without a vote, it was clear that most of the participants wanted Kaminer to run the meeting. And in the stream of his words he got angry and the following words escaped his mouth: "See in what times we are living! Who participates, for our many sins, in our meetings! A fellow, who earlier would not have dared to push among important people and would not have had the chutzpa to open his mouth in front of Torah scholars, now jumps to the head and gives us opinions!"

These words were like oil to the flames. Gutman got up and said: "Please, gentlemen, allow me to respond to the words of defamation and insult that I heard from the mouth of Mr. Fiszman. He thinks, no doubt, that he is still living in a time when the aggressors in the city ruled the masses and rode upon them as on the back of an animal. Those times have passed never to return. We will no longer allow anyone to ride upon our backs and to make use of his cream as he sees fit; Mr. Fiszman included himself among important people – what is your importance? – Is it in the fact that you eat the large head of a mullet and another eats fish-paste? What advantage do you have over the others? Those who work with the sweat of their brow to find their daily bread are more important than all these parasites who live off of others."

Such talk had never been heard in the hall of the community committee, which had been ruled, up until now, by the most assertive members of the congregation without interference, and the secular authority had also supported them.

There was a noise in the hall. The participants in the meeting divided into two groups of rivals. Those who had gathered dispersed in the midst of yelling and curses without taking any decision.

However Gutman came out of there as the hero of the day. Everyone saw him as a man without fear and who knows how to tell the bare, unvarnished truth. On the one hand, people started to respect him, and on the other hand, to fear him.

Judel Gutman's friend was Josef Goldszajder. He was also a painter. But he was more of an expert in his profession than his friend Gutman. He wanted to be called an artist-painter. He would say: "I learned the art of painting in Switzerland."

[Page-145]

And truly his sense of taste and beauty were very developed. Everyone recognized and admitted the fact that his work was better than the work of other painters. Precision, order and seriousness were some of his traits. These qualities, together with the taste that dwelled in his soul gave him a certain importance in all circles. These qualities of his were expressed in his entire life, in his speech, his dress and also in his work. Therefore, he was more successful at his profession than his fellow painters. Anyone who wanted the walls of their homes painted with quality and knowledge would give it to Goldszajder, and they were certain that he would neither cheat them nor allow any work of his to stand that was not of quality. People did not bargain with him; they gave him the payment he demanded; in their opinion, he was worthy of receiving a higher wage than that paid to other painters, since he invested more energy, strength and even greater expenditures in his work.

He and Gutman were partners in contracting work; however on small jobs for private individuals, each of them worked separately.

They were also friends in their public work. The one did not oppose the other in public. Seen from the side by other people they were considered to have one skin, having the same opinion and outlook. At meetings and gatherings one saw them always together. If one requested the floor, it was clear that the other would do so afterwards.

However, whoever had ties of friendship with them knew that there were deep differences of opinion between them. The harmony and peace between them, which were so obvious, were only superficial. Whoever investigated and knew the essence of their souls learned that before us here were two different types, whom it was impossible to merge and knead into one dough. Gutman had a selfish personality, in all of his deeds and activities, he first of all sought advantage for himself.

In contrast, Goldszajder was devoted to the ideal that motivated him to action without noticing his own self interest. The first was warm tempered, easy to anger, prepared to assault his fellow for a slight injury to his honor; the second had a moderate temper, relaxed, defended his views and opinions calmly and logically, careful of others' honor. Gutman tended towards Zionism, Goldszajder, in contrast, tended towards "The Peoples' Party" ("Folkisten") and was one of the disciples of Noach Prylucki and was indifferent to Zionism. Local affairs had his chief attention, and he would devote his free hours to activities that would elevate the condition of the workers, the artisans and the poor of his city.

Sometimes serious disagreements would break out between these two friends; however Goldszajder did not want to reveal a secret, to raise the curtain and show what was going on behind the scenes, and did everything to make peace between himself and his friend. He valued peace above all. Disagreement and hatred were despicable in his eyes. As a person with a sensitive nature he wanted to ply a smooth and straight path without bumps or crookedness.

I will bring an example here that will demonstrate Goldszajder's character.

The year after World War I, America sent food for the starving Polish population. For the Passover holiday, the Jews received flour for baking Matzo from America. A certain amount of Matzo was received by the Artisans Union for distribution among its members. Every member had to register in the office of the artisans and according to the number of souls in his home, he would receive a portion of Matzo.

[Page-146]

Among those who were dealing with this matter were some who suggested that the members of the committee, who work and devote their time to the matter of distributing the Matzo should receive a double portion.

However, Goldszajder expressed his opinion against their suggestion, saying, that it would not be honest, that those who stand close to the community plate enjoy more than those who are distant from it do. They have no advantage over others. They must not demand a prize for the fact that they work and devote their time to the benefit of others. They are more able to do community work, it is their duty, therefore, to give of their strength and time for the benefit of the public.

Goldszajder, as one of the committee members who supervised the Jewish "Popular Bank", guarded this financial institution like the apple of his eye. He guarded it from destructive elements that attempted to penetrate into it and to turn it into their own private territory.

Goldszajder's relatives in Canada kept trying to persuade him to leave Europe and immigrate to America, where he could find a good life. He was tempted by their words, left Kielce and set off for America. He left his family behind. He didn't want to bring them until he knew the conditions in the new place, and whether these would allow him to manage and live a regular and proper family life there.

However, American life did not suit him, he could not adjust to the giant machinery that has the general name "America", which swallows millions of immigrants into itself and blurs their distinctions and denies their character and their initiative and turns them into an automatic machine and work force. This life was alien to him. His spirit tended towards individualism. He wanted to be an influence himself, and not be influenced. Being a personality with a definite shape – that was his ideal. Personality – that is the main thing. The concept "personality" was so high and exalted in his eyes that he was willing to give up the material benefits that American life promised him. Over there in America – so he thought – he would remain without shape, merged among the masses for his entire life.

This perspective drove him back to Kielce, to his birthplace, to the place where he found a broad field for his actions.

But after returning, he did not live long. A terminal disease attacked him and sent him to bed. After he had twisted with agony for several months, he died.

The people of the city, who had cherished him in his life, honored him greatly at this death. The local rabbi and activists of the city eulogized him and expressed their sorrow over a loss that would not return, at the death of an honest activist who was devoted heart and soul to community affairs.

A new faction started up in the Artisans Union that had a leftist direction; the chief spokesmen in this faction were the Strawczinski brothers. Szymon, the younger brother, was especially notable, since he had a talent for speaking and an educated tongue. They functioned as the opposition to the leaders of the artisans. At every meeting they would make their appearance as the chief critics of the activities of the committee members and would condemn the faults and mistakes of the members of the administration and the damage that they were bringing to all of the laboring workers. But their influence in the city was negligible and not noticeable.

[Page-147]

The Artisans Union, which later changed its name to Artisans Club, did important work in the area of raising the laborer and worker from his low social status and it was also an important factor in elevating him in cultural and aesthetic areas. It introduced the representatives of the workers to various public institutions, and there they were treated seriously. All of these caused an improvement in their material state to a noticeable degree, even though, this latter was dependent upon the political situation of Polish Jewry.

The anti-Semitism that started to make waves among the Poles, with its slogan "Sawoi do Sawgo" – "prefer your brother to the stranger", which gained preeminence in Polish circles, caused the Polish population to turn its back on the Jewish artisan, who was impoverished by this and found himself forced to take a wandering staff in his hand and to emigrate over the sea, if he was fortunate enough to get a visa.

In such a political situation, the artisan's organization was essential. With joined forces they made the effort to withstand the waves of anti-Semitism, which attempted to swallow them up. The "Peoples' Bank" gave them credit, they developed mutual aid and their strength grew slightly in the war against the consequences of anti-Semitism.

The Merchant's Union in Kielce

When the independent state of Poland was declared after World War I, the Jewish merchants faced severe problems, that it would have been difficult for any one individual to solve on his own. There was an urgent need for the merchant class to organize and defend itself in concert against the waves that arose to depress and humiliate it.

Poland, despite its natural wealth, was always battling to balance its budget. The Jewish merchant class was a "milk cow" in its eyes, and all the governments that were established in Poland levied a tremendous burden of all sorts of taxes upon the Jewish merchant. Not a few collapsed and fell under this weight.

The merchants, therefore, organized into a special unit. The merchants of Kielce also got up and founded themselves a union. The task of this union was to function as a representative of the merchants to the government, to defend the individual from the arbitrariness of the treasury clerks who would levy huge sums as income tax, periodic tax, property tax and war profits tax on the Jewish merchant, to establish a merchant's bank which would give credit to the small merchant who needed money, and to elect from within its ranks a representative to the central government chamber of commerce, and to form a center to which the Jewish merchant could turn to get advice, clarify situations, where he would not feel himself isolated in his troubles.

[Page-148]

The living spirit of this union was Herman Lewi, an enlightened industrialist, with energy and initiative from a family with roots in Poland going back for generations. He did not know any rest, at the call of a friend he was always ready to come and help him as much as he could.

Next to him were other merchants like Benjamin Lew, Aszer Kazlowski, Mejer Ajzenberg and others.

The merchants respected their union and willingly registered as members. At every annual meeting words of praise for the directors were heard and the criticism was limited to technical matters.

In the first row: (from right to left) Herman Lewi, Mejer Ajzenberg, B. Lew, M.P. Kaminer, Josef Kohen, A. Piotrowski.
In the second row: R. Rafalowicz, Welisz, M. Horberg, Judel Kaminer, E. Justman.
In the third row: Mosze Ajzenberg, Mosze Kaufman, Fiszel Kochen, Icak Rapaport, J. Gutman and S. B. Goldman

[Page-149]

The Commercial Club

During the period after World War I, the Jewish intelligentsia in Kielce grew. In part, they came from Galicia, and in part were local. The number of Jewish doctors, lawyers and teachers grew. Not all of them were connected to parties and unions; they were unaffiliated, and therefore decided to establish a club that would serve as a center for all those who wished to spend their free time in pleasant company, which they would enjoy, which would entertain them, in which they could get to know one another in an atmosphere free of the political controversies and serious matters that were current.

In 1932 this club was founded and called "Civilian Club", which showed that every citizen could find something he wanted here: a reading room for those who wished to spend their free time reading newspapers; a games room in which players could sit, and where they could play dominos and chess and other games. A place was also found for those who enjoyed pleasant conversation, and from time to time a speaker came to give a lecture on literature and art.

This club was a favorite of the Jewish inhabitants, and the number of those visiting grew over time and it became also a cultural center. The enlivening spirit of this club was Mosze Kaufman. A Jewish merchant, on Sabbaths and holidays he wore silk clothing; in his youth he was also a Chassid, and he did not lose a degree of Chassidism even afterwards, when he began to keep company with enlightened and educated people. He was a Jew with a sense of humor; he always had a Jewish joke ready to tell. When he spoke, he continued to imitate the Chassidim in their gestures and facial expressions.

It was pleasant to speak with this Jew. He knew how to spice up ordinary conversation with episodes that were both funny and entertaining.

The Jewish Banks in Kielce

The anti-Semitic method of the government and authorities in Poland was to disturb and injure mainly the economic life of the Jews.

This method was expressed, first and foremost by the levying of heavy taxes on the commerce and production of the Jews (periodic tax, income tax, etc.) and with the well-known slogan of "obszam" – according to the expletive of one of the ministers in the Pilsudski government, that he objects to pogroms against Jews, but economic oppressions – "obszam" (certainly, certainly). According to these government patterns, the government banks "Bank Polski", "Bank Gospodarstwa", "Krajowgo" and others, as well as private Polish banks barely extended any credit to Jewish merchants, industrialists, artisans and in other professions. Running a business in Poland without credit from a bank, at a time when all of the wholesale trade and even the retail trade was conducted with notes whose redemption was many months away, was totally impossible – a kind of "cut off the head and not die"; and that is actually what the authorities intended – to remove the Jews from the economic cycle, especially from the trade and manufacturing of the country.

At that time Polish cooperative banks were being founded with a central bank "Bank Zwiazlcu Spolek Zarobkowych" at their head. This bank received large sums in a government loan whose purpose was to strengthen the cooperatives of the workshops and the commerce of the Poles, who, according to the desire of the authorities, were supposed to inherit the places of the Jewish merchants and artisans.

[Page-150]

The situation became more difficult from day to day; and then the American "Joint" [Jewish Joint Distribution Committee] arrived to help the Jewish population in Poland and founded a central Jewish bank in Warsaw called "Bank dla Spoldzielny", whose goal was to encourage the establishment of Jewish cooperative banks in every city and town, which would help with credit for the Jewish merchant and artisan.

A bank like this was founded in Kielce as well, called "Bank Ludowy" (Popular Bank). At its head, during its existence stood Messrs. Berza Blumenfeld, Icak Mejer Rajzman, Dawid Rozenberg and others.

This bank developed nicely; it encompassed many hundreds of artisans and small businessmen who joined it as members (the bank gave loans only to members) and for about ten years it was a blessing to the lower middle class Jews of Kielce.

The main activities of the bank, aside from disbursing loans from the monies it received from the "Joint" via the central bank ("Bank dla Spoldzielny") in Warsaw, focused mainly on collecting the savings of the Jewish population, so that the Jews would not deposit their savings in the Polish banks ("P.K.O.", "Bank Polski" and others) and would thus practically be contributing to their own dispossession of commerce and manufacturing, rather, that they deposit them in the Jewish cooperative bank - and thus help the Jewish economic classes and established their position and their situation via inexpensive credit.

Understandably, these activities were a great blessing for the entire Jewish population in the city. The "Bank Ludowy", however, concentrated in its activities only on the artisans and small businessmen (the grocers). The middle classes enjoyed credit from this bank only a little bit; and then there was the demand and the necessity to found banks that would serve these classes as well. Banks like these had to be founded as large banks (of shareholding companies), but since it was not possible to receive a permit from the Polish government to found a private Jewish bank, the entrepreneurs who were establishing these banks had to use the law of the cooperatives, which allowed any group of 10 people to found any cooperative they wanted, i.e., also a cooperative for giving out loans to members and for other banking activities (with almost no exceptions). For this sort of cooperative one did not need a special permit.

In this manner several banks were founded, technically cooperatives, and actually private, the most important among them was the Commercial Cooperative Bank ("Spoldzielczy Bank Handlowy"), which was headed by Aharon Josef Moszkowicz and Jakob Fridman and whose manager was Elazar Arten; the Discount Bank ("Bank Diskontowy") headed by Chaim Wajnryb and Herszel Sercarz; the Credit Bank ("Bank Kreditowy") headed by Melech Engelrad, Mejer Zloto, and Mosze Kohen; the Loan Bank ("Bank Porzyczkowy") headed by Mordechai Fiszel and Judel Kaminer and others.

All of these banks brought relief to all the Jewish inhabitants of the city; for, as we mentioned, they filled a very important role in gathering the savings of the Jewish population and distributing them as loans to the various economic classes of Jews and having them flow into the financial cycle funds that would otherwise have gone to the coffers of the Polish banks and would have been another means of depriving them of their economic positions.

[Page-151]

According to the law of cooperatives in Poland, every cooperative was required to be under the supervision of the Cooperative Council of the Treasury or of a Cooperative Oversight Union ("Zwjonzek Rewizjeny") recognized by the government. The council or union had to audit all the activities of the cooperative once a year and to confirm its balance.

In Poland there were three Jewish cooperative unions; one in Warsaw of the cooperatives of the "Joint", the second in Lwow headed by members of the Sejm (Parliament), the Zionist activists Dr. Henryk Rozmarin (who was later the Polish consul in Tel-Aviv) and Dr. Fiszel Rotensztrajch; and the third in Warsaw, around which the cooperatives of the "Agudat Yisra'el" clustered.

The "Ludowy" bank belonged to the Warsaw union of the "Joint", the "Handlowy", "Diskontowy" and "Kreditowy" banks, which were headed by Zionists, belonged to the Lwow union, and the "Porzyczkowy" bank to the "Aguda" union.

As we said, the banks underwent a precise audit every year of all of their activities and their financial condition and base was always strong.

The cooperative unions we just mentioned put out their own newsletters – monthlies. The name of the "Joint", Warsaw-based union's newsletter was "Di Kooperative Bewegung"; the Zionist union in Lwow had two newsletters/monthlies, one in Polish called "Paszglund Spoldzielczy" and another in Yiddish "Der Kooperator".

A member of the editorial board of these two newsletters was Elazar Arten (manager of the "Commercial" bank) and his articles aroused considerable interest in all of the Jewish cooperative circles, and sometimes also in Polish government circles.

In one of his articles, which was published in 1929 in "Paszglund Spoldzielczy", and was later copied in the daily press ("Nasz Paszglund" and others), he suggested exempting the savings funds, which were deposited in the cooperative banks, from income tax and from the interest which were due on these savings, in order to encourage the ordinary person, in this manner, to take his savings out of the "sock" and the "mattress" and to deposit them in a cooperative bank.

This suggestion found a welcome audience in the economic circles of the government and the Treasury Minister gave the instruction to exempt these savings from income tax and the interest, without consideration for the amount of the savings of each person; and together with this to require the cooperative banks with total secrecy towards all of the government institutions regarding the identity and name of each depositor or owner of a savings account.

In 1931 there was a great crisis in all branches of the economy in the state of Poland. This crisis was evident also in the banking industry in the state, in all of its variety.

[Page-152]

First, one of the largest banks in the state "Bank of Commerce and Industry" ("Bank dla Handlu i Przemysl"), which had branches in nearly every city and town, stopped making its payments. After that the commercial bank in Lodz, which also had branches in many cities in the state, Kielce among them.

However, the Jewish cooperative banks received the worst blow, which shook up their existence, not from the bankruptcy of these Polish banks, but from the stopping of payments of the "Joint's" central bank for the cooperatives ("Bank dla Spoldzielny") in Warsaw, headed by the well-known activist, Dr. Kalumel. This bankruptcy undermined, first and foremost, the foundations of the popular banks.

When this bankruptcy became known among the popular classes, which made up most of the savings depositors in these banks and in the popular bank ("Ludowy") in Kielce, a fearful race began of the depositors and a demand of returning the deposits all at once. No bank in the world can stand up to such a demand without government backing, which can step in and help at a serious time like this.

The fears and the demands for the return of the deposits of hundreds of thousands of depositors spread like a contagious disease among everyone how had savings in the banks and especially in the Jewish cooperative banks and caused the destruction of their financial state in every way.

Aside from the savings funds, all of the banks also had monies from collections on notes and documents, which were given to the banks and whose value went into the checking account of the people who had handed in the documents for collections; these monies also were a large part of the cash flow of the banks which was lent to the members. The moment the banks were full of depositors all day long who demanded the return of their money without consideration if its maturation date had arrived or not, the people handing in collection documents stopped coming to the bank (they transferred their custom to the Polish banks), the money in their checking accounts they withdrew in its entirety and they too, with these actions of theirs, helped to undermine the existence of the banks.

Also those who owed loan money to the banks used this opportunity of chaos that took over all the Jewish banks and evaded paying back what they owed with the excuse that their credit had suddenly been cut off in all of the banks, and they didn't have any way to meet their obligations.

All of these circumstances caused a stoppage of payments of all the Jewish cooperative banks in all of the cities of Poland, including Kielce.

As we said, the first to stop its payments was the Popular Bank, ("Ludowy"), after that the "Bank Kreditowy" and the "Bank Diskontowy" were forced to follow suit and finally, the "Spoldzielczy Bank Handlowy" surrendered as well, after fighting for its life for a long time and returning most of its deposits in full.

After the destruction of these banks, new Jewish banks were established in the thirties, among them Dawid Rozenberg's private bank with a government license, and the banks "Spoldzielnia Kreditiwa Kopczow i Przemyslowczow" (Merchants and Industrialists Credit Cooperative) with Szmuel Lewartowski and Kalman Kluska at its head and the householder's bank whose manager was Chaim Judel Ajzenberg.

These banks developed and existed until the outbreak of the war in 1939.

המועצה, ההנהלה וחבר הפקידים של הבנק הקואופרטיבי למסחר בקילץ

The council, directorate and staff members of the
Cooperative Commercial Bank ("Spoldzielczy Bank Handlowy") in Kielce

[Page-154]

Rabbis, Religious Leaders and Scholars

Translated by Judy Montel

Edited by Warren Blatt

Rabbis of the Kielce Community

The first rabbi and chief of the rabbinical court of the Kielce was the Gaon Rabbi Tuwia Gutman son of Rabbi Dawid, chief of the rabbinical court in the community of Ostrowiec. This rabbi was one of the outstanding Chassidim of Kock. His lineage went back to the Sha"ch [Rabbi Shabtai Kohen] and the Rama"h Z"L [Rabbi Moshe Iserlis].

I will note down here the list of his lineage according to the list of the chief of the rabbinical court in Plonsk, which was printed there entitled "Kontras Beit Tuvia" in his book "Birkat Kohen".

- One) Rabbi Tuwia Gutman HaKohen, chief of the rabbinical court of the holy congregation of Kielce.
- Two) son of the Gaon Rabbi Dawid HaKohen Z"L chief of the rabbinical court of the holy congregation of Ostrowiec.
- Three) son of the Gaon Rabbi Izrael HaKohen chief of the rabbinical court of the holy congregation of Alexander [Aleksandrow Lodzki] and the holy congregation of Pinczow, the in-law of the Admo"r of Kock.
- Four) son of the Gaon Rabbi Zew HaKohen, chief of the rabbinical court of the holy congregation of Szczekociny and Pinczow.
- Five) son of the Gaon Rabbi Icak Kac [Kat"z is an abbreviation of "Kohen Tzedek"] Z"L, known as Rabbi Icak Charif, author of the responsa "Keter Kehuna", rabbi in Pinczow.
- Six) son of the Gaon Rabbi Dow Berisz Kac Z"L, son in law of Rabbi Awraham Abele Z"L chief of the rabbinical court of the holy congregation of Pinczow and the holy congregation of Opatow.
- Seven) son of the Gaon Rabbi Icak Kac Z"L, chief of the rabbinical court of the holy congregation of Podhajce [Krzemienic], author of the book "Gevurot Anashim".
- Eight) son of the Gaon Rabbi Mosze HaKohen Z"L, son-in-law of the Gaon Rabbi Menachem Mendel Margaliot.
- Nine) son of our rabbi, pillar of instruction, author of "Siftei Cohen", Sha"ch.
- Ten) son of the Gaon Rabbi Majer Aszkenazi ZaTZ"L, rabbinical judge in Frankfurt am Main.

This is the lineage of the first rabbi of the holy congregation of Kielce. Also his spouse, the Rebbetzin, was from rabbinical and eternally righteous stock. She was the granddaughter of the Gaon Rabbi Jehoszua Fejwel Teomim, chief of the rabbinical court of the holy congregation of Przemysl, son of the Gaon Rabbi Jona Teomim chief of the rabbinical court of Metz, author of the book "Kikayon deYona".

Besides his ancestral lineage, Rabbi Tuwia Gutman HaKohen Z"L had his own lineage. He was a genius in the Torah and left behind him many compositions in scriptural casuistry and innovations. He was a favorite of his congregants, and all of them admired him and were proud of this rabbi of theirs. And the elders, who were fortunate enough to know him during his life, said his name with awe and great admiration.

He died and was gathered to his forefathers, 26 Shevat, Friday, eve of the holy Sabbath, in 5662 [February 5, 1902]. Upon his tombstone the following words were engraved:

> Aha! We have lost our genius, our wreath has been removed!
> Ha! Murder in our bones, our blow is critical.
> Trembling in our waists, our glory has descended to the earth!
> Pure and upright in the midst of his flock, he was acclaimed.
> When the community was founded, he was crowned with the rabbinical crown
> by men of character.
> Clear faith, straight thinking were matched in his heart.
> His voice was like honey from his mouth, sweet to those who visited his
> garden.
> He set times for Torah study, dove into the depths of its waters,
> And the renown of his greatness became known. With your strength you
> acquired knowledge in its study
> And you inherited your ancestors' genius. Therefore, in the Eden of their
> spirits, the Glory of God gathers you up.

After the death of Rabbi Tuwia Gutman HaKohen Z"L, the rabbinical seat of the holy congregation of Kielce was occupied by the Gaon Rabbi Mosze Nachum Jerusalimski, author of several books of responsa: "Minchat Moshe", "Birkat Moshe", "Be'er Moshe", and "Leshed HaShemen", a commentary on Maimonides.

Rabbi Jerusalimski

In this outstanding rabbi the characteristics in which scholars excel were united – love of Israel, love of the Torah of Israel and love of the land of Israel.

[Page-156]

Rabbi Jerusalimski was one of the first "Chovevei Zion" and a fan of political Zionism, however, due to his official position he could not participate actively in the Zionist endeavor, which was considered "not kosher" by the authorities and the Chassidim, who then held the reins of the community authority. But the home of this outstanding rabbi was wholly filled and instilled with the ideas of the rebirth of the nation and the family members held Zionism in esteem and fondness. In general the home of this rabbi was an ultra orthodox, nationalist and intelligent home.

Rabbi Jerusalimski, in his studiousness and the firmness of his opinion exemplified a type of genius himself, one who stands above all the petty affairs that separate people from one another.

All of the various Chassidim, even the Gur Chassidim, who looked suspiciously at every rabbi who was not from their own group, admired and respected him, saw in him a man elevated above the common folk, a strong personality who did not compromise his views, did not know how to flatter the rich or prostrate himself before the authorities as many of the rabbis used to do in those days.

These qualities of his earned him the respect of the authorities as well, their representatives would visit his home at any opportunity, and he too was often a citizen guest in the home of the district governor. From these connections he aimed to gain advantages for the members of his community and to gain respect for the rabbinate. In 1910 he was elected as the representative of the district rabbis at the convention of rabbis in Petersburg, which was called by Prime Minister Stoliapin, at which he defended the national affairs on the agenda with courage, and his name was then acclaimed among the Jews of Russia and Poland.

His excellent sermons filled with Jewish ethics and national content influenced their hearers and entered the hearts of the masses.

On Saturday afternoons, for the third meal, all of the Torah students in the city would gather to hear his sermon that encompassed all the types of rabbinic literature, from the books of the legal arbiters to the books of Kabbala and philosophical books such as "Guide for the Perplexed" and "Kuzari". In such sermons he demonstrated an amazing expertise.

His essays and responsa gave him broad renown in the rabbinical world and people would send him questions from the ends of the earth in order to hear his opinion, since the conclusions he reached from his various considerations was one they considered to be a deciding opinion.

His heart was alert to every bit of suffering of the individual and the community. He never prevented himself from helping anyone impoverished. His home was open to anyone needy. A preacher or itinerant speaker, the author of a collection would get his signature on his composition, and in general – any person who needed any kind of aid, all these would first turn to the local rabbi, and he received everyone graciously. Everyone left him satisfied, for they had found adequate response to their requests.

However, there were instances, where the goodness of his heart, his excellent qualities caused him unpleasantness sometimes. Many took advantage of his qualities for their own good without regard for the consequences, which could hurt him and cause his honor to be demeaned. I will describe one such incident below:

[Page-157]

During the elections to the third Duma a Jew from Warsaw, practically a Pole, and a socialist named Jagelo was elected as a delegate from Poland's capital, Warsaw, to the Russian legislature. This event angered the Endeks; they were dissatisfied that a "Shabbes Goy", who was enslaved by the Jews, represented Warsaw. In order to teach the Jews a lesson for their brazenness the Endeks declared a boycott upon them. The Polish newspaper "Dwo Grosza", which was founded at the time to wage a war against the Jews, publicized the anti-Semitic venom and conducted the "boycott" propaganda against the Jews all over Poland, in the cities and in the towns, in the villages and on the estates. The priests gave especially invaluable aid to the Endeks in this propaganda; they preached hatred and poison against the Jews from their pulpits. The unenlightened masses were aroused when they left the churches. There were incidents of crass assaults upon Jewish passersby as well as upon peddlers who set out their wares on market days. The Jews were beaten with cudgels, and their wares were trampled and destroyed. The Jews in small towns suffered from the anti-Semitic propaganda especially, in places where their Christian neighbors were under the influence of the priesthood.

In those days, the rabbi of the town of Skala in the Olkusz district came to Kielce, Rabbi Icak Natan Sztark, and visited at the home of Rabbi Jerusalimski, in order to ask his advice about the boycott, from which his flock was suffering greatly. With great tears he laid out his tale before the rabbi; he described the series of sufferings his community was undergoing, being beaten and incited against by a new priest, who had arrived in the town and was inciting his flock against the Jews. Under the influence of his incitement not only had the Jews lost their livelihood, but when they ventured out of doors their very lives were threatened, their Christian neighbors showered them with stones and abused their victims.

Rabbi Jerusalimski was moved and horrified to hear these words and immediately called the writer of these lines to be a witness to the words of the rabbi of the holy congregation of Skala, and requested him to translate into Polish a letter that he composed to Bishop Augustin Lusinski.

In this letter, to the head of the head of the church in the Kielce bishopric the accusations of the rabbi of Skala against the local priest were laid out and the Bishop was requested to influence the priest who was under his authority, to stop conducting anti-Semitic propaganda, and it expressed the hope that his honorable reverend the Bishop would, of course, remember his words, which he had delivered to the Jewish delegation, which had greeted him the day he arrived in Kielce to serve in the high position of the shepherd of the community: regarding the words of the rabbi, who had blessed him then upon his arrival, and who had quoted among his other words the verse: "and God will seek out the persecuted" and requested him, to institute peace between the Christian community and the Jewish community and stand at the side of the persecuted, the Bishop had responded: "I respect the man who is created in the image of God and do not discriminate in this regard between a Christian or a Jew". He promised to always defend those who were cheated, whether they be members of the Christian or Jewish communities.

In this letter of appeal these words were mentioned. And based upon them, the hope was expressed that at a time that a boycott campaign was being conducted against the Jews, he would stand by those being persecuted and would quiet the fire of discord.

[Page-158]

After a few days a response to the letter was received, written very politely and in which the bishop promised to conduct an inquiry in the matter and to report the results to the rabbi without delay. Interestingly, the response letter of the Polish bishop was written in Russian, while the appeal had been in the Polish language.

Several weeks passed – and there arrived a brief letter, written in a dry and official style, addressed to the rabbi, not from the bishop himself, but from his Consistorium, that is, his religious court, in which it said that after a thorough and precise investigation it turns out that the accusations that the rabbi claimed against the priest in his letter were false. Even the rabbi from Skala, the chief accuser, who was summoned to the investigation to the city of Olkusz by Smulka, the local deacon, denied the matter entirely and claimed: "these things never happened". Noting the results of the inquiry, he finds the matter closed, and need not be dealt with further.

This reply was a serious blow to the reputation of the rabbi. The denial of the rabbi of Skala cast aspersions on the rabbi of Kielce, as if he was informing on the Christian priesthood without sufficient foundation and as if he was inventing accusations against them for some other purpose. Horrified to the depths of his soul by this terrible incident, the rabbi could not let this embarrassment, caused by the rabbi of Skala, pass without mention, and he turned to the rabbi of Olkusz, Rabbi Menachem Mendel Rozensztrich Z"L and asked him to meet with Deacon Smulka and to explain to him that in fact, he had appealed to the Kielce bishop only at the request of the rabbi of Skala, and that apparently, this rabbi had only denied the matter before the committee investigating the matter out of fear, and therefore, the deacon must inform the bishop in Kielce that the words of the rabbi in Kielce were true and the denial of the rabbi of Skala must not be taken into account.

Several days after the aforementioned rabbi met with Deacon Smulka and gave him the content of Rabbi Jerusalimski's letter, the rabbi in Olkusz received a written answer from the deacon, that the Bishop of Kielce understands all the details of the matter and has no quarrel with the rabbi from Kielce. The rabbi from Olkusz passed this on to Rabbi Jerusalimski and the latter wrote a second letter to Bishop Lusinski, in which he expressed his certainty that the bishop understood the motives that caused the rabbi of Skala to deny the accusations he had made and thanked him for responding to his request and dealing with this matter, whose results would no doubt be for the good, and added, that knowing the nobility of the bishop, he was sure that this incident would not ruin the excellent relations that had, until now, existed between the two community shepherds. This letter received a response in the name of the bishop that he too agreed with the opinion expressed in the letter and the friendly relations continued as they had before.

Several months passed, and a letter arrived addressed to the rabbi from the leadership of the Jewish community of Warsaw, signed by Rabbi Joel Wagmajster, which announces that a convention of Christian clergyman is to take place shortly and the question of the "boycott" against the Jews is also on its agenda. The decisions that would be made at this convention regarding this question, would be crucial, for the church still had a lot of influence on the masses of the Polish people, especially upon the peasants, who made up the vast majority. In this letter, the rabbi was requested to intervene with the Kielce bishop, who was to participate in the aforementioned convention, and to endeavor to influence him to express his opinion against the boycott and against the general anti-Semitism that the Endeks spread so energetically among the Polish population. In this letter it also stated that the representatives of the Warsaw community received promises from several leading clergymen that their opinions would be in favor of the Jews, therefore it would be desirable if a large portion of the participants in this convention express their opinion in our favor, and in this way, remove the sting of the "boycott" which was devastating Jewish commerce.

The day the aforementioned letter arrived was a day of great turmoil in the home of the rabbi: the rabbi was marrying off his daughter, and he and all of his household were preparing for a long journey to the city of Kostopol in the Ukraine, to the wedding of his daughter. The rabbi was greatly embarrassed. On the one had, he could not neglect the matter, upon which the benefit of the community depended, and on the other hand, he must travel to the wedding of his daughter, which could not be postponed to another date. With no choice, he decided to send a letter of petition in the matter to the bishop. The composition of the letter was once again entrusted to the writers of these lines. And since the rabbi did not have time to wait for even a brief time, since all the members of his family were ready for the journey, it was necessary to send the letter to the city of Kostopol, to the address that the rabbi had given him prior to his journey and there he would look over the content of the letter and put his signature upon and from there he would send it back to Kielce addressed to the bishop.

However, a great error occurred here. Such things are always done discretely, in person, and are not put down in writing. Things that are in writing are destined to become known.

The decision of the heads of the Christian church regarding the boycott remains unknown until today. All of their meetings were held behind closed doors, and no political or social decision was publicized. The church periodical "Church News" published the decisions that directly effected the affairs of the church, in which cracks had begun to show. The movement of the Mariovites had begun to have an effect among the Polish population and threatened the unity of the church. But the content of the letter that was sent by the rabbi to the Bishop of Kielce was published later in an anti-Semitic newspaper, "Dwo Grosza". This newspaper attacked the Bishop of Kielce, Augustin Lusinski, with curses and libels, calling him: "slave of the Jews", "Shabbes Goy", who was on the side of the Jews who aspire to take over Poland and who cause many misfortunes to the Poles. And as proof of its claims this vulgar newspaper brought excerpts from the letter, in which the rabbi of Kielce requests the bishop, the friend of the Jews, to support them.

And from that day forward, the relationship between the rabbi and the bishop ceased.

In the event, the rabbi did have to appeal directly to the bishop one more time for the benefit of his brethren, members of his flock.

It was at the start of World War I. In 1914 during the month of Av [July-August] the first Polish legionnaires entered Kielce headed by Pilsudski. A battalion of Cossacks, which was encamped north of the city, chased the legionnaires out of the city. The Russian commander levied a penalty on the city totaling one hundred thousand rubles, as punishment for the gracious reception the city's inhabitants had held for the Polish legionnaires, and threatened to bomb the city if they did not supply him with this contribution within twenty four hours.

[Page-160]

Meanwhile, the Cossacks were set free to entertain themselves "Pogoliati".

Life was quiet in the city, the shops were closed and shuttered, the gates to the houses were locked. The inhabitants were hidden in their rooms and were afraid to come out.

The Cossacks began breaking the doors to the shops and looting their wares. Polish youths accompanied the Cossacks, in order to show them which shops belonged to Jews, and there they would break in and wreak destruction; they would pass over the shop of a Christian. In this manner the shops of the Jews were looted and the Cossacks did not harm the shops of the Christians.

The Jews were in great distress, since at the beginning of the war the Poles had incited the Russian soldiers against the Jews.

In such a situation the rabbi could not sit quietly hiding in his isolated corner. As the head of the community he felt in his warm heart the sorrow of his congregation, the suffering of each and every individual touched his heart and moved him to action.

When the rabbi saw the next day that the Cossacks' looting, directed by the Poles, were not ceasing, and the shops of the Jews were falling victim one after another, he arose and went, accompanied by a semi-official person, Chwat, the teacher of Jewish Religion at the Russian government Gymnasium, to the bishop to request him to publicize an announcement to the Christian inhabitants, to cease to aid the Cossacks in the looting of Jewish property.

The bishop was upset and emotional to hear the accusations that the rabbi made against the young Polish rabble and promised, that he would order an announcement immediately in all of the churches that every Pole must refrain from such despicable acts, and also influence others, not to abet such criminal activities.

The rabbi did not remain satisfied with the bishop's promise, but also appealed in this matter to the commander of the Russian army and informed him of the looting that was being done on Russian citizens by the Cossacks.

To the joy of the Jews, the Austrians and Germans arrived in town and the Russian army left the city.

The Jews breathed easier, went out of their homes, opened their shops. The Poles didn't understand German; in contrast the Jews, knowing the language of the Germans grew closer to them and did business with them. The Germans knew how to approach the inhabitants of the city. And the Jews were no longer anxious about looting and violence.

However, the Germans did not remain in Kielce for very long. The Russians started a major offensive near Warsaw and the Germans were forced to retreat to Krakow.

[Page-161]

Bad days then began for the Jews of Poland in general and the Jews of Kielce in particular. Deportations from places close to the front began to take place; the Polish informants became worse and worse and the results were very hard on the Jews. Military tribunals were handing down death sentences to innocent Jews every day. The army commanders with great pleasure accepted false libels, that the Jews were busy spying for the enemy, since it gave them an excuse for their failures in the war.

Next to the city park a gallows were set up, and the death sentences were executed there. The rabbi was forced to be present when the executions took place. He knew that the victims were holy martyrs, who were being killed only because they were Jews.

Every time the rabbi returned home after a death execution upon a Jew he was white a chalk, horrified to the depths of his soul. His heart nearly broke to see the disgraceful death that awaited the Jew, who confessed before him in his last moments. If he had only had the opportunity he would have given all he owned and also his soul, just to save the life of a Jew ascending the gallows without having committed a crime. He attempted time and again to endeavor to speak to the general in favor of those sentenced; however, each time he left him in a terrible state. The general yelled at him crudely reprimanded him for this action, for troubling him from his work. Instead of influencing his flock not to aid the enemy, not to spy for them, he came to plead the case of the criminals, who betray their homeland and provide the enemy with knowledge of the movements of the Russian army. At this opportunity he spewed forth a kettle of filth upon the Jews, curses and accusations. The rabbi left him depressed, broken and shattered.

Such horrible sights affected his health, from day to day he became more frail and weak, his strength left him, he could not sleep, he constantly saw the faces of the condemned before his eyes and the question that penetrated to the abyss: why? wherefore? was expressed in their faces.

The rabbi's family began to fear for his life; they knew that if he stayed here in a city close to the front and continued to be present at the executions of innocent Jews, his life would be in danger. Therefore his sons, some of whom lived in Russia, decided to take their father to where they lived, saying that he would find rest for his devastated soul, his nerves would heal. And there he would live until the fury of the war passed.

The rabbi left Kielce with his family and traveled to their in-laws, the rabbi in the city of Churol [Poltava gubernia, now Khorol, Ukraine].

But there too his heart did not calm down nor was he able to find peace. From a distance he saw the suffering of the Jews, the deportations, the death sentences, read and heard the disgraceful conspiracies and the accusations being brought against the Jews. His heart broke, and his soul departed in purity on the 29th of Sivan, 5676 [30 June 1916].

When the terrible news reached the inhabitants of Kielce of the death of their rabbi and leader, they all felt that their glory had passed, their magnificence was gone. The mourning among the members of his congregation was great. A bitter dirge was held for him in the synagogue in which his exalted sermons had been heard.

His apartment remained in Kielce with its furniture and his rich library for a long time, everyone who passed by it was enveloped in a great sorrow that the place had been abandoned and a great light had been put out, that from that place had shone its glorious rays upon all the members of the community.

[Page-162]

And until today, Kielcers wherever they are remain proud of the man who was their rabbi, of Rabbi Mosze Nachum Jerusalimski Z"L, author of books in scriptural casuistry, a maker of regulations for the benefit of his congregation, a lover of Israel and a fan of the movement of the rebirth of the people of Israel in their ancient homeland.

Rabbi Jerusalimski did not spend a long time serving as the local authority and rabbi of the holy congregation of Kielce; however, his name remained identified with the Kielce community. In the Jewish world, the name is commonly mentioned, Rabbi Jerusalimski, the rabbi of Kielce.

The Rabbinical Writ Appointing Rabbi Jerusalimski as the rabbi of Kielce

We have gathered together, we the undersigned, heads of the congregation of our community, leaders of the city, respected and important as well as those who carry the burden of the taxes of running the city and with the agreement of all the inhabitants of our city, may Zion and Jerusalem be rebuilt, we hereby unanimously elect to set the crown of the rabbinate of this here community of Kielce upon the head of the rabbi who is a genius, a fortress and tower, sharp and expert, Sinai and uprooter of mountains, his good name is known over distances, the glory and magnificence of the generation, veteran and pious, his palate is full of sweet things etc., etc., the honor of the holy name of his glory our teacher the rabbi Mosze Nachum Jerusalimski, may he live excellent and lengthy days, Amen, the rabbi who is currently head of the rabbinical court in the holy congregation of Ostroleka and who was confirmed by the government according to the Ochwola which was on Wednesday, portion of "Beha'alotcha", the 13th of the month of Sivan of this year, and we allotted in honor of the crown of the Torah a set salary totaling one thousand and five hundred silver rubles aside from rabbi, cantor and "shamash" and all the income from the city which belong to the head of the rabbinical court, rabbinical authority of this locality as is customary in all the cities of the Diaspora of Israel.

And the aforementioned honorable and magnificent genius will accept the position upon his shoulder to administer our congregation and to shepherd the sheep of his flock along the waters of the springs of the Torah and of knowledge to stand the glory of the Torah upon its pedestal and to be well known and glorious.

The court of justice will be established in his home in the company of the arbiter of justice of this here congregation who will come to the home of the crown of the Torah every day at a regular time. And for his eyes to look over all the groups of the city's inhabitants which were already established and which will yet be established in the coming days to guide them in the circles of justice and to tend them in the straight and proper path. The general point of the thing for the genius rabbi aforementioned to be the living spirit in the wheels of all the city's needs according to the Torah and fear of God, to stand in the breach and to strengthen every bolt. And at the end of the first year he will be given two thousand silver rubles every year. This writ of the rabbinate will stand in effect until the time three years from the day noted below, and with God's will when God approves our path may he strengthen our hands to continue this writ of rabbinate for the years that are approaching us for the good and God, may he be blessed, be an aid to him and to us to succeed in all of his paths and our paths to raise our glory in honor and the glory of all the inhabitants of the city may be raised and go forth for a blessing, and for success and for peace unending until the coming of Yinon speedily in our day, Amen.

With all this, we have agreed with a whole heart and willing spirit and all is legal and standing.

Motz'ai Shabbat Kodesh [Saturday night] before the first day of the portion "and who he chooses he shall bring near to him" [Numbers 16/5], 20th of Sivan, 5662 [1902] in this here Kielce, may God protect our city. –

Simcha Bunem Izraelski, Awigdor Rajzman, Eliezer Tenenbaum, Chaim HaKohen; Mendel Ajzenberg, Icak Kaminer, G. Miszpienki , Szmuel Pietrowski, Szmulik Rajzman, Jakob Maliniak, Mosze Jechiel Bester, Mejer Ajzenberg; Dawid Hasman; Jakob Hilel Paserman, Mosze Piotrkowski, Lajbusz Blacharowicz, Szamaj Hakohen Kalichsztajn; Dawid Zylberszpic, Mosze son of rabbi J. Slawatycki, Szlomo Jakob Miodowicz, Mosze Albirt, Josef Szlamowicz, Mosze Lewkowicz; Izrael Szmul Alpert; Joske Fiszman; Baruch Moszenberg; Icak Icza Balicki; Naftali Hakohen Elencwajg, Icak Majer Goldberg, Szmul Aba Balicki, Azriel Pukacz; Mordechai Rozenberg; Fejwel Finkelsztajn; Jechiel Szajnfeld, Dawid Gedalja Szafir, Awigdor Litauer of the house of the wealthy departed rabbi Chaim Tykociner Bosterlenka, Ch. Alter Marberg, the holy Chaim Dow Hirszzon, Cwi Jehuda Abramowicz, Izrael Majer Szafir, Menachem Dow Piekarski, Motel Szafir, Chaim Kaner, Chaim Tencer, Icak Mejer Beserglik, Jechiel Michl Hakohen, Szlomo Cymerman, Icak Cwi Kaminer, Anszel Frajtag, Awraham Isocher Garfinkel; Jehuda Lajb Alpert, Mordechai Bornsztajn, Szymon Sosnowski, Mosze Dawid Ajzenberg, Szlomo Beser; Jehoszua Heszel Cwajgel; Jechezkel Paparsztak, Zecharja Rozenberg, Sz. Ajzenberg; Jakob Icak Grynberg; Mejer Horwicz son in law of Rabbi Chaim Hakohen, Motel Bimka; Josef Zylbersztajn; Chaim Wajntraub; Echezkel Bimka, Baruch Josef Hakohen Elencwajg, Izrael Mejer Cytryn; Aharon Korngold, Szlomo Ajzenberg, Jehuda Judel Rotszild; Aharon Emanuel Goldberg; Josef Grynberg, Mosze Kohen Adler, Josef Szymon Hejn; Szmuel Hagerman; Henich Lewkowicz, Mane Kohen; Awraham Ber Ajzenberg, Jechezkel Partinski, Jona Hakohen

Szapiro, Mosze Mordechai Frohman, Michael Mejer Minc, Icak Mejer Kaner, Icak Mejer Beser; Hersz Mazupe; Awraham Josef Bester; Josef Korngold; Icak Icza Ladowski; Pinchas Hakohen Zaherman; Mosze Zew Lipko; Mosze Cwi the ritual slaughterer Recht, Szlomo Rubinsztajn, Motel Feldman, Mordechai-Gimpel Moskowicz, Icak Mejer Elazar Cukerman, Josef Icak Rubinsztajn, Szlomo Zylbersztajn, Jehuda Lajbusz Golembiowski, Dawid Feldman, Icak Gerszon Awraham Bekerman, Alter Dajtelcwajg, Mosze Josef Almer, Jona Wajsman, Fiszel Aszer Kazlowski, Josef Zauerman, Jeszaja Herszberg, Awraham Chaim Bekerman, Chaim Szloma Kohen Adler, Lejbusz Liberman, Szmuel Fejwel Ladowski; Szachna son of Dow Priwlan, Cwi Tenwurcel, Doberisz Bimka, Awraham Icak Zylbersztajn, Mordechai Josef Wajcman, Nota Gotman; Jakob Szlomo Moszkowicz, Jom-Tow Lipa Cwi Kaminer; Hersz Mordechai Granek, Awraham Ladowski, Icak Mejer Szajnfeld, Szmuel Aharon Garfinkel, Elazar Kohen, Berl Elencwajg, Jakob Josef son of the Gaon Rabbi Doidislaw, Cwi Hersz Grinszpan son of Rabbi I., Chaim Jehuda Ajzenberg, Zew Wolf Holejner; Szmuel Jegier; Szlomo Zalman Brak; Cwi Arje Albert; Izrael Mejer Heszel Goldberg, Elimelech Zylbersztajn, Chaim Szydlowski, Chanoch Henich Kaminer, Berl Sztrozberg; Szmul Gat; Nete Zew Wajsbaum, Izrael Ajzik Kind; Jakob Manela; Reuwen Edelsztajn, Dawid Garfinkel, Eli Mejer Chmelosz.

[Page-164]

We the leaders of our congregation, may God protect it, confirm and stand by the signatures of our congregants and with God's will the crown of Torah may it live long and prosperously in our city and his honor will be revealed to us, then all those who have not signed below will come to sign their names. Mosze Menachem Menli Hakohe Fefer, Elija' Naftali Ajzenberg, Mosze Chaim Kaminer, Icak Becalel son of the late rabbi Dawid may the memory of a righteous man be for a blessing, the head of the rabbinical court of here in Kielce.

Formulation of the Regulations Instituted by Rabbi Jerusalimski Regulations for "Melamdim" [Teachers of Children]

We the teachers of this community of Kielce accept upon us with an oath and solemn obligation to go about the matters of education with faithfulness as it has been the custom in the Diaspora of Israel from generation to generation and not to combine into any unions or union and not to institute any new regulations that had not been the custom up until now, except if there should be something between us we will bring a witness before the Rabbi, the Gaon, the head of the rabbinical court may he live many long and prosperous years and his court and they will arbitrate between us.

In addition we hereby accept upon ourselves with the agreement of the Gaon head of the rabbinical court may his candle shine, and that of his court that no "Melamed" should go to the householders on matters of education before the holiday, that is, from the interim days of the holiday at all. – All this we accept upon us of our free will without any insistence or force upon us to follow the aforesaid with all our strength.

And the signatories Tuesday, the portion of "Nitzavim-Vayelech" 5666 [Autumn, 1906] here in Kielce. Hilel Oberman, Jehuda Judel Rotszild, Lajbel Gertner, Jechiel Dawid Chroberski; Simcha Bunem Wirzewa; Berisz Beker, Mordechai Mendel son of the Righteous Arbiter of Chmielnik, Naftali Ajzenberg, Jakob Cukerman, Mordechai Charendorf, Zew Fuks, Menachem Mendel Bornsztajn; Zisza Biderman; Lajbusz Mendel; Luft; Mordechai Goldszmid, Zelig Grinszpan; Baruch Szaul Roterband; Jehoszua Szlomo Leszec; Jedidja Gnat, Motel Szternszos; Wolf Horwicz, Icak Mosze Gut, Baruch Auerbach, Mordechai Malianski, Mordechai Menachem Gepner.

When there were additional "melameds" in our city who had not yet signed the regulation and holy obligation and solemn oath of a letter which had been written on the other side of the page on Tuesday, the portion of "Nitzavim-Vayelech" 5666, they gathered at the command of the rabbi, head of the rabbinical court all of the "melameds" who had been added at the end of Elul in the year 5671, the portion of "Nitzavim-Vayelech" on Tuesday, Wednesday and Thursday [Autumn, 1911] to his rabbinical court and they are all the signatories below and they accept upon themselves with solemn oath with all force and authority all of these regulations, which are elucidated on the other side of the page without any change at all and all was done with good will and the agreement of the rabbi and his court.

Signed on this day here in Kielce.

[Page-165]

The Baker's Regulation

We the bakers of here in Kielce who have signed below have gathered together in the matter of a mitzvah and taken upon ourselves not to make leavening or dough on the holy Sabbath nor to prepare on the holy Sabbath other needs of baking, such as to heat up water on the Sabbath for baking during the week. The general principle is to be careful in the matter of observing the holy Sabbath in the bakeries even by non-Jews. And only to start the entire activity of the baking on Saturday night after the time of Havdala. And all this we accept with the ban and oath of the rabbi may he live a long and prosperous life and his rabbinical court and it is forbidden to us to do anything underhanded to cause preparation of leavening and any of the remainder of the labor of baking be done on the holy Sabbath, but contrariwise, that we are each obligated to observe one another carefully that each should be careful in the bakeries with regard to the commandments of the holy Sabbath in all of its details.

And this we shall do of our own good will without any release in the world and we have read over the above material and with this we sign below on Wednesday, the 24th of the reckoning of the children of Israel, AT"R of this community of Kielce.

> Signature of Mosze Goldblum
> Signature of Elazar Godfrid
> Signature of Josef Wasser
> Signature of Baruch Sternzys
> Signature of Izrael Icak Boruchowicz
> Signature of Mejer Micnmacher

After the death of the Rabbi Gaon M.N. Jerusalimski Z"L, all the members of the community turned their eyes towards the son of their first rabbi, Rabbi Gutman HaKohen Z"L, Rabbi Awraham Abele, who was a witness to the death of Rabbi Jerusalimski Z"L, head of the rabbinical court in the Kielce community.

The Rapaport family, a rabbinical family, descendants of a line of Gaonim, sent its glories to many communities of Israel, and was a home for Torah and elevated virtues. And without any objection from any side whatsoever, Rabbi Abele Z"L took the throne of the rabbinate in the Kielce community.

All members of the congregation respected and admired their rabbi, Rabbi Abele. He spread his wings over all parts of the community without consideration for their party affiliation. While he himself was pious and strict, he was not a zealot, and would embrace the free thinker with the same affection and love with which he embraced the Chassid and the observant. His method was: "Not by fire, and not with the noise of God, but with a small still voice".

In these times, he would say, when neglect has grown and the overthrowing of the yoke of Torah and commandments has spread so much, there is no place for zealotry. Zealotry will add strength to the flame, oil to the fire. Therefore he was also non-political; he wanted his influence to reach all parts of the congregation. In fact, his heart leaned also towards "Agudat Yisra'el" and also towards Zionism, especially, to that part of it that rallied to the banner of the Torah. Willingly he allowed every preacher, speaker, propagandist and Zionist activist to speak in the synagogue. There was an incident when even Icak Grinbaum, despite his anti-religiousness, spoke in the synagogue when he visited Kielce.

He didn't want to become involved in the rivalry between the parties who were scurrying around the Jewish streets, and would say: since every party seeks the nation's welfare, this chooses one way and this chooses another; in the end, the ways will unite – and from all of them the people's redemption will come forth. Therefore he was affectionate to everyone; everyone pronounced the name of our Rabbi Abele with a sort of fondness that also had a little pride in it that the Kielce community had merited that such a rabbi, comfortable with heaven and comfortable with people, should stand at its head.

[Page-166]

HGR"A Rapaport, may the memory of a righteous man be for a blessing

His sermons and speeches matched the qualities of his soul. In his sermons, he did not preach morality with a voice of fire and brimstone, with threats and punishments; but would spread out the words of our sages like a dress, show, with good taste, the great light that continues to shine forth from our holy Torah; he would reveal the elevated morality that is a part of the practical commandments; he would explain to his listeners the holiness with which the Torah inspires any Jew who studies it for its own sake; he would prove with graceful words that the end goal of the rules of the Torah is to elevate people above materialism and brutishness and to instill good qualities in them.

His words and sermons contained moral notions through which he attempted to influence his listeners, who would arrive at the synagogue in great crowds on the days when he was preaching a sermon to the members of his congregation.

He would appear also as the featured speaker. As the local rabbi, as the spiritual shepherd of his community it was his duty to participate in the prayers that were held in the synagogue on holidays for the welfare of the state and the welfare of its rulers. At these opportunities the rabbi charmed those gathered there, among whom were also representatives of the authorities, with his speeches, which were lovely in form and sublime in content. Among his words one could discern the flowering of elegant style and national pride was also evident.

It was a wonder to many that this rabbi, who devoted all his time to the study of the Torah, found time to also adopt a modern style and knowledge about the world just like the authors and speakers who did this for a profession.

This is the spiritual figure of our rabbi, a figure full of grace and simplicity, with whom people were comfortable.

Also the members of his rabbinical court were suited to his temperament. He influenced them with his exemplary personality. He was their model in the way he behaved towards the plaintiffs and defendants who came to him with their arguments and disagreements. Rabbi Alter Horberg, who was called "Alter who hands down decisions" and was an excellent sermonizer, studious and well versed in the treasures of the Torah, and Rabbi Herszel Grinszpan, a modest Chassid, but full to the brim with the Talmudic discussions of Abayeh and Rava and in halachic decisions were outstanding members of his rabbinical court.

On matters of license and prohibition [*heter ve issur*] Rabbi Abele Z"L took the part of those who advocated lenience, he took the property of the Jews into account, lest it be lost.

[Page-167]

The land of Israel was his passion; he yearned to send first his son to the land of Israel, so that he might make a place there for him as well and in this matter he contacted the chief rabbi of Tel-Aviv, Rabbi Ami'el Z"L, asking him to aid in obtaining him a certificate. However, in the meantime, the war broke out and the fate of his community was his fate as well. The long chain of rabbis, of which Rabbi Awraham Abele HaKohen was an important link – was terminated.

The Admo"rs of Kielce

The Kielce community grew, developed materially and spiritually. What did it lack? The holiness of righteous men was lacking, heavenly pious men. The community needed the Admo"rs to sanctify the place. And indeed the community began to attract the righteous from nearby locales and they came to instill honor in the growing community and spread the rays of their glory directly upon the members of the congregation and sanctified the place and its inhabitants.

The first to arrive in Kielce was the Admo"r from Checiny, Rabbi Chaim Szmuel HaLevi Horowicz Z"L. I will write down his elevated lineage below:

One)   this righteous rabbi was the son of the holy Rabbi Elazar, Z"L.

Two) son of the holy Rabbi Cwi Hersz, who guided the holy flock in Lublin after his father.

Three) son of the righteous and holy rabbi who was well known as the "Chozeh of Lublin" [the Seer of Lublin] exemplar of his generation Rabbi Jakob Icak Halewi Horowicz may the memory of a righteous man be for a blessing. And so on until the family of our rabbi, the holy author of the "Shnei Luchot Habrit" [The Two Stone Tablets]. On his mother's side, the Admo"r of Checiny was a grandson of the holy Rabbi Josef Epsztajn from the new city – Neu Stadt – who was known by the name "the Good Jew" – "Der Guter Jud", who was the son of the famous righteous rabbi, exemplar of his generation Kalonymus Kalman Epsztajn, who led the chassidic community in the holy community of Krakow, author of the commentary on the Torah called "Ma'or VaShemesh".

The Admo"r of Checiny had many Chassidim in the cities of Poland who gathered around him. His sons and grandsons as well were crowned with the crown of Admo"r and became famous and well-known Admo"rs in their own right, and hundreds and thousands of Chassidim flocked to them as well.

The Admo"r of Checiny was a unique personality. He occupied himself with the revealed more than with the hidden [mysticism]. He would say: "The hidden things are for God and the revealed things are for us…etc." [Deuteronomy 29/28].

[Page-168]

He would not speak "Torah" during a meal, as is the custom among the Admo"rs. He revealed his innovations and discoveries in the secrets of the Torah only to special individuals who were worthy of it, whose minds absorbed the hidden aspects of the Torah, and with them he would seclude himself for hours; and they would publicize the greatness of their rabbi among the people. Even to Chassidim whose level was not so high, he was none-the-less a pillar of fire at whose light they warmed themselves. He influenced them with his brief pronouncements that were full of ethics. And in general he taught the paths of worshiping God to his audience of admirers by means of his behavior and habits.

He was fond of Torah scholars with his whole heart; when he saw a young man of talent who persevered in his studies he would make him an intimate and debate matters of Abaye and Raba [talmudic sages] with him as if they were contemporaries.

He was the only Admo"r of his time, if I'm not mistaken, in Poland, who had a subscription to the newspaper "HaTzefira". Aside from the regular issues of the newspaper he also received all of the supplements: the books of CZ"S [Chaim Selig Slonimsky] and N"S [Nachum Sokolow]. One of his young aides, Motel Pinies, or "Bochur", as the rebbe called him, brought him the newspaper from the post office everyday at eleven a.m.. His opponents, the Gur Chassidim, gossiped about him, saying that he was bringing heretical words into his home, however he paid no attention to their vexing words, and continued to read the Hebrew press. Those close to him excused this custom of his, which was difficult for them as well – could one read the words of CZ"S and N"S, which were considered heretics, - yet they themselves would open the "Yad HaChazaka" of Maimonides and take out the page on which the proof of CZ"S to a holy chapter was printed this month – but, they would say, the rebbe suffers from constipation and he spends a lot of time in the "house of honor", and so that he doesn't in the meantime think of words of the Torah, he read the news of the day in the newspaper which occupied his mind and thus he didn't think about holy words in such a place.

Whatever the reason and the explanation – reading "HaTzefira" and intelligent articles of CZ"S gave the rebbe of Checiny information about the world at large and also about the sciences. The rebbe would state in advance, for instance, when a solar or lunar eclipse would be. The innocent Chassidim, when they heard from their rabbi that on such-and-such a date and at such-and-such a time there would be a solar eclipse, or on a certain night – a lunar eclipse, partial or full, were amazed and ascribed this information to the divine inspiration that hovered over their rabbi. These innocents didn't realize that the rebbe drew his information from the newspaper that he read.

The court of the Admo"r in Checiny was notable among the other buildings of the city. Along the southern wall of the rebbe's house there was a garden in which there was hut in which the rebbe would sit during the summer days and learn Torah without being disturbed. The sounds of songbirds would mix with the sound of the Torah, which came forth and went up from within the hut and made a wonderful harmony.

The inner workings of his home were arranged in good taste. The rebbe had a special sense of beauty. The furnishings of the house and the table settings were according to the newest fashion. And in general, his manner, his clothing gave off a special charm.

[Page-169]

His Chassidim, those who lived in his home and his aides knew the attributes of their rabbi who was very strict about the qualities in which Torah scholars excel; therefore they attempted to sooth his mind with a nice apartment, with elegant vessels. They also arranged for him to have a special mikve [ritual pool] in his yard. It was very deep. Fifty steps led down into it. The water in it was clear and cold as ice.

This Admo"r had a magnificent carriage and he drove it like one of the counts.

After the fire that broke out in Checiny and which destroyed half of the houses in the village, including the house of the Admo"r, the rebbe moved his dwelling place to Kielce. However, from that time the breadth of thinking left him. He did not find the comfort, and particularly the quiet and restfulness that he needed in the new place.

Kielce had the honor of housing the Admo"r of Checiny for only a few years. During World War I he passed away. In 5676 on the 18th day of Tevet [December, 1915], his soul departed in purity. Thousands of admirers from the area came to his funeral, among them rabbis, leaders of the community. There was a great mourning in the city. On this day the shops were closed; everyone ceased their labor and came out of respect for their rabbi, who had, in his lifetime, been an advisor, a shield and a patron to them. Over his grave his Chassidim built a "tent" in which they set a memorial stone upon which they engraved the following words [the initial letters in Hebrew spell out his name]:

> Hoi, my father, hoi holy trunk, my chariot and knight!
> Tens of thousands of Israel will come here and cry out,
> With bitter weeping call: Hoi my genius and holy one!
> Wailing: Hoi generous one! Hoi our suns have gone out!
> Have mercy on the meek, the ill and the distressed.
> They despair of life, of every physician and advisor,
> They will bring their bones to you, the pressure and the burden.
> Hurry to save them from every illness.
> Sunk in its abominations, thus begins the illnesses of the soul
> Then hurry to come to the shade of his holiness, -
> And you will be relieved and drawn out of trembling and filth;
> Even washing their foreheads to save them.
> To the thousands of Chassidim and those of bitter spirit aside from them

With prayer he offered them redemption, advice and strength;
Try a miracle and a sign and save them from their trouble,
Remove them to well being and turn trouble to redemption.
Many did he turn from sin and return to truth,
To his work, holy worship an enthusiastic soul.
Shot his arrows at them until they went
Until they threw out their abominations and dressed in humility,
Glowing in the light of faith, in the light of the awe of heaven,
He enthused the hearts and souls of Israel and sanctified them.
Righteous Ones are called alive even in death.
To this Tent of Meeting will go forth all who seek God. [TBCV"H]
May his soul be bundled in the bundle of life

[Page-170]

And every year on the anniversary of his death, hundreds of Chassidim and admirers come to the grave of their righteous one, light candles and leave notes upon the tombstone and give "redemptions" to his widow, the Rebbetzin, the righteous woman, who lived many years after her husband's death.

The Kielce cemetery was significantly elevated by the "tent" of the first Tzaddik that was established there. The soil of Kielce was honored that in its dust a pure and holy body lay, and with this the city, which had earlier been considered an impure city by other Jews, was also sanctified.

After the death of the Admo"r of Checiny the Chassidim crowned the son of the deceased Z"L, Rabbi Eliezer, to take his place. His eldest brother, Rabbi Heszel was appointed to the rabbinical seat in the city of Olkusz during their father's lifetime.

However the rebbe Rabbi Eliezer didn't live long, the war years impoverished the house of the Admo"r, shortage was a constant visitor to his family. At this proximity to the battlefront, which was close to Kielce, the support of the Chassidim ceased. Although the homeowners in the city sent their donations to nourish the rebbe's house, but "the pinch did not satisfy the lion", and donations could not supply the wants of a house with many people in it. The rebbe's house, which in former days had been generously fed began to slide down and down. And the rebbe, Rabbi Eliezer, died on the even of Shavuot, 5679 [1919], and his honorable rest is in his father's tent, and upon his tombstone the following words were engraved:

Beloved and pleasant in their lives
Death cleaved and connected the holiness of both;
A righteous man has been lost from Israel, and a man of God from humanity
Heart rends the space, for the pious have lost their honor
Water shall drip from every eyelid, and the cry of God's congregation be
    borne
For a righteous one and leader of thousands has fallen in Israel
Qualities and attributes cry out, who will guide us in the future?
Our rabbi, a man of goodness, who will allow us to hear your pleasant words?
    Hurry his candle
His chimneys are seen to be darkened
The sky is overcast and his sons are extinguished.
Wisdom is here, old age is not, for this our hearts are woe!
The days of his life are a garden, from the garden of Torah order he has gone

> to his Garden of Eden.
>
> The day of the eve of Shavuot, year of "Ateret" [acronym of year rearranged means "crown"], the crown has been removed from our heads.
>
> 49 to the counting he prepared himself in purity to receive your Torah.
>
> Heavens – be destitute, may the earth grieve, for there is no defender in our midst
>
> What shall I testify? How shall I console thee? For as great as the sea have we lost
>
> And all those who know of his righteousness and beloved attributes call out.
>
> A tombstone is too small to contain his good deeds.
>
> May his merit stand forever, and that of his holy forefathers.
>
> The memory of righteous and holy ones as a pleasant incense, as a sacrifice. Who comes to the tent and his soul speaks, the prayer and the merciful one will raise his redemption.

[Page-171]

After the death of the Admo"r the Chassidim crowned the brother of the deceased, Rabbi Szalom; but he too didn't live long. In 5680, the 18th of Cheshvan [Autumn, 1919], he died and they dug him a grave in the tent of his father and upon his tombstone the following is engraved:

> The earth shook on the day that the guards of the house of martyrs perspired,
>
> His lesson was completeness and staying with his deeds of holiness, they were the glory of martyrs
>
> Son of his father and an authority on the three sections of the Torah, from a lineage from the holy of holies
>
> A great and holy prince and righteous man has fallen, in a family of holy sheep.
>
> The skies darkened, flickered and went out; who controls his commandments in the earth and heavens.
>
> The grace of his awe, the uniqueness of his respectful action, his sanctification to the God of the heavens.
>
> Roaring, shaking, and calling out his loss to the Jews.
>
> Those who accompany the righteous and who crowd together in the shade of holy ones.
>
> May his merit protect us, he went up to the heights in the midst of his days.
>
> The memory of righteous and holy ones above to the heavens elevated father and sons.

After the death of Rabbi Szalom, his brother-in-law Rabbi Icak Szlomo Z"L was elevated to the position of Admo"r. However, during his life his glory fled, the magnificence of the house of the Admo"r of Checiny was deflected. It continued to exist; yet this existence was already miserly and unknown. The generations had changed; the younger generation did not flock after the Chassidim. The courts of the great Admo"rs pulled he congregations of Chassidim to their centers. For the less valued among the Admo"rs only the elderly artisans and old women were left, who supported the houses of the Admo"rs with their redemptions and donations.

Of the grandsons of the Admo"r of Checiny may the memory of a righteous man be for a blessing, the most well known are: the Admo"r of Piaseczna, the son of the Admo"r of Grodzisk Z"L, and the Admo"r of Pilc [Pilica], the son of Rabbi Eliezer Z"L; both of them perished in the days of the Shoah that overtook Polish Jewry.

The Admo"r Rabbi Motele Twerski z"l

The Admo"r Rabbi Motele Twerski also came to settle in Kielce as well, who was known as "The Rebbe of Kuzmir". He was:

One) the son of Rabbi Awraham, the Magid of Trisk, author of "Magen Avraham".

Two) the son of Rabbi Morechai Motel, the Magid of Czernobyl, author of "Likutei Torah".

Three) the son of Rabbi Menachem Nachum, the Magid of Czernobyl, author of the book "Ma'or Einayim".

Four) the son of Rabbi Cwi Hersz

Five) the son of Rabbi Nachum Gaon.

[Page-172]

Rabbi Twerski

This Admo"r was a totally different character than the Admo"r of Checiny. The Tzaddik Rabbi Motele Z"L mostly dealt with mysticism. His teachings were filled with acrostics and gematrias. His Chassidim were noted not for their studiousness but for their enthusiasm in worshiping God; their prayers were extremely devout. Also their feasts to celebrate a mitzvah – had an element of divine worship in them. Prayer, song, eating and drinking – everything for them was a kind of holy service. In every action and endeavor one must direct one's intention. In every word, in every letter and symbol – in everything there are secrets and mysteries. A person must always take care lest he damage the upper worlds, God forbid, by a foreign thought, a careless word or a dishonest action.

This rebbe was very careful of purity, purity of the body and soul. He would lecture to those who came to him with "notes" of great redemption. A blessing, request for mercy for someone ill would cost those who needed them a high price. He gave no aid for free, it was difficult to get even advice out of him without paying for it.

Many were amazed at this manner of his. They would ask: "For whom is he hoarding the money? He has no sons? Perhaps, his admirers said, that there is a deeper intention hidden in this policy. The rebbe said that a man who has some desire, a request from God, and who cannot make a sacrifice of money for this thing he is requesting, this is a sign that his request isn't serious, since it isn't worth it to him to sacrifice even a small part of his money for it, therefore, he isn't worthy of the blessing or the request for mercy on his behalf. "God is close to all who call him, to all who call him truly," says the Scripture [Psalms 145/18]. This addition "to all who call him truly" comes to instruct us that the call must be from the soul and spirit and not just with the mouth, for then the blessing and the prayer will be for naught.

[Page-173]

The "redemption" the rebbe received was not for his own benefit. He himself was satisfied with little, but for the good of the petitioner. "A pure and broken heart, God, won't despise". The thought, the true and serious intent do their work and do not return empty handed.

No one knew for what purposes he used the redemption monies. But after his death, when the Chassidim went to search in the drawers of his closets, to find the treasure, the hoard, which he left behind him, they found barely anything.

The clowns in the city said that one of his Chassidim, who slept in the house of his rabbi at the time he died, had taken the treasures, which were hidden in a place known to him, without anyone noticing.

A tent for the Admo"r of Kuzmir Z"L was built in the Kielce cemetery as well, the land next to the graves of the holy ones gained sharply in value, for many wished their bones to be laid next to the righteous ones after their death and jumped upon the plots which were next to their tents.

The Admo"r of Pinczow

At the beginning of the war, the Admo"r of Pinczow, Rabbi Chaim Mejer Finkler, brother of the holy Rabbi Hilel of Radoszyce arrived in Kielce. The two were the sons of the rabbi Gaon Rabbi Icak, who was the son-in-law of the holy rabbi the famous exemplary Rabbi Isachar Ber of Radoszyce. The Admo"r of Pinczow was a genius of Torah, of the revealed and the hidden. A righteous man, foundation of the world, he fasted and mortified himself for decades. He composed many articles on mysticism. He did not live long in his new dwelling place. He died on the 29th of Shevat 5677 [1917]. A tent was set up in the cemetery for this Admo"r as well.

After his death, his place was taken by his son, the righteous rabbi Eliezer. A few years before the outbreak of the war he moved his household to Sosnowiec, where he died in 5696 [1936]. This Admo"r had two sons, well known public activists in Kielce. The elder, Rabbi Pinchas (Pinja), a scholar and man of excellent attributes who later took his father's place, and the younger, Rabbi Icak.

When parties were established in Israel, the Finkler brothers devoted themselves to public-party activity, Rabbi Pinja Finkler turned to the right and was active in "Agudat Yisra'el" which was founded in Kielce at the time. Rabbi Icak Finkler turned a bit to the left and became a Zionist, a "Mizrachi" Zionist.

[Page-174]

The two brothers began competing with one another; when Rabbi Icak founded the "Mizrachi" cheder, called "Yavneh"; Rabbi Pinja founded the "Yesodei Torah" cheder. One recruited souls for the "Yavneh" cheder and the other for the "Yesodei Torah" cheder.

At the community elections they both appeared on different lists, one on the list of the ultra-Orthodox and the other on the Zionist list. And since they were in the first places on the lists of candidates, they were both elected to the community council. And there the two brothers would knock heads over public affairs. The elder brother would demand that the community authority pay attention only to the religious needs of the Jewish inhabitants of Kielce; the younger brother, contrariwise, demanded that the community authority take care of all public matters and needs, aside from local matters, which took first place in the tasks of the community, the council must also notice national affairs, allot financial budgets to the Zionist funds, aid and support the impoverished pioneers who were planning on moving to the Land of Israel, etc.

The tongue of Icak Finkler, who was active in party affairs from his youth, was quite acute. In debates he would speak at length. When he spoke about the tasks of the community he would lecture the council members about his demands for the entire group that had sent him.

His words, which were spoken with tremendous enthusiasm and with incredible pathos, influenced their audience, especially the gallery, which gathered to hear the arguments at the meetings of the community council, which had been elected democratically. Their ears heard things that until then had never been heard within the walls of the community building.

**The righteous Rabbi Eliezer Finkler,
may the memory of a righteous man be for a blessing**

[Page-175]

In his energy, in his fierce desire and with the help of the representatives of the artisans union he was able to institute new procedures in the community authority, to entirely change its face.

In general, the younger Finkler was a man of initiative and energy. When he was planning to execute some endeavor, he did not rest or sit quiet until he had brought the matter to fruition.

To a certain extent he had an influence on the formation of the public life in Kielce during the years after World War I. He was one of the enthusiastic supporters of I. Grinbaum in his project to create a bloc of national minorities in the Polish Siem and conducted energetic propaganda during the elections to the Polish Siem in favor of the national list. Rabbi Icak Finkler was the type of activist who cannot remain limited in a narrow sphere, and who seeks activities with a grand scope; he desired to break out of his frameworks; however his strengths were concentrated and his abilities limited. Every time the desire awoke in him to take off to new heights, his wings were clipped and he remained in his place. This was the tragedy of his life, as he once confessed to the writer of these lines. Aside from this, he was oppressed by loneliness. He would eat at the table of his father, the Admo"r, he hadn't a family of his own, no wife, no children. After the death of his father, the Admo"r, his fans and those who followed his advice began to treat him like a man of influence and an Admo"r.

The Admo"r Rabbi Dawid Goldman (the Rebbe of Chmielnik)

A third Admo"r lived and was active in Kielce, the Rebbe of Chmielnik of the Goldman family. This Admo"r was the son-in-law of the Gaon Rabbi Awraham, head of the rabbinical court of the holy congregation of Bialobrzegi, son of the Gaon Rabbi Jeszaja of Prague and the grandson of the righteous holy rabbi, exemplar of the generation Rabbi Icak, the old Rebbe of Worki.

Aside from his ancestral lineage he also had his own lineage. He was a great scholar and was blessed with generous and exemplary attributes.

In his youth he was a merchant and owner of the "Radislaw" estate. However, the outstanding Chassidim of Worka had their eyes on him, they recognized his holiness and began treating him like a man of inspiration. They turned to him in times of trouble, gave him notes and redemptions, learned gracious attributes from him and the ways of worshipping God.

Finally, he moved his dwelling to Kielce, bought himself a house on Neue Welt Street and began holding "tables" like one of the great Admo"rs. As a merchant, he was well versed in the ways of commerce; therefore, for the most part, merchants would turn to him to consult with him about their business affairs.

One of his sons, Rabbi Jeszaja'le was a rabbi in the nearby city of Bosk [Busko-Zdroj], known for its healing springs. His second son, Rabbi Mendel, continued to work in commerce, he was a merchant of "Finland" wrapping paper. He died in a train accident near Lublin during World War I and was buried in Lublin. The Admo"r of Chmielnik died in 5684 on the 16th of Cheshvan [Fall, 1923]. after the death of the Admo"r, his son, the rabbi from Bosk came to Kielce to take his place. His grandson, Simcha Bunem, the son of Rabbi Mendel Goldman Z"L, was elected, a few years before World War II, as chairman of the Jewish community committee in Kielce.

[Page-176]

These Admo"rs were famous to a well known degree even outside of their own regions and they had an influence upon broad circles of admirers. Aside from them, Admo"rs of lesser weight also came to settle in Kielce, who did not so much influence as they were influenced. All of their merit was the merit of their forefathers. On the strength of this merit they were granted the title "Tzadik" and received notes and redemptions mainly from women, who were not used to discriminating between one "Tzadik" and another. They would congregate around the gates of the "Tzadiks", whose managers and aides knew how to spread miracles among the masses of the people.

The Admo"r of Suchedniow

The Admo"r of Suchedniow also came to live in Kielce. Suchedniow was a small settlement which was no longer a village, but not yet a city. During World War I living in small places was dangerous because of their proximity to the battlefront, which kept moving from place to place.

It was especially difficult for the Admo"rs to live in rural cities. They got most of their income from "redemptions" that people from other places donated to them. However, during the war, travel was restricted and the income of the "righteous ones" suffered as a result; therefore, they moved their dwellings to the large city which had a major concentration of Jews. In the large cities there was more security for one's life as well as more readily available income.

The righteous Rabbi E. Rabinowicz of Suchedniow

[Page-177]

The Admo"r of Suchedniow of the Rabinowicz family was descended to Rabbi Natan Dawid, the Admo"r of Szydlowiec, and his lineage even reached Rabbi Jakob Icak of Przysucha, famous as the Holy Jew.

He married off his eldest son, Natan Rabinowicz, to the daughter of a wealthy man from Checiny named Mosze Szif. This wealthy man, who had accumulated a great amount from the grain trade, was known all over the region as a great miser. He had a large estate next to Kielce called "Markowizna", and a large steam mill. He also had a stone house and garden in Kielce.

Mr. Szif had an only daughter, who stood to inherit this entire fortune. Since he wished his fortune to be in faithful hands, he married his daughter to the son of the Rabbi of Suchedniow.

After the death of the wealthy man, his son-in-law inherited his entire fortune. The family of the heir was great. His wife was blessed in the fruit of her womb. His household expenses were great. The rabbi's son was not at all capable of managing the estate economy. His servants became wealthy at his expense. The fortune, which his father-in-law accumulated over decades grew smaller and smaller. Rabbi Natan began to work in commerce; however, he was not successful at this either, he sank into debt, and in order to pay off his creditors he began selling off parcels of his great estate.

After his father's death, he saw no other way but to take the place of the deceased, to be crowned with the crown of "Rebbe", and he was a studious man of character.

Kielce received into its gates the Tzadik Rabbi Ozer Awraham Josef of Rakow as well. He was of the same family as the Admo"r of Suchedniow, the Rabinowicz family.

In the line of Admo"rs who chose Kielce as their seat, this Admo"r stands towards the end. He had no Chassidim worthy of the name. Country people came to ask his opinion and to lay before him the troubles of their heart and to request a cure for all of their ills. Righteous women were his main admirers and would bring him their redemptions. They said: "For he is a Tzadik from a line of Tzadiks, and he has the power to save."

On the 24th of Iyar, 5685 [Spring, 1925], the Tzadik of Rakow died. His eldest son, Rabbi Cemach put on the cloak of Admo"r after his father's death. For every affliction and every trouble that might come he had a special cure. A book of cures, he said, which he received in an inheritance from his holy ancestors. He used these cures the way a physician might use a medical text, and on the strength of them he performed wonders and signs.

Aside from these people mentioned, Rebbe Lajbeniew Twersky was in Kielce. He was from the famous family of the Czernobyl Admo"rs, which drew its lineage from Rabbi Nachum of Czernobyl. Rabbi Lajbeniew was the son-in-law of the wealthy man of Kielce, Reb' Chaim Kaner, a merchant in leather and overshoes, this merchant was an enthusiastic Chassid who crowded into the shade of the Rebbe of Kuzmir. He had an only daughter and he married her to the son of holy ones.

His son-in-law was a man who enjoyed life. He did not mortify himself with fasting. He kept the saying of the sages: "A man will yet have to answer for not taking pleasure in the things he saw with his eyes." Therefore he would spend most of the hours of the day on the rules of the meal in the company of young Chassidim who wished to worship God with joy.

[Page-178]

Even after the death of his wife, he remained in Kielce in the home of his father-in-law in order to educate his orphaned daughter.

After a short time, he married the daughter of another wealthy man, the daughter of Mejerczik of Dzialoszyce. Then he left the home of his former father-in-law for an apartment of his own and began to behave like and Admo"r, as the next in line of Rabbi Motele Z"L.

His name immediately gained repute in the area and Chassidim began flocking to Rabbi Lajbeniew, to the Kielcer Rebbe. Afterwards, he also traveled to America. The American Jewish newspapers gave him a lot of publicity. This trip overseas brought him much blessing.

With this Rebbe Lajbeniew the line of Admo"rs that Kielce housed in its midst is ended.

On their account the Jewish population of Kielce was increased; they attracted the inhabitants of the surroundings into their circle by virtue of their holiness, and they gave the Kielce community a unique form, because the added their own characteristics to its general shape.

Formerly, Kielce was considered an unclean city. The appearance of the righteous men within its walls sanctified it and gave it an added gravity, which acted upon certain circles of the surrounding communities.

Kielce continued to grow at the expense of the small communities, which shrank socially and culturally.

Chassidim, Scholars and Men of Action

Let us mention here the names of several of the outstanding Chassidim and the excellent scholars, who were worthy of the name and title with which their fellow citizens crowned them. Their piousness and studiousness were not superficial, just for show, but they represented the true Chassidic type. In their Torah, in their divine service, in their business affairs, in their behavior in their own homes it was evident that their souls were hewn from a noble world. They didn't use the cloak of Chassidism and the label of the Torah in order to browbeat others; but, on the contrary, in order to benefit others, to serve as an example of a Jew who is whole in his qualities. Zealousness was far from their hearts. They never participated in activities that could cause dissent; they did not annoy their opponents, but tried to draw near them and influence them. They did not push among those who leapt to the head of the congregation; they were withdrawn, modest, their entire honor was in hidden things.

[Page-179]

Rabbi Emanuel Sowkower

Rabbi Emanuel was one of the greatest of the true Chassidim and of the great Torah scholars. A man who adopted the qualities of his teacher, Rabbi Mejer Jechiel of Ostrowiec ZTZ"L. He enjoyed this world little. He and his family lived in poverty and want. But his soul was glad, a smile was always playing about his lips. The pleasures of life were strange to him, for he found the satisfaction of his soul in the innovations of the Torah. For him, the affairs of the Torah were the pinnacle of pleasure in life. The rest of the affairs of the world with all of the material pleasures and enjoyments were mere vanity in his eyes, empty of meaning, that are can only distract the mind from the true pleasure, which he found at moments when some difficult matter in the Gemara became clear to him or he thought of a way to mitigate some severity of Maimonides.

He was beloved by people, for they saw in him a man whose soul is pure and elevated above other Torah scholars. He truly learned Torah for its own sake, since he saw in it the purpose of man.

Rabbi Jechiel Szajnfeld

Rabbi Jechiel was a textile merchant, an agent of Poznanski, owner of a large factory of textiles in Lodz.

Rabbi Jechiel was the son-in-law of Rabbi Judel Kaminer of Checiny, the father in law of the Admo"r of Gur, author of the "Sfat Emet", ZTZ"L. Of course he was an outstanding Gur Chassid. Aside from his lineage, he was the son of a respected family, and was himself an exemplary man. A great scholar, well read in all of the treasures of the great sea of the Talmud and spent nights and days on affairs of the Torah and divine service, on prayer, purity and attempted to everything in a whole manner. He would scatter charity as much as he could. He especially supported Torah scholars.

In the city he was considered an upright man, who regarded the money of others as dearly as his own. He was careful in his speech, lest a falsehood escape his mouth even by accident. With these qualities he acquired the trust of the members of his faith and those who were not members of his faith. Poznanski the manufacturer entrusted him with goods worth one hundred thousand rubles; and he was certain that he was putting them in trustworthy hands, for a man like Jechiel Szajnfeld would not be irresponsible with the money of strangers.

All the members of the community, whether Chassidim or enlightened, respected him, even though he himself ran away from honor.

The director of the Lodz bank branch in Kielce, Mr. Merber, said: "I respect the opinions and outlook of Mr. Szajnfeld, for they are serious and are not just for show."

"I," he continued to say, "according to my education, according to my social status, even because of my knowledge cannot be of one mind with him; however this does not prevent me from respecting the opinions of others, when I see that they are a part of their essence, they flow from the root of their soul, and there isn't any hypocrisy or counterfeit in them."

With these attributes and other excellent characteristics Jechiel Szajnfeld Z"L acquired the affection of all the inhabitants of the city. Even his opponents didn't dare to insult his honor.

[Page-180]

Rabbi Szmuel Hakatan [the Small]

Among the Gur Chassidim Rabbi Szmuel Hagerman was also notable, and he was called "Szmuel HaKatan". He passed away in middle age.

This was a type of unique Chassid, he stood out in his retirement from the matters of this world; his eyes were always cast down to the ground so that he not, God forbid, look at a woman. His side-locks were wet from the waters of the mikveh [ritual bath], for his was very careful in immersion and purity. His heart was full of love and affection for every Jew and he was always ready to help anyone needy with his own money and with charity he collected from others, who were moved to open their hands and give their donations by his words which came from the heart. He could not imagine that a man could eat and be satisfied, could fill his own belly when another was suffering from hunger.

And therefore one could often see Rabbi Szmuel HaKatan walking around and collecting charity in order to satisfy the soul of hungry people, to purchase necessary medicines for impoverished ill people, to host guests. He himself observed the saying of the Mishnaic sage: "All whose actions are greater than his wisdom – his wisdom will last." He was not satisfied with the study of Torah alone, but wanted to keep the intent of the Torah, to multiply charity, mercy and tenderness among human beings. He was also beloved by all circles of the inhabitants. Even though the clowns of the city sometimes teased him for his excessive retirement and would treat him like a "pious fool", in fact, he was not a fool at all; his intelligence was always evident in his words. But since his innocence reached an extreme, the name "Szmuel HaKatan", which, by the way, he received because of his height, became the nickname for an idler.

Rabbi Eli Nachum's (Rotenberg)

Rabbi Eli', also an outstanding member of the Gur Chassidim, a scholar and exalted soul, merchant, owner of a dry goods shop, was scrupulous in observing the commandments, being strict with himself even on permissible matters. In his shop he would not take money from the hands of a woman in order not to touch her flesh.

He ate only meat purchased from a reliable butcher, one he trusted not to feed him meat from an animal that had suffered from adhesion of the lungs [which would render the animal's flesh unkosher]. He was careful to pray at the proper time and set aside a regular time for the study of Torah. People said of him that he was "pious in all his actions" [Psalms 145/17]; comfortable with people, he was not one who searched out other people's misdeeds. He would say: "instead of looking at the flaws of others, look at your own". "Know that if there is no flaw in your behavior, if you continue this way, you will influence others in any case and serve as an example to many." – And truly the man was an example and model for many others.

Rabbi Szlomo Icak Binental

Rabbi Szlomo Icak was the son-in-law of Rabbi Mejer Jechiel Gotfrid, ritual slaughterer, Z"L. He was one of the Grodzisk Chassidim, a pious man whose piousness was not evident. At first glance he was a simple Jew, a tradesman, buying and selling, a man of modest habits. Many did not know how far his piousness reached.

[Page-181]

He had a small grocery shop and aside from this he also was a grain merchant on a small scale. From the farmers who came to his shop to buy kerosene and salt, he would buy the sack of grain that they brought with them to the city to sell. From this trade he made his living and raised children in the manner of all of the Jews.

This was his habit on secular matters; but his habit on holy matters was not visible. Before dawn, when the inhabitants of the city were sunken in sleep, he would rise early for a "Tikun Chatzot" [Midnight Learning Vigil] and afterwards he would study Torah until daybreak and the time for prayers.

During the day he was concerned with the cares of a livelihood, therefore he stole the sleep from his eyes and dedicated the hours of the night to the study of Torah. His face always expressed a sort of sadness; laughter never appeared on his lips; from his chest from time to time deep sighs burst forth, as if he was worried about the exile of the Shechina [presence of God] or the tyranny of the Diaspora, which distracts the hearts of many from divine service; and it could be that he was troubled by his own deficiencies in prayer and the study of Torah. But in truth, he was not deficient at all, and when an opportunity to observe a commandment presented itself, he never missed it; he always ran to perform any commandment, great and small alike.

Rabbi Szymon Tenenbaum

Rabbi Szymon was the son of Rabbi Benjamin Tenenbaum, or Benjamin "Buzek", as the inhabitants of his city called him. His maternal grandfather was Rabbi Mordechai Fiszel, one of the great Chassidim and scholars of the city of Checiny. This Rabbi Szymon was a Gur Chassid. But in his opinions and outlook he was their total opposite. The Gur Chassidim were known in Poland as zealots who ignored those who were not their supporters, and considered themselves the creme de la creme of Polish Jewry.

Rabbi Szymon took issue with them and would expose their flaws in front of them. He would say: "Every single Jews is a limb of the national body; we must treat every Jew with affection and love. Pride is the worst attribute."

His heart held a great affection for the Zionists, especially the pioneers who were devoting their lives to the homeland, who were saturating the soil of the holy land with their blood and sweat. "What great merit they have," he would say, "that they themselves accepted the obligation to live and make fertile the wastelands of our country, from which we were exiled, and to prepare a homeland for the children of the Diaspora for whom the ground of the lands of their dispersion has begun to burn beneath their feet." And when people scorned him and said: "But the pioneers are those who have thrown off the yoke [of the commandments], who violate the Shabbat, eat unkosher foods – and how will they bring about the redemption?"

He would answer and say: "Whoever is busy building the land – is exempt from the commandments." And immediately bring a proof to his words: "For also during the fourteen years of the conquest and division of the land during the days of Joshua bin Nun the children of Israel were exempt from the commandments."

In spite of straightened circumstances and lack of livelihood, he was always in a calm and merry mood. A smile never left his lips. The joy of life came to him from his love of Israel.

[Page-182]

His friends, the Chassidim in the "sztibl" once wanted to excommunicate him because of his strange opinions, but they didn't dare to carry out their plot, because in his actions and customs he was as one of them, they couldn't find in him any deviation from the ways of the Chassidim, for he was careful with even a tiny bit of anything forbidden; he was scrupulous to a hairbreadth's degree with each and every commandment that fell upon him to perform; they could not find any flaw in his actions. Therefore they contented themselves with putting about the lies that he was not entirely sane and that he had some problem with his brain and they it is not worth dealing with him and paying attention to his nonsense.

However Rabbi Szymon was one of those early Chassidim whose Chassidism was not counterfeit, acquired by imitation, but was the essence of their soul, their soul was quarried from the world of love, the world of loving-kindness. They had to be what they were - true to their nature and soul.

Eli' Rebbe'le

I will mention here the name of a Chassid who was known in the city of Kielce as Eli' Rebbe'le. He was the son-in-law of a baker in Checiny, a town close to Kielce. This baker had an only daughter and he married her to a Torah scholar. The strength of this son-in-law of his was not in the disputations of Abaye and Raba; in contrast, his strength was great in Chassidism. Serving the Creator with prayer and beseeching was to him the main task of a Jews.

And thus his prayers were lengthy. His prayers were not like the prayer of Hannah in her day, in the sense of "only her lips moved and her voice was not heard" [Samuel I, 1/13], but he shook worlds with his prayer. All of his limbs participated in it, in the sense of "all of my bones shall say" [Psalms 35/10]. He would stamp his feet, clap his hands in the air, on the wall, on the table, blink his eyes, and his entire body would tremble and shake. From his mouth came all sorts of sounds: yells, screams, shrieks, groans and sighs, grinding teeth, wails, cries.

It seemed to those who watched him from up close that this man who was standing at prayer wrapped in his prayer shawl was doing a vicious battle with all of the forces arranged to block the path of his prayer and prevent it from going straight up to the heavens. However, truly his worship was aimed at another purpose: to reach the level of "cancellation of what is", to drive away the evil thoughts, which arrive during prayer to confuse his mind and heart.

People, when they saw the manner of his behavior, began treating him as a Tzadik [holy man] who is destined to be revealed over time in all of his greatness and glory. Artisans, Torah scholars and old men began gathering around him on the Sabbath for the third meal. In the dark evenings his movements and grimaces had an even stronger effect upon those gathered. Women came to him with "notes".

Among the common people he was already bestowed with the title of "Rebbe". But since he was short and young, they used the diminutive "Rebbe'le". Who knows if he wouldn't have really reached the level of Tzadik and Admo"r if not for one incident, which all at once took him down from his status and holiness. And this was the incident the decided the fate of Reb' Eli' in life.

[Page-183]

On Friday nights it was Eli' Rebbe'le's custom to remain in the study hall where he prayed, about an hour after the service, in order to go over special Sabbath learnings [Tikunei Shabbat] and read the chapters of the Zohar and he would arrive home when the Sabbath candles were already dying and flickering in the candlesticks.

His father-in-law, a simple Jew, a baker, who was up at night all during the week because of his profession, would sit next to the set table and doze. His mother-in-law and wife would read "Tzena Ureina" and wait for him to arrive from the study hall in order to eat the Sabbath meal with him.

During the early months, his father-in-law bore his odd behavior with much patience, even if in his heart he was annoyed with him for the disturbance he caused him in the Sabbath rest he yearned for all week. The baker would make light of any insult to himself by saying: "If my son-in-law has lengthy prayers, it is all for the sake of heaven and there is no place to complain to him." And in order that they not eat in darkness, they would light large candles.

However, once on a Friday night his son-in-law tarried in the study hall longer than usual. The baker had already had time to awaken from his sleep, the mother-in-law and her daughter had already gone over the weekly portion in "Tzeina Ureina" – and their "Kli Yakar" [Precious Vessel – also the name of a commentary on the Pentateuch] had still not arrived. Finally the candles also went out, the room was dark and black, the challahs and the wine are ready on the table – and waiting for a blessing.

And then the door opened – the scholar enters. "Good Sabbath!" "Good Sabbath!" The "Shalom Aleichem" song, etc, his voice is heard in the darkness of the room in a joyful gladness, as if light and glory were spread around him.

The baker did not contain himself and with some annoyance asked his son-in-law: "Why did you spend such a long time in the study hall? The candles went out and now we must eat in the dark."

"You have darkness, for me it is light", - Rebbe'le answered surely and continued to read the "Ribon Olamim" by heart and sang "Woman of Valor" fervently and earnestly read the Zohar for Friday night. Sanctified the wine and in the light of the moon he and his household ate the Sabbath meal according to the law. Between each course he sang Sabbath songs.

His mother-in-law and his wife were simple Jewish women, innocent and didn't say a thing. In their innocence they thought that it was supposed to be that way. Who can understand the secrets of holy men.

However the baker was not light-minded like gullible women who believe anything. A doubt crept into his heart, if all of the deeds that his son-in-law does weren't in fact some sort of distraction in order to be considered a miracle working Tzadik by others. And he decided in his heart to test him, if his words were honest, that even in the darkness his son-in-law was in light or whether he was just fooling people.

The following Friday night, his son-in-law was again late in returning from the study hall, the candles went out, the darkness wrapped itself around the room. The baker whose nerves were very aggravated, went and opened the door to the cellar, which was in the middle of the room under the floor. The women didn't notice this.

The door opened. "Good Sabbath!" he didn't have time to repeat his greeting again when – "Trach!" an abyss opened at his feet, and he fell and went down to the cellar. Fortunately for him, it was not a deep cellar, and the Rebbe'le was not physically injured, he only received a small blow.

[Page-184]

The baker, with a cry of victory and satisfaction that this experiment worked out, called to his son-in-law: "This is the result of stubbornness; the stubborn man damages only himself. On the Sabbath there should be light and joy for the Jews, not darkness and sadness. This is a punishment from heaven; now you won't say: "It is light for me!"

Embarrassed, the Rebbe'le came out of the cellar, didn't say anything, he realized in his soul that his father-in-law had set a net at his feet to trap him. The matter became known outside the walls of his home as well; the entire city was talking about the event.

From then his honor descended in the eyes of the masses, they stopped coming to him for the third meal on the Sabbath; the women also stopped coming to him with notes. He himself learned that he was not worthy of the degree of a Tzadik if such a small matter could all at once remove him from his stature in the eyes of the people.

But even afterwards, he did not change his behavior, he continued to pray with a noise and a ruckus, he read much in the Zohar and did not speak of daily matters on the Sabbath.

When he ceased to be supported by his father-in-law, he became a matchmaker, would make matches and over time would also sell fortunes. In his praise one can say that until the end of his days people respected him for his exaggerated piety.

A quality of security was instilled in his heart to a great degree, which was communicated from him to people who came in contact with him.

He had an only daughter and he married her to a Torah scholar. The father-in-law crowded into the shade of the Admo"r of Radoszyce and the son-in-law – in the shade of the Admo"r of Alexander.

This son-in-law, whose name was Mosze Chaim Jakubowicz, made an effort to attain the qualities and habits of his father-in-law as well; however he was not successful in his endeavor to echo him in all details. For the former, his behavior was like a second nature, the attribute of his soul, from which he could no longer be released; however for the latter this behavior started only after battle, effort and strain. It was clear that he wanted to imitate his father-in-law without having any emotional need for such behavior himself.

The Alexander Chassidim found in him nothing lacking and included him in their ranks, gave him a position in life, the position of a "melamed" in their congregation. They gave their sons to him and he taught them Gemara and commentaries. And in general they respected him and considered him one of the outstanding Chassidim of their community. He succeeded in his holy work, the teaching bore him fruit. As he was without children and had little expenditure, he also saved himself a bit of capital. The citizens of his city considered him a well-to-do man.

In the city of Kielce there were many other Chassidim. Some of them did not expose their piety to public view and some of them did not enter into my sphere, and their names did not reach my attention. I have mentioned here, therefore, only the names of the Chassidim who were closest to me, and whose homes I visited. I saw their behavior with my own eyes. I have noted here in an objective manner the impression they made upon me and did not come to make any value judgements. I described them as they were. My intention is to hand on to the generations a sketch of the face of the Kielce community, therefore I chose from each and every class a few characters that were selected not just to teach us about themselves, but about the whole from which they were extracted.

[Page-185]

To complete this, I will present to the readers also several characters of scholars for whom the Torah was their art, and who were the glory of the Kielce community.

Rabbe Isachar [Ritual Slaughterer] Goldrat z"l

Rabbi Isachar was the son of Rabbi Mordechai son of Rabbi Szlomo Z"L, a rabbinical arbiter in the Kielce community. Rabbi Isachar was a high class scholar and teacher. He publicized his innovation on the Torah in writing and orally. His articles on the laws of ritual slaughter gave him a reputation in the rabbinic world, especially his book "Minchat Isachar".

Rabbi Isachar Goldrat

However, he was not famous just among scholars, whose profession it was, he was well known for his great expertise in the treasures of rabbinic literature; but even those who devoted most of their time to work, labor and commerce enjoyed his talks on Jewish law and lore. On Sabbaths and holidays he would interpret the weekly portion, "Midrash Raba", "Midrash Tanchuma", The Sayings of the Fathers in excellent taste for the householders and artisans and inspire in the hearts of his audience faith in the holiness of our Torah, in our national mission, hope for our future and in doing so elevated their low spirits, strengthened the hearts of those who suffered from the enslavement of exile, from the yoke of a difficult livelihood.

Even though he was not an open supporter of the Zionists – his stature in the community did not allow him to be counted with any political party – in spite of this a strong love for the land of Israel beat in his heart as well as for those who were occupied with and taking care of rebuilding it. He expressed to me many times his fervent desire to move and settle in the Holy Land. To this purpose he sent his son, Awraham Goldrat, to the land of Israel, a member of the first Knesset and one of the leading spokesmen in the camp of religious labor in Israel, to make a place for him and pave him a path for coming as well.

However, this desire of his did not come to pass, for death came first. The inhabitants of Kielce gave him great honor at his death and his memory remained as a blessing among those who he had influenced with his Torah, and who had an opportunity to sit in his company.

[Page-186]

Rabbi Alter Josef Baruch Horberg

Rabbinical arbiter and head of the rabbinical court in the Kielce community until the arrival of the Shoah. Great in Torah and an excellent sermonizer, he attracted the young men and taught them rabbinical debate. In his speeches and sermons he influenced the Jews of Kielce greatly. He was the son of the righteous Rabbi Icak Becalel, who was the head of the rabbinical court of the holy congregation of Bosk.

Rabbi Alter Horberg was also expert in matters of commerce and the merchants would bring him their arguments and disagreements, and he would mediate between them to the satisfaction of each and every one.

Rabbi Szmul Blumenfeld, son of Rabbi Izrael Sofer Z"L, also came from Kielce and he served as a rabbi in several communities in Polish towns and was famous for his expertise and the sharpness of his mind and could settle every difficult matter in the Talmud.

His son, Rabbi Josef Baruch Blumenfeld moved to the land of Israel and served as the head of the rabbinical court on the community committee of Tel-Aviv. His second son, Szlomo Blumenfeld, also moved to the land of Israel and he serves as a member of the Kashrut committee of the community committee in Tel-Aviv.

**Rabbi Icak Mejer Tauman and Rabbi Josele Chelmner
and others deep in a Chassidic discussion**

If I were to try and make a note of all of the names of those who were famous in the Kielce congregation and its environs as great in Torah, the list would be too long. I will only mention a few of the most outstanding ones, Rabbi Mosze Trajman or Rabbi Mosze Aharondl's, the son-in-law of Rabbi Aharon Cytron HaLevi Z"L, a rabbinical arbiter in the Kielce community. Rabbi Cwi Grinszpan, a rabbinical arbiter and member of the rabbinical court of the community. An innocent man who spent days and nights studying the Torah. Rabbi Mordechai (Motel) Nachum's (Rozenberg) a great Torah scholar and a Chassid and the son of Rabbi Izrael. Rabbi Mosze Gutfrajd, ritual slaughterer, who had a sharp mind, of the Chassidim of the Admo"r of Ostrowiec, in whose shade scholars gathered who were able to enjoy his sophisticated innovations, which amazed his listeners. Rabbi Jehoszua Heszel Ajlenberg, son of Simcha Bunem the "melamed", principal of the "Yesodei Torah" cheder in Kielce. Rabbi Gerszon Zew Wulf, principal of the "Torat Chesed" yeshiva in Kielce, the son in law of Rabbi Chaim Dow, Z"L.

As well, one must mention among the Chassidim and men of action, Rabbi Icak Mejer Tauman, the grandson of the author of "Chidushei HaRI"M" and the brothers Rabbi Mosze'le and Rabbi Josele Chelmner (Chenciner). Both were excellent in their qualities and good musicians, famous prayer-leaders. The younger, Rabbi Josele, had a reputation in Poland as a "Ba'al Musaf" [one who leads the "Musaf" prayer on Sabbaths and holidays] in the court of the Admo"r of Gur. He perished in the Shoah in the Lodz Ghetto.

These scholars and Chassidim and their many friends made sure the coals were not extinguished, shared their wellsprings with others and were a valuable addition to the Kielce community.

[Page-188]

Parnassim, Benefactors and Public Figures

Aside from Chassidim, studious people, there were benefactors who lived in Kielce who donated a portion of their wealth for the benefit of the public. I will mention the most famous of these here, those whose names were known beyond the bounds of Kielce and were known throughout the country of Poland. And also some of the simple householders, benefactors who were involved in public life, who serve as examples of the average Jew of Kielce.

Rabbi Mosze Pffefer Z"L

Rabbi Mosze Pffefer was in his actions and deeds an outstanding man among his fellow citizens. He stood at the first line in the Kielce congregation with his wealth, with his multi-faceted personality and with his endeavors, at the initial foundation of the of the community the man got up and gave a tremendous push to its growth and development.

He was not an industrialist, but still did much to improve the economic situation of the Jews of Kielce. As a contractor, lumber merchant, owner of the "Nichczyc" estate, he employed Jews from his community in all of his businesses.

This man is worthy of expanding upon also to perpetuate his memory for the coming generations.

Rabbi Mosze Pffefer was a personality which is hard to find today, even among the leaders who have ambitions of standing at the head of the nation. In him, in this exemplary man, Torah and greatness were combined in one place. He aroused respect with his external appearance, his facial expression and the assertiveness of his opinions. Nobility shone from his eyes and his manner of speech. His gestures and manners were those of an aristocrat born and bred. He dressed as one of the Chassidim – and a special charm flowed over his clothing, which gave him additional glory and grandeur.

He had a talent for speaking. He spoke the Polish language fluently and spoke it like one of the Polish nobility; he also spoke fluent Russian. Every opportunity showed him to be a gifted public speaker.

A Jew, who had not studied in school, all of whose education had been received in "cheders" and the study hall, was wise enough during his life not only to amass a great deal of wealth, that was estimated at half a million rubles, a tremendous amount in those days, but also to acquire himself an education to a degree well known, to learn the national languages, which allowed him to appear in polished speeches in public places in front of high level personages.

The Jews, the inhabitants of Kielce, respected him and admired him not only because his home was wide open to anyone needy, or for the donations he scattered about for the general good, but mainly because he was the glory of the congregation. The community glorified in him. It was an honor to the community to be led by such a superior man. Mosze Pffefer, this name was a symbol of nobility, honor and generosity.

[Page-189]

When he started out, he was a contractor, supplied building materials for the building of the Warsaw-Vienna railway line. After that, when he had acquired some capital, he became a lumber merchant. Finally he also bought a large estate "Nichczyc".

Due to his large business he came into contact with the Polish nobility and also with the district authorities, and in these circles he was respected and taken seriously. The authorities appointed him as a member of the district council.

In his business negotiations he kept his word; his mouth and heart were as one; his spirit was upright without any mental crookedness, without the slyness of peddlers, without hidden agendas, his Jewish mind, mixed with the traditional attitude of respect for the "Poretz", was attractive to the "Portzim", the estate owners who included him in their company.

His attitude towards his fellow Jews was devoted and loyal, he was involved with them, participated in their joys and mourning. The masses of Jews considered him their patron, their protector, who had the power to avert an evil decree the authorities were plotting to send against them. And in general, they said of him: "Mosze Pffefer is close to royalty". And indeed he was active and did much for the benefit of the members of his community. First of all, many families, inhabitants of Kielce, found their livelihood with him. Some of them as clerks and some of them as supervisors in his many businesses. Because of him, the number of Jews in his city grew larger. In his household, "melameds", teachers, artisans and many of his impoverished relatives whom he supported with regular allowances found work.

Mosze Pffefer was an outstanding type of those Jews, the wealthy, the leaders, who lived in previous generations and used their wealth not only for their own good, but also for the good of their fellows. And it was they who stood by their brethren in the dark days and enabled them to withstand their poverty and trials. Although there were meager, under-funded philanthropic societies like "Bikur Cholim" [Visiting the Sick], "Hachnasat Kalah" [Welcoming the Bride] and others whose entire existence depended upon a miracle and whose aid to those failing among the community was like nothing at all. Wide ranging social aid was not on their agendas nor was it possible.

In those days, the wealthy man was like a solid dike, towards whom all eyes were turned. Also within the home of Rabbi Mosze Pffefer his generous wife Ester'l, may she rest in peace, gave help to all those who turned to her.

However, the generosity of Reb' Mosze Pffefer's heart was not satisfied with petty philanthropy. He had his eye on great endeavors, whose value would not just be for moment, but for generations to come. He saw that the Kielce community was developing and growing and did not have a public synagogue. The members crowded into private apartments, in "shtiblach", or in the study hall, a low building that was about to collapse of age. Pffefer arose and build upon the community lot a splendid synagogue that would do honor to himself and his community.

The authorities, headed by the district governor, were invited to the ceremony of setting the cornerstone. On this festive occasion, Pffefer gave a speech in Russian. The ceremony made a great impression upon all of those gathered, and the honor of this benefactor went way up.

[Page-190]

On the day of the consecration the joy of the community members was very great. They saw before them a minor temple built with much splendor. An iron fence surrounded it with stone steps by the entrance. The inner organization gave the building an atmosphere of holiness. Everyone who entered was surrounded with a sense of mystery. A sense of awe and feelings of holiness were awakened in him.

Also at this opportunity Pffefer gave a speech in Russian, in the presence of the authorities. In his speech he quoted the words of King Solomon, who spoke before the congregation of Israel on the day of the consecration of the temple. He emphasized in his speech that in this minor temple they would pray for the welfare of the rulers and for the welfare of the country, for that is the commandment from our prophets, and we observe their edicts. From the day we were exiled from our country and were scattered among the nations of the world, we pray for the welfare of the rulers and ask for the good of the country, for peace for them – is peace for us as well. He continued and said: "This synagogue will be open before all people, to Jews and to non-Jews, for one God created us and all of us – our eyes turn to him in our prayers."

This speech aroused great applause from the entire audience. The district governor shook the speaker's hand and expressed his thanks to him in the name of the government for his generosity.

The Jews, full of joy, returned to their homes, convinced that their community had been elevated by the endeavor of this philanthropist.

Meanwhile, new times came. A new generation arose. New streams conquered the hearts and minds of the young people; and they not only did not give proper respect to this generous man who was elevated above others, but they began to mock him and put down the value of his activities.

The fifth year of the 20th century arrived. The liberation movement, which had made waves throughout mighty Russia, also did not pass over Kielce. Parties and factions arose, and they removed the champions of the people from their elevated positions.

The new generation, Zionists as well as all sorts of Socialists, began to treat people like Mosze Pffefer with scorn and indifference. The early ones called him a "Ma Yafit'nik" for the way he groveled before the "Poretz" and before whoever held authority. The national renewal movement demanded that everyone, first of all, have an erect posture, a recognition of self-value, courage and forthrightness in demanding human rights. Groveling, a justified request that is framed in the language of begging, in weak language, in a low tone, all these attributes of exile were hated by the nationalists.

Mosze Pffefer, who in their eyes was an outstanding example of the older generation, appeared lowly to them, wholly lacking in respect. And on the other hand, the leftists, the revolutionaries, saw him as the representative of the class they hated and fought against, whose time had past and which needed to make way for the working class, and therefore it is a commandment to beat it into the ground.

In order to describe the relationships that formed at this time between the activist elements in the Kielce public and Mosze Pffefer, I will mention on episode here that will show us very clearly the revolution that took place then in the minds and hearts of the younger generation which was educated by the influences of the Zionists and the socialists and which adopted their slogans.

[Page-191]

In the elections to the second Duma [Russian parliament] in 1907, the election battle in Polish society was conducted between two large parties, the Endeks (Nationalist Democrats) and the Progressive Polish Party. The first used anti-Semitic slogans, and had great influence upon the Polish masses, for the Catholic clergy supported this party.

The second had not yet been swept away by the anti-Semitic current and in order to increase its strength, when it went out to campaign, it wanted to draw the Jews into its ranks.

These two Polish parties conducted their election campaigns in Kielce as well. Kielce was a bastion of anti-Semitism. The Endeks found fertile ground for their activities there. The Progressives made up only a small minority. The most notable members of the Progressives were Papiwski, a dentist; Artwinski, a pharmacist; Riger, editor of the newspaper "Echo Kielcka"; and a few others, representatives of the workers party PPS who were simultaneously representatives of the Kielce Progress. With their meager forces they could not go out to do battle against a strong party like the N.D. party, which held most of Poland in the palm of its hand, therefore they turned to the Jews, who also had no chance of winning, with a proposal of campaigning together, united and integrated into a single election list. The mediators between the Polish Jews and Progressives were the assimilated Jews.

An early meeting of voters was called in the hall of the "Achiezer" society that was next to the synagogue, for purposes of public relations and propaganda among the Jewish population. The main goal of the meeting was explaining the topic of the elections to the Jews and to emphasize the advantage that would accrue to the Jews from the cooperation with the Progressive Poles.

Representatives of the Progressive Party were also invited to this meeting. The initiator of the meeting was Mosze Pffefer, who opened it and suggested electing the lawyer Majzel as chairman of the meeting, an extremely assimilated man. (By the way, it must be noted here that this Majzel converted out of Judaism before his death).

Immediately voices of protest were heard from among the audience: "We don't want an assimilated chairman who is distanced from the Jews and their affairs".

Pffefer was astounded at what his ears were hearing. How many efforts had he invested until he was able to bring this lawyer to a meeting of Jews; the presence of Poles at this meeting was what moved him to come and participate in it; also, the opportunity to be a candidate for a delegate to the Russian Duma tempted his sense of importance and he agreed to honor the meeting with his presence; and suddenly he sees, that in the eyes of the Jews who usually prostrated themselves before him when they came into his office, he was now of little value and not worthy of the respect that even the Poles, in their meetings, did not withhold from him.

Furious from the insult, that the wearers of long "kapotes" [the long Chassidic coats] dared to throw at him in the presence of the Poles, he grabbed his hat and prepared to leave saying: "Apparently I am not wanted here, this is not my place."

[Page-192]

But Pffefer and the Poles stopped him, calmed him down by saying that most of the audience admire and respect him, and the calls had come from some insolent young men whom the Zionists had confused with chauvinist ideas.

After the voices were quieted, Pffefer gave a fiery speech against those who had disrupted the meeting. He said: "The Jewish meetings were always notable for lack of order, yells and disagreements until they became a fable and a paradigm: 'Jewish Meeting' was a symbol of argument and chaos. However new times have arrived. We the Jews have also received the right to vote from the government. The duty, therefore, is for us to demonstrate to the nations and the ministers that we are worthy of these rights. First of all," he continued, "I demand manners from you, I invited this guest to this meeting, the respected and admired "Mecnas" who is a glory to our city, and all its inhabitants without any difference in religion hold his name dear. He is my personal guest in my apartment, and I demand that you elect him to the chairman of this meeting, for whatever the 'ba'alhabayit' [owner of the house] tells you to do – you do! I am putting this matter to a vote: whoever wants Mr. Majzel to be chairman, raise his hand."

Of course, after a speech like that, the assimilated man received an absolute majority.

Consoled by Pffefer's speech and the results of the vote, Majzel was willing to receive this honor from the audience and agreed to lead the meeting. When he took his place, he began to express, as is customary, words of thanks to the audience for the honor they did him. However he was not able to finish his opening words – he was immediately stopped by new voices, more energetic cries than the earlier ones: "Yiddish! Speak Yiddish! This is a Jewish meeting!"

These calls made the chairman very embarrassed and he turned reprovingly to Pffefer for giving him such a burden that he could not bear. Drops of perspiration appeared on his brow and rolled down his face. His expression showed shame. He was at a loss, didn't know how to get out of this uncomfortable situation. He was especially ashamed in front of the Poles, who were participating in this meeting.

However the Poles understood more of this matter than the assimilated Jews. To the Poles, the demand was a legitimate one. At a Jewish meeting the speakers must speak in a language that is understood by the audience. One of them, Riger, the newspaper editor, got up and declared that he also supports this demand that the speeches be in the Jewish language.

The chairman then announced that he relinquishes the honor and is leaving the running of the meeting for the simple reason that he doesn't know the "Jargon". It was a mistake on the part of the audience who elected him, and a mistake on his part for accepting the role of chairman in a meeting so entirely foreign to his spirit.

Pffefer tried to quiet things down. He again took the floor and declared: "We are Poles of the faith of Moses, and the Polish language is our language, and we must use it in public gatherings." Such words, coming from the mouth of a Chassidic Jew, who had also not compromised on the kippa and did not sit with his head uncovered, stirred things up even more.

[Page-193]

Only after a compromise decision was reached which stated that every person was given permission to speak in a language that was comfortable and desirable to him and according to the demands of one of the audience that words that are not comprehensible to him must be translated into a language he understands, did the voices quiet down.

The chairman ran the meeting for only a short time. He saw and was confronted with how lowly and scorned was the glorious Mecnas in the eyes of the new generation, which was meeting him for the first time in its life; he could not take the assaults and frequent attacks and the disgraceful names that were the lot of those of the speakers who were assimilated.

After a short time, Majzel left the meeting, and Pffefer conducted it to the end. Jews spoke, Poles spoke. There were no more interruptions, there were no more obstructions, finally a combined committee, Polish-Jewish, was elected to tend to the elections and to conduct propaganda among the population.

Majzel who left this meeting shame-faced and depressed, wanted to restore his dignity, which, from now on, was in danger, he got up and publicized an announcement in the local Polish press that he was retiring entirely from the matter of the elections. The Endeks who wanted to increase their strength put him on their list, believing that he would draw the votes of the Jews in their favor.

The propaganda on both sides was conducted with great energy. On the Jewish street the young people were active with great enthusiasm. Chassidim, assimilated Jews, Zionists and Socialists united in order to defeat the Endeks. In these elections the members of the Hassenbajn family, the father and his son the lawyer demonstrated especially great activism, they devoted themselves wholeheartedly to running the campaign, did not spare effort or money on the elections. They sent special messengers to small villages to bring the Jewish voters to the district capital where the elections took place.

It was very difficult to arouse the village Jew, preoccupied with his own affairs, to treat the matter of the election with anything other than indifference, and he wanted to first of all know what good would come to him from the matter, and if it was worth the expenditure and traveling to the district capital, where the balloting was. And in general, a fear to stick one's head into a dark place, to interfere in a matter that one didn't understand. It took a lot of effort and bribes of money for such a Jew to agree to travel to the city in a farmer's cart to fulfil his civic duty. In spite of all the great labor that the Jews of Kielce invested in these elections, the Endeks won. The Polish Progress was limited in those days to a narrow circle of intellectuals, and their connection with the Jews was to their detriment. By doing so they distanced from their camp also the classes, which were close to them in spirit like the laboring classes. The hand of the Jew in the middle – ruined their list in the eyes of every Pole.

After these elections, Mosze Pffefer saw himself as humiliated and removed from the height of his position and his greatness not only in the eyes of the Poles, who began demonstrating their anti-Semitism and their scorn towards the community leaders, but also in the eyes of the Jews; he had especially lost his appeal with the younger generation. Pffefer's faith in his method, the method of concealment, the method of the assimilated Jews who called themselves "Poles of the Mosaic faith" was weakened.

[Page-194]

He attempted to salvage his standing in the Kielce community. In his desire to demonstrate to the members of his community that he too was aware of the spirit of the times and that nationalism also had a place in his heart, he invited the writer of these lines to teach the son of his old age, Jeszaja, Hebrew language and grammar. This step was supposed to be a sign that he was no longer ignoring the demands of the times.

However, rage leapt upon him from another place, and he could not dwell in Kielce in peace.

As mentioned earlier, Pffefer built the synagogue upon the community lot, and here a creditor found a place to demand his debt.

Between Pffefer and Reb' Mosze Chaim Kaminer there was constant opposition. The reasons for their conflict were varied. Some of them personal and some of them public and some of them due to the hunger for power over the Jewish population of Kielce. The question: "who was ahead?" injected venom between them. In any case, this was not a difference for the sake of heaven.

Kaminer, who was then at the head of the community, brought a legal suit against Pffefer for building the synagogue, which was his private property, upon a public lot and demanded to clear the lot or turn the synagogue over to the community.

The disagreement ignited and had an effect upon the Kielce public as well. The congregation divided into two camps. Each one of the rivals had his own side. Kaminer and his faction looked for any opportunity for excuses to besmirch their rival justifiably or not.

Finally Pffefer grew tired of the squabbling and arguments, which were destabilizing the community, and he decided to leave Kielce. A few years before the outbreak of World War I, he moved to Warsaw.

The matter of the synagogue was settled in favor of the community. The entire building was given over to the congregation on the condition that a part of its income be dedicated to supporting the impoverished relatives of Reb' Mosze Pffefer. Berisz Pffefer, an old man, one of his relatives, came to function as a second "gabbai" of the synagogue with a regular salary.

In Warsaw, Pffefer retired into his own private affairs and we didn't hear about any public activity on his part.

However, at the end of World War I, the name of Mosze Pffefer came up again in the area of political activism; not in the area of Jewish activism, but in broader areas. He entered the royal council as a delegate.

At the end of the war, the Germans seeing that the cycle of battles was not going in their favor, attempted to draw to their side the minorities, which had previously been subjugated to Russia and during the war were under German occupation. To do this, they granted them autonomy and self rule. For the Poles they created a "National Council" whose members were not elected by the people, but appointed by the German authorities according to the lists that they were given by the gatherings of estate owners and by the municipal magistrates of the large cities.

The task of the "National Council" was to conduct the internal affairs of the state.

[Page-195]

A number of Jews also entered this council. Pffefer also became a member of this council for the estate owners wanted to demonstrate their liberalism and decorated their list also with one Jew and they chose Pffefer, who owned an estate and was worthy of receiving a mandate.

In the deliberations of the council, Pffefer once requested the floor regarding an important matter that was then on the agenda. At the start of his words, he apologized and asked forgiveness for allowing himself to express an opinion about a matter of importance to the country in spite of his being a Jew.

His manner of speech and his prostration before the Gentiles in this legislative institution aroused strong protests from his Jewish friends, who saw an insult to themselves in these stammering and defeatist words of a so-called representative of the Jews.

Noach Prylucki, the representative of the Jews of Warsaw, stopped the speaker with a call of protest and requested the chairman to remind Pffefer, that all the members of the council are equal in rights and one must not apologize for the expression of an opinion about any subject.

The attitude of scorn and disdain of the Jewish delegates towards Pffefer embittered his spirit and removed from him the courage to express his opinion and finish his speech.

In addition to this insult that he garnered in the legislative house, an unpleasant surprise awaited him in the street as well. The Jews, who heard his words in the gallery, went out to the street to wait for Pffefer, and when he left they assaulted him calling "Ma Yafit'nik" and "Buz" [Shame]. Hurriedly, he hid in a carriage that was waiting him in front of the legislative house and left the place.

This insult depressed him very much. He took ill from the surfeit of sorrow and did not recover from his illness.

His death did not arouse any echo in the Diaspora of Israel. However, the Jews of Kielce mourned his death. In their eyes, Reb' Mosze Pffefer remained an outstanding man who had with his actions and endeavors given a tremendous push to the rapid growth of their community and left himself a memorial due to the splendid synagogue he built for it.

The Zagajski Family

The Zagajski family belonged to the benefactors of the city who earned a special reputation, who have already been mentioned on earlier pages of this book, and therefore I will not expand upon them here. I will mention only the charitable and merciful endeavors that members of this family founded and which were a glory and honor to the Zagajski family and the Kielce community.

- One. An old age home, a charitable institution, which was a blessing for elderly people with no one to care for them.
- Two. A building for the orphanage in which abandoned orphans found shelter, education and care and which had existed previously in a rented apartment which was not appropriate for such an institution.
- Three. Three. A study hall for the inhabitants of the city – Hawser Square and its surroundings, a place for prayer and Torah.
- Four. A road to the Jewish cemetery so that those accompanying the deceased would not sink into the mud during the rainy season.

These were the notable activities of the members of this family, aside from their daily acts of charity and kindness.

[Page-196]

Many other Jews from Kielce excelled in acts of charity and kindness, and it is not possible to list them all; we will mention below several of them who stood out in public life.

GIMPEL MOSZKOWICZ, an ultra-orthodox Jew from those close to the Admo"r of Radomsko, owner of a large business selling flour and very generous with charitable and public needs.

His son **AHARON JOSEF MOSZKOWICZ**, one of the Zionist activists, member of the Kielce municipality on their behalf, active in many charity societies such as "Linat HaTzedek", the orphanage and others.

MORDECHAI DAWID KRYSTAL, owner of a factory for wooden flooring, a Chassid who was a well educated benefactor to the public good. His son, Wolf, was a well-known musician in Poland.

His son-in-law **AHARON GRANDAPEL**, one of the leaders of the Zionists in Kielce, moved to Israel after the war and died here.

MEJER AJZENBERG, the son of Reb' Josele Ajzenberg (Kaczka), a public activist, was especially devoted to the Talmud Torah and the orthodox schools as well as to the mikveh [ritual bath] and public bath in which he invested much of his money and labor for the good of the public.

The brothers **ICAK AND JOEL KLAJNMAN**, owners of sawmills for lumber and lumber expert, philanthropic Jews who donated generously to public needs and charity.

JOSZKE (JAKOB JOSEF) ROTENBERG, son of the rabbi of Wodzislaw, an authority and arbiter, owner of a wholesale business for kerosene and representative of international fuel companies, a man with a good heart and very generous, a host in the style of Grandfather Israel.

His son **MOSZE ROTENBERG**, who inherited his devotion to public causes from his father. Regarding his activities in Israel and outside of it we have already made mention in earlier chapters. Arrived with his family in Israel and died here. Also Joszke's daughter, Hena Mincberg and his grandchildren from his son Jehuda who died during the war in Russia, moved and settled in Israel.

JAKOB SZAJNFELD, son of Reb' Jechiel was also a wholesale kerosene merchant, of the benefactors of the city. Two of his sons, Szalom and Aharon moved to Israel before the war and settled there.

JOSEL FRIDMAN, owner of flourmills, of the leading citizens of the city, donated to every charity and public need most generously.

PALTIEL FIRSTENBERG had a large family, known for his public and social activity. One of his sons, a doctor, and his daughter, are in Israel.

SZEFTEL TAUMAN, son-in-law of Jakob Zagajski, great-grandson of the Admo"r of Kock, an educated and well-read Jew, with a sensitive soul and spirit, participated in all of the charitable endeavors of the Zagajski family.

LEON RAJZMAN, owner of a factory for flooring, one of the important benefactors and philanthropists in the city.

MENDEL LIFSZYCZ, from a well-known Chassidic family, owned stone quarries and lime kilns, one of the founders of "Linat HaTzedek", active in many of the charitable and helping institutions.

DAWID LEWARTOWSKI, one of the important Chassidim of the Admo"r of Checiny, son of a good family and an arbiter, excellent prayer leader, with a warm Jewish heart, he and his wife Chana-Sara excelled in giving charity in secret. He dealt in wholesale commerce in kerosene, pickles and salt. The father of Szmuel Lewartowski and the father-in-law of Icak Kirszenbaum, about whom we spoke in earlier chapters.

At the consecration of the "Home for the Aged",
donated by the Zagajski family

Among those present: In the first now: Z. Kluska, B. Lew, the rabbinical judge Reb' C. Grinszpan, Rabbi Rapaport, Rabbi L. Twerski, C. Zagajski, Waldberg ; I. Kirszenbaum.
In the second row: H. Goldberg, W. Wajnryb, Icak Klajnman, N. Ostrowicz, M.D. Ajzenberg, Ch. Zagajski; J. Paserman; A.J. Moskowicz, A. Ehrlich.
In the third row: B. Sokolowski, Jechiel Zagajski, and M. Kaufman

[Page-198]

PINCHAS ZAJDE, a textile wholesaler, benefactor and active in all the public institutions. His son Mejer was an active Zionist. His younger son Jehuda – one of the leaders of "Poalei Zion" (left) in Kielce, his daughter Fajga (Fajngold) was a devoted Zionist, his second daughter, Manja, a dentist, lives in Israel.

SZMUEL ABA BALICKI, owner of a textile business, active member of the public and charity institutions. His daughter Casza (Zilber-Ewen) is in Israel.

The brothers **MORDECHAI AND SZMARJA MACHTYNGER**, lumber merchants, men of excellent characters and fine qualities. Szmarja moved to Israel before the war and built several houses in Tel-Aviv. The son of Mordechai, **IZRAEL MACHTYNGER** fell in the battle for Gaza in 5717 [1957].

AWRAHAM FINKELSZTAJN, one of the important Zionists in the city, a generous man, comfortable with people and active in many social societies.

ELIEZER TAUMAN, the son-in-law of Eli' Naftali Ajzenberg, owner of a large textile business, one of the respected citizens of the city, donated generously to all of the charitable and social institutions. His son Josef moved to Israel before the war and serves in the navy as an engineer with the rank of major, and is also an assistant-lecturer at the Technion in Haifa.

Zyskind Herman

ZYSKIND HERMAN, a native of Warsaw, son-in-law of Lajbel and Malka Lea Goldszmid, a Torah scholar with a sharp mind, one of the great textile merchants, manufacturer and owner of a private financial institution, member of the committee of the merchants association and the supervising committee of the Jewish Gymnasium, one of the founders of the Charity Fund to aid the little man, the peddler and the artisan. He visited the land of Israel with his wife Szewa (Batszewa); they bought a house in Tel-Aviv and were getting ready to settle here. They had to travel to Poland and were stuck there when the war broke out. His sons received a Zionist education, studied at the Hebrew Gymnasium in Kielce and continued later at universities abroad. Today they are in Tel-Aviv and work in academic professions: Dr. Awraham Herman, a pediatrician, Jechiel Herman, a lawyer and Dr. Jakob Herman, a gynecologist.

Pinchas Zloto

Among the inhabitants of Kielce who influenced the form of its Jewish life the figure of Reb' Pinchas Zloto stands out.

A native of Wygoda, Kielce District (his father - an estate owner, a descendant of Rabbi Yom-Tow Lipman Heller, author of the "Tosfot Yom-Tov"), in his youth, Reb' Pinchas moved to Suchedniow, near Kielce. Here he worked in trading kerosene and lumber and crowded into the shade of the Admo"r of Suchedniow, Rabbi Elimelech Rabinowicz, ZTZ"L. During the period of World War I he moved to Kielce together with his rebbe. Here he found himself fertile ground for developing economic initiative. First he worked manufacturing whitewash, later as a representative of beverage companies, and finally as one of the directors of a cooperative credit institution.

[Page-199]

The father of a large family (2 daughters and 8 sons) he gave his children a traditional-nationalist education. While he was one of the well-to-do citizens of the city, Reb' Pinchas ran away from honor. He wasn't an active Zionist worker, but his heart and pocket were open to the needs of the Zionist movement, Hebrew culture and the settlement of the land of Israel. It was natural that his son Mejer was one of the outstanding public activists in the city, one of the founders of the Hebrew Gymnasium and more, his son Natan, one of the first young people from Kielce who moved to the land of Israel in 1920 and put down roots there (today, one of the respected citizens of Nes-Ziona), his son Hilel, one of the loyal members of the Union in Tel-Aviv, his son-in-law – Jehuda Kopf – one of the founders of the Revisionist movement in Kielce (today – in Tel-Aviv, a jurist, secretary of the civil branch of the district court).

Pinchas Zloto

There was in him a nice combination of assertiveness and gentleness. The man was very strict, both towards himself and towards others. He was strict about physical cleanliness and spiritual purity, and on the other hand, there were not many like him who had pity upon others in distress and who gave charity in secret. He worked his whole life with Christian forest owners and manufacturers, but was not one of those whose stature bowed in the presence of the "Goy". In his patriarchal figure, his assertive behavior, in his commercial honesty and even in the strict Polish accent – he aroused a feeling of respect in all who came into contact with him.

He made sure his daughters married sons of good families:
His first son-in-law – Rabbi Izrael Feferman, HY"D, was a well-known merchant in Kielce. His second son-in-law, Rabbi Awraham Aba Kopf HY"D, an arbiter, son of a Chassidic family, one of those close to the Admo"r of Modzicz, ZTZ"L. He was granted that his son Jehuda (see above) moved during his lifetime to the land of Israel and settled there.

Reb' Pinchas died during the period of the Shoah (1940), however he was granted a natural death and even a respectable funeral, one of the last in which the inhabitants of the city could give public expression to their sorrow.

May his memory be blessed.

Natan Dawid Zajfman

Many of the veteran inhabitants of Kielce remember the wonderful figure of Reb' Natan Dawid Zajfman, one of the first members of the community in the city. A good Jew, a quiet and modest man, gifted with exalted qualities, he enjoyed learning and working and helping others already in his youth. And even if he was not the wealthiest man, his home was open to anyone needy. This house was full of bubbling life, for there were many children in it and they had many friends from the most excellent families of the city.

Natan Dawid Zajfman owned a large shop for clothing, furs and textiles in the center of the city for 55 years.

[Page-200]

His name was well known as that of an upright man who kept to the tradition and was a loyal Chassid of the Rebbe of Radoszyce. He was a loyal friend to many charity and aid institutions, in which he was active. Towards the end of his life he was granted "nachas" [pleasure] from his sons and family members and was especially proud of his son Jakob who moved to the land of Israel with a group of immigrants from the "Shomer HaTza'ir" and was one of those who built Kibbutz Ein HaChoresh in the Chefer Valley where he still lives today.

Natan Dawid Zajfman

Of his other children, his son Mosze Zajfman was notable as a founder of "HaZamir" and "HaShomer" in Kielce, and he was seriously injured in the pogrom in 1918, he devoted much of his time to public activity as a member of the committee of the merchants association and the board of the Popular Bank in Kielce. In 1933, he immigrated to Paris and was very active as the chairman of the organization of Kielce natives in that city until his death in 1954.

His third son, Kalmen Zajfman, an agronomist by profession, excelled in rehabilitating the pioneer farms "Grochow" next to Warsaw, during the war, during the war this pioneer farm supplied vegetables to the Warsaw ghetto. At this post of his he fell together with the rest of the martyrs at the hands of the Nazi murderers, may their name be erased.

[Page-201]

Leaders of the Kielce Community

Translated by Judy Montel

When I come to commemorate the Kielce community in this volume, I feel it is incumbent upon me to mention the names and activities of the people who were privileged to stand at its head and conduct its affairs.

The leaders of the Kielce community were not, for the most part, the most aggressive members of the congregation, who ruled their flock with a strong arm for their own pleasure and advantage, like those the authors of the time usually embarrassingly described in their books. The young community of Kielce did not have tradition or possessions. At its head stood mainly simple and kosher people, who were unanimously elected by the Jews of the city who turned their public affairs over to them in the opinion that they were in good hands.

The first communal leader was Reb' Lejbusz Lewkowicz, who was called by the inhabitants of Kielce "R' Lejbusz Feuer", since he had lived in a village in his early years and acquired the attributes of village farmers in his manner of speech, gesture and manner of living; it was noticeable that he was from a Polish village.

This simple man excelled in good qualities. Simplicity, fear of God, love of Torah scholars and support of them, doing charitable and merciful deeds – these commandments gave him the love and trust of all of the inhabitants.

He married his daughters to Torah scholars, who established splendid and extensive families in Kielce: the Kaner family, the Paserman family and the Bukowski family.

In his generosity he set aside part of his house as a prayer house; this was a great necessity for the Jews of Kielce in his time, before a synagogue had been built for the community members.

After him, Mejer Sztunke, one of the important homeowners in Kielce and one of the first to settle there, served as head of the community. He was active in public and charitable affairs. No poor or needy person left his house empty-handed. He founded the Chevra Kadisha [Burial Society] in the new community and was one of its most active members.

Since there were still no public baths in the community and also no kosher mikveh, Sztunke arranged a mikveh and bathhouse in his home for the use of all the city's inhabitants.

His memory as a benefactor, activist, someone who created the Kielce community and brought it out of its infancy remained for a long time with the veteran inhabitants of the city, who used to tell stories and jokes about him. I will bring one instance here, very typical of his type of thinking.

[Page-202]

Once before the Passover holiday, R' Mejer Sztunke became deathly ill. His sons, who were not as strict about the commandments as he was; didn't notice the ruling of selling the "chametz" [leavening] to a gentile. Meanwhile, Passover was over, and the patient improved and returned to his activities, to his beverage shop, brandy, beer and wine. When he discovered that this "chametz" had not been sold to a gentile before Passover, as he usually did every year, he went to Rabbi Gutman, the local rabbinical authority, to ask him what to do in this matter.

The rabbi gave his ruling: "Chametz that has been in one's possession through the Passover – it is forbidden to take any pleasure in it."

What did R' Mejer do? He stood on the bridge that spanned the river Silnica, which flowed in front of his house, took bottles of brandy and barrels of beer and poured them into the water of the river.

The peasants, who were passing by stopped at the sight, also Jews came out of their homes to see this performance. The goyim saying to one another: "This Jew is out of his mind; he is destroying such precious and wonderful fluids with his own hands." They removed their hats and stirred their arms above the river to try and catch a bit of these beverages in their hats and pour them straight into their mouths.

To the Jews who were watching Sztunke kept repeating: "Chametz that has been in one's possession through the Passover – it is forbidden to take any pleasure in it." This performance continued until the shop was emptied of the drinks.

R' Mejer son of R' Icak Sztunke died on the 19th of Cheshvan, 5673 [Fall 1912]. One of his sons, Dow Berl Sztunke, followed in his father's footsteps and was one of the respected people in the congregation of the Jews of Kielce.

R' Mosze Chaim Kaminer Z"L functioned as the head of the Kielce community for a long period of time. He was more elevated than his predecessors were in his lineage and his social standing. A son of the Jewish "aristocracy", the son of R' Judel Kaminer of Checiny, owner of the "Podzmecza" estate. Mosze Chaim was the brother in law of the author of "Sfat Emet", the famous Admo"r of Gur, whose fortress protected most of the Chassidim in Poland. This great connection alone already put him on a high level above the people.

However, he also had personal qualities, which gave him added respect not only among the Gur Chassidim, but also among the rest of the Jews of Kielce. His external appearance, his assertive opinions, his intelligence, his expertise in the experiences of the world, his relations with the authorities, all these qualities gained him status and respect; and everyone admitted that it was good and appropriate for him to lead the community which had managed to grow in the meantime and take on a more definite form.

Even though he was not among the wealthy people of the city, his home was always open to the needy, to anyone who held out a hand. The grandson of the Admo"rs, who came to request charity on the merit of his ancestors, an emigrant, passing through the cities and villages, equipped with letters of recommendation and letters which testify to his wealth and honesty beforehand and his poverty now together with a request to support him generously, an author, who came to collect signatures for his book which is about to be published and in his hand endorsements from all of the sages and rabbis of the generations – all these have Mosze Chaim Kaminer's address in their hands and first knocked upon his door thinking that they would not leave his home empty handed. He kept to the tradition of his ancestors doing much charity in Israel.

[Page-203]

It happened once that the mailman brought a large package of pamphlets to his house. As a man who was distracted with his own business and public affairs, he didn't have time to look at them and see what their worth and contents were.

When I came to his house, he turned to me and said: "Please go and see who the author is of these books of moral instruction and I will send him their cost." When I took a look at them I told him: "These books must be burnt, they are the books of heretics; the missionaries distribute them to Jewish homes in order to capture souls in annihilation." Kaminer in his way was already willing to send the author the money of their cost without even looking at their contents!

I remember that when, in 5653 [1893], the cholera epidemic broke out in the cities of Poland and wrought devastation in the assembly of Israel, there were Jews who wandered in terror of the epidemic from cities which were infected to villages the disease had not yet reached and thus spread the germs of the epidemic.

In those days, M.Ch. Kaminer traveled together with the sanitary committee from village to village in the Kielce district and explained to the Jewish inhabitants the regulations of the committee, which had been established to preserve the health of the population. They listened to his words, since they respected him, and his advice and instructions were heeded.

As a government contractor, he paved sections of roads between Kielce and Krakow, came into contact with the authorities and in certain instances he was able to influence them to the benefit of Jewish affairs.

In his public activities, his generosity, his position in the center of the Chassidim he had great influence on public affairs and community procedures.

The clowns of the city used to say: "In Kielce, two camps have won public opinion: Public opinion of the Christians has been won by the Endeks and Jewish public opinion – by the Gur Chassidim, with Mosze Chaim Kaminer at their head."

However, from the day that the Zionist movement arose in the Jewish street, criticism also arose against this control of the Gur Chassidim in the running of community affairs. The Zionists, as enlightened democrats, wanted to introduce light into the public institutions. As advanced nationalists they wanted the community authority to deal not only with religious affairs but also with general national affairs: improving education, increasing productivity of the masses, etc. Therefore, they demanded the broadening of the community's responsibilities and activities; it needed to include, they thought, all of the charitable institutions, the cemeteries and Chevra Kadisha, the ritual slaughter and so on, which then were still private or public fiefdoms and were not included in the areas for which the community authority was responsible.

[Page-204]

Even though under the Czarist regime the community didn't have the authority to introduced any changes in the regulations which the central authorities handed down to them, these demands made appropriate propaganda material, to besmirch those who led the community in the eyes of the masses. The Zionist slogan: "Conquer the communities!" was accepted by the Zionists of Kielce.

After years of public relations, the Zionists succeeded in conquering the community several years before World War I and making its chief one of their comrades, the banker, Jakob Nowak. He was an outstanding Zionist. He dedicated an entire building for the use of the local Zionists, who moved from place to place, since they didn't have their own apartment in which to do their work.

Jakob Nowak was an enlightened man and at the same time he clung to the tradition and hopes of his people. Even though he was a wealthy man, he did not follow the path of assimilation, as did most of the wealthy Jews of the time. The Zionist idea took him over and he was devoted to it with his money and his soul. And his end proves his beginnings. He was a whole Jew, and as a Jew he suffered in exile.

At the beginning of World War I, the supreme Russian Commander, Nikolai Nikolewicz, accused the Jews of spying for the enemy and he captured the leaders of every community and held them hostage and he sent them as prisoners to the Russian districts where they were held in prison as criminals. If not for the help of the Russian Jews who made enormous efforts to free them from their prisons and thus to ease their fate, probably they would have all rotted in their poverty and suffering. Only thanks to the brotherly help of the Russian Jews did some of these hostages manage to return home after years of wandering.

I said "some", since not all of them managed to see their homes again; many of them died in foreign lands from a surfeit of trouble and wandering.

Also the bankers from Kielce, Jakob and Henryk Nowak were among the hostages. Henryk Nowak died in Moscow, far from the members of his family and members of his community. His brother, Jakob Nowak, returned to his city and home cast down and shattered in his soul and didn't live long after his wanderings. On the 18th of Iyar, 5679 [1919], Jakob son of Szlomo Nowak Z"L died. He lived as a Jew, suffered as a Jew and was a victim of hatred of Jews. May his memory be blessed!

During World War I, Isachar Berisz (Berza) Blumenfeld led the community. He was a modest activist, a homeowner, far from party rivalries. He was the son-in-law of R' Simcha Rajzman, owner of a large estate in the Kielce area. The community members looked to him as someone worthy of holding the honorable position of community "Parnas", because during the crazy days of the war sufferings he was very active quietly, without loud noises in the area of aid and charity to the needy, the refugees and those who were torn from their homes and families.

His public activity, which stemmed from love and mercy, from participating in the sorrows of his fellows, gained him a good reputation with all sections of the Jewish inhabitants, and everyone treated him affectionately.

[Page-205]

When the "Popular Bank" (Bank Ludowi) was founded in Kielce with the help of the American "Joint", whose purpose was to rehabilitate artisans and small grocers via inexpensive credit, Blumenfeld was appointed to head this financial institution. He ran the bank faithfully, not for any reward. The bank developed under his direction, its members increased and its turnover grew. He guarded this financial institution like the apple of his eye. His seat in the bank was a permanent one, he did not take his eye off of it, and endeavored that not even a penny of the community funds go astray.

This community leader was the last in the Kielce community who was elected to his post according to the old Czarist regulations, according to which only property owners had the right to vote in the elections to the community authority.

In independent Poland [post-1918], the Jewish community was founded upon democratic elements. A council of twelve members was elected in general elections. The council selected a community authority from within itself. During this short period, from the day of Polish independence to the outbreak of World War II, the matter of the heads of the community depended upon the strengths of the parties that participated in the elections. The party that won the election battle also elected the community leader from among its members.

In the years after the Balfour Declaration [1917], the Zionists prevailed in the elections and it was they, in partnership with "HaMizrachi" and the artisans, who dominated in the community.

During this period, the following sat on the seat of community leader: the Honorable Icak Mejer Rajzman, Cwi Zagajski, Dawid Rozenberg and Zew Kluska. The last community leader was from another camp, from the chassidic camp, Simcha Bunem Goldman.

I will describe the personality and quality of spirit of each of the community leaders here in a few lines, may their memory be engraved in this memorial book. They are worthy of having their names remain as a blessing to the members of the coming generations. Every one of them gave of his energy and strength, his knowledge and talent for the good of the community he led; every one of them yearned to elevate the members of his congregation materially and spiritually, to provide appropriate educational and charitable institutions and also introduced general national matters into their sphere of activity, such as allotments to the national funds, supporting pioneers who were moving to the land of Israel and others. Certain sums for these purposes were included in the community's annual budgets. In general, everyone was aware of any national event and responded to it, as is appropriate to a limb of the national body.

Icak Mejer Rajzman was the son of a glorious and famous family in the city. A descendant of R' Szlomo Rajzman or Szlomo Cwatil's, a benefactor in the Checiny community, who built a splendid study hall for the learning of Torah and prayer in 5622 [1862], a grandson of Simcha Rajzman, owner of a large estate in the Kielce area, son of Awigdor Rajzman who was one of the respectable members of the community.

[Page-206]

I. M. Rajzman was elected by the Zionists, excelled in his speaking ability with which he influenced his audience; an enlightened and educated man who knew how to conduct public affairs. Over time he also became known as the director of the "Popular Bank".

Also his wife, principal of a school for girls, did much to give her students national values.

The Zionists accepted Cwi Zagajski, "HaMizrachi" representative, as well. He was one of the wealthy men of the city and a great benefactor. He and his brother Jakob Z"L founded the "Home for the Aged" in Kielce and other institutions, as I mentioned earlier.

Dawid Rozenberg, a Zionist from his youth, from the day he was conscious he held the Zionist banner in his hand. A speaker and debater of talent, he would appear at every convention and meeting. His words made a considerable impression, for they were spoken with logic and pathos.

He was also a member of the municipal council, where he defended affairs of the Jewish public and its honor with fierceness and courage, which we had not previously seen in our representatives when they came to speak in the name of the Jews who sent them.

Rozenberg made many souls for the Zionist idea, especially among the young who admired him. He could not tolerate lukewarm Zionism, and therefore followed the Zionism of Ze'ev Jabotinsky, whom he admired heart and soul.

By profession he was a banker, he served for time as the assistant director of the commercial Lodz bank, Kielce branch; over the years he was also the director of the Popular Bank in Kielce. He excelled in the extent of his knowledge not only in banking, but in many other areas as well. His keen glance, his rapid grasp helped him orient himself in each and every subject and express his opinion regarding the question being debated.

Finally he founded a private bank, as the first and last Jew in Kielce to receive a concession to found such a bank from the Polish government. Even when he owned a bank he did not cease his work in public affairs.

Dawid Rozenberg was the most popular Jew in Kielce. He was active in all of their affairs and all of their needs. Everyone, from whatever party they belonged to, held him in esteem.

He grew up on the soil of Kielce, lived its life, aspired to elevate the members of his community in spirit and in fact, did much to improve the lives of the worker and the artisan; therefore everyone became fond of him. Whenever necessary, at every opportunity he was chosen to be their mouthpiece and representative, and he fulfilled his mission faithfully, may his memory be blessed.

R' Zew Kluska was a man who kept his word. From his youth he was devoted to the Zionist idea, he went through all the stages of the development of this elevated concept, didn't abandon the camp even in the days of major crisis that Zionism went through. He believed with perfect faith that the rebirth of the nation in its homeland would come to pass one of these days. This faith caused him to work devotedly in the Zionist movement.

[Page-207]

When he saw that life in the Diaspora was becoming more and more difficult, that anti-Semitism was growing stronger and the ground was falling away even beneath his own feet, he liquidated his Diaspora life and moved with most of his family to the land of Israel.

The only son of his Chassidic parents, he had a traditional education, after his marriage at a young age he was numbered among the ranks of the Chassidim; however, the national movement of rebirth swept him into its ranks and he was one of its most active and devoted members. His piety did not stop him from battling against his Chassidic and pious fellows who eschewed Zionism.

He was one of the founders of "HaMizrachi" in Kielce. In the Mizrachi he found a broad field of activity, he also found satisfaction there for his soul which clung to the tradition of his ancestors on the one hand and which yearned for rebirth on the other. The love of the Torah and the love of the land of Israel were united in him to one enthusiastic passion.

His friends recognized his excellent qualities, which dwell in the heart, elevating a person from the depths of selfish life and elected him to a position of honor in their community, to head the community; and he served the members of the congregation faithfully.

Here in Israel he is also respected and the natives of Kielce appreciate him, see in him an honest activist and show him signs of affection and admiration at every opportunity.

The last community leader, R' Simcha Bunem Goldman, was from the Chassidic camp. His father, R' Mendel Goldman was the son of the Admo"r R' Dudel of Chmielnik. This worthy lineage is what swayed people in his favor to elect him as the leader of the Kielce community.

As anti-Semitism grew all over Poland, and especially in Kielce, the hands of the Zionists grew weak in their local activities. Even Grynbaum gave up in his battle with the Polish Sejm [parliament] and left for Paris, and afterwards moved to the land of Israel. Thus all true Zionists also put their hearts and minds to moving to the land of Israel; almost everyone came to the recognition that there was no hope for Jews in exile. Many of the Zionists liquidated their businesses and moved to the land of Israel, even though all of those who led the Zionist movement opposed Jabotinsky Z"L's "Evacuation" plan. Those who remained in exile were no longer interested in local public activity, they viewed it as Sisyphean labor which bore no fruit.

At the time the Chassidim succeeded in conquering the public positions that the Zionists had abandoned. They received a majority in the community and also in the municipal council the only Jew elected came from their camp.

This is how Goldman was placed at the head of the community, a man from the tree of Tzadiks, of pleasant temperament who responded to the sufferings of others; a benefactor whose house was open to the poor. However, he did not excel in the qualities needed by a man who is conducting public affairs: a fierce desire and encompassing knowledge that includes public needs and the manner in which they are satisfied – these qualities he lacked. Others influenced him, and therefore his personality did not arouse the same respect that is usually given to the head of the community. He served the community until the outbreak of World War II.

[Page-208]

When the disease of the century, the Nazi murderers, invaded Poland, the Jews were their first victim; first and foremost they set their impure hands against those who led the communities, especially against those who didn't want to cooperate with them in the destruction of the members of their communities, these they abused, tortured them to death. They were the first martyrs who gave their souls for the sanctification of God's name and they are worthy of their names being engraved in golden letters in the national pantheon.

Every one of them served his community according to his talents and to the best of his ability. The image of all of the community members crystallized in the leader of the congregation.

When the enemy came to wipe out Israel, most of the community leaders did not flee from their posts to save their own souls, but stood their ground firmly in the battle and gave up their souls sanctifying God and their people.

The author has not yet come to evaluate the activities of the community leaders during the destruction of the Jews in Poland; but according to the information that reached us, the stand of each and every one of them in the face of the enemy was courageous and worthy of respect; they gave their lives and did not desecrate the honor of their people. The head of the Warsaw community, the engineer Czerniakow Z"L and the Kielce activist Dr. Mosze Pelc Z"L are specific examples of the general rule.

The "Gabbaim" of the Chevra Kadisha of the Holy Congregation of Kielce

The occupation with the dead was always one of the commandments that was kept with affection and devotion in all of the Diaspora of Israel. For the death of an immediate relative even the high priest would become impure. The accompanying of the dead is one of the things that a person eats of their fruit in this world, and is also rewarded in the world to come.

The honor of the dead was very precious to every person in Israel. Everyone would endeavor to care for the dead according to his status, to sew him a shroud of expensive cloth, to dig him a grave in a place that suited his status, to hold a proper funeral and graveside speech. The Chassidim also have a custom of making circuits around the deathbed.

In the cities, aside from the official Chevra Kadisha there was also a special "Chessed Shel Emet" [True Lovingkindness] society which took care of the dead who were impoverished, abandoned, without any relatives and brought them to a Jewish grave.

In each and every community the Chevra Kadisha was the most important of all the aid societies. Only the most important homeowners were accepted to it, god fearing. Not everyone was worthy of caring for a deceased Torah scholar.

[Page-209]

The "gabbaim" of the Chevra Kadisha in particular had to excel in good attributes and to have the trust and affection of the city's inhabitants.

On the evening of Hoshana Raba [the seventh day of Sukkot] a meeting of the members of the Chevra Kadisha took place in Kielce, in which the gabbai and his assistant were elected. On Shmini Atzeret [the eighth day of the holiday] the gabbai would hold a large kiddush in the morning for all of the members.

I did not intend to describe the role that the Chevra Kadisha played in the Jewish community. The Jewish authors of the previous generation wrote prolifically in this area. My goal, due to the task before me, is to make a memorial to the people who led this important society in the Kielce community, and I drew the purpose and essence of this society in Jewish life in a few lines.

The Chevra Kadisha in Kielce was founded by R' Izrael Mejer Szafir Z"L, the brother-in-law of R' Mosze Pffefer Z"L, and R' Mosze Dawid Ajzenberg, who was called Mosze Eli' Naftali's.

The community was still in its infancy, it did not yet need a society with many members. A few of the important homeowners got together at the time: those mentioned above, and a few others, like R' Josef Szwicer, R' Mejer Sztunke, R' Szmuel Jakil the baker and took upon themselves the job of filling the tasks of a Chevra Kadisha.

As is customary among Jews, one weeps and gives funerary oratories for the deceased. When the dead is still fallen upon the ground and also at the time of burial the cries and shrieks of the keening women and those who were related to the deceased go up to the heavens.

The members who take care of the dead were mostly people with a sense of humor and in the presence of the deceased they liked to joke and lighten the sadness that hovered over those present to some extent.

And in order to strengthen their spirits and chase away the sadness that crept into the heart when faced with death, at these moments they would take a drink of very strong brandy of ninety six proof, which excites the blood and sends it flowing in the arteries of the limbs at a quick tempo. The shrieks and wails became ordinary sounds to them and in this way they could do their job properly and according to the law.

Thus have members of the Chevra Kadisha done forever, and the people of Kielce were no exception.

In the Kielce Chevra Kadisha the following people served as gabbai consecutively: R' Mejer Ajzenberg, R' Mosze Ajzenberg, R' Joske Fiszman, R' Icak Rapaport and R' Heszel Goldberg.

From among all of these, R' Mosze Ajzenberg and Heszel Goldberg were the only ones who devoted nearly all of their days to the tasks of the Chevra Kadisha. They were veteran activists in this area. Here I must note that R' Mosze Ajzenberg was active also in other areas of community affairs, as I have mentioned above. And even so, he dedicated much of his time to the Chevra Kadisha activities. Heszel Goldberg, in contrast, was wholly involved only in the matter of "Chessed Shel Emet". He was the gabbai of the Chevra Kadisha for many years; the ability to care for the dead he inherited from his father, R' Mosze Goldberg, who was also one of those who care for the dead.

[Page-210]

Heszel Goldberg, who had capital, and who lived off of his rents, did not have to worry about a livelihood; therefore, he could dedicate most of his time to this sort of activity. In the morning hours one would see him in the market with his staff in his hand, or at the shop of R' Icak Kopel or in the book and stationery shop of R' Icak Kaminer, awaiting the call to fulfill his duty as the gabbai of Chevra Kadisha, to choose a grave for the deceased in accordance with his status, to oversee the Jewish cemetery and keep it up in a proper way and see that there be a paved road leading there.

The cemetery, which was a distance out of the city, did not have a paved road leading to it for a long time. In the fall or during the rain, reaching the cemetery was very difficult; there were cases in which the cart carrying the deceased sank in the mud and it was difficult to extract it from there.

Due to Heszel's constant endeavoring and with the aid of a generous family, the Zagajski brothers, the road was paved that became a blessing to those accompanying the dead and also to the thousands of visitors came, sometimes from distant places to visit the graves of ancestors. The visitors to the Kielce cemetery grew numerous especially after the righteous Admo"rs found their resting places there: The Admo"r of Checiny, the Admo"r of Kuzmir, the Admo"r of Pinczow, the Admo"r of Chmielnik, the Admo"r of Suchedniow and the Admo"r of Rakow, may the memory of righteous ones be a blessing. On the anniversaries of the deaths of these righteous people hundreds of men and women flocked to pray at their graves.

In the last years before World War II, when anti-Semitism grew stronger in the state of Poland, the fury of various anti-Semites pounced upon the Jewish cemetery of Kielce. It was not enough for them to assault the Jews who were alive, but they also cast their eyes and sent out their unclean hands to desecrate graves, to shatter tombstones. Sometimes they even dared to throw stones at those accompanying the deceased from behind the walls.

The parcels of land that bordered the cemetery, which formerly were owned by Jews, passed into the ownership of Poles; the Jewish cemetery suddenly found itself surrounded by Polish settlements in which anti-Semitic venom also fermented and they made a mockery of the mourning of the relatives of the deceased by imitating their wails. The Jews were already used to the actions of these rioting vermin and ignored them in silence without any sort of response.

This was the situation before the war. During the war the executioner came upon the living and the dead. Cemeteries were plowed under, the tombstones taken to pave sidewalks and roads.

What never happened in the darkest days of the Middle Ages – happened in our very own times!

Entire communities were erased from the face of the earth without a trace, and without the remnants of tombstones in their "Eternal Homes" (as cemeteries are called in Yiddish), and the fate of the Kielce community was the same as the fate of the rest of the communities of Poland.

Gabbaim of the Synagogue

Synagogues existed in each and every community of Israel. In every place in the Diaspora of the exile, since Jews had to gather together in a minyan [quorum] their first concern was the building of a small temple which would serve as a center for all of the affairs of the community. The Jews united in the synagogue. The individuals became a generality, a congregation, a community with various functions.

[Page-211]

There, within the community was hidden the secret of the existence of the assembly of Israel for such a long period of time, a period of two thousand years, scattered among the nations, expecting their trampling feet at every moment. The synagogue filled not just a religious role in this matter, but also a great national role. It safeguarded the unity and existence of the people of Israel in exile.

Wherever they arrived, Jews began to build a synagogue, immediately after finding homes. In some of the cities of Poland there were very ancient synagogues, which were built in different styles of architecture. These synagogues were always witnesses of the settlement of Jews there. The equal side of them all was the investment of excessive labor and care by their builders in the decorations and furnishings. Evident in all of them is the energy and affection with which the congregation set about decorating the ceiling, the walls, the doors, the windows, the bima, the holy ark and the rest of the holy accessories.

The content of the engravings and drawings are taken from the scriptures and from the landscapes of the land of Israel. Engraved on either side of the Holy Ark were the four holy animals. On the ceiling the twelve signs of the zodiac were drawn; the walls were decorated with scenes from the lives of the patriarchs, landscapes of the holy land, plants of the land of Israel and so forth.

Whoever entered a synagogue was imbued not only with a spirit of holiness but also with the atmosphere of the land of Israel. He saw figures with his own eyes about whom he had read in books and whom he mentioned in his prayers. In this way the land of Israel took hold of his affections, yearnings and nostalgia for it awakened in him and it was not forgotten during the long period of exile.

Also the young Kielce community did not rest or feel quiet until it was fortunate enough to see a synagogue within its borders. A lovely and splendid building, which honored it and its surroundings.

As was mentioned earlier, the well-known philanthropist R' Mosze Pffefer Z"L, one of the best of the city's sons and builders, built the synagogue. But the finishing work, the decorations and interior design and furnishings, the community did on its own several years later at its own expense. They invited painter-artists from Warsaw and they executed their work with good taste and charm. From that time onwards, the synagogue of the Kielce community was one of the splendid buildings and those who visited it from other places were full of praise and respect for those who took part in its building and improvement.

In this synagogue there were gabbaim, the elect of the congregation, who oversaw the internal procedures and the respect of the holy place, that it not be desecrated by arguments and fights, which usually take place in public assemblies. Of course, those elected to be gabbaim were only those who were suited to the position, those who were accepted and held in affection by most of the congregation.

And here are the gabbaim: Mendel Ajzenberg, Simcha Bunem Izraelski, M. Grynszpan, Icak Kirszenbaum, Baruch Moszenberg, R. Finkelsztajn, Josef Orbajtl, Mejer Zloto, Josef Ziunczkowski. Of them, Mendel Ajzenberg, one of the veteran inhabitants of Kielce, from the family of activists who shaped the community, functioned for a number of years as the gabbai of the synagogue. The congregation was content with his manner of conducting the synagogue and his behavior with the community of worshipers.

[Page-212]

I will not be considered a gossipmonger over the merits and qualities of each and every gabbai. It will be enough if I say in general that they were people who did not seek out honor, they served the community faithfully and guarded the synagogue like the apple of their eye; each and every one of them added to the grandeur of the synagogue some personal component. One endeavored to make the entrance to the synagogue arranged properly; another planted decorative trees around it. One took care of the choir, ensuring it functioned properly.

A new gabbai came and glanced around him to see if the previous gabbais had left him an area to call his own. When he found that everything was in order, he went and arranged a uniform for the members of the choir.

Grynszpan emigrated from Kielce and settled in Germany, in Frankfurt on the River Main. Towards the end of his life hie moved from there to the land of Israel and lived there to his last day.

The synagogue also suffered not a little from the anti-Semites. The local haters of Israel saw that the Jews had built themselves a grand building as a synagogue upon the soil of Kielce, where previously they had been forbidden even one nights sleep on this ground; they were jealous of them and organized a group of thugs whose job would be to bother the Jews at prayer. During the prayers they would throw stones and shatter the windowpanes. There were instances in which Jews came to worship in the synagogue in good health and returned to their homes injured and bandaged. The Polish police never found those who carried out these events of desecration of holiness and did not react to them at all. In order to evade the danger, the gabbaim took it upon themselves to install metal grills over the windows to catch stones of the hoodlums so that they would not hurt the panes of the windows.

Finally, the Shoah arrived and together with those who built you and who sanctified you, you drank and drained the cup of poison. Impure ones came and desecrated and defiled your halls, your temple, your Torah scrolls in which on white parchment was written by a pure and holy scribe the moral injunction: "Thou shalt not murder", and many other laws and commandments, whose content was love and mercy to others.

The Jewish synagogue! What have these evil impure ones done to you! My heart breaks inside of me, when I hear the abominable things that were done within your holy walls.

Jewish Members of the Municipal Council

In this chapter, dedicated to the people who lead the Jewish public institutions in Kielce, I will include a short list of activists who worked and fought for the benefit of the Jewish community and its institutions within the walls of the Kielce municipality.

According to the constitution of the independent state of Poland, all inhabitants of the state without difference of race or religion had the right to vote passively and actively for the municipal councils and their communal authority.

[Page-213]

The Jews used this right and elected municipal council members and also entered the municipal authority themselves.

The Jewish members of the municipal council of Kielce were well-known activists in various areas and I have mentioned their names and attributes a number of times in this book; among them, the following were especially outstanding in their devotion to their work at the municipality and city authority (the "Magistrat") in favor of the Jews R' Benjamin Lew and R' Mosze Rotenberg, an Agudaist and a Zionist who both moved to the land of Israel and died in Tel-Aviv, and Dr. Mosze Pelc. I will mention here only Dr. Pelc, since with his energy and knowledge, his expertise in the needs of the city in general, he left a mark on the activities of the municipality. And in his defense of the Jewish population that the majority of the municipal council not neglect it, he gained a reputation among the Jewish inhabitants of Kielce.

To the extent that anti-Semitism grew stronger in Poland, to the same degree Jewish representation grew smaller in Kielce on the municipal council.

In order to decrease the number of Jews elected to the municipal council, the authorities annexed many villages in the area to the municipal authority of Kielce, calling them suburbs of the city. In this manner, the number of voters grew. Finally, they began to use other means: distorting the names of the voters, in order to disqualify them later; not including Jewish names in the voting lists; using terror tactics during the voting itself. Things reached a point that only one Jew got into the last municipal council before World War II, Simcha Bunem Goldman, instead of ten members who had been in the first municipal council.

But even in days when things were running properly the Jewish institutions, which were supposed to receive allotments from the municipality just like the Christian institutions, were neglected. Even in instances when the council, under pressure from the Jewish members, budgeted paltry sums for the use of the Jewish institutions, the Wojewoda (Province Governor) came and cut the allotment drastically.

Thus, for instance, in the fiscal year 1929-1930 the council budgeted a total of 7,400 gold coins for the use of the Jewish institutions, the authorities came and changed the allotment to merely 4,300 gold coins.

The Jews were always neglected by both the municipality and by the authorities, which cast narrow eyes on the Jews, lest they enjoy the municipal income to the same degree as the Christians, even though this income came mainly from the Jewish inhabitants of the city.

[Page-214]

Authors and Scientists

The Kielce community, the youngest of the Jewish communities of Poland still managed to produce authors, scientists and journalists from its midst like one of the ancient communities. Some of them even earned an international reputation and were published on two continents: in Europe and in America.

Fiszel Bimko

Fiszel Bimko was a Yiddish author and playwright, the son of a shopkeeper in Kielce, his name became famous in Poland and in America after he emigrated and settled there.

The amazing thing is that Bimko received no education, he attended no educational institution whatsoever; he developed on his own and his literary talent increased from level to level until he was famous as an outstanding author and extraordinary playwright.

His father, a grain merchant, never knew the concept "literature"; but he had one trait that is very important in an author. He had been blessed with a most developed imagination, and he made use of this strength of his once even to solve government problems. He heard that the Polish government was grappling with the question of the currency, how to improve its currency which was not linked to the gold standard. Old Bimko got up and composed a "Memorandum" in spoken Jewish – Yiddish – for he knew no other language – in which he proposed a plan that was annotated and explained the matter from every angle, according to which the government treasury could be rehabilitated and to save great amounts of gold which could serve its currency; Polish currency would be repaired. This plan gained the attention of the government after it was translated into Polish.

A rich imagination and momentum his son also had, and these made him an author in Israel. However, not only his heritage played an important role in the development of his writing talents, fate had a hand in this also. For the sin of participation in the liberation movement in 1905 he was sentenced to prison. While he was in jail he read prodigiously: the stories of Mendele Mocher Sforim, I. L. Peretz and others. He swallowed their contents whole like unripened sheaves, and they aroused his slumbering talents. While he was still a prisoner in jail, he tried his hand at storytelling. He wrote a story there called "Di Aveira" [The Transgression]. It is based in a Chassidic setting. The buds of talent are visible in this work of his; and if it was still green fruit, it already revealed signs of a literary power, a talent for observation accompanied by the sweep of the imagination.

[Page-215]

He was especially successful when he began writing plays. The Jewish actors in the Warsaw-Lodz theatres took his plays and performed them before the Jewish audiences, who received them with great applause. The types of lives that appeared before their eyes were familiar and well known to them.

His play: "The Thieves" remained part of the theatrical repertoire for a long time. Since he was the son-in-law of a horse trader, he knew all about the lifestyles of the various horse thieves, he entered their circles, learned the language of the thieves. Using his powers of observation he penetrated the depths of their souls, and with artistic talent could put living figures from the world of thieves on paper.

The Jewish press printed reviews of the performance of this play. All of the critics were of the opinion that they had before them a force that drew material for his mind's vision not from some second hand vessel but directly from the life and nature that surrounded him.

In America his literary talent was also recognized and Bimko had a major role in American-Jewish literature.

The Kielce landscape had a great influence upon him. Even when he settled in America he was unable to shake free of the impressions he had received from his environment in his childhood. Mountains and hills, forests and fields of grain, meadows and orchards, streams and waterfalls turning it a varied and spotted carpet. On the edges of the horizon here and there some rows of huts straggle along which look like boxes from a distance.

In his walks in this landscape his soul was enriched by color and sights and formed it into the soul of a creative artist. In every one of his stories landscape scenes appear of their own accord, which his soul absorbed during his childhood days.

Szlomo Berlinski

Sz. Berlinski was a Yiddish author who was younger than Bimko. He was born in Checiny, a small town in Kielce district; Kielce raised him and it was there that he sprouted wings, the wings of imagination, which are necessary to a man who is meant to be an author in Israel.

He also didn't receive any education in childhood; he didn't even learn in a "cheder" for very long. His father, one of the Chassidim of the Admo"r of Checiny, was an agent and lived in poverty all of his life. The poverty that filled his home left its mark upon the spiritual makeup of this sensitive child.

In one of his autobiographical stories in which he describes the lives of the Jews in his native village, he sets before us a scene that emphasizes the shabbiness in their home with clear lines.

Summer, Sabbath, after naps. The men, women and children go out to walk between the fields that are outside of the city. Everyone is wearing their holiday clothing. Those who wore new shoes picked up their feet as they walked as if they wanted to show the others and tell them: "See what nice steps I take in my new shoes that shine from blacking!"

[Page-216]

And he, the child, sits next to the window that overlooks the road and watches the passersby, and among them he sees his friends, they too are dressed and shod, walking out to breathe fresh air in the fields. The boy's heart breaks within him, he also yearns to go out; but he is barefoot, he has no shoes; how can he show himself outside on the Sabbath barefoot like one of the "Shkeitzim".

His father sits at the table and reads "Chapters of the Fathers". His dull and monotonous voice brings a dark pall to the house. Outside, everyone is cheerful and gay.

The child turns to his father with the question: "Father, when will I also have shoes?"

In such an impoverished home Berlinski lived in childhood and in youth. Therefore, it is no wonder that he later found an arena for activity among those less fortunate in life, among those who earned their bread with the sweat of their brow and live in miserable circumstances in dark and dank cellars. For all that, it is among them that he found sparks of light and tenderness, which illuminated the darkness of their lives and gave them meaning and content in their poverty and want.

In his articles and stories he aspires to give meaning to the mute sorrow of those with miserable lives, wasting away in their poverty without a sliver of hope or a mite of consolation.

The inspirations for his literary activity were the scenes of poverty, depression and lowliness which his soul absorbed during childhood and which he lays out before the reader. With his keen eye he penetrates into the very center of things and of the sights and reveals hidden aspects. He does not see the objects and phenomena as they appear to the naked eye; his associations amaze us in their richness and multi-hued variety.

He settled in Israel after the Shoah, which came upon European Jewry. And here too he does his literary work and from time to time publishes his creations in which critics find real and valuable subject matter.

Leon Finkelsztajn

The third author who was hewn from the soil of Kielce was Leo Finkelsztajn. He was different from the two mentioned earlier in that in his childhood and youth he was educated in general educational institutions and also attended the university at Krakow.

I knew him from his time in Kielce. He was then an alert and sensitive young man, with a quick grasp, interested in philosophical questions, active in youth circles and appearing as a speaker at meetings. His speeches were full of information and content. He frequently mentioned the names of the philosophers: Spinoza, Kant and Nietzsche. He began his literary activity while still in Kielce. He wrote a play in Polish called "Broken Wings" ("Skaszydla Zlamna") and Polish actors performed it at the local theater

[Page-217]

And here there was a coincidence and Noach Prylucki was invited to Kielce by the "Artisans Union". Several members wanted him to organize a branch of the peoples' party in Kielce, - "Folkes-Partei" – that he headed. Prylucki then came into close contact with the young Finkelsztajn and saw that he was talented and could use his abilities to spread his party's ideology among the masses of the Jews. Prylucki took him to Warsaw, gave him a position in the artisan's bank. There in Warsaw, Finskelsztajn began to act as an activist in the peoples' party.

His name became especially well known when he was elected in the capital, Warsaw, as a "Parnas" in the Jewish community. His articles appeared in the Polish-Jewish newspaper "Nasz Paszglond", most of them about philosophical matters. He also wrote in the Yiddish monthly: "Literarishe Bleter".

When the Nazis invaded Poland he escaped to Soviet Russia. There he became close to the Jewish authors and absorbed communist opinions from them.

He returned to Poland and saw the destruction of Polish Jewry with his own eyes, began to work for the Jewish committee in Warsaw, but could no longer live in Poland, which had turned into a giant graveyard for its Jewish inhabitants.

He traveled to America and afterwards to Argentina. There, in the large Jewish communities, he hoped to find himself again, but the travails of the journey weakened his strength, his health was unsettled, and he died in Argentina. People from Kielce mention his name affectionately; his talents were developed in their city and he was flesh of their flesh, bone of their bone.

Feiwel-Artur Lewi

The Kielce community also produced from within its ranks educated people of renown. They did not receive the appropriate or necessary preparation in their childhood and youth, which might have paved them a way to science and wisdom. On the contrary, their parents never even dreamed that a spark of talent and a thirst for knowledge and science was hidden within their children and did not notice the attributes of their children's souls. They were too sunk in worries of livelihood. And once their children outgrew the age of "cheder", they handed them over to the artisans. To seek another goal for their children, according to their spiritual strengths and their abilities – they could not conceive of such a thing, worried as they were all day with earning a living.

However, this is the way of the spirit, even if iron barriers bar its way to the wider world, it will break out with force and insist upon its own correct path in life.

Feiwel Lewi can be our example of this phenomenon of life. He was the son of a tailor, did not receive any secular education in his childhood, only religious education in a "cheder". He did not learn to read and write there. When he grew older, he worked as a typesetter in a printing press.

Yet his spirit yearned to break free of its framework. The secrets of life and social questions occupied his mind from a time when he was still very young. He began to read books, taught himself the Hebrew language, penetrated into the depths of the questions that were then on the agenda in Yiddish and Hebrew literature and that were discussed in the press. At every meeting and convention Lewi would express himself.

[Page-218]

In those days, before World War I, the Jewish press and literature were mainly pro-Zionist; and on the Jewish street the Zionist movement was noticeable and very active; therefore, it was obvious that Lewi, as a young man seeking an outlet for his stormy soul, found his place in the ranks of the Zionists.

However, in public and national activity he did not find enough spiritual satisfaction, he aimed for a broad education, for spiritual wholeness.

When he was twenty years old he devoted himself to textbooks and began to study the principles of mathematics, the rules of grammar, geography, history and the natural sciences. He studied diligently and continuously, for he had one goal in front of him – receiving a matriculation certificate, which would allow him to attend university.

After the war he traveled to Warsaw; there he hoped to attain his goal more easily – for all the educational institutions were in the capital city. Meanwhile, he was an auditor for free at the popular university. There he discovered that the areas of science are as great as the sea, and the human mind cannot grasp them all at once.

Lewi, who had been preoccupied with the question of life since his youth, chose the new branch of science, biochemistry, so that he would be able to deepen his investigation into the secrets of the forces of life and in this way he aspired to quench his thirst for knowledge.

In Warsaw he did not find the scholars in this field, since the university in Warsaw after World War I was just then beginning to gather its forces which were scattered in various countries.

To this aim, Lewi decided to travel to France and study further in the scientific area that he had selected as his life's goal. Success shined its face on him, he married the daughter of a wealthy man in Warsaw. His wife's parents, when they saw his great desire for science and wisdom, sent him to Paris at their own expense. There he studied and advanced in his favorite subject. He worked and did research in the laboratories of internationally renowned scholars. And as was always his way, he invested all of his energies and all of his resources, his entire being into this branch of science.

The expert professors, when they saw their student so full of blessing paid special attention to him and allowed him to work in their laboratories and to use their instruments. He investigated hormones in particular, which fill an essential role in the living body. Afterwards he published an essay in which he revealed important matters in physiology.

After several years he returned to Poland as a scholar. The newspapers wrote about his discoveries in the scientific area of chemistry. Lectures about the quality of discoveries of the young chemist could be heard on Polish radio.

The Polish government, even if it was normally anti-Semitic and removed Jews from their positions, gave F. Lewi a very important position on the recommendation of its president Moszczicki. He was appointed inspector of sanitary conditions in the army and in factories; according to his decisions the amount of food calories necessary to maintain health in the army ranks was settled.

[Page-219]

At a convention of Polish chemists in Poznan, at which the president of the country J. Moszczicki participated, Lewi was one of the most important lecturers.

Feiwel Lewi, who I saw for the first time at the age of twenty, strolling in the city park with a Russian mathematics book in his hand, and he kept repeating aloud: "what is addition?" "tszeto takuja slorznja?" and acquiring the four mathematical operations, information that a student in the first grade of elementary school has to know, was after a few years a scholar, and inventor, famous within the country and out of it.

Lewi was able to escape to America, to his brother, who had emigrated there in the days of the national liberation movement, in 1905. Over there, in America he continues to work in his profession and to take an interest in the fate of the refugees of the Shoah, his fellow townsmen. He became famous in America as well and there too they gave him the title of professor.

Mosze Manela

A modest scholar who did not seek fame was Mosze Manela. He also did not receive even elementary education in childhood. His father, an impoverished "melamed", lived from hand to mouth, was forced to hand his son over to artisans so they could teach him a craft that would support one who plied it. M. Manela learned tailoring and until he was seventeen was busy with this craft.

However, in the depths of his soul other desires were hidden. As the grandson of a long line of rabbis, experts in the Torah, whose lineage reached the "Siftei Cohen" (the "Sha"ch"), he also had a natural tendency towards academic matters from birth. Simple craft, which demands from a man only the force of the muscles, and in which spiritual forces take no part – did not satisfy his spirit, which was hungry for knowledge; his abilities from birth and before demanded their satisfaction, development and completion.

He was gifted with an amazing memory, quick grasp and over all with a great thirst for knowledge and wisdom.

But his father, a sickly man, burdened with children, did not pay any special attention to him. He gave him to "melameds" and there he received knowledge in Talmud, rabbinical arbiters and scripture and after he reached bar-mitzvah age he was handed over to a tailor to learn a profession that could support him.

I remember one fact that serves as an example of his extraordinary abilities, which he displayed when he was still a small child. His father, wanting to demonstrate the talent of his four year old child, brought him to the rabbi's house and there stood him upon the table. And the child declaimed by heart and translated in to Yiddish the prayer "Baruch Shmaya" etc. that is read when the holy ark is open and which is written in Aramaic. Everyone was astounded at the sight and sound. By his manner of speech it was clear that he also had understanding of the words he spoke.

[Page-220]

However at the same time that he learned the craft, he acquired languages and knowledge in the subjects of the high school curriculum. When he was sixteen he took the exam at the Jewish Gymnasium in Kielce and entered the 8th grade. When he finished the Gymnasium he went on to university and immediately became famous among the students as a first class mathematician.

After the death of his father he took it upon himself to support his widowed mother and her orphaned children. Naturally good hearted, he sacrificed his future on the altar of a son's responsibility to his orphaned family. Instead of continuing in his profession and continuing to study in scientific areas as his teachers at the university recommended, and to reach the level of professor, he was satisfied with the degree of Magister [Master] in Mathematics and Physics and entered the Hebrew gymnasium in Kielce as a teacher, in order to support his family and to enable his brothers and sisters to have a decent education.

At the same time, he continued to do research in his field of science, participated in the conventions of the scholars and gave lectures in higher mathematics and physics. During the last summer before World War II he participated in a convention of mathematicians in the city of Radom, in which Szwiantoslawski, the Minister for the Peoples' Education also participated, and among others, Manela also lectured, and his lecture won the first prize.

He had a dissertation all ready, an encompassing composition about subjects in higher mathematics and he was supposed to present it to the faculty of professors in order to receive the degree of doctor of philosophy and humanities, and then the war broke out, which brought about the terrible destruction to the Jews of Poland, and the Jewish scholars were its first victims.

Those of his students who moved to the land of Israel remember the name of their teacher and educator with affection and admiration, who asked nothing for himself, and who took great pleasure if he had an opportunity to come to the aid of others.

In Kielce several other young people lived and worked who had begun to show signs of talent as authors and as journalists, but the fell together with all of the Jews of Poland before they were able to sprout wings and to fly on the winds.

I will mention their names here and may this memorial be a marker for these precious souls:

Mendl Krakauer

A young man with imagination, a philosopher and Hebrew writer, published a book, his first work, which described the life of a young man who lived in a time of a battle of ideas and views, of different ideologies, and he wandered and felt his way among them without having a compass to know which was the correct way. Religious, national, socialist questions meet one another; parties and factions arise; each of them with their own teachings, their own beliefs. The young man is lost in a flood of the ideas and programs since he has no authority he can trust. Krakauer did much in the cultural arena among the youth of Kielce.

[Page-221]

Chaim Rzylony

Chaim Rzylony, a secretary in the community committee and an outstanding Zionist, editor of the newspaper "Kielcer Zeitung", had journalistic talent; his popular articles made an impression upon their readers.

Lajbl Rudel

Lajbl Rudel from the Revisionist camp. A young man of literary talent, he published articles in the local newspaper and in "Moment" of Warsaw, afterwards he became a member of the editorial board of the Warsaw newspaper "Express" and was also a reporter for the "Forwarts" and "Tag" in New York. He excelled especially in his reporting about the pogrom at Przytyk, which were published in all of the

American press. He was one of the important fighters in the Warsaw ghetto, saved many Jews from death, among them people from Kielce by sending them through the sewage system from the ghetto out of the city, and his name is blessed among those who sanctified heaven and their nation in their courage and died the death of the brave, may god avenge his death.

[Page 222]

Folk Artists

In Kielce there were also artists who did not gain an international reputation, since they did not have those kinds of demands; but the local Jews considered them artists gifted with special abilities and honored them as people who increased the joy in their homes and would bring pleasure to those invited to a family celebration and add a grandeur to any party. Artists such as these were not educated in academies, they developed on their own, studied and reached their degree of excellence.

R' Anszel Szpilman

Anszel'le Klezmer was famous in the city of Kielce and its surroundings. This diminutive of his first name was used to express affection and admiration for the man who bore the name.

The "Klezmers" in every city and town in Poland filled an important role in the life of each and every community. If the plastic arts were neglected among the Jews due to the ban: "make no graven image", the musical art, singing and playing, were extremely developed among them. Those who played instruments, the cantors and their choirs brought life, joy and pleasure to the Jews. There was no wedding in Israel, even among the poorest of the poor, in which the Klezmers and local cantor didn't participate.

Among them were also great musicians, who, despite not having learned musical theory and the art of playing at a conservatory, became virtuosi by virtue of their own developed talent, and the sense of music that was instilled in them from birth.

The general reputation of the Jewish "Klezmers" was admired even in the circles of the Polish aristocrats. At their feasts and parties the Jewish "Klezmers" also played. The great Polish poet Adam Mieckowicz in his collection "Pan Tadeusz" admiringly and affectionately describes the character of Jewish player R' Jankel Cimbalist, a devout Jews and at the same time an enthusiastic Polish patriot, who plays the Polish anthem at the balls of the nobles in spite of the danger of being convicted as a traitor to the throne.

[Page-223]

In a more limited way, Anszel'le Szpilman was also a virtuoso like this, the first violinist in his orchestra. He acquired a complete technique in his profession. With his violin he would play and successfully perform the complicated composition of famous composers. He would pull all sorts of strange and unusual sounds from the strings of his violin: sounds of songbirds, sounds of domestic and wild animals, the wind in the forest trees, the waves of the sea, and in general, any sound you wanted.

When he stood upon a table with his violin in his hand, it was as if he and his violin were part of one body. He stood erect, his fingers moving over the strings, moving and shaking, pure sounds coming from them, sometimes sad, beseeching, which stirred the heart of the listener. You could hear the spasms of body and soul: weeping, yelling, groaning, wailing, crying. And sometimes, from the strings of his violin happy and gay notes poured out, full of joy and celebration. You could hear the sounds of victory in them, cries of joy, tenderness and comfort, elevation of the spirit and the soul.

Listeners charmed by these notes would pick up their feet of their own accord and dance; their hearts were filled with unending comfort and pleasure. Love and friendliness shone upon their faces, feelings of joy filled their entire beings, great song burst from their mouths, their hands joined in the communal dance. And thus they would dance, drunk with joy until their feet refused to obey them.

This was the power of the fiddle when Anszel'le Klezmer played it. His violin worked wonders. When he played the "Darkecha" on his fiddle before the bride was welcomed to the chupah [wedding canopy] the eyes of men and women filled with tears they were so moved. What could not be heard in this splendid tune? The troubles of the many and the troubles of the individual, the outpouring of the soul, the justification of the son before his father, sounds full of beseeching. And the tune continues on until it ends with salvos of victory. Feelings of happiness overcome those gathered – and all ends well.

A Jew who married off his daughter did not spare money and did his best to ensure that Anszel'le Klezmer and his friends would play at his daughters wedding, for besides this adding splendor and beauty to the general joy of the marriage, Anszel'le's participation in his family celebration was considered an honor to the host.

In every celebration of a mitzvah: the party of finishing the study of a volume, the party that was held in honor of arrival of some important guest, at every family celebration, Anszel'le was invited to glorify and decorate the party.

When the representatives of the nations gathered in St. Remo and confirmed the Balfour Declaration, there was great joy in the Diaspora of Israel; many saw "Atchalta DeGe'ula" [the beginning of redemption] in this.

In Jewish communities national celebrations were then held. Synagogues held thanksgiving prayers and read the "Hallel" prayer of praise. The Kielce community also held a popular celebration with much splendor. At this opportunity Anszel'le and his orchestra appeared in the synagogue. And within the walls of this minor temple the players thundered with their instruments and filled the space of the holy place with the sounds of praise and thanksgiving, which reminded the congregation of the Levites on their platforms during the time of the Temple in Jerusalem.

[Page-224]

Elevation of spirit, spiritual joy of a two thousand year old hope which was beginning to be fulfilled took over the synagogue from within and without. The melodies of Anszel'le did much to aid in spreading this mood among the massed congregation who gathered to hear the news of the redemption.

Josef Rajzler (Josele Badchan)

In Kielce a "badchan" [jester], who was famous in nearly all of the cities of Poland and was known by the name of "Josele Badchan" lived and worked.

At the time that theatres were not very common in the cities of Israel, the "badchans" would satisfy peoples' need to laugh and have fun. There was no celebration in Israel in which the "badchan" did not participate. The "badchan" would entertain the groom and the bride; he was the one who chastised them and called them to repent before they entered the wedding canopy; he scattered praises and compliments, congratulations and good wishes to the young couple, the in-laws and all of the invited guests; during the eating and drinking he would entertain the dinner guests with songs, jokes and witticisms. He would dress up and perform a well known character who was famous there and would imitate his manner of speech, his gestures, his gait and his habits and would make the guests laugh. The "badchan" was even allowed to expose the flaws of the respected members of the community with thin and transparent hints.

The "badchan" also entertained the Chassidim in the courts of the Admo"rs at all of the celebrations of mitzvah. He would chase the sadness from the hearts of the pious and righteous.

The story of the "badchans" among the Jews of Poland has not been taken up by the authors of Israel. The "badchans" are worthy of having a complete and comprehensive composition dedicated to them. For they introduced the times of comfort and moments of joy into the bitter and sad lives of the members of the exile. But I, due to the labor that I have undertaken, mention them only in passing for the sake of "Josele Marszilik".

This Josele was not a simple "badchan" but a jester among jesters. He was a genius at his profession, an outstanding artist. Had he entered the theatre, he would doubtless have been one of the most famous actors in the world. But he was a Chassidic Jew, who wore silk clothing on the Sabbath and wore a "shtreimel" hat, and on the high holidays he would lead the prayers and with his pleasant and endearing voice arouse emotions of devotion, awe and repentance in the hearts of the congregation. – Such a Jew would never even dream of the theatre. He found his satisfaction in his role as a "badchan".

It was pleasant to hear his improvisations, his rhymes. He would stand before the groom or before the guests and make up rhymes, include epigrams, Jewish laws, sayings, amazing acrostics, "gematrias", rise up to higher worlds and immediately descend to a bottomless pit, all of it clear to him from the entrance to hell up to the gates of paradise, from the battle of Gog and Magog until the feast that will be held for the righteous in the world to come at which the meat of the wild bull, the whale and preserved wine will be served them. The audience stood amazed and astounded by the expertise and the force of this short fellow. With open mouths and craned ears they heard and listened to his rhymes and his songs.

[Page-225]

This Josel Badchan was also a member of the local "HaZamir". For his profession belonged to the arts in an obvious way. And "HaZamir" fostered art. He would read aloud to the audience in the "HaZamir" auditorium from the works of "Shalom Aleichem."

The works of this author are full of lively and fresh humor, the funny element rules them; and Josel the Badchan would in his manner of reading, his facial expressions and gestures add twice as much of his own contribution to the funny reading material.

I was once present when he read "The Gymnasium" by Shalom Aleichem. The listeners nearly burst from the laughter he roused in them. The laughter attacked everyone and it was difficult to find release from it. I had never heard such popular laughter, which burst from so many mouths with great strength, accompanied by tears and which took over every aspect of the human body, – as the laughter that took over the auditorium during the reading of Josel the Badchan. It seemed as if the air was saturated with laughter, and it broke to pieces in the thunder of laughter. People would forget their problems and sufferings at such a time, and their worries and give themselves over to the laughter, to do with them what it would. The world took on a charming aspect in their eyes. If life gives a man such pleasurable moments – one cannot despair, life is worth living. Better one hour of comfort in this world than piles of promises for the world to come. – thus people thought in their hearts when they left this occasion.

This was the power of Josel the Badchan. A short Jew, pale, wearing a "shtreimel" on Sabbaths and holidays like one of the Chassidim, snatching "songs" from the rabbi's hands, and together with this, he had an amazing talent to create characters, rhyming verses, to sing beautifully; to make jokes and gladden hearts.

These attributes gave him a reputation in the entire region. There is not doubt that if Josele the Badchan had developed his talents and abilities with appropriate exercises combined by comprehensive education; had he done professional training, he would have reached a high level of stage actor. Certainly, he would have earned himself a reputation as a famous actor in the great theatres of the world.

However, he lived in the Jewish village, he remained in his narrow circle, he used his abilities to gladden and entertain simple people, who had no concept of theatre life, and this role he filled with wisdom and knowledge during his lifetime.

The elders of Kielce still talk about him today and speak favorably of his memory.

"Josel Badchan" – they say – "that was a force! That was an artist! The actors of today don't even reach his ankles." With such words they appreciate the personality of the "badchan" who was their favorite in his lifetime, and remained firmly in their memories even after his death.

[Page 226]

Portraits and Characters

Translated by Judy Montel

Rabbi Mosze Mendel Walden

Reb' Mosze Mendel Walden son of Reb' Aharon Walden, author of the book "Shem HaGdolim HaChadash" [The New Book of Great Ones] was a bookseller. He was of the type that Mendele Mocher Sforim described so well in his fiction and presented to us perfectly.

However, there was a difference between the Kielce bookseller and Mendele's character. Mendele's character was a nomad: he traveled from city to city, town to town with his skinny mare pulling a cart full of books. Mosze Mendel, on the other hand, knew the meaning of a good rest. He sat there in his shop among the piles of his books and waited for a customer to come in. He would say: "Vai to the merchant who goes from door to door with his wares! A merchant whose honor is precious to him and who respects his business awaits buyers in his shop."

In his shop were all sorts of religious books: prayer books for every day and for holidays, books of women's beseeching prayers, prayers of repentance and dirges, books in Yiddish about the weekly portion etc. Among the books of the bible one could find in his shop Pentateuchs with 32 commentaries, a few of the books of the prophets, with Ivri-Taitch (translation into Yiddish). Of the scriptures he had only the "Tehilim'lach" [Little Psalms] required by every householder in Israel. Also a few of the Gemaras required by the students in the "cheder". Sometimes we could also obtain some of the books of casuistry there: "Sha'agat Arye", "Pnei Yehoshua", "Noda B'Yehuda" and others; but these only arrived at his shop in used condition.

Thus, for example, when one of our acquaintance departed to the world of all goodness and willed his son books of Gemara, arbiters and bible, what was the unfortunate heir to do? At first he allocates a place for them in some corner; however, after a while, when a thick layer of dust has accumulated upon them he says: "why should these names take up space in my home?" he then turns to Mosze Mendel and the latter removes the "leavening" from his home.

It once happened that a Polish priest entered his store. He wanted to purchase a Hebrew bible from him. At first Mosze Mendel was frightened: "what did a priest want with his shop?" he said to himself, and his heart pounded in his chest as in the "Gazlan". He was probably there as part of a plot. However, it became clear immediately clear that the "heathen" had come to do business, and harbored no bad thoughts. The word "biblia" which came from the priest's mouth frequently calmed him and the fear left him entirely.

[Page-227]

Via a small window that connected to the kitchen, he called his wife Sara. She wiped her dirty hands on her apron and appeared before the priest. The women usually know the national language more than the men do. In the market, they come into contact with the peasant women who bring their produce to the city and the Jewish women learn their language from them.

She understood the priest's desire without any delays. In a pile of old books that were heaped out of order in a corner of the shop, she found the "biblia" and handed it to the priest. In answer to the priest's question the woman mentioned a round sum: a silver ruble. The priest did not bargain, paid the ruble, took the book and went on his way voicing a parting to the couple who stood astounded in the shop.

It had never happened that a buyer had given them the entire price that they asked of him; a price – by nature went continually down until it reached a level from which it was not possible to lower it any further. And who was the innocent who would pay the full price?

From that time, Mosze Mendel understood a principle in life. He had always been troubled by a serious question: "why do the Jews choose to dwell among the gentiles? Why don't they pack up their things and move to the land of Israel, the land that has only Jews?" Now he found the answer: a Jew cannot make a living except from "Goyim".

From then on, whenever a Jew entered his shop to buy a prayer book for daily or holiday use or such things and took a long time to bargain, Reb' Mosze Mendel would say: "Oy Va'voi for me and my wares if my customers were only Jews; happily there are gentiles among my customers as well; priests come to my shop! Say what you will, but I will tell you, you can't make a living from Jews, bounty and income come from the heathens!"

Reb' Chaim Jehoszua Lewensztajn

One of the Jewish inhabitants of Kielce who was gloriously and respectfully known was Reb' Chaim Jehoszua Lewensztajn. This exceptional man had unique qualities and all of the Jews of Kielce held him in high regard and affection.

In spite of his being a religious man – a Sokolowi Chassid – he owned a pharmacy and was expert in all sorts of medicines and was the support of many of the sick poor, who came to him on medical matters that troubled them instead of going to a doctor who would demand payment.

In general he was always willing to come to the aid of anyone who turned to him, even if this help of his meant some inconvenience, effort and money he did not stint any of them in order to help his fellows.

[Page-228]

Aside from this he acquired an excellent reputation in his profession as a "mohel" (one who conducts circumcisions). He was an expert without parallel among the "mohels", he performed the circumcision, the "pri'a" and "metzitza" [ritual segments of the circumcision] in an instant; in this way the infant being circumcised did not even have time to make a sound. According to the rules of hygiene he removed the old means of antiseptic from use and only used the means accepted among the doctors. This holy labor he always performed for no reward. He settled in Kielce before World War I. He died in the fullness of his days and the Jews of Kielce did him a great honor at his funeral. In spite of the fact that he had lived in Kielce only a short time he had still circumcised thousands of children and left a glorious reputation behind him among Kielcers as one of its most excellent and favorite citizens.

Mosze Ajlbirt

Mosze Ajlbirt was fortunate enough to be famous in his city not for his great wealth; he had fame during the time that he was a mere peddler, who offers his meager wares for sale on market days. His name became well known not because of the silk stockings with which he equipped the daughters of Israel and the daughters of the gentiles inexpensively. The praise for the stockings must be accounted not to his credit but to that of his spouse, a woman of valor who stayed in Lodz most of the weekdays, acquiring damaged goods from the manufacturers at cheap prices and sending them to Kielce to her husband. Many jumped at such goods, especially among the young women.

So what was the main reason for his fame? For if you ask anyone of the citizens of Kielce: "Do you know Mosze Ajlbirt?" he will look at you in amazement as if to say: "Of course! Who doesn't know Mosze Ajlbirt?"

Not his wealth, not the silk stockings and also not Saski the pharmacist's big building that became his portion gave him renown in the city, but – his voice. His voice made him famous among all segments of the Jews of Kielce, especially among the women. His wonders and achievements in song were especially notable during the High Holidays, when he stood in front of the ark during the Musaf prayer wrapped in white. Whoever did not hear his "Netaneh Tokef" or the "Hayom Harat Olam" might as well have never heard singing and vocalizing in his life.

And Mosze showed his strength not only on the High Holidays; also on a regular Sabbath, when the spirit of song and melody rested upon him, he would stand up in front of the ark for the "Kabalat Shabat" prayers. Pleasant of melody in "Lecha Dodi" he would sound the voice of love and release that end in sounds of joy and enthusiasm. His soul had been quarried from the source of music and song. In spite of the fact that he was a businessman, preoccupied with buying and selling, with repaying notes at the banks etc. he found spiritual satisfaction only in music.

It once happened; for example, that his shop was full of customers, his wife and her assistants were all occupied with selling socks and silk stockings.

[Page-229]

And suddenly, in such a time of commotion the angel of music appears and whispers a pleasant melody to Reb' Mosze. The latter sneaks away from the shop, leaves his wife and her assistants, the silk stockings and the selling of them, stands there in the market and hums the new "nigun" [tune].

And Reb' Mosze's acquaintances knew that on the coming Sabbath, Mosze will sing it for them all with much embellishment in the house of prayer when he stands in front of the ark to lead the prayers.

Aszer Friszman

Ten measures of jokes and clever riddles came down to the world, the Jews took nine of them, and one measure was divided up among all the nations. This attribute with which the Jews were graced was a well-known ingredient of theirs against the troubles in which they lived in the darkness of their lives in exile. In the bitterest moment, at a time when a murky nightmare was sullying the soul of the Jew, his friend came along and with his jokes and witticisms he would introduce a speck of light, a spark of joy into his darkened spirit, and the power of such a spark was enough to save spirits from bitter blackness.

Also in the city of Kielce such a joking man lived and his name was Aszer Friszman, from the family of the author Dawid Friszman. Wherever Friszman was standing a group of people immediately collected around him to hear his jokes and jests, and immediately the sounds of laughter would burst out among them, which made a person of Israel forget their trials and tribulations.

Friszman's material circumstances were not the most glowing: he sold lottery tickets and when his own fate did not work out – his circumstances were most dire, but in spite of this he was always overflowing with jokes and witticisms, as if all of the difficulties of life were a joke to him.

For a while he was a member of the Chassidim, wearing long clothing and praying in the "shtibl" of the Chassidim of Rosprza. But superstitions were distasteful to him; he made especial fun of those Chassidim who told of miracles and wonders that they saw with their own eyes at the various Admo"rs.

Once he sat in the "shtibl" on a winter evening after the Mincha and Ma'ariv prayers among a group of Chassidim who were telling one another of the wondrous acts of the righteous ones. When they finished their stories, he opened his mouth and said: "Now I have understood the verse in Psalms [Psalms 149/1] 'Sing a new song to God, his praise is in the congregation of the pious [Chassidim]'. If his praise is in the congregation of the Chassidim, that is to say, if the Chassidim praise their rabbis with the same praises with which they praise God, therefore one must sing a new song to God."

When the Zionist Association was founded in Kielce, he was the first to lend them a hand: the idea of rebirth enchanted him and because of Zionism he was forced to leave the "shtibl". However, even though he came into the company of the Zionists and was friendly with people who were liberal thinkers, in spite of this he continued to hew to the ancestral traditions and customs. Once he met an "avrech" [married Torah scholar], formerly a Chassid, sitting with his head uncovered and drinking tea. He turned to him and said: "I have been debating with myself for these fifteen years regarding the problem to find rabbinical permission for "uncovering the head"; and you, apparently, found the permission easily. Perhaps you would be willing to reveal to me the source of the 'permission'?"

[Page-230]

He would say in the name of an "apikors" [heretic] whose custom was to not fast on the Fast of Gedalia for three reasons, which were:

    a. if he (the apikors) were to be killed, Gedalia would probably not have fasted for him; and therefore why should he fast for them killing Gedalia?

b. if Gedalia hadn't been killed back then, in any case he would not be alive any more today; and the main reason:
c. since this is not a fast that is more serious than the Day of Atonement; and since he doesn't fast on the Day of Atonement, how can he fast on the Fast of Gedalia for this would be an insult to the honor of that holy day.

His clever jests found their way among the city's inhabitants and earned him the reputation of a clever and educated man, and till this day, when Jews of Kielce meet in Israel or abroad, you will hear one of them say to the other: "Aszer Friszman used to say…"

His sons also inherited a sense of humor and joke from their father. His son Dawid excelled especially among them in this regard, of all of them only Dr. A. Friszman who is in Israel remained alive.

Mejer Cetel

There was a Jew living in Kielce who became very famous, not just among the members of the covenant, but also among the gentiles, and not just among simple people, but among the ruling classes as well. He became famous not because of his great wealth; he was impoverished and not well-to-do, a simpler peddler, who bought chickens or a geese from the peasant women who came to the city in order to later sell them to the householders for a small profit.

Could it be his great wisdom that earned him a reputation in the country? But why would you find wisdom in a poor peddler? The wisdom of the downtrodden is scorned; and even he himself didn't concern himself with wisdom; he didn't know how to tell the difference between wisdom and foolishness. In his eyes, Reb' Mosze Arindel's, who handed down rabbinical decisions in the city, was a wise man, and the rabbi of the city is the wisest of the entire congregation, for whom no hidden thing is not understandable, he yearned to hear their words, which were holy in his eyes.

He himself never bothered his mind with questions: what belongs up and what belongs down? He was a simple man, he followed the ways of his ancestors, prayed three times a day, not forgetting to spit in "Aleinu". On the Sabbath after a nap he would read Psalms in public in the synagogue. The moods of the world did not concern him, they were above his conception.

[Page-231]

But then what gave him fame and honor in spite of it all? For his external appearance didn't contribute to the matter. How could a poultry salesman have anything to do with glory and splendor? The hair on his head was filled with feathers, his beard was sparse; his clothing – a worn "kapote" shiny with use; not all of his external appearance had anything in it to bring him honor and respect.

However, in spite of this he was the only one among the Jews of Kielce who was decorated with the symbol of honor of the state of Poland, and who, in all of the celebratory parades was placed in the front row by the Poles next to their most honored citizens and who was pointed at by people saying: "That is a Jew who did a great service to the country of Poland."

And how did he reach this greatness? A simple occurrence that Reb' Mejer didn't notice to begin with, and which, after a while, he forgot about entirely.

At the beginning of World War I the first to enter Kielce were the Polish Legions with their commander Pilsudski at their head. The Russian occupying force left Kielce and encamped in the village Dombrowa and dug itself in there between the hills.

The inhabitants of Kielce received the Legions with pomp and circumstance. The Russians, when they saw the Legionary force was not large, decided to encircle them and take them hostage. They sent platoons of Cossacks in every direction and began shelling the city with heavy cannon. The Legions, sensing the danger that awaited them, began to retreat to the west and south in the direction of Kraczowka and Bialogon. They scattered in the forests and attempted to reach the main camp, which was encamped about thirty-five kilometers from Kielce at Jedrzejow. However, for many the roads were blocked and they were forced to hide in Kielce proper. In spite of the fact that the Russians returned to Kielce and occupied it for another three days, in spite of this, not a single Legionnaire fell into their hands. The Legionnaires who remained in the city mingled easily with their fellow Poles.

However on the road leading southwards in the direction of Checiny three Legionnaires ran into a Cossack platoon; soon the Legionnaires were surrounded with no way out. In order to save their lives, they jumped through a fence into a fruit garden, which was leased by the aforementioned Mejer Cetel. They asked him for shelter from the Cossacks who were chasing them.

This simple Jew, who was full of the spirit of Judaism from his mother's womb and from birth and the commandment: "Do not stand upon the blood of your fellow" operated within his subconscious, didn't think much and hid them in his hut in the garden. For three days they sat in the hiding place, and the Jewish gardener brought them bread and water. On the fourth day, when the Russians had completely retreated from the city to the Warsaw side, the Legionnaires came out of their hiding place and wrote down the name of their savior as a memorial.

Years later, when Pilsudski's men took over the government, these three Legionnaires were also elevated.

In those days, the three great men remembered the sensation of the Jew of Kielce, they recalled that he had saved them from the wild Cossacks and wanted to get some political gain from this fact. They themselves came to Kielce to give the honor and respect due to the Jew who participated in such an obvious manner in the Polish war of liberation.

[Page-232]

In the square before the municipality building, next to the tomb of the Unknown Soldier, the leaders of the authorities gathered and with great pomp decorated Mejer Cetel with the symbol of honor for his excellent service to the liberation fighters.

From that time, Reb' Mejer Cetel became a Polish patriot and was invited to every celebration and every parade and would walk in a row together with the veteran Polish fighters.

But a few years before the outbreak of World War II anti-Semitism among the Poles became much stronger due to the influence of the Nazis; and the disease of anti-Semitism, which spread among all of the classes and also in the ranks of the leadership, hurt Mejer Cetel as well. Once when he returned from some parade, decorated with his symbol of honor, one of the Polish thugs assaulted him and tore the medal of excellence from his clothing, crying: "Jew – to Palestine!"

Mejer Cetel came home depressed. Suddenly he had fallen from a high level into a deep pit. And thus he returned to his grey life, the life of a poultry salesman in Israel.

Kalman Gejst the Zionist

We never knew who Kalman Gejst's ancestors were, but he himself was known by the entire city. He was especially easy to find in the homes of the Zionists; there, in the company of the people of Zion he felt at home.

And the two sides gained mutual benefit from these visits: Kalman would receive news in the homes of the Zionists about the progress of the movement in the world and what was happening in the land of Israel; the Zionist matrons would use him for their various chores, he would carry their baskets from the market, he would carry the "Cholent" to the baker on Friday afternoon, etc.

And aside from the Zionist news, with which he was enriched in these homes, he would also receive material reward: a slice of bread, a cup of tea, sometimes a hot dish. But for Kalman the material reward was just a side issue. Being in the company of the Zionists was his greatest reward. He saw in Zionism the essence of his life. All of his conversation and speech, all of his thoughts and resources were devoted to just one thing – to Zionism.

Kalman's main ambition was to move to the land of Israel. For this goal he gave up on many things a person needs, neglected himself and did not even learn a profession which could support its owner. He also did not marry, even when he reached middle age. What point was there in having children in the Diaspora: If God willed it and he succeeded in moving to the land of Israel, then he would start a family there.

He admired the pioneers and the leaders of the Zionist movement his entire life.

[Page-233]

At first he was at the vanguard of those opposing the Revisionists, but when he saw that the people of authority within the movement were not helping him to get a permit to move to Israel, he changed to the camp of Jabotinsky.

However, redemption did not come from here either, and poor Kalman, the innocent and devoted to rebirth of the people did not stay alive and was not redeemed!

* *

These characters which I have introduced in this book are not here to teach about themselves, but to teach about the generality.

The part they all had in common is the special coloration with which the Kielce landscape imbued its inhabitants. Broad hearts and souls, alertness of thought and feeling were typical characteristics of the Jews of Kielce.

It is no wonder, therefore, that the Zionist movement found its place in Kielce immediately in its first period. Cultural and social institutions were established as soon as the community was founded.

The Kielce community was a shining pearl in the framework of the communities of Polish Jewry, a precious stone embedded in the crown of Israel!!

[Page-237]

The Story of the Ghetto and Liquidation

Beginning of the End

At the end of the summer of 1939, when Hitler commanded his minions to invade Poland, the Jews were filled with fear. They knew and felt what to expect from this enemy, who publicly declared his plots against the Jews. There then began a widespread movement of the Jews from the western districts to the eastern districts. And as the enemy armies progressed towards the interior of the country, thus the extent of the stream, eastward towards Russia grew. All of the roads, all of the paths were filled with refugees and were a target for the airplanes of the enemy, who flew low and destroyed them with various munitions.

Also within the area of the occupation there was – at the start of the war – internal movement from place to place. Families from Warsaw, Lodz, Sosnowiec and other places came to Kielce. The Kielce community that had numbered twenty three thousand souls grew at the start of the war and the number of people reached thirty thousand, even after a large portion of its permanent residents fled to rural cities on the Russian side.

Kielce did not suffer greatly from the bombs of the enemy; aside from a few buildings that were destroyed or damaged, there were no signs of war in the city.

On September 4th the Nazis entered the city and the Jewish population felt the yoke of the oppressor immediately during the first few days. The city leaders were captured and taken to jail as hostages; they were responsible for ensuring that all the commands and edicts that were given to the Jews would be filled exactly and completely on schedule. They were frequently exchanged, so that no one was sure that it would not be his fate to be a hostage. The oppressors gave the Jews collective punishments of enormous sums, confiscated their apartments and possessions, took their children to forced labor etc.

Not long after this a command was given that a Jew was forbidden to manage a commercial establishment, shop or factory. The Nazis set Aryan commissioners in every shop and factory that belonged to Jews, and they treated the Jewish property as if it was their own.

To begin with they would transfer some monthly amount to the owner of the property; however, once the goods had been sold and others did not replace them, the shop was closed and its owners came out without their property and didn't even receive a minimal payment with which to maintain their families.

Commissioners were also appointed to the large properties of the Jews to collect the rents from the lodgers, and the owner was allotted a miserable sum for his livelihood.

These edicts limited the means by which the Jewish population could get income.

In addition to this the Nazis decreed that everyone must turn over to the authorities the foodstuffs in their possession. The division of the food among the inhabitants was assigned to the municipal authority. The Jews were forced to hand over all of the food that they had prepared for themselves for lean days.

[Page-238]

From now on the Jewish population was in the grip of hunger. It was not enough that the allotted food ration was very small, but the Jew was deprived even when he received the food ration, for he was pushed and shoved out of the line and was beaten and kicked; many times he came home empty handed without bread for his hungry infants.

The religious Jews with beards and side-locks suffered especially; they were a target for the arrows of scorn of the S.S. who strolled arrogantly in the streets of the city. Such a Jew who came to their attention did not get away cleanly if he fell into their hands. One such instance out of thousands will be told here:

Once in the month of Tevet Jews were going to a warm "mikve" in the morning, as was their habit in normal times. Polish "shkeitzim" went to the S.S. men and told them about it. The S.S. were happy that they had a good opportunity to mock the Jews. Accompanied by Polish gentile men and women who came to see the sight, the thugs entered the "mikve" and with the whips in their hands they chased the bathers, naked as the day they were born, out into the courtyard in front of the synagogue. A signal was given to the "shkeitzim" and "shkeitzot" to throw snowballs at the miserable and freezing Jews, who ran about the courtyard looking for cover from the barbarians' attacks. This incident was photographed by the Nazis, who always took care to always send their loved ones in Germany scenes of their acts of courage towards the Jews.

This was the first stage of the Nazi's cruelty towards the Jews. In this stage their goal was to weaken and humiliate the Jew, in order to take from him the strength and ability to protest against his torturers.

At this stage there were several individual murders, whose goal was to sow fear among the Jewish population, during those days the sons of Sercarz, Jakob son of Dawid Manela and others, whose names did not reach us.

Although there was a period of time that the Jews deluded themselves that the rule of the Nazis over the Jews was changing for the better. A commandant came to Kielce who began drawing the Jews to him and giving them economic positions. Thus he gave Jechezkel Lemberg the export of eggs. He and his assistants were given the task of buying eggs in the Kielce region and turning them over to the economic committee for export to Germany. Jakob Kohen of Checiny was given such a role for the export of leather, and others were given similar positions with regard to grain, feathers etc. For a while these Jews were busy with their tasks, and they didn't just profit themselves, but found jobs for other Jews. The word went out that the Jews of Kielce had found relief and reached even the Jews who had fled eastwards and many of those began to return to their place of origin.

But not much time went by and the situation regressed to what it had been formerly. That commandant, who had had mercy on the Jews, was removed from his position. And the one who replaced him was a crude and ruthless man, who came to take revenge upon the Jews for having enjoyed his predecessor's rule. Those who had been working at exporting goods to Germany were accused of embezzlement, they were arrested and died under terrible torture. Their property was confiscated and their families were left without bread.

[Page-239]

In spite of all of these murderous attacks, the Jews of Kielce could bear the suffering and torment. The got used to the sights of death, adjusted to a life of starvation; the rich sold the remnants of their former wealth to bring food to their homes. The poor went to forced labor in order to maintain their own lives and those of their children.

This situation continued until 1941, until the entrance of the United States and Soviet Russia into the war, from that day forward the attitude of the Nazis towards the Jews changed entirely. Until now they had not wanted to appear before the nations of the world as public murderers and had done their acts of murder under the guise of punishments for breaking the law.

Now, when they were cut off from the world and large areas of Europe, Asia and even Africa were under their control, they felt themselves to be rulers of the world and able to do whatever they wanted to with the Jews.

They went about the work of liquidation with Germanic method according to a plan prepared in advance.

First of all, the enemy didn't want the Jews to be scattered and mingled among the Christian inhabitants, but concentrated in one place. In this way, he could be sure that his prey would not escape him, and thus the ghetto was created.

Jailing the Jews in the Ghetto

In Kielce the northwestern part of the city was allotted to ghetto.

The Jews were forced to leave their homes, to leave their furniture and all of their possessions and to move to the ghetto within a very short time. Aside from the plot of destruction, the Nazis intended to use the creation of the ghetto to take over the possessions of the Jews; and indeed those who wanted to save something of their property and delayed in their apartments a little bit after the time that had been set were shot on the spot.

In the ghetto – in this crowded area the Jews lived a bitter life. The hunger and crowding took their toll, and disease and epidemics killed many people. Leaving the ghetto was strictly forbidden and the delinquents who risked their lives and went out to search for food for their children usually never returned. They were shot on the way.

To ensure that their orders and decrees were fulfilled exactly, the Nazi authorities set up a Jewish council in the ghetto with a Jewish police alongside it, who had to ensure that the entire Jewish population followed every decree and command. Thus, for example, a command was given to hand over hundreds of strong young men, suitable for backbreaking work for forced labor. The council with the aid of the police fulfilled this command precisely.

[Page-240]

As one of the survivors of Kielce, Szymon Celcer, reported, the head of the Jewish police was Rzymnowoda and his deputy was Szindler (a German Jew) and the two of them behaved very decently in fulfilling their duties, and most of the rest of the members of the police were decent people. However, among the policemen there were also those who were agents of the Gestapo, headed by Johan Szpigiel, Proszowski, Bialobroda, Strawczinski and others, who harassed the Jewish population very much and their behavior was like that of the Nazis themselves.

The Germans killed Rzymnowoda at the end of 1941 and Szindler in 1942 when the population was deported to Treblinka.

The first council head was Dr. Pelc. Once he was given an order to give shots of poison to the ill and weak who were in the hospital to get rid of them in a manner that appeared to be natural and not arouse fear among the Jews. Dr. Pelc refused to carry out this cruel order. The Nazis put him in jail. From there he was sent to the extermination camp in Auschwitz. However his behavior did not serve as an example of sanctifying God's name to the rest of his fellow doctors. This satanic order was carried out by two other cowardly doctors. Afterwards it was the turn of the orphanage and they demanded that their caretaker bring all the orphans outside and arrange them in a row, in order to transfer them to another building. The caretaker and the children did not know what awaited them and went to death with childlike innocence. When they arrived at the place the murderers commanded the caretaker to strip the children of their clothing. The executioners spared the clothing of the poor children, that they not be lost with the victims.

The caretaker refused to carry out the executioners' order and called out: "Despicable murderers, God's vengeance will find you for spilling the blood of innocent children!" and with these words she jumped into the pit in which she was immediately shot. After that the executioners began shooting the children and throwing them into the pit.

Then the head of the Gestapo, Hamfel, came up and said: "Don't waste so many bullets; use just one bullet per child!" and he shot the children one at a time until they all fell dead.

Before the enemy began to liquidate the ghetto, he wanted to remove the Jewish intelligentsia from there, the doctors, the lawyers and the schoolteachers.

For this purpose an order was given that all of the people of this type should congregate outside of the ghetto at a certain place, since they were about to be sent to places where they needed doctors and educated people.

With the aid of the police the doctors and the rest of the professionals were removed to the Jewish cemetery where they were all shot to death. The young doctor Fiszer, who wanted to take revenge on his murderers before his death grabbed a tombstone and cracked the skull of the head of the Gestapo with it.

The Ukrainian guards, the Gestapo and several of the Jewish police, who had been recruited from the underworld joined forces to wreak havoc on the inhabitants of the ghetto.

However, the life force of the Jews was very strong. Gradually the Jews got used to life in the ghetto. The head of the Jewish council after Dr. Pelc was Herman Lewi, a Kielce industrialist. A social department was organized by the council whose job was to give aid to the sick, the weak and the needy in general.

[Page-241]

With ingenuity and various tricks they brought food into the ghetto. People sold their clothing, their kitchen utensils etc. The Christian peasant women would bring foodstuffs to the barbed wire fence and receive in return clothing, kitchen utensils and other things. The young and those with muscles who were capable of difficult work would leave on foot every morning for the nearby labor camps, to "Ludwikow" and "Henrikow" and return in the evening. On the way they would sometimes get food and bring it to their parents and children.

In spite of the murderous blows the Nazis bestowed upon those who hid food among their tools, they still did not stop bringing food into the walls of the ghetto and thus temporarily easing the hunger pangs of those who were trapped there without hope of being saved.

There was an attempt by several young men who left the ghetto and joined the Polish leftist underground, which was hiding in the forests around the city. The active ones of them were: Hermansztat, a teacher of gymnastics in Mrs. Wolman's Gymnasium, Fajnsztat and others; this underground saved several people here and there when the ghetto was liquidated; but due to informers from the right wing Polish underground, they were captured by the Gestapo in the end and murdered.

The inhabitants of the ghetto eventually became so weak that they started viewing life and death apathetically.

Liquidation of the Ghetto and Destruction of the Population

And finally the third stage arrived, the day of the liquidation of the ghetto. The bitter day, 9th of Elul 5702 (22 of August, 1942), on which the community of Kielce was destroyed, is engraved on the hearts of survivors of Kielce as an eternal day of mourning.

Fear fell upon the inhabitants of the ghetto. News had reached them of the great killing that was being done among the Jews of the area. It was hard for them to believe the rumors, for the Nazis would conceal their satanic intentions until the last moment. But the air was saturated with fear and terror.

With frozen expectation they awaited some command which would arrive from outside. The fear of the adults passed also to the little ones. The children crowded into their mother's laps fearfully.

Only the Chassidim, the elderly, whose faith had not yet been shaken, read Psalms and prayed for the decree to be averted.

And then the ghetto was surrounded by a chain of Ukrainian and Latvian soldiers. The Jewish police was given a command to bring the Jews out of their apartments and line them up in the streets of the ghetto.

An order was given that every one of the deportees could take with him luggage weighing ten kilograms. It was forbidden to cry aloud. Whoever did not obey this command would be shot on the spot. Everything must be carried out in order, in military discipline, quietly, without complaint.

[Page-242]

The Jewish police was responsible for the accurate execution of all of the orders.

That day no one left the ghetto; even those who worked in the labor camps remained in the ghetto that day.

When all of the Jews of the ghetto were standing in order on Jasna field next to Zganaska street in long rows, those who had work cards were removed from their midst, they were allowed to remain in their places. Among them were many who had work cards but didn't show them, because they didn't want to be parted from their families; what happened to those closest to them, they decided in their hearts, would happen to them as well. They would share one fate.

The deportation of the Jews of Kielce took place over thirty-six hours. The ghetto was divided into three areas; every area was emptied of Jews over twelve hours.

Trains were standing on the tracks ready to swallow their victims. One hundred and fifty souls were put into every freight car. The cars were locked up. The heat and stifling atmosphere, the terrible crowding without a drop of water made these poor souls choke and many died on the way. The dead and the living intermingled.

During the liquidation of the ghetto there were several instances of Jews who did not want to leave the place where they had been born and their ancestors had been buried and chose to die there. Among them was Mrs. Wilner, the daughter of Cwi Zagajski, who didn't want to leave the ghetto under any circumstances and was shot where she stood. The secretary of the community, Baruch Sokolowski, turned to the Jews at the train station and said: "My brothers! We are being led to be slaughtered; know what you must do…" one of the Gestapo heard his words, shot him and killed him where he stood.

The rabbi of the Kielce community, Reb' Abele Rapoport Z"L, then turned to the members of his congregation with his final words and said: "From time to time I would reprove you for every fault I noticed among you; now I request your forgiveness if I injured your honor. I see that the entire congregation, all are holy; for God has chosen you to sanctify his name, as our ancestors of old sanctified his blessed name. Let us all confess."

When the train reached its destination, and the poor things left the death cars, they were led to a large courtyard that was surrounded by barbed wire.

There in the courtyard the murderers began to sort the arrivals. They chose the strong and those with a profession: barbers, carpenters, metal workers, cobblers and tailors, from among them, since from them the oppressors could squeeze out the remnants of their strength with hard labor, and those they left in the camp thinking that the victim would not escape their vicious fangs. Whoever arrived in the Treblinka extermination camp did not leave it alive.

Those who remained alive for the time were used for various work: extracting gold teeth from the mouths of the victims of the gas chambers, sorting their clothing by type of weave, shearing the hair of the women, etc. Whoever wanted to lengthen their lives for a little bit was forced to perform such cruel actions with accuracy under a hail of beatings that fell upon them from every side by wild animals in human shape. Those who were marked for destruction were commanded to strip off their clothing in order to be bathed and then go to work.

[Page-243]

At first the poor things were gladdened when they heard they were to go work, but they immediately learned to their horror that they had been caught in a satanic plot.

The executioners began pushing their victims en masse into the narrow corridor into which dark chambers opened. Once the victims were shoved into the chambers, the doors were shut, the gasses were turned on, and after a few moments the bodies of the martyrs were removed via the chambers' openings on their other side.

In this satanic way the Jews of Kielce fell sanctifying God's name together with all the Jews of Poland and their ashes were scattered over the fields of Treblinka, Auschwitz and locations of similar killing. It must be mentioned here that a youth of Kielce, Zalcberg, was among those who revolted against the oppressor at Treblinka. As a result of this revolt several dozen Nazis were killed and what was more important – several Jews escaped and as living witnesses could let the world know about the horrors of the camp.

The city of Kielce was emptied nearly entirely of its Jews. About one thousand five hundred Jews remained there, among them a few hundred veterans of Kielce, and the rest – were Jews from other cities and even countries, who had been brought to Kielce by the Nazis as professionals in various areas who had been assigned a special area in the ghetto.

Every morning the latter would leave on foot for work and return in the evening; sometimes they had to walk for many kilometers to reach their work place. They had little to eat and their work was difficult, and therefore it is no wonder their numbers dwindled. If one of the forced laborers became too weak to go to work he was sent to Auschwitz and immediately to the gas chambers. Many therefore hid their weakness or illness and continued to work with their remaining strength until they fell down, never to rise again.

From time to time, other groups would arrive to supplement the lack in the number of workers in the camps.

Those who succeeded in keeping their place used all sorts of tricks to find sources of nourishment, at night they would go through the apartments of the Jews which had been emptied of their inhabitants and find their remnants of their kitchen utensils, and other things, and they would trade these utensils for food, and in this manner they would lengthen the days of their impoverished existence.

As was mentioned earlier, after the liquidation of the ghetto the member of the Jewish police and the members of the Jewish council, that was headed at that time by Messrs. Herman Lewi, Gotlib and Trager still remained. But they also became irrelevant in the eyes of the Nazis and were liquidated cruelly.

Those who remained in the ghetto were destined to be tormented by the horrible episode of the destruction of their children in front of their eyes.

Sara Karbel, one of the Shoah survivors who lives with us in Israel, describes the destruction of the last children of Kielce:

[Page-244]

On the 23rd of May, 1943, at day break, the Jewish police came and knocked on the window of my room calling: "Gather at the inspection yard!" We already knew the meaning of such a command.

In our city there remained about a thousand people who worked in the labor camps, among them forty five children and infants.

The mothers, who worked in the labor camps outside of the city, would leave their children under my care as a childcare worker. Among the infants was also my baby, Girza, a sweet girl with light-blue eyes and golden hair.

Frightened by the policemen's order I left my room in haste. I held my Girza under my coat. I took her from her cradle when she was asleep and I was terrified she would wake up crying. After me came my husband Irwin and my brother Mordechai. When we arrived the yard was full of Jews standing in line, everyone pale and anxious. Across from us, in rows, stood the gendarmes, the S.S. men and the Gestapo. There was silence in the yard.

Suddenly the command came like thunder from the heavens: "Hand over the children!" The entire world swirled within me; in shock I knew only that the children were in the hands of the S.S. men being dragged by them to a small neglected hut that stood on the side. All of my being concentrated on one thing: "my daughter is hidden under my coat, who will save us?" My strength left me. Six hours we stood erect. And meanwhile all of the children in the hut are screaming and crying. The bigger ones among them begging before the German gendarmes: "Let us come out!" showing the remnants of their hands and saying: "we are capable of work!" But those evil ones had sealed ears; they did not respond to their screams, closing the windows and the shutters, so that their voices wouldn't reach us. But we hear, if not with our ears, in the depths of our hearts. And my little girl is still with me. I turn here and there, wanting to hide from the looks of the evil dogs, perhaps I will be able to save my only one!...

And then came the bitterest moment in my life – a Ukrainian policeman noticed me and came over. He grabbed the girl forcefully from me and carried her by the collar of her coat across the entire yard. Everyone burst forth: "Girza, Girza!" There was no one in the entire camp who did not know my sweet little girl. I remained shocked. I no longer saw my husband and my brother. I saw only the golden hairs of my little girl disappearing from my eyes into the death hut.

The adult Jews who stood in order were divided into four groups and sent to labor camps: Blizszin, Skarzysk, Pjonki and Strachowica. The group I was in was sent to the factory for iron products in Ludwigszuta near Kielce.

And that night, the children were brought to the cemetery in Kielce where they were murdered without mercy.

Dear children! How you were cut down by a cruel hand!

At the last moment, they didn't see the eye of a loving mother; before the innocent eyes only the murderers could be seen. May God avenge their blood!"

Six children, who climbed upon the roof of the hut and hid there, were saved by the few Jews who still remained in the city. They took them, hid them from sight, and took care of them until the city was completely emptied of Jews. The fate of those six children is still not known.

List of the last children to die in Kielce

	Name	Age		Name	Age
1.	Ajzenberg Lulek	5	24.	Jezwicki Ester	13
2.	Aleks Lea	11	25.	Jezwicki Chana	9
3.	Bugajer Fred	5	26.	Jezwicki Szmuel	10
4.	Bornsztajn Menachem	12	27.	Kasrielewicz Riszja	8

5.	Bornsztajn Chana	10	28.	Lederman Saran'ke	4
6.	Berkowicz Manos	7	29.	Lender Mina	9
7.	Goldblum Aharon	1 ½	30.	Laks Saran'ke	6
8.	Goldblum Joszijahu	7	31.	Minc Lili	7
9.	Goldberg Zola	2	32.	Mendelbaum Chawa	5
10.	Gurewicz Zygmunt	3	33.	Sapir Mercel	3
11.	Grosberg Pola	10	34.	Fajnmeser Ceszja	5
12.	Grojbrad Sara'nke	5	35.	Francek	14
13.	Grynberg Zew	4	36.	Proszowski Irena	7
14.	Grynberg Josef	7	37.	Fridman Icak	5
15.	Hofman Anja	8	38.	Cypros Bronek	7
16.	Wajnberg Plejusz	2	39.	Klinberg Dawid	5
17.	Wald-Liprent Karol	1 ½	40.	Klinberg Chana	11
18.	Zauberman Fajbusz	1 ½	41.	Karbel Gisela	1 ¼
19.	Zylbersztajn Dora	12	42.	Rozencwajg Gisela	5
20.	Zylbersztajn, Miljusza	5	43.	Rozencwajg Januszek	6
21.	Chmielnicki Izrael	3	44.	Rajter Zuszja	7
22.	Chmielnicki Rozia	4	45.	Recht Menachem	5

23.	Charson Miatek	2			

On 25.11.45 several parents of the little martyrs, seven mothers and three fathers, gathered in the cemetery in Kielce. We had already been released from the Nazi nightmare. We set up a memorial stone on the joint grave of the children a grey stone, but in our hearts it is engraved as a stone of blood. We will never forget them, the flowers of our souls. The day of your death will remain a memorial day for us forever!

One of the Rechtsman family demonstrated touching sibling loyalty. Wishing to save his little brother, he put him into a sack among his work tools. And daily on his way to the labor camp and back he would carry him in the sack; and the child remained quietly inside without moving, all day. It occurred to no one what a treasure the laborer was carrying upon his shoulder. And thus the child was saved and the two of them were finally able to move to Israel. Such deeds are worthy of being engraved upon the memorial book of the nation.

The wicked Nazis used various tricks to discover the hiding places of the Jews; they would give a price to anyone who discovered such a hiding place.

[Page 246]

Once they published a notice that they were giving permits to leave for every Jew who wished to move to the land of Israel.

Several Jews who were hidden in cellars and whose lives were always in danger; as well as those who as possessors of Aryan passports were in constant fear of betrayal, all these trusted the words of their oppressors and came out of their hiding places – and were caught in the trap that the enemy set for them.

We will mention here only one name, the head of the "Judenrat", Herman Lewi, who lived in Kielce also after the liquidation of the ghetto under a Polish Christian name – he too fell victim to this satanic plot of the Nazis. Thus, the few Jews of Kielce continued their dismal existence, forced laborers at the factories and the labor camps, fluttering always between life and death until 1944, until Lublin was occupied by the Russians.

Of all of the labor camps in which the Jews of Kielce worked, the camp at Skarzysko was the worst and most difficult. Very few succeeded in leaving there when the hour of salvation came.

Here one of the survivors describes the conditions there and the tortures the laborers suffered at the hands of the manager von Hecht.

The day after we arrived there the managers came to the barracks and began to choose people for work. We immediately felt that we had arrived in a hell hole. The men were sent to various factories that were located there. I saw human skeletons: men and women, dressed in faded rags and on their faces – terrible despair.

The strongest men were sent to a factory that manufactured pikrin, that is the powder that is used to make mines.

On the first day I couldn't work. I felt a choking in my throat, I coughed, and my eyes streamed with tears.

The laborers were weakened to such an extent that they had to stop their work, every day they removed dead bodies from there. No help was extended to the sick, not even water to ease their thirst would the accursed wicked ones give them. Whoever continued at this work for three months would become damaged in their body and especially their lungs.

The work managers hurried the laborers to work without pause for eleven hours. Whoever stopped their work for a moment, to straighten their limbs, received a cruel beating. Every inch of ground in this camp was saturated with the blood of those tortured.

The daily food ration of the laborer was a quarter kilogram of bread and potato soup. No wonder the workers were frequently hungry.

Among those supervising the labor camp were also two from Kielce: one named Ajzenberg, who was a member of the underworld even when things were normal, and the second named Markowicz, he and his wife were the cooks in the camp. The were sent to Auschwitz also, finally, and died with their brethren in the gas chambers.

[Page-247]

The murderous Nazis chose the yard outside of the synagogue as the place for their acts of cruelty against their victims. The yard was surrounded by a barbed wire fence. The synagogue itself was desecrated by the hands of the unclean when they perpetrated their disgusting deeds in it. But the yard they reserved as a place of purgatory for the poor things who fell into their unclean hands.

When the rumor reached the ears of the Jews working in the camps about the Russian advance, hope stirred in their hearts that they would be saved in the near future. They were convinced that the liberation of Kielce by the Russian forces was a matter of a few days. They didn't know that the Russian advance would be halted by the Wisla River for six months. Many of the forced laborers could not contain their impatience and began leaving the labor camps; some of them escaped to the nearby forests, hoping they would succeed in organizing into partisan groups there and await the arrival of the Russians. Some of them tried to find shelter and places to hide in villages, in peasant homes. But both erred in their judgement. The Russians took a long time to come; these refugees were mostly felled either by a bullet of the Nazi enemy or the axe of the Polish peasant.

Finally the Soviet forces crossed the Wisla River and approached Kielce. The Nazis evacuated Kielce and the few Jews, the forced laborers they transferred to Auschwitz. And again, when the Red Army approached Krakow, all the prisoners in the death camp were transferred to the interior of Germany, to the concentration camps at Dachau, Buchenwald and Bergen-Belsen and others. Many died on the way from hunger and suffocation.

Of all of the glorious Jewish community of Kielce a few dozen young men and women were all that was left. All of them broken and degraded in body and spirit.

Those that were survivors of the camps didn't want to return to their former habitations, whose earth was saturated with the blood of dear and precious souls.

But the world was cruel to them: at first they were held in camps; the gates of the land of Israel were locked in their faces. The intention of the great powers was to force them to return to their country of origin; and if not, if they didn't agree to return, they could remain in the camps until they were sick of it.

Some of them were tempted and returned to Kielce. Refugees also began returning from Russia, and also from the area, a few remnants of the death began to gather and find a place to dwell in Kielce; a small community that numbered a total of close to two hundred souls, began to organize. They chose a committee from among them that was entrusted with the various actions of a community that wishes to renew its existence. The kashrut committee and the aid committee began to do their jobs. There was a chance that in Kielce at least a small kernel of the grand community that had been destroyed would continue to exist.

However, the Poles looked meagerly at the Jews who were about to renew their lives. They were afraid lest they were thinking of demanding the return of the loot that was in their possession. There were some who feared the vengeance of the Jews for their participation in the murderous acts against them.

[Page-248]

In addition to these, the soldiers of General Anders arrived and began spreading hatred and venom against the returning Jews who supposedly wanted to reconquer Poland. The Polish oppressors stood in amazement:

Where were so many Jews coming from? – in the end, they rose up and spread a conspiracy that the Jews were murdering Christian children in their desire to be revenged against the Christians for the murders that had been perpetrated against them and their children.

And indeed, their wicked propaganda fell on fertile ground.

[Page-248]

The Pogrom in 1946

Translated by Judy Montel

On the fourth day of July, 1946, the fifth of Tamuz, 5706, armed Polish rioters, among them also communists, attacked the Jewish committee house on Planty Boulevard where most of the small Jewish community gathered, and began injuring and killing without mercy. No one came to the aid of the Jews. And they could not even defend themselves since the day before the police had taken the few revolvers that were in their possession.

The police of course, came much later, after the rioters had already scattered after committing the murders.

The results of this pogrom were terrible: forty-two murdered and many injured. All of those who were then in the Jewish committee house were either killed or injured.

And this was the epilogue of the hatred of Jews in Kielce. The last sacrifice of a group of Jews, remnants of a community that had numbered twenty five thousand souls, proved again why Hitler had chosen Poland as the place for destroying the Jews of Europe. He knew that in this country he would find loyal assistants to carry out his satanic plans.

This pogrom, which came as a slap upon the tiny group of Jews who had escaped the hands of Hitler, may his name be erased, cast fear upon the remnants of Polish Jewry who began to flee back east to the camps.

And thus Kielce was emptied entirely of its Jewish inhabitants. The Kielce anti-Semites had their wish – they murdered and also inherited!

Although the Polish government sent a committee of inquiry to the place immediately, among whose members was also Adolf Berman, the government advisor. The committee took evidence from the injured, the policemen and others. As a result of the activities of the committee nine murderers were condemned to death and several dozen to various terms of imprisonment. The laborers who were incited by the anti-Semitic manipulator who stood at the head of the police were sentenced and punished for their carelessness; but the instigators of the riots – not only were they not punished, but they were promoted.

Let us mention here the thug and murderer, the officer Subcinski, he who organized the Kielce riots, and was later promoted by the Polish authorities to manager of the office of foreign passports.

[Page-249]

The Jews who crowded the foreign passport office suffered greatly from this outstanding anti-Semite. After causing the pogrom against the Jews, he cruelly did not allow them to leave the country that was saturated with Jewish blood.

In 1955, nine years after the pogrom in Kielce, Jan Rozanski, who had been the secretary of the Polish security police, was sentenced by a special court to five years imprisonment for abusing his authority (among other things, for refraining at the time from indicting those responsible for the riots in Kielce).

Rozanski, the son of one of the editors of the "Haint" of Warsaw, stood, at the time at the head of the investigation the authorities conducted after the pogrom.

We also bring here a description of the ceremony of the unveiling of the monument upon the grave of the victims of this pogrom in the Kielce cemetery. It is translated into Hebrew from the letter of one of the inhabitants of Kielce, Lajzer Fiszman:

"There is no longer a sign of the Jewish blood that sprayed upon the walls of the house on Planty Boulevard. Whitewash has covered the disgrace of Polish Kielce, but the sorrow and the rage of the Jewish people will not be forgotten.

In the streets of Kielce young Christian men and women stroll gaily during the morning hours.

In a side alley next to the main street at the same time, at 20 Marechale Foche Street – leaning against the wall a few dozen men and women. Black bitterness is on their faces, the are like mourners – but they are Jews, who have come from Warsaw, Lodz, Czestochowa and Radom to visit the graves of the martyrs of Kielce, to honor their memory on the first anniversary of their murder.

There is no longer a Jewish home in Kielce to receive the guests, they stand, therefore, in the street and wait for a passenger vehicle to take them to the cemetery.

At one o'clock in the afternoon we reach the cemetery, a field open in every direction, without a fence.

A row of graves meets our eyes, covered with a black scarf. Our knees grow week, our eyes are misty, the sorrow of the nation hovers over this place.

– "Thou shalt not murder," sounds the voice of the sad master of ceremonies, the voice of Magister Ajzenberg. "Thou shalt not murder!" This edict was received by the Christian's as well; but in the name of Christianity, the murderers cut into these victims – the accuser cries out…

– "Yitkadal veYitkadash" – a young pale voice is heard, the brother of the murdered Albert. It is difficult to hear the words, for massive tears choke his throat.

The district governor of Kielce approaches the grave, Major Wiszlic. As the first citizen of the district he has been given the honor of revealing the monument. And here, the covering is removed from the monument, and to the eyes of those gathered a stone is revealed: Forty two martyrs who were murdered on the 5th day of Tammuz, 5706, in Kielce, may God avenge their blood.

[Page-250]

And after this inscription come thirty-two names of those murdered (the names of the remaining martyrs could not be identified).

Major Wiszlic says: "I reveal not only this stone, but also the disgrace of Polish Kielce, as well as the great sorrow of the Jews of Poland."

A representative of the central committee of the Jews of Poland, the engineer Rozenman, demands a trial against the instigators of the pogrom in the name of the Jews of Poland.

The coffins of the victims are set down in a joint grave

At the cemetery, the representatives of the Polish democracy in Kielce express their participation in the sorrow of the Jews of Poland.

A representative of the Polish worker's party, P.P.R., gives a speech. He recalls that his party always fought hand in hand with the Jewish workers for the freedom of man. This murder was aimed not just against the Jews, but against the Polish worker battling for liberty and equality.

The representative of P.P.S. repeats the words of the Polish minister Katczrowski, who said last year upon the martyr's grave: the pogrom was not only a stab in the back for the Jews but for the entire Polish people.

[Page-251]

The representative of the farmer's party declares in the name of his party that the Polish farmer condemns the Kielce pogrom.

The representative of the democratic party turns to the Jews gathered there and says: "Let us try to forget what happened in the past; to the extend that forgetting comes more quickly, it will be easier for us to build democratic Poland with our shared strengths."

In the name of the Polish army, a young officer declares: "Today, the 4th of July is a difficult day for a Polish soldier who was a witness to the riots in Kielce. The Polish soldier, who fought for a free and democratic Poland will continue to fight in this country against reactionism. Today, the 4th of July remains a day of mourning for the Polish soldier."

The words of the representative of "HaShomer HaTza'ir" in Poland, Poznanski, were moving. He requested from the Polish children who were in the cemetery at the time they bring flowers and lay them on this grave, and also upon the grave of the young children who were murdered in their tenderness.

The ceremony is over and the Christian visitors leave, but for us the Jews it is difficult to part from the cemetery, as lonely and neglected as we are. A thought persists in our minds: will this monument be the last memorial to the cruelty of those who hate Israel? Will the Polish children cast flowers upon this slab or – stones?

This monument bears witness...

[Page-252]

Closing Words

With this I conclude my words about the holy community of Kielce. This community, like the rest of the communities of Israel which were destroyed and extinguished – its name will not be erased. The members of the community perished sanctifying God and their people and their memory will echo forever.

In a small way this book will also serve to honor the memory the martyrs of Kielce, serve as a sort of monument of paper to their ashes, which are scattered over the face of the fields of Poland.

My strongest wish was to help in erecting a memorial for Kielce among the other communities of the Diaspora, which were erased from the face of the earth. It was as if the characters stood before me and demanded their presentation.

And therefore I went about the task and wrote down only things that were clear to me, in which I actively participated or to which I was an eye-witness. In describing personalities I tried to be as objective as possible, and if I have erred in any places – please, may the reader forgive me.

I had no grudge, God forbid, against anyone of the Jewish inhabitants of Kielce. I was fond of everyone, each one with his virtues and faults, with his positive attributes and his weaknesses was as a part of my, as flesh of my flesh, we were all like members of one family.

But on the other hand, I didn't want to present them as perfect angels. I brought them in this memorial book as they actually were, without additions of glitter and rouge. A true description, I believe, of people, public activists, does more to praise and honor them than exaggeration and apostrophe would.

With a heart full of affection to those who were – and who are no more, to those who were granted to move to the land of Israel and who work to build it, I went about this task. I will admit, that this labor has given me great emotional satisfaction. On the one side I found revealed to me anew a long life story, in which I too was a participant to some degree, and this was a tremendous experience for me. It was as if my life was happening again, and all of the events and incidents were being experienced once more. This work took me, in imagination, from the world of the present to the world of the past, from the Holocaust and horror that took place in our times to days of gaiety and light. I could distract myself for a moment from the terrible catastrophe which happened to the Israelite nation and to me in its midst.. Besides my friends and relatives who were chopped down in the Shoah, lost to me were my dear sons, whose souls were tied up in my soul.

In this work I have found a small portion of comfort from the deep sorrow that afflicts my soul. Would that we all find comfort in the redemption of the entire land of the people and the land!

[Page 253]

Testimony of Mr. Jechiel Alpert

(Formerly a member of the Jewish Committee of the Kielce District)

Up to the middle of 1945 a significant number of Jews gathered in the Kielce area, but due to the hostile attitude of the Poles they left the places they were living and moved to Kielce. One day the Poles in Kielce threw a hand grenade and injured 3 Jews. One of them was Eliahu Knobel. We appealed to the political police and they gave us a guard. When I appealed to the district governor asking what to do, we were advised to speak to Bishop Kreczmark. We appealed to the Bishop and after being put off several times he received us. The conversation lasted about an hour, but he said that the priesthood now had no influence over the masses, especially since many Jews were taking positions as clerks and treating the Polish population disdainfully.

On Thursday, 4.7.46 when morning arrived we were informed that the police had arrested a Jew accused of kidnapping a Polish child and holding him for two days in a cellar. When I heard this I went to Dr. Kahana, chairman of the community committee, demanding that he go to the police and have them release the Jew. Dr. Kahana returned and said that the police promised to release the imprisoned Jew, who was half-crazy. In the meantime, many Poles had gathered next to the offices of the community committee at 7 Planty Street and when I went to the window I saw that the police had arrived. I was informed that it was their intention to conduct a search in the community offices, in order to find the Christian children who had vanished recently and about whom it was suspected that they had been killed by Jews. I immediately telephoned the security police, since I saw that the police were explaining something to the Polish crowd and I suspected them of inciting them about this conspiracy. A Jewish army captain came immediately, Mr. Mora, and I saw that he was demanding identification from one of the policemen, one of those who was among the inciters. The policeman refused to show him his identification. I went to Captain Mora and he told me that the child who came to complain that he had been kidnapped and held in a cellar had pointed to a building that had no cellar. This captain told me that it was all falsehood and lies, and promised me that it would all be worked out, in spite of the fact that thousands of Poles had now congregated and the officers of the security police had totally vanished.

At 11:00 a.m., while I stood in the community office, I heard shots, and was told that the army had arrived to scatter the mob that had gathered. We were sure that the army was shooting in the air, so that people would disperse, however suddenly a bullet penetrated my room in the community office, and then I understood that they were not shooting to disperse the crowd, but at our office. Dr. Kahana turned to the window and saw an army captain K.B. ("Korpus Bezficzenstawa") and asked him what was going on here. But the captain did not want to reply to his question. I left the office and went out to the stairwell. There was a Christian girl standing there who was yelling: "You have it good! You killed Jesus and now we will repay you. You have drunk our blood enough!" When I insisted that she leave the office a soldier came over to me and said: "Leave her alone, otherwise we will take care of you!"

[Page-254]

In the same building there was a kibbutz of "Ha'Ichud HaZioni" [The Zionist Union]. At 11:30 a female member of the kibbutz, Ewa, burst into our offices shouting: "They are killing in the kibbutz!" I ran to the second floor with Dr. Kahana and there saw soldiers armed with Stens. They insisted that I go down to the yard outside of the house. I refused, even though I did not yet understand that the army, who had come as if for our security were actually the ones who began the pogrom. After several minutes, an injured fellow from the kibbutz called Wisznicki was brought from the kibbutz. Around the same time our friend Herszke Wajnryb was murdered in the kibbutz. Of all the O.B. officers meanwhile only one officer remained with us, a Jew called Albert.

At about 13:00 there was a lull. During the entire time we were in telephone contact with all sorts of people from N.K.W.D. and we asked them to come to our aid. They refused claiming that they didn't have people in the Polish army uniform, and on the other hand, they couldn't send forces in the Russian uniform so that the Poles wouldn't say that the Russians were killing Polish workers. Meanwhile a Polish army officer appeared who demanded that we hand over our arms. After he took my pistol from me, he demanded all of the bullets. I went up to my room, and then I found that my room was already totally destroyed, and everything that had been in it was stolen and wrecked, there was no longer anyone in the kibbutz that was across the way, and everything was destroyed. There were two rooms there and a corridor. The soldiers entered shooting via the corridor, and afterward to the first room, and from there to the second room shooting. And thus they killed and injured the young people who were there. When I went back down from my room I heard shots and screams, we went into the room and sat on the floor, since we feared shots through the windows. We heard the telephone ring. Dr. Kahana, who had been waiting the whole time for a call from the district governor, entered the room that had the telephone in it, which was already partially destroyed, so that the telephone itself sat on the floor. Dr. Kahana was forced to stretch out on the floor and he began the conversation. Suddenly, soldiers burst into the room, shot at him and killed him instantly. In the same incident Pinchas Ajzenberg was injured. When those of us in the room next door heard the soldiers bursting into Dr. Kahana's room we closed the door to our room and moved a closet in front of it to prevent the soldiers reaching us. However, we immediately heard their shouts: "Open the door, otherwise we will shoot through it!" We were therefore forced to open the door. Soldiers entered immediately shouting: "Hands – up!" "Go out!" We left the room between two rows of soldiers who were posted on the two sides of the corridors, guns in hands, and searching us, incidentally, they took everyone's money from them. When I went down the steps a Polish citizen assaulted me yelling: "He wanted to kill me!" and then gave me a blow to the head. Down in the yard Polish soldiers were standing, who grabbed every Jew who came down and threw him to the mob. When I saw that I stopped and sneaked back upstairs. Upstairs I met several young men who had also returned and after a consultation we decided to go down after all, since upstairs there was a greater danger of falling into the hands of the murderers. I went down first and looked around carefully to make sure some soldier wasn't waiting for us in ambush.

[Page-255]

Then a Polish officer came over to my wife, who had been with me, together, the entire time, and reassured her: "You see that nothing happened to your husband." She meanwhile saw 2 soldiers wearing my shirts. And when she mentioned this to the officer he laughed and denied it. I went down to the yard with my wife, where a lieutenant colonel stood speaking Polish with a Russian accent. He told us that all of the Jews had been taken to jail. When we asked what would become of us, he responded that when the cars returned, they would take us as well. Since the jail was very close to where we were it was clear to me that there would be no need of the cars, I therefore suspected that they had executed the Jews. In the presence of the aforementioned officer a Polish soldier came over to me and said: "Is today enough for you for the Polish blood, or do you want more?" While I was waiting in the yard, the O.B. captain came over to me and wanted to take me in an open jeep, but the aforementioned lieutenant colonel would not agree, the mob that roared all around numbered, to my estimate, approximately 20,000 people. In the meantime a truck arrived which took us to Foche Street, t the home of the O.B. officer. The rest of the Jews were transferred to various places, some of them to the stadium, some to O.B. and some to other places.

According to the news we later received, at 13:00 they already knew in Warsaw what was happening in Kielce. The next day, on Friday at 11:00, Mr. Albert, the Jewish officer of O.B. came to me at the home of the O.B. officer and told me that a delegation of American journalists was about to go to the hospital, and requested that I meet with the delegation and that I not tell them that the pogrom was conducted by the army and the police, in order not to damage the good name of the Polish government. In addition to this I would have to identify the bodies of those killed. I agreed, on the condition that I was given an excellent guard. When I arrived at the hospital on Aleksandra Street, I went into the morgue, which was filled with corpses. To my sorrow, I was not able to identify many of them, since the faces of those killed were altered until they were unrecognizable. Among those I identified were Dr. Kahana, the brother-in-law of Jechiel Zagajski, Fajnkochen, Izrael-Mosze Ajlbirt and others. The members of the delegation spoke among themselves in English. From the expression on their faces I understood that they were very moved (one of them did not even hide his tears). They attempted to calm us. I gave the journalist who was so moved the details I knew. By the way: among those killed was a young girl, not from Kielce. This girl had been in Bosk a day earlier. During the course of the riots we called on the telephone and told her not return to Kielce. To our sorrow, she returned and was killed. Her friend who was delayed in Bosk was saved from death.

I later visited the hospital, where I found 80 wounded and about 40 killed. The officer I was living with told me that the commander of the O.B. Sobczinski, who was supposed to bring the cadets from the O.B. officer's school in Slowik, near Kielce, to control the mob, had kept them for an hour and a half lecturing them. In the opinion of that officer, this was done intentionally. The same day Antek Cukerman arrived in Kielce who visited the hospital together with me and returned to Warsaw immediately. In the evening the Central Committee of the Jews of Poland arrived by airplane, together with the director of the Joint, Mr. A. Bejn and Messrs. Adolf Berman, Zelicki and others.

[Page-256]

We began to discuss what to do about the survivors still remaining in Kielce. We decided to transfer the seriously wounded to a hospital in Lodz, and the lightly wounded to leave in place so that they could give testimony in the police investigation. On Sunday Mr. Mordechai Gertler came to me and told me that the wounded in the hospital had declared a hunger strike, demanding to be removed from the municipal hospital, fearing that the Polish nurses would poison them; they were also unable to calmly bear the military guard. The injured demanded that a Jewish doctor be brought to care for them. I went to the O.B. requesting that they give me a car with an armed guard in order to drive to Czestochowa, a place where there was a Jewish doctor at the time. In spite of all of my efforts, I could not find a Jewish doctor who was willing to travel to Kielce. I then turned to a Jewish nurse, Helena Majtles, who agreed to come with me immediately. When I returned to Kielce, I barely made the funeral of the holy martyrs, in which the chief army rabbi, Dr. Kahana, the Polish defense minister, Rackiewicz and others participated. The memorial service was conducted by the cantor M. Koussevitsky.

The next day we transferred the wounded to the O.B. Polyklinika and Nurse Majtles took responsibility for their care.

On Tuesday the first military trial took place against 10 civilian rioters, among them one who was a police sergeant. Among other things they were accused of the fact that on that day, Thursday, 4.7.46, searching for Jews in all sorts of other places in the city and killing them, among the victims was also Icak Prajs and also Mrs. Fisz with a three week old baby. The aforementioned sergeant, together with a driver and another civilian who helped them, took Mrs. Fisz out of the city and shot her and the child to death. During the trial the judge asked him if he himself shot them or if he had given his rifle to someone else for the killing. The policeman answered: "How could I hand over my weapon to a strange civilian?" The policeman declared that he sniped and shot at the woman from a distance of several hundred meters, the judge asked him: "Why did you also kill the baby?" to which the accused answered: "I couldn't leave the baby alive since his mother had been killed." The court sentenced 9 defendants to death, and one woman to 10 years of hard labor. The sentence was carried out the next day.

The same Thursday, 4.7.46, the rioters also attacked the Chestochowa-Kielce train; the engine driver slowed the train's progress intentionally, all of the Jews were forcibly removed and killed. When I later appealed to the district governor to give me the number of those killed he responded that the number was not known to him.

I remained an additional several weeks thereafter in Kielce and finally went to the police demanding a guard, and I transferred the Kielce survivors to Lodz. Only a few people remained there.

During all of the weeks that we still remained in Kielce, additional investigations of the police and of the investigating judge took place. The results of the rest of the trials are not known to me, for we were not allowed to be present at those trials. It is worth mentioning that after the riots the police arrested many of the Polish public servants. In is interesting by the way, that the funeral and hospitalization expenses of the wounded were covered by the Central Committee of the Jews of Poland.

[Page-257]

The Jews of Ostrowicz were lucky: on Thursday, 4.7.46, when they heard of the riots in Kielce, they quickly notified the Zionist Organization Center in Warsaw, from which a vehicle was sent immediately with an armed escort, which transferred all of the Jews who were in Ostrowicz at the time to Warsaw.

On the first anniversary we erected a monument upon the graves of the victims. The District Governor, Major Wiszlic, representatives of the Zionist Organization and the Central Committee of the Jews of Poland were present.

Jechiel Alpert
Chairman of the District Committee of the Zionist Organization "Ichud" in Kielce
and member of the district committee of the Jews of Poland for the Kielce District currently in Holon, 36 Hamefade HaEzrachi St.

Ten Years to the Kielce Riots

Rabbi Dr. Kahana Dawid, Lieutenant Colonel
(in "HaTzofeh" 27th Tammuz, 5716 [1956]

When I open my bundle of written sketches from 1946, a year after the end of World War II, I am astounded and cannot believe my eyes. Can such a thing be?!

Not even a full year after the destruction of the evil empire – the rule of the Nazis in the country of Poland – when it seemed that the land was quiet and at rest, and that now the few survivors who remained could return to their dwelling places and live there without fear, to rest and renew their strength after the years of suffering and wandering. And suddenly the fury of the Polish "Black Hundred". Every single day horrifying news arrived in Warsaw at the seat of the Polish community committee at 6 Twarda Street about murders and assaults upon individual Jews, on entire families in cities, in villages and towns who had dared to return to their homes and demand their property back from their neighbors – their Polish inheritors.

The entire nation, and especially the nationalists among them, who couldn't stand the new regime, had decided to vent their fury upon the surviving remnant and to execute and complete Hitler's labor, may the name of evil ones rot.

[Page-258]

But the utmost pinnacle of hatred towards the eternal people was reached by the Catholic inhabitants of the infamous city.

On the Thursday, the fourth of July, 1946, it happened.

During the morning hours an 8 year old boy called Henryk Blaszczak passed through the city's streets with his father and told all the passersby that the Jews had held him captive and tortured him for two days in a certain cellar at 7 Planty Street, meaning to kill him and suck his blood. He described how he was miraculously saved and how he was able to escape the claws of the murdering Jews. The rumor took wing and for several hours went through the entire city from end to end.

At ten o'clock in the morning an enormous crowd gathered which first numbered several hundred people and by the afternoon hours reached the thousands, on Planty Street next to building number 7.

About 250 Jews in the city of Kielce lived at the time, some of them survivors of the Shoah and also some who had returned from Russia. Most of them lived on Planty Street in building number 7, the building of the Jewish committee and the community, the building of the "Ichud" kibbutz.

The organizers went through the crowd, inciting them to storm the building and kill the Jews calling out slogans "Death to the Jews! Death to the murderers of our children! Let's finish Hitler's job!"

The Jews shut themselves up in the building, blocked all the entrances and the windows and prepared to defend their lives with the few weapons they had. At about 12 a group of armed policemen (militiamen) arrived headed by police sergeant Wladislaw Blachot, who was sent by the police headquarters to disperse the mob and calm spirits. Blachot called to the Jews to open the gate and allow him and his aides enter. The besieged Jews sighed with relief, they thought their savior and redemption had arrived. But to their astonishment and bitter disappointment, Blachot commanded them to hand over their arms and to go down to the yard below.

As the investigation revealed, Blachot was the only policeman who was truly sent from the police, his "aides" were simple murderers who had dressed up in military uniforms. When the Jews refused to go down, Blachot began to beat their heads with the gun in his hand saying: "The Germans did not have time to exterminate you, but we will exterminate you." Once the signal had been given by Blachot the mob stormed the building, broke open the doors, the window shutters, came in and began beating, killing and wiping out everyone they reached, whether with a pistol, by hand by wood splinters and stones or iron spikes which had been prepared and brought by the organizers in their advance planning, back during the early morning hours.

At the same time the mob spread through the city streets, removed Jews from their homes and killed them on the spot. A great mob swarmed over the train station, the rioters organized into platoons and checked all of the trains that arrived in Kielce, people whose faces looked Jewish were removed from the cars and killed in a horrifying manner in front of the entire throng.

[Page-259]

Only towards the evening did military forces that had arrived especially from Lodz, succeed in gaining control over the rioters. That same night nearly 80 people were arrested.

The following day, on Friday morning, Minister Radkiewicz, in charge of the internal security of the country, arrived in Kielce accompanied by the chief prosecutor Domb. He held several consultations, gave urgent instructions regarding a special military court to try the first defendants accused of murder. The same day, the police commander of Kielce, Zagorski, was arrested, as well as the commander of the security forces in the district, Major Sobczinski, the district commander Lieutenant Colonel Kuzminski. They were all responsible for the blood bath.

After the Sabbath, Saturday night, I flew to Kielce accompanied by several members of the Committee of the communities in Poland in order to evaluate the riots from up close and take down evidence from the survivors.

The funeral was held on Monday, the 9th of Tammuz, 5706, on July 8th, 1946. Masses of people participated – nearly the entire city. I looked at their faces and tried to read in the expressions of the participants, of those standing crowded on both sides of the street through which the funeral passed, it was hard to say that these faces showed regret or sorrow. On the contrary, a hidden a sly smile would peep out at me from the crowd, and that is what accompanied me until the cemetery.

The Jewish cemetery in Kielce stood in its full and horrifying destruction that afternoon. Among the remnants of broken tombstones that lay around everywhere, among the half-opened graves, a giant mass grave had been dug which contained forty-one coffins. The coffins were lowered into the grave and the eulogies began.

The series of eulogies was begun by Dr. Adolf Berman, who spoke as the representative of the Central Committee of the Jews of Poland, after him Minister Kaczorowski spoke for the government, Professor Gorcki spoke for the League Fighting Racism and they both expressed their deep sorrow. They both spoke about the terrible shame that the Catholic inhabitants of Kielce had brought upon their people and country.

The grave was covered. Cantor Moshe Koussevitsky prayed the "El Maleh Rachamim". The terrible tragedy of the ruined Jewry of Poland was expressed in the pure sounds. The mourners said Kaddish, and the last of the speakers was the writer of these lines, who spoke in the name of the committee of the holy congregations in Poland.

33 bodies of men women and children were identified, some by witnesses and relatives, and some by documents which were found in their clothing. Besides these there were another eight coffins of shattered bodies, which were not identified and who were buried as anonymous victims. Among them, one body with a number of the Auschwitz concentration camp on its arm – 2969B. Six died of their wounds in the Kielce Hospital a week after the funeral. A total of 47 victims.

On July 11th the first group of rioters was tried before a special military court. The instruments and tools of destruction used by the rioters as they conducted their "task", pipes and iron bars, hoes, stones, poles, three bloodstained shirts and two pistols, were exhibited on a special table before the court.

[Page-260]

I sat in the courtroom, watching the faces of the accused. They all sat with their heads down, not daring to lift their heads and to look into the faces of the judges and the audience members. And here are several images of the accused:

Antonina Biskopska, a young woman of 26, mother of a child aged 4. On the bitter Thursday she left the house, passed in front of the mob and called "death to the Jews!" and incited the mob to kill the "rzids". Together with others she threw stones into the building at 7 Planty Street. With a trembling voice she described that indeed this was what happened, but that she is a weak woman with weak nerves. She heard that the Jews murdered a Christian Polish boy and could not contain herself. Something pushed her to go out and join the mob. Biskopska received ten years in prison.

Eduard Jorkowski, forty years old, educated and a member of the symphony orchestra in Kielce, marched at the head of the mob like someone conducting an orchestra and yelled: "Men, forward, death to the murderers of our children!" Jorkowski tried to prove that he had been drunk that day, but the judges proved the reverse.

Julian Poksziwinski, 43 years old – his bloodstained shirt was found on the table of exhibits. He stepped with his feet upon the stomach of an injured woman who was lying on the road in a puddle of blood. Poksziwinski did not even try to justify himself.

Dorarz – a blond fellow of 18, he split the skull of a Jew at Planty Street with the stone in his hand. Dorarz admitted the accusation, expressed remorse and wished to ease his sentence. He received life imprisonment.

Here is a group of four – all of them from the middle class: policeman Stefan Mazor, owner of the Kazimierz Nowakowski bakery, the cobbler Jozef Sliwa and the shopkeeper Antoni Proszkowski. On that Thursday they took the woman Regina Fisz and her baby from the building, dragged them to the forest, robbed her of all her possessions – 17 dollars and 3 gold rings. After the robbery they killed her and the baby with the iron bars in their hands. The entire group was sentenced to death.

11 death sentences were carried out by the special military court on the same day.

All of the Polish newspapers (there was free press in Poland at the time) came out with headline articles with energetic and sincere protest against the rioters. Everyone blamed and condemned the Polish reactionaries, and especially the leaders of the church who could have protested and didn't all protest – except for the well known periodical of Mikolaiczik, "Gazeta Lyudowa".

On July 9th the newspaper "Gazeta Lyudowa" published an announcement in Mikolaiczik's name, that he was indeed horrified by the murder in Kielce, but in his opinion, the entire matter needed serious investigation. And what particularly bothered him – the reasons that led the people to such a thing. In his opinion it would be possible to discuss the matter and draw conclusions only after an in depth investigation and inquest.

[Page-261]

The announcement of the head of the Catholic church in Poland, Cardinal Halond, was without shame and full of barbed remarks against the Jewish people. After pressure from foreign journalists, the Cardinal published an opinion, which stated: The Catholic Church opposes all murder and condemns it without consideration of its causes and source. With regard to the murder of the Jews in Kielce, the Cardinal believes that the reason for it was not the hatred of the Polish people towards the Jews, there was no room here for anti-Semitism at all. At the end of the vague announcement it said that the Cardinal opposes the role of the Jewish people in Polish social life. There are too many Jews in key government positions, too many high-ranking officials, too many officers in the army. And here the Cardinal revealed his true face and true position. Pretending to justify the rioters, they acted in accordance with the position promulgated by the Catholic Church, let the Jews not intervene in the internal lives of the Christians....

Ten Years to the Riots in Kielce

L. Lenman ("HaBoker" 27.7.1956)

At this hour, when the eyes of the entire world are turned towards Poland in which at this very moment a dramatic uprising is taking place in Poznan against the communist oppressors, the calendar has uncovered the anniversary day of sorrow and deep pain, which recalls to our memories a chilling chapter in the long bloody accounting that, to our sorrow, has not yet ended, between the Jewish people and the Poles. On the 4th of July, 1946 42 Jewish souls were cruelly slaughtered in the Polish city of Kielce, men women and children, and dozens of others were seriously wounded. This date has been set in the post-war history of the Jews of Europe not only because of the frighteningly large number of victims in the Kielce riots, but much more because of the special circumstances of that cruel drama, which brought about results of a truly historical nature. It is worth spending some time on them and looking back at them from the perspective of ten years.

And when we renew the events of the fatal riots themselves in our memories, we recall, first and foremost, that it began with a provocation, that criminal hands prepared and executed according to the "best" examples from the darkness of the Middle Ages.

On the 1st of July, 1946 the 8-year-old child, Antony Blaszczik [sic] disappeared in Kielce, and all of the Polish inhabitants searched for him. After three days, the child was suddenly found, and told everyone that the Jews had grabbed him, held him in a dark cellar, stabbed him with nails and wanted to slaughter him.

Around the "tortured" boy a large mob congregated immediately that was "coincidentally" armed with iron bars, pitchforks and stones. The mob besieged the new Jewish committee building that worked for the benefit of the few Jews of the remnants who had gathered in Kielce and the area who had returned from the camps, from hiding places, from villages and also – from the Soviet Union.

[Page-262]

The Jews who were inside the building closed themselves in with the shutters and telephoned unceasingly to the police headquarters to send aid. After several hours, chief of police Sobczinski arrived accompanied by several sergeants. They entered the building and took the few rifles and pistols the defenders had from the members of the Jewish committee. The policemen explained that they were doing this so that the arms the Jews had would not provoke the rage of the mob even more; and as to protecting their lives – "The police of democratic Poland already know how to safeguard you..."

And indeed it did know how to safeguard: when the policemen had just left the building with the arms they had taken from the Jews in their hands, the pogrom began. The wild mob burst inside, assaulted the defenseless Jews and murdered them all, and threw the bodies of the members of the committee out of the window to the street where the mob fell upon them and tore them to pieces.

At the same hour the fire of the pogrom took hold of the entire city: gangs armed with iron bars and axes broke into apartments of Jews, robbed, set on fire, and murdered every Jew who fell into their hands. The pogrom went on until late in the night. The rioters even put a "guard" at the train station checked the trains that stopped at the station on their journey, removed a number of Jewish passengers from them and murdered them.

While Jewish blood was flowing in Kielce, I was in Warsaw, and those hours of horrified expectation of the news that the authorities had finally taken control of the situation were etched very deeply in my memory. For in Warsaw the matter had become known early: a few hours after the pogrom began General Wictor Grosz, head of the Foreign Ministry's information service for foreign journalists had called a meeting of the newspaper journalists and told them about the terrible events, and added that "up until know we know of ten Jewish fatalities." He promised, that the authorities would do everything to restore order, but that this wasn't easy since thousands of people were participating in the assaults and that "there is provocation taking part in the riots, which is conducting all of the incitement and determination against the new popular Poland."

And order in Kielce and the area was reestablished only the following morning. The army took over the city. Several dozen Poles, who were caught in the very "act" of killing, were arrested and jailed. Three days later an urgent trial took place for 12 thugs who were found to be the major culprits. When they were brought to the courthouse their clothes were stained with the spilt blood.

The trial was conducted swiftly. Most of the accuse confessed that they were part of the mob "that wanted to take revenge upon the Jews for the torture of a Christian child." One of the rioters used the following typical words: " – I thought there were no more Jews in Poland… that the Germans liquidated them forever… but they started to come back, I don't know from where… and they even began repeating their old crimes… and therefore we got angry, me and the other Poles…"

The young Polish prosecutor concluded his accusatory speech with a few sentences: – The accused are all Poles. I am also a Pole and the elevated court is also made up of Poles. They are Catholics, and I am Catholic, and I am ashamed to be Polish and Catholic like them… I feel upon me the terrible shame, which lies upon all of Poland and all of the Catholic world… there are no extenuating circumstances for their horrible actions…."

[Page-263]

Nine murderers were condemned to death and hanged the next day.

All of these details I took from an article I sent at the time from Warsaw and which was printed in "HaBoker" on the 29th of July, 1946.

I did not travel to Kielce and I did not see the faces of the murderers with my own eyes. The director of the information of the Foreign Ministry invited me to fly to Kielce on the special airplane with the rest of the reporters, but I remained in Warsaw as I wrote in that same article. I admit that I didn't travel to Kielce, even though it was my journalistic obligation.

But especially as a man who was born and educated in Poland, I couldn't go. As a man who had finished Gymnasium in Warsaw as well as higher education, for whom Mieckiewicz and Slowcki were impressed deeply upon his heart… and for whom Rzromski and Orzszkowa shone their glory upon the days of his youth… I could not make myself stand face to face with human beings (these are also called "human beings)… who had torn my brothers and sisters into pieces. These were not professional criminals from the underworld; not bandits, robbers, thieves who had a record of other crimes. No, in Kielce the Jews were murdered by average Poles. From all circles and classes. Barber and musician, baker and construction worker, militia sergeant and merchant. That is, Poles of the same sort that I met every day, every step and every yard on the tram and the bus.

From the time I had returned to Poland, together with thousands of Jews returning from Russia, I had been subjected to a fierce debate and propaganda, which tried to convince us that only the Fascist Poles aided the Nazis in the destruction of the Jews of Poland. They, "Anders' Men", who opposed democratic Poland, also opposed the rehabilitation of Jewish settlement in Poland. In contrast, the average Pole, the man of his people, was honest, straightforward and good. One must just gain his support for the new democratic regime and he would be the best we would have…

This is what not only the Polish leaders of the new regime claimed, but also – and perhaps mainly – the Jewish leaders of a certain position. Leaders who didn't cease to speak and persuade, that here was a new Jewish settlement "flowering and flourishing with new life," for which we must found and build cooperatives, factories, children's homes and clubhouses…

– Therefore, the readers will please excuse me for not traveling to Kielce myself and not looking at the faces of the Polish murderers, who were not members of the underworld, but from those same good Poles among who we were now being called to live and with them to build a new Poland, better than its predecessor.

Today, is there anything much to add to these lines, which were written ten years ago under the fresh impression of the pogrom in Kielce?

When you look back from the perspective of ten years, it is necessary, first and foremost, to express satisfaction that in the dramatic argument whether to remain in Poland or not, the healthy popular sense of the Jews won out. After the Kielce riots over 100 thousand Jews left Poland, and the vast majority of them live healthy and normal lives in Israel. Seeing the renewed wave of anti-Semitism on the rampage in Poland once again, we must regret that so many Jews were misled by false leaders, who persuaded them to resettle upon the soil of Poland, saturated with the blood and tears of the Jews. And the serious question: why has the fury of the Jewish people not yet reached the false preachers: those who supported – those who misled?!…

[Page-264]

Kielce

Translated by Mark Froimowitz

Kielce was a large Jewish center where, before the war, there lived 22,000 Jews. But the economic and cultural position that Jews occupied here far exceeded their number. The picture of Kielce was Jewish. The long street beginning at the railroad station and running till far past the city center and all of the cross streets were thickly settled with Jews and occupied by Jewish stores. The signs over the stores, the houses themselves, the people on the streets - Jews and Jewishness. Though the pre-war Polish powers compelled the Jewish manufacturers to remove Jewish workers and to replace them with Polish ones, the Kielce industries remained Jewish and Kielce was dominated by the Jewish family Zagiski, the owner of the large lime kilns that supplied lime for all of Poland.

Kielce did not have those deep traditions of the old Jewish cities like Lublin or Krakow. She was the youngest Jewish community in Poland. Until the Polish "rebellion" in the year 1863, there was not a single Jew in Kielce. After the removal of the prohibition for Jews to live there, a Jewish life was established in the course of a short time which, from that time on, increased continuously until the great catastrophe of 1939.

Because of her youth, Kielce did not have famous Yeshivas and Talmud Torahs. Here, Jewish life developed more under the influence of trends toward Polish culture. Also later, the Jewish secular culture did not hold back her great ambitions here. However, Kielce was a city with a Jewish heart, the same Jews as in Warsaw and other cities, the same readiness to sacrifice, the same tie to Jewish qualities and Jewish ways. Just the opposite, because of her upstart status, the wallets of Kielce Jews were more open than in other cities. As if she wanted with charity and generosity to atone for her lack of a Torah tradition.

Among the Kielce Jewish citizens, the largest influence was Zionism. But, other Jewish political parties also had an honest share here. And, just as in the other cities, the Kielce Jews believed that they were building an eternal place, and in that eternal place would play out all Jewish salvations. They would, they believed, through their arduous work, build a Jewish state in the land of Israel, to shape the socialist revolution in Kielce. They would free themselves and others. And, in Kielce itself, they would have deeper roots than until now.

Now I have come to Kielce and found all that Jews have created. But of they themselves, of the Jews, I found only a few. Literally, only a few Jews. And not in their houses did I find them, but only accidentally, the way that one meets people in a bus depot.

Here, it is the opposite of other cities. There is vast movement. The streets are filled with people. For those who did not know the city before the war, it will look normal. He will not recognize that vivaciousness and creativity has been taken away from the population.

It was – beginning in 1940 – when in Kielce were found 28,000 Jews. When after the take over of Poland by the Germans, the Jewish wandering began. Better said, the Jewish running. Several thousands Jews fled Kielce. They were running to the Soviet side toward Lemberg. Later, many of them came back in order "to die in their own bed". Jews also came from nearby towns. Two thousand Jews came from Lodz and from the Lodz province. On the eve of Passover 1941, 28,000 Jews were locked in the ghetto. Compared with other cities, the Kielce ghetto was large enough. The local Polish leaders asked the Germans to designate a large ghetto since overcrowding causes the outbreak of epidemics from which everyone suffers, including the Polish population. The Germans accommodated the request of the Polish city fathers. However, they later realized that what the Polish leaders want is against the politics of the Germans. They, the Germans, need epidemics and the largest possible gas chambers. They cut Warsaw street off from the ghetto and the crowding made epidemics a natural annihilation before they had activated the "A *produktive* " [translator's note: not known]. An epidemic of typhus breaks out which takes 4000 victims.

In the ghetto, however, a much worse epidemic breaks out, degeneracy. An assimilated Jew, Herman Levi informs on the president of the Jewish Council, Dr. Moshe Pelz, who did all things possible to lighten the lives of the Jews in the ghetto, that he is working against the German power. Dr. Pelz is sent to Oswiecim (Auschwitz) where he dies in the gas chamber and he, Herman Levy, takes over the leadership of the Jewish Council like a plain Gestapo agent. He also, after his "accomplishments", dies in November 1942 in the Oswiecim gas chambers. The youth in the ghetto prepare an underground movement. However, the same dark process repeats itself as in all other Polish cities. Against the Jews are not only the Germans. The Jews are completely alone. The Polish organizations have help from abroad. They have weapons, but they do not want any contact with the Jews. The ghetto remains with empty hands and without any hope of someone's help from the external world. Except for those lying in wait for Jewish boys, the internal enemies, the Jewish police. The ghetto is too crowded to allow someone to do something in a conspiracy.

The 20th August 1942 begins the end of all hopes. The German "Zondercommando" with the Ukrainian, Lithuanian, and Polish helpers occupy the ghetto and, within several days, they liquidate the Kielce community. The "norm" is six thousand Jews a day. The command is to kill more Jews on the spot. In the time of the "resettlement", the streets, the houses, and the bunkers are flooded with Jewish blood. Thousands of dead Jews are scattered in the streets. A wild slaughter goes on for a whole week. Every second day, 6000 Jews are brought out - on the 20th, the 22nd and the 24th of August. At the end, there remain in the ghetto not more than 2,100 Jews. Among them, 45 children from the police, the doctors, and the Jewish Council.

When 600 Jews fall to the last transport, they become the complement of left behind workers and 1500 Jews are confined in the Kielce work camp [translator's note: There was a Hasag slave labor camp in Kielce]. With their hands, the German murderers gather together the plunder. Here, the Jews will live until their work ends. Left are only the young, strong ones. They now begin to prepare themselves intensively for a revolt. The organizers are David Bachwiener, Gershon Leftkowich and the younger Chmielevski. They manufacture weapons by themselves . David Bachwiener makes grenades by himself. But, a provocateur places himself in the movement, that is Yahan Spiegel, a Vienna Jew, the chief of the Jewish police in the camp. He wins the trust of the organizers and they confide to him their plans. Yahan Spiegel believes that, by giving away the organization, he will win life for himself and his family. He gives the organization into the hands of the Gestapo and all fall the death of holy martyrs. Later when the Germans liquidate the work camp and they send the provocateur to Oswiecim, he dies there at the hands of two religious Jewish boys, the brothers Shlomo and Yehuda Perl from Kielce.

The Jewish community of Kielce no longer exists. After the war, she conducted herself for life. A few Kielce Jews saved themselves in Russia. The remainder came out from the German camps. 400 Kielce Jews came home and wanted to start anew as was done 80 years ago. But, the Polish population had decided not to allow any more Jews in Kielce. The triumph of the German murder of the Jews was also their triumph and they would not allow it to be pulled from their hands. And they made a pogrom against Jews in 1946 upon a pattern of a "resettlement" from the German-Ukrainian "Zondercommando".

The current representative of the Jews in Kielce, Isadore Cohen leads me to the house where most of the victims fell. He tells me that the tactics of the Poles were well thought out. Precisely as the pogrom was planned out before hand. With appropriate propaganda in the streets. And the pogrom was carried out through the unified power of all of the Polish strata. They killed the Jews leisurely in cold blood while they were sure that no one would interfere with their work. Hoodlums from their security forces also participated in the pogrom.

The central power liquidated the pogrom. About ten pogrom perpetrators were shot. And even several officers of the security forces were punished for their "slow interventions" at the time of the pogrom. However, the father of the pogrom, Bishop Hlond remained in Kielce. And Jews ran away over the borders. They have had, call it, enough, of Kielce and this land as all that was dearest is crushed and destroyed.

In Kielce are left about 20 Jews, Jewish boys and girls, whom in the streets you will not recognize as being Jewish. Where do these Jews live? No one knows. When I came to Kielce, a policeman on the street informed me that, if I was looking for Jews, they must live near the security forces, because they are afraid to live just anywhere in the city. And indeed, in a house near the police station, I found three apartments where Jews lived. In the small rooms is the bed with the table and oven together. There, in the evening, I had a meeting with the whole Jewish population of Kielce. I was on no account able to determine what holds this score of Jews here. From one woman, I heard that she is there temporarily.

She is battling a Polish woman about her sister's child whom the Polish woman will not return. Several boys occupy themselves with selling Jewish houses. One young man declared to me that, in any case, the Jews have lost the war, so what difference does it make how one's few years end. Sitting here are about a score of Jews as in a station from which one can come and go away. But the passengers are, in any case, homeless, to where should they go?

Characteristic of the Kielce Poles is this. After the Germans were driven away, they took upon themselves to destroy what the Germans had not yet destroyed. The Germans had polluted the Kielce cemetery. They had made it into an execution place. They had polluted the fence with Jewish gravestones. After the driving away of the Germans, Polish hooligans took to the fence and, in the course of several days, completely wrecked it. Now the Jews have built a new fence and erected at the cemetery a memorial for the murdered Jews during the German occupation and during the pogrom.

The large beautiful synagogue was converted by the Germans to a warehouse in which was found the bedding of the Jews after the "resettlement". The entire huge building was filled with Jewish pillows and comforters. After the liberation, the synagogue was converted by the Poles to a toilet for peasants who come to the large synagogue plaza with their wagons on market day. When I, with the mentioned Isadore Cohen, went together to look at the synagogue, we found there a group of Polish schoolchildren who had taught themselves to aim with stones in the remaining panes of glass in the windows. That was the successor generation to the hoodlums who dug up tens of graves in the cemetery and robbed the gold teeth of the dead. They are the offspring of those who took hundreds of gravestones from the cemetery and dragged them away to their homes for building purposes.

The second synagogue in Kielce – Zagiski's synagogue – was converted to an iron warehouse.

All that happened in Kielce after the liberation was a liquidation of every trace of the Jews. The pogrom in Kielce was a continuation of the liquidation of the remainder of the large Jewish community. A total of 500 Jews remained in Kielce and the murderers destroyed also the remnant of the escapees and with that ended the history of Jewish existence in that city.

[Page-270]

The Day of Mourning in 5666 [1906]

After the bloody riots that occurred in Russia against the Jews during the months October –November 1905 and the incitement against them which grew stronger at that time, it was decided, according to the suggestion of the genius rabbis Rabbi Cwi Hersz Rabinowicz of Kowna, Rabbi Eliezer Gordon of Telz; Rabbi Mosze Danoszewski from Slobodka and Rabbi Israel Mejer HaKohen from Radin Z"L to call for a public fast on the even of the new month of Elul 5666 in the entire country of Russia. The fast was then declared all over the world.

We hereby publicize herewith the exhortation letter that was published at the time by the rabbi of Kielce, the genius Rabbi Mosze Nachum Jerusalimski Z"L, in its original form:

B"H Tuesday, portion of Matot-Mas'ei, 5666. Kielce.

With regard to the holy, elevated most high idea that came to the minds of the acclaimed genius rabbis of Lita, may they merit long and excellent days, having a general mourning fast on the eve of the new moon of Elul which is approaching for the good, here this thing is truly a worthy and necessary matter, good and of benefit and all agreement by a body in this matter is redundant, except in that whoever is able to help to transform this thing from the potential to a reality, is obligated with a holy and moral obligation to attempt with all the efforts of his strengths and as far as he can reach in order to bring to action, and in this I am together with you in one mind to endorse this with all the warmth of my Israelite body and soul, for who is the man whose eyes do not shed a sea of tears and his heart not be broken into shards over the terrible tragedy which has befallen the house of Israel during the preceding days, however, the gates of tears shall not be locked. We don't have in our strengths but a mouth, and if we have also sinned to the Lord our god and our transgressions have piled high, we will please repent with willing heart and soul for He is very forgiving.

My brothers children of Israel, brothers in trouble! Let us gather together with the wind of all the ends of the earth, the places where we have been scattered, let us unite in our prayers and our fasting for one day –on the even of the new moon of Elul which approaches for the good. All of the Israelite people will pray on this day and will fast and will repent before the dweller of the heavens from the depths of the heart and we will then be in surety that the prayers of the entire holy congregation of Israel will not be returned unanswered and may we be speedily redeemed materially and in spirit, and a redeemer will come to Zion Amen.

Mosze Nachum Jerusalimski head of the holy rabbinical court of Kielce and the region

This letter was published in a general notice of the great ones of Israel and in all of the synagogues and houses of worship the general fast was kept strictly, and even more so by all of the inhabitants of Kielce.

[Page-271]

The Diary of Rabbi Jeruzalimski From the Days of the First World War

Translated from the Yiddish by Jerrold Landau

The diary of Rabbi Moshe Nachum Jerusalimski of blessed memory, from the time of the First World War, transcribed from a manuscripts by his son David Yonah of blessed memory and given to us to publish by his son Shamai Dov Yerushalmi (Jerusalimski).

This Memorial

These words describe in brief one one-thousandth of what I experienced during the days of turmoil, beginning from the 8th of Menachem Av 5674 until I came to my son in Kharal on the Tuesday of the Torah portion of Acharei Mot-Kedoshim, on the 6th of Iyar 5675 [1].

On Thursday of the week of the Torah portion of Devarim (5674), the general mobilization began, about which we could not even begin to physically understand how we were sitting in fresh air [2]. At first at 12:00 midnight, when the "Beis Din" [3] departed for Kielce, I noticed the local shochet (ritual slaughterer). That Friday, there was a panicky flight from the surrounding countryside. Throughout the entire Sabbath day, the roads were filled with departing Christians. On Sunday the 10th of Av, despite the fast, all the Jews fled from the surrounding countryside. At night, when I felt quite weak from the fast, I received a telegraph, sent from the factory in Kharal, with the sorrowful news that my daughter-in-law Chana Rozia was with her daughter Rivka – who had taken seriously ill, and is in need of great mercy. The telegraph was written with many errors and was completely unclear. The tribulations that she was going through were indescribable.

In the morning, on Monday of the Torah portion of Vaetchanan, they summoned me from Kielce, telling me that I should come quickly. That night, when I arrived home broken, drenched from a heavy rainstorm, I found the whole city enveloped in fear, for many known reasons. I speedily arranged a Get (bill of divorce) for a Jew – a soldier who had to travel [4] shortly. On Tuesday night, there was a panic in town over the first arrests that took place in connection to the shortage of small currency, and everybody knows about the difficulties that that issue raised. I quickly issued a ban on hoarding copper and silver coins, and thanks to that, the innocence of our Jews in this connection was demonstrated. On Wednesday, 13th of Av, I went to see the governor regarding that issue and other issues. (Before I saw him in person, I had a serious discussion with his assistant, a discussion which seemed to present a favorable opportunity in my mind.) He answered each matter appropriately. He informed me about the telegram that he sent at that time to the general governor, in which he requested that the population remain calm.

On Thursday of the week of the Torah portion of Vaetchanan, at night (on the 25th) [5], the governor Ch. Ligin left Kielce, and the next day, on Friday, all of the higher and lower officers followed. It is difficult to describe the fear that this event instilled in the city, as well as another frightful happening: the sudden liquidation, based on an ordinance from the higher authorities, of the entire liquor reserve for a few million, and the open burning of all kinds of documents from the national archives, and other such items. That same day, the magistrate appointed a civic militia from all segments of the population, which would begin its activities on Tuesday of the Torah portion of Ekev (July 29), and would maintain its duties until the arrival of the "Sokolen" (the privileged Polish militia which united with the Austria-Hungary army, who were expected to march into town very shortly carrying their flag. On Wednesday, there was a shootout between the "Sokolen" and the Russian cavalry. The next day, on Thursday the 14th of Av, strongmen from our brave militia came, and a difficult battle took place between the two sides in close proximity to the city. One side took up its position on the "Karczawka", and the other on the hill near the Jewish cemetery. Many victims fell in the city. The battle took place for one hour until the Austrians were repulsed. After a short break, about an hour later, a special emissary from the magistrate came to me bearing the very unfortunate news that the president of the city has been arrested, and the city commandant has imposed upon Kielce a contribution of 105,000 rubles. The deadline for the contribution was 5:00 p.m. Obviously, the entire city was in great danger. The weeping and lamentations of the wives and young children could be heard on all the streets… Hearing this made the hair stand on edge and caused a shudder through the heart… After a great deal of effort, and with the help of certain acquaintances, I was able to pay the contribution down to the last groszy, ant there was some relief in the city. Shortly thereafter, at evening on the following day, Friday, the peace was disturbed by a certain segment of our militia… The damage was estimated by the magistrate to be 200,000 rubles. Thanks to the intercession of the Greek Orthodox priest, peace prevailed until midday. However, shortly thereafter, in the evening, the Poles proclaimed that revenge would be taken against the Jews, which means that they were preparing for a murderous pogrom… I ran to the bishop at nightfall. He, along with his assistants, urged the public to hold their peace and to live freely with everyone. Thanks to this, peace prevailed until the next morning.

On the Sabbath day of the Torah portion of Ekev (22 Av, August 1) a frightful thing took place… The Austrians entered the city. A terrible slaughter broke out, continued until 8:00 p.m. on Saturday night. Victims fell like flies around the city and in the city itself, causing terrible scenes in several places… There was no humanity, and great distress. Whoever did not hear the shooting and thunder, and whoever did not see the disarray in the city, -- has not witnessed destruction. The darkness of Saturday night continued through the next morning, the Sunday of the Torah portion of Reeh, which given over to sweat and terror, and to various tribulations which cannot be written about. On the Monday of the Torah portion of Reeh, some of the liar-specialists attempted to terrorize the population by starting a false rumor, apparently as an ordinance from the highest commander, that in two hours the entire population, men, women and children, must leave the city. This rumor spread through the city like a thunderbolt. Who knew what kind of bad fortune might be coming! As is shown, from all of the false rumors and confusions that were issued regarding Jews, the worst was that one of the sides was "retreating". That moment served as an opportunity for all of the tribulations and ill fortune that took place for a variety of terrible reasons in many Polish cities, particularly Radom, Kornacice, Zamosc and others. Only G-d in his great mercy could assist us in leaving the city. Most of the residents remained put in their places.

On Tuesday of the Torah portion of Reeh (August 5), the Austrians with the "Sokolen" came to Kielce. About two weeks later, the German "Landstrum" arrived, and put up three different flags. They remained with us until Thursday of the Torah portion of Ki Tavoh, on the 4th of Elul (August 29) [6]. During that month, many events took place that left a large imprint upon the hearts of the Kielcer residents. On Friday of the Torah portion of Shoftim, Mr. Herschel Preis was arrested along with several other people. They were freed two weeks later. On Tuesday of the Torah portion of Ki Tetzeh, those who resided in the building of the governing authorities and who required support through my intercession from the Jewish committee were gathered into the well-known "Komisarsz" area. Thanks to G-d may He blessed, I was able to leave in peace. On Thursday of the Torah portion of Ki Tetzeh, A. Wachsberg and his son N. were arrested. They were later freed. On Thursday, I spent a dark night with the elder Greek Orthodox priest, and the next day, on Friday of the Torah portion of Ki Tavoh, the Russian army marched triumphantly into Kielce. That same day, the "Sokolen" killed two Jews along the way, whom they had chanced upon. They hung them in the forest that was near the village of Petkowice. I first found out about this on Friday night during the time of prayers. This matter and other matters caused a great deal of discussion in town. That same day, the accident took place with the well-known Birnzweig, who aroused the Polish crowds many times that they should beat any Jewish passer-by on the Sabbath of the Torah portion of Ki Tavoh, men and women. The priests tried to calm him down somewhat. That same Sabbath, all of the Jewish stores remained open, for they had to provide all needed provisions to the Russian army who were crowding into the city. On Thursday of the Torah portion of Nitzavim (26 Elul) the governor and his assistant, along with all the ruling officials, arrived by train. They met up with Jews outside the station, who greeted them with joyous shouts of "hurray". The governor extended his hand to me and thanked the Jewish community in his name for the enthusiastic reception. As can be imagined, the city became calmer (only in the shops on a few side lanes was there some temporary unrest). The two days of Rosh Hashanah were, with G-d's help, peaceful, spent in calm supplication and worship. On the day of Shabbat Teshuva [7], Tishrei 6, 5675 (September 13), the governor suddenly appeared with his assistants and all of the officials, and a dark bitterness fell upon all of the Kielcers. On Sunday night, there was a fright over the announcement that was pasted onto the railway station, that a special train would come on Monday during the day. A rumor spread that there was an order from the high officials that we would have to leave Kielce. It is impossible to write in this diary what was took place that night in the city. (Here, as in the surrounding cities, a large, fierce battle broke out.) Even though the chief of police posted notices, one could not trust the widespread, frightening announcements that, on Monday, half of the community would have to leave Kielce on the train and be dropped of somewhere along the way. The other residents convinced me to hold my peace, as there would be no traveling.

On Tuesday, the eve of Yom Kippur, we heard loud cannon shots that frightened the Kielcer community. Later, we found out that they were breaking apart the railway lines with dynamite. In the confusion, in the midst of the sounds of gunfire, I immersed myself in the mikva [8], in order to accept the holy fast day and the holy Kol Nidre night upon myself in purity. From all sides, one could see the great fires that broke out in the villages surrounding Kielce. We spent the night in holiness, intermixed with fear and terror – for the unique souls it was an uplifting religious experience… On Yom Kippur morning, the terrible battle got stronger. One could hear the sound of artillery during the time of the prayers. At around 11:00 a.m., the Germans stormed into Kielce… They set up their heavy artillery guns on Warsawer Street. The Great Synagogue was surrounded by cannons.

The Russian army retreated from the city in haste. The prayers finished in the Great Synagogue by 1:00 p.m. I gathered a larger crowd of people around myself, and we prayed for the entire day. We could hear the shooting throughout almost the entire day. During the time of the Avoda, as we were reciting the words "Achat", "Achat Veshtaim" … [9], the artillery stopped, as if they were saying with us the words "Achat", "Achat Veshtaim"… During the day, a command was issued by the German commandant that all of the stores must be opened, as the Jewish bakers must provide bread for the German military. At Neila time [10], the general called together all of the Jewish butchers and shochtim at the magistrate. At night, at the conclusion of Yom Kippur, the entire brigade of German soldiers arrived, who were in charge of the life of all of the Kielce residents.

On Thursday the 5th of Tishrei (September 18) [11], the German soldiers grabbed whomever they found on the streets, either Christians or Jews (among everyone, they also grabbed my Binyamin, but a little later, they found someone else who would work in his place, and they freed him). They were conscripted to repair the railway and the artillery wagons. On the same day, I received a request from the commandant via the magistrate that the stores should remain open, and in return for fulfilling the request, he would be responsible for my well-being [12].

On the Sabbath prior to Sukkot [13], I was called to the commandant, as he wished to insure that the Jewish bakers would shortly begin baking bread. Dr. Lewi from Berlin was with me at the time. He had the feeling that they would be satisfied with the oral assurances that we would give. The magistrate would transmit the assurance to the officials, who would issue the command to all the bakers.

At this time, the German-Austrian soldiers concocted various libels, about which it is difficult to discuss. As far as I am concerned, they would make people "defer". At that time, a significant number of the Poles, our blood-enemies, assisted in making the situation difficult for our Jews. For example, one can bring the terrible accident in Staszow, which everyone knows about: On Yom Kippur, a quorum of eleven pious, proper Jews worshipped together not far from the city. At the time they were there, a gentile set a house on fire, and the members of that quorum thought that this was done as a treacherous activity. All the proofs and pleas that they were innocent of that disgusting deed were for naught. On the holy day at Neila time, they were brought out to the field be shot. Ten of them were shot on the same day, and the prayer leader was hung. It is not possible to write at all about the libels that took place at that time in Poland in general, and in the Kielce region in particular.

Prior that time, when the German-Austrians wanted (even though the economic situation was good) they invented pretexts, for which the Jews were arrested for spying. Among these were the father and son Kaufman, and N. Wachsberg, who were freed only after a great deal of intercession. There was also the libel with the feldscher [14] Ch. Singerman who was arrested at night in the middle of the street, and immediately taken to the magistrate, where he was killed in a terrible fashion.

A few days after the burial, they wished to perform an autopsy on him; however by presenting reasons, and through intercessions, this did not take place [15]. Two Jews of Checiny were also arrested: One of them was found with explosive materials in his store, which caused an explosion that killed two people and injured the homeowner. Explosive material was also found by the second. Both were freed after a monetary fine was imposed. Prior to this time, there were many professors from Berlin and Breslau (Wroclaw) in the Kielcer hospitals who had it good with us, including Prince Joachim, Professor Oppenheimer of Berlin, and Adjunkt Bodenheimer from Cologne. They were all counted among the popular residents, and were mentioned with pride. During the period from Yom Kippur (September 17) until the 17th of Tevet, in particular on the week of the Torah Portion of Lech Lecha (14th of Cheshvan, October 18), they made preparations to flee [16]. (On the same day, an Austrian Gendarme came to me with an urgent request that the Jewish stores must open at this moment. If not, he would shoot. My prayer quorum was at the point prior to the reading of the Torah. They left the Torah scroll on the table, and hurried to insure that their stores would be immediately opened.) The same day, a Jew was arrested for carrying on a conversation with a converted soldier [17]. At 11:00, I was called to the magistrate regarding a loan of 10,000 rubles that was imposed on the Jews by the magistrate. Sitting there, one could see the removal of the flags and the retreat of the German Austria-Hungarian army. After the Sabbath they ignited the train station and all nearby buildings. They city was light as if it was day. On Sunday of the Torah portion of Vayerah, the bridge and the "Herber" railway line were destroyed by dynamite. The other bridges and buildings in the area of the Kielce railway station were in great danger, and were only saved by a miracle.

It is difficult to write about the confusion that took place that day. On Monday of the Torah portion of Vayerah (13th Cheshvan – October 20) at the time that we were sitting in the Beis Midrash arranging the loan for the magistrate, one heard the massive retreat of the Germans, Austrians and "Sokolen" with their equipment and automobiles by way of the Warsawer Street toward the Krakower Road. Thereafter, a fierce battle broke out. The bombardment was heard from the town of Maslow, not far from Kielce. The next day, the Russian army entered Kielce with songs of victory. A service took place in the synagogue to mark the victory. This took place on October 21, on the day that the Kaiser was kicked off of his throne. Kielce and the surrounding area were filled with Russian soldiers.

In truth, at the outset, Kielce and its vicinity were calm. Only later did G-d's punishment fall upon us. The Poles, our lifelong enemies, contrived a variety of false, lowly libels against our Jews. For example, a good portion of our army had confidence in that speech, which brought with it a great deal of victims. Every day, we heard tidings of fresh tribulations that took place in the surrounding towns in general, and in particular from the towns of Suchedniow, Lopuszno, Bodzentyn and others. These were tidings that would tear at the soul... In several places, our brethren were punished with beatings... It came to such a point that the old Stopnitzer rabbi, Rabbi Y. may he live long, was sentenced to the death penalty; however he was saved prior to the execution of the sentence... Every detail is fitting to be written about in a large book – "a history of mankind" so to speak.

On Friday night of the Torah portion of Vayerah (18th Cheshvan, October 25), I was suddenly summoned to the commandant. I went to him, and he angrily asked me why two Jews were found possessing liquor, which they sold to the soldiers. He then announced why I was being arrested. He then clarified the situation, indicating that he does not think that this is worthy of arrest, for they never arrest the innocent; especially somebody such as me, who is an intercessor before the authorities and all of the regional offices are pleased with my honest work – therefore he would treat me with more gentleness. I told him that, through my clerical offices, I would insure that the Jews no longer sell liquor. He was satisfied and let me go home. Indeed on the Sabbath, during the services that took place to mark the victory of our army, I spoke a few earnest words and imposed a "strong ban" on those who sold liquor, and also upon those who know about that business but do not inform. The selling did indeed cease.

On Monday of the Torah portion of Chayey Sarah, at 4:00 p.m. (the 27th) the governor arrived in an automobile along with the official of the gendarme. They arrived completely unexpectedly; therefore I was not able to greet them appropriately.

On Tuesday (21 Cheshvan, October 28) during the middle of the prayers, a great crowd came to me in the synagogue with crying and wailing, for they had heard about the sentencing of Yitzchak Hecherman (who was known as a G-d fearing person, an honest man) to death by hanging. The lamentation filled the synagogue. The children grabbed me around the neck with weeping and wailing, which shattered me... I decided what to do. I ran to the official of the gendarme, who was located in a hotel. I saw him only for a few minutes. He wrote down the names of those who were arrested, whose names he knew. On the same day, at 12:00 p.m. I went to see the governor and his assistant. He was very friendly to me, and he informed me that my request that I had placed on Monday to allow Jewish nurses in the Jewish hospital would be granted. As I was leaving from there, the official of the home-police met me along the way and informed me that there was an order from the commandant that I must come to the jail at 3:20 p.m. My heart began to beat loudly, as I understood that a death penalty was to be carried out there... I do not know with what type of powers I was able to arrive home in peace.

When the set time approached, as I was parting from my family, I said that who knows if I would come home at all. I felt as weak as a small child... I felt that I had no energy to hold up. Along the way, I strengthened. I said to myself that perhaps they had called me for something else. Only when I approached the jail, which was on Cziste Street near the town hall, did I see that they had erected a large gallows there... At that moment, my eyes became dark, and my feet underneath me became crooked so that I could not stand still on the spot... My friend Avraham Wachsberg, who was walking close to me, led me into the consular office along with some superintendent... As I entered, the general arrived in order to carry out the sentence. Shortly, they would carry out the procedures of the death sentence in the consular office by means of hanging: Yaakov Hecherman of Kielce and Shmuel Moshe Astrian. They read out the death verdict to them, and told them that they had the rights to speak to me about anything. The Radomer [18] wrote out a will regarding his estate. Then they confessed... [19] Obviously, I shed a great deal of tears as I explained to them the power of repentance at such a time. The Radomer shouted out that he was innocent of the charges for which he had been convicted. The Kielcer requested that I study at least one chapter of Mishna for his soul. I requested of the general in my name, in the name of the Radomer, and in the name of the entire Jewish committee that he permit them to be brought to a Jewish burial in the Jewish cemetery. He answered that this does not depend on him, and that one must submit a request to the higher authorities. I did so.

(However to my sorrow, three days later, on October 30, I received an answer on an official document, number 721, that my request has been rejected.) Oy Vey! [20] I will never forget those minutes! I mean the reading of the sentence, the writing of the will, the recitation of confession, and over everything, the look in their eyes… together with the shrieking and wailing of the Radomer's wife as they separated her from him, and the carrying out of the hanging outside… After I told them that they should accept their fate, that their deaths will serve as an atonement for all of their sins, and that just before their deaths they should shout out "Shema Yisrael" [21], I fell down like a stone. Then the general convinced me that I do not need to fulfil his command of witnessing the execution – and I remained sitting in the consular office. (The well-known deputy Puriszkewicz, who was at that time present in Kielce, stood outside at the time of the hanging.) I arrived home greatly troubled and weakened. I lay in bed for ten days. For a long time, that which I heard continued to ring in my ears… For very long did the terrible picture stand before my eyes…

On Wednesday, they tried the rest of them: Yitzchak Hecherman and his brother-in-law Eliezer Kahn along with his son Moshe. All of them were freed with G-d's help, except for Moshe, who was sent to Vitebsk for the entire duration of the war.

Shortly thereafter, a few days later, Szaragder was arrested. He was sent to Vitebsk. Later, in the city itself and its surrounding areas, as well as in other regions, mass arrests of Jews took place. It is impossible to ascertain the number of trials, the number sentenced to prison, exile or other penalties… Not one day passed where a tribulation did not take place, one greater than the next; but the army did maintain the calm.

In truth, the Jewish population of Kielce did a great deal for the wounded soldiers. That same week of the Torah portion of Chayey Sarah (October 30), the Jewish committee opened up two "czainies" [22], one on Krakower Street and the second on the Russian Street, near the train station. Even though they were opened primarily for the wounded soldiers, with the permission of the governor they also accepted our own people from the beginning of the war and thereafter. These places did their laundry, and many Jewish daughters served as medics. (For a while, the military authorities commanded that no wounded be kept in the Jewish hospital, but later, the administration permitted the healing of the wounded, and requested a greater number of medics from us.) The Red Cross granted the Jews a grant of 1,000 rubles. At that time, the Jewish citizens committee was approved by the governor "to help soldiers wounded at war". (I worked on this committee with all my might, together with all of its members and my children). The military, which passed through the city by the thousands, behaved in a friendly manner toward the Jews, and the city and its environs were calm. This is the way things were through the end of the month of November. On Sunday of the week of the Torah portion of Miketz, on the first day of Chanuka (November 30), the peace was disturbed by an accusation by the Polish masses, causing great damage to the Jews. The next day, on the second day of Chanuka, I went to the governor. I obtained 500 rubles from him for the benefit of the Jewish war victims. I had a discussion with him regarding various matters, the same matters that I had discussed with the former high governing officials. Thank G-d, on that same day, posters were put up by the commandant indicating that anyone who would harm another's property would be tried in a military court. Thanks to this announcement, calm returned.

My health situation became much weaker, and therefore my dear children from Kharal [23] sent me letters and telegrams requesting that I come to them, take a rest from my sorrowful work, and spend the bitter days with them. I requested a leave from the governor. On Wednesday of the Torah portion of Vayigash (December 10), the governor granted me a leave of two months. Since at that time, one could only travel by ox [24] and such a trip was fraught with danger, the trip was postponed. In the meantime, fresh disturbances came. The situation of our army remained good, but the battles became fiercer. Every day, we could hear the shooting from the police area. The number of those arrested also grew at that time. At the end of December, many hungry and thirsty Jews arrived from the entire vicinity…

On the Sabbath of the Torah portion of Shemot, I was sitting at the Third Sabbath Meal (Shalos Seudos), and many of those refugees were around my table. I glanced at their worried, darkened faces, and a deep sadness overtook my heart, and rivers of tears flowed from my eyes… At that time, I firmly decided: I could not be complacent in that place. I could not leave my embattled brothers in such a terrible situation. The next day, I informed the city representatives that I intend to remain with them until after Passover, with G-d's help. From that day, I undertook hard work on behalf of the community. (The number of refugees later reached 3,000 souls, aside from the local wounded from the war, numbering several hundred families.) The work greatly affected my health, since I worked with all my might. The donations from the Kielcer residents did not cover the great expenditures that we made. I requested support from the Jewish assistance organizations, from philanthropists in the large cities of Russia, and from the central assistance organizations in Switzerland. Our dear brethren, who excelled in their warmth and mercy, sent their support generously. The work of the committee to assist those downtrodden in spirit required even greater energy and courage from my weakened person. I did not have any rest, neither during the day or during the night, as I did all that was possible.

On Tuesday of the Torah portion of Beshalach, I received the first thousand rubles, telegraphed in from the Petrograd central committee to assist the war wounded. I received ongoing general contributions from that prestigious committee. (This does not take into account the donations from the others cities, which I intend to discuss in detail later.) Therefore, may they be blessed by G-d with all good things.

That same week (of the Torah portion of Beshalach, on the 15th of Shvat – Tu Bishvat, January 17th 1915), a bitter event took place upon us, that left its imprint upon me forever. On Friday night, when I took advantage of the sweet Sabbath delight to study my lessons [25], two superintendents came to me – one from prison, and the second – a resident, with a document stating that I should come to the prison at 5:00 a.m.. This was a preparation for the same type of thing that took place on Tuesday, 25th of Cheshvan [26]… Of course, this did not permit me to sleep. Throughout the night, my bed was drenched with tears… I hurried around the entire morning, so that I could arrive at the designated time. However, there must have been a misunderstanding regarding the documents of the commandant, and nobody came to the jail. First, at 6:00 a.m. a "convoy" arrived with a document from the commandant, indicating that the sentencing was to outside of the city, and that the rabbi should accompany him to the place of execution. I had to go by foot (with my secretary Wachsberg) behind the "convoy" for a long distance, farther than Zageiski's factory) [27]. They were already waiting for me, and I was not able to run along with the soldiers… The general who was conducting the sentencing remarked to me that they had held up the carrying out of the sentence on my account for an entire hour… I answered that I had presented myself at the jail at the designated time. I wanted the convicted man to recite the confessional, but the official did not see it as appropriate, for the document stated that I was only to accompany the convicted man to the place where the sentence was to be executed. The general explained to me in a gentle fashion that, in his opinion, they should not stop me, and that I can do as I wish, provided that I go out of there immediately after the confession. The convict was Efraim the son of Yosef Eliazd of Sosnowiec. His wailing during the confession still rings in my ears… (He was the only son of his parents.) Even though I left prior to the deed, and I did not see the execution of the sentence with my own eyes, I heard the volley of gunfire, which left a deep imprint upon my heart. Tired and broken, almost in a faint, I arrived home at 9:00. At 12:00 noon, prior to the Sabbath day meal, as soon as we had finished our prayers, I went together with the communal officials to the vice-governor. He took out his anger toward the people of Israel upon me… His spear-like, sharp words pierced my wounded heart, so that I was not capable of answering him anything at that time, until a later time when a favorable opportunity arose. (This was much later, when I came to the governor for a communal matter. At that time, I gave him a clear and sharp answer, an answer that was fitting to the mood at that time.)

The next day, on Sunday of the Torah portion of Yitro, I saw that announcements in large print had been posted about the death penalty on all of the main streets. This incited a great hatred toward Jews…

This caused various false libels, contrived by our evil neighbors. Oh how did they make such designs, all together!

On Monday of the Torah portion of Teruma (Adar 3, April 3) someone from Lublin Gubernia was shot – Reuven Shlomo the son of Shmuel Licht from the village of Hodel. I could not leave the city on account of my weakness, so I sent my assistant, the judge Rappaport. From the time of those trials and those that followed, the hatred became stronger. Various new libels sprouted up. As is known, many people were arrested, and many were sent to far off places... The good G-d should have mercy and honesty should prevail before the virtuous court.

As I mentioned at the outset, what I have brought down is only one part in a thousand of that which took place to us. This is how it was in reality. It is impossible to describe everything. I want to only describe the shooting that we would hear every day from the surrounding positions. The Germans began to drop many bombs from their airplanes, which fell around the city every day. The bombs fell in the city itself as well as the vicinity. Many were wounded, and some were killed. The fear that this caused is difficult to describe. Who could carry on a conversation while the sun still shone – for one had fear to even walk out on the street. We had only cloudy, grief filled days... as far as I remember. On the Sabbath of the Torah portion of Shmot (December 27), the day was filled with grief. I had gone to request from the governor on behalf of Avraham Wachsberg who had been sent to Tomsk [28]. As I approached the governor's office, the sun came into view, and the Germans began to drop bombs from airplanes. The soldiers began to shoot at the airplanes. I ran into the crowds, who were hurrying to the houses and yards.

I also remember the 1st of January. I went to greet the governor for the New Year. When I was in the yard of the governor's office, an airplane flew very close by. I entered the governor's office, and ... as soon as I was inside, a large bomb exploded near the office. The explosion was so strong that the entire office shook... I thought that the entire building would collapse, G-d forbid, but thank G-d, nothing was damaged. From there I went to the official of the gendarme to greet him as well, and to ask a favor of him on behalf of somebody. Thank G-d I arrived home in peace. I saw no living being on the street, for nobody would go outside unless it was a cloudy day.

During that time, we continued to live. We lived with the shooting of the artillery, which was used to attack the airplanes. Prior to the cannon shots, they would shoot with rifles as a warning to not go out on the streets. We even lived with that! Somebody went out on the street along his way, and got in the way. The good G-d saved us from death and let us have life, but not a peaceful, happy life... The arrests and deportations to far off places increased each day... Who can talk when the highest commander issued an order to appoint "civic zsalasznikes" [29] from the gubernias: Kielce, Radom and Lomza – all of Poland shuddered, seeing that the regime had always sympathized with us; while our bad neighbors with their accusations were guilty of our ill fortune; and who knows what further they will plan against us!

On the Sabbath of the Torah portion of Pekude (February 23), three eminent members of our community of Kielce were arrested: Mr. Henryk Nowak, Alter Maurberger, and M. Fuerster. They brought in all of the "zsalasznikes" from the surrounding towns of the Kielce gubernia, numbering 25 eminent Jewish citizens.

On Tuesday of Rosh Chodesh (the New Moon) Nissan those who were gathered in were sent to Poltava. Thirteen "zsalasznikes" were sent out of Radom, including eminent rabbis (one of them was my relative, Rabbi Twersky from Pakszownica. Later, my friend, the Staszower Rabbi, Rabbi Graubard, the author of "Chavalim Baneimim" was expelled.) The latter were deported to Czernikow. From the news that arrived from there, it seems that the regime lightened their sentence and permitted them to dwell in the local old age home, under the supervision of the community representatives. In Poltava, they were treated as true prisoners. It is difficult to describe in writing what the situation did to our Jews. Along with this, there was a command from the military authorities that all Jews who arrived in the cities after the liberation from the Germans (that is, after December 22) would be sent away a distance of 200 miles [30] from the front lines. Along with that ordinance, in that pre-Passover period, they began to arrest hundreds of Jews along with their families. Later, the situation eased, for they decided to deport only those who came from other gubernias, but not those who came from other cities from within the gubernia.

Later, on account of the many illnesses that took place, an ordinance was issued that the war refugees must leave the areas near the places of battle, and settle in designated places in the Kielcer gubernia. In Kielce itself, where the number of refugees was very large, they permitted refugees to remain. (Who can describe the difficulties that took place in Kielce due to the illnesses that circulated. People dropped dead, mainly among the refugees. I wanted to do a good deed toward the convicts who had not been brought to a Jewish burial. The sanitation committee decided that, for sanitary reasons, the corpses of those who were hanged in the city itself, and left to lie in the city in places where people walk, must be removed. Only the police, who were to carry out the ordinance, decided that the convicts should be buried "very deeply". They decided that even from a sanitation viewpoint, there is no reason to fear.)

As it was – the turmoil deepened. The entire pre-Passover period was filled with agony. I placed a request with the headquarters that they permit the thirteen Torah scrolls that were left behind in Lopuszno to be brought back by Jewish soldiers. (Regarding this, I placed an oral request to the home authorities, asking them to place a request with the high headquarters.) Two days before Passover, I received a refusal from the highest commander. However, the corps commander acceded to my request to be allowed to send Passover matzo to the soldiers on the front. He received me very nicely, and issued the appropriate command. In accordance with the order of the high command, matzos were provided to the Jewish soldiers along with their military rations (indeed, two of them sent to Christians as well). We sent 12 pounds to each soldier [31]. They charged a cargo fee of 3,000 rubles. Thus did G-d help our brethren, who are merciful people, descended from merciful people. The refugees were granted a significant sum of money prior to Passover, on the accounts of the committee. The work of the committee (especially for me, the general chairman and the city rabbi) was beyond human capabilities. Then, difficulties arose for the masses of exiles from many Jewish families, difficulties that are difficult to write about.

On the 13th of Nissan during the day, the day prior to the evening of the search for Chometz [32], as well as the next morning, we heard heavy cannon fire. On the eve of Passover, toward evening, the cannon fire ceased, and Passover was, thank G-d, calm. The holy community was able to observe Passover in a fitting manner.

After the festival, I began to make arrangements for my journey. There were many obstacles. In order to oversee all of the communal matters, two assistant chairmen were appointed: M. Ch. Kaminer and Dr. Lewensohn. They were sent to the governing authorities to be confirmed. I requested a leave of two months from the governor. Prior to that time, the expulsions increased, as did the number of homeless. The expenditures of the committee were exceedingly large. The mind would become confused in trying to keep account. It was as difficult as the splitting of the Red Sea to arrange all of the necessary matters prior to the journey. This was the situation until the Sunday of the Torah portion of Acharei Mot Kedoshim (Iyar 2, April 5).

On Sunday, the 2nd of Iyar (April 5), I received a document from the police chief that was issued by the commandant, asking me to come at 3:00 to the consular office of the city prison, in order to assist two Jews who were sentenced to death by shooting with their confessionals: Fishel Bleicher and Avraham Gincberg. I came at the set time. They confessed with rivers of tears... I then accompanied them (in a horse drawn wagon) for several miles outside the city, where the sentence was to be carried out. (A Pole was shot along with them.) Prior to the shooting, the man with the passport in the name of Avraham the son of Moshe Gincberg from Miechow clarified to me that he was from Tomaszow, and that the correct name was Westman. I recorded this in his certificate.

I arrived home in sorrow and pain, and I continued on with my work. The next day, on Monday, I was brought the certificate of leave for two months signed by the governor, his assistant, and the home committee, from April 7 until June. The preparations for the journey took the entire day. On the next day, on Tuesday, I rendered the accounting of money that came into my hand for the benefit of the Jewish committee of Kielce.

From Petrograd	13,000 rubles
From the Warsaw communal committee	1,000 rubles
From Niezhen, Yekatrinoslav, Poltava, Vilna, Perm, Samara, White Field [33], and Kharal	2,150 rubles
Dr. Safer's contribution	300 rubles
Deputy Kanowolow (aside from 300 portions Of food every day)	500 rubles
The Governing Authority	900 rubles
Monthly contributions and private donations from Kielce itself	1,521.22 rubles
Total	**19,371.22 rubles**
From Warsaw	3,000 rubles
From Petrograd	3,800 rubles
Total	**6,800 rubles**

That same day, I met in Kielce with the city chairman and all of my dear friends. Who can write down on paper all of the wishes and blessings that many of them bestowed upon me! All of them lived with the hope that the situation would improve, that the regime would see the truth regarding all of the false accusations that have been placed upon us. Who knows more than I do about how the Jews are faithful subjects to the regime, and pray for its wellbeing! Even during the time when the Germans and Austro-Hungarians invaded us, and when we were not free, as we were generally, to gather in synagogues – many Jews gathered in my small home synagogue to recite the sections of Psalms that were generally recited for the "peace of the government". There, we recited the special prayer, and prayed in a heartfelt fashion for the well-being of the Czar [34] and his family, and for the wellbeing of the fatherland. We prayed that the Russian army would return from the battlefield crowed with a garland of victory.

Each Sabbath and festival, we prayed for the well-being of the regime, as we are required to by the Torah [35]. On the Sabbath that immediately followed Passover (26 Nissan, 28 May [36]) a crowd of approximately 10,000 Jews gathered in the Kroiser Synagogue of Kielce to hear the reading of the words of thanks from our Czar to the Jewish community of Kielce, delivered to me by the general governor of Warsaw. Everyone stood and listened with respect as I read the thanks from the highest authority, which the Czar sent as an answer to the telegram that we sent via to the Czar's offices via the governor on the day that the opening of the home for homeless children, at which time we held a service for the wellbeing of the family of the Czar.

Following the reading of the thank you, we recited a prayer to the Master of the World, requesting health and happiness for his majesty the Czar and his high family, for the well-being of the entire land, and for the Russian army, that it should return from the battlefield coronated with a great victory.

We all left the synagogue with shouts of hurray, and with the hope that we would see the end of all of the libels that have been placed upon us by our enemies. We hoped that they would see the truth, that we are faithful servants of the regime, and we wish them every success, though which we hope that our own situation would be secured – Amen, may it be G-d's will – as all Jews ask of G-d.

On the same day that I took leave of Kielce, on the Tuesday of the Torah portion of Acharei Mot Kedoshim (6 Iyar, 7 April) the news reached me that in Poltava the regime eased the arrest of the citizens of the Kielcer Gubernia (and some of the Radomers) who were sent there as "zsalaszniks". The lightening of the arrests meant that they were freed from prison and were permitted within a week to find private houses – this is also for the good!

I left Kielce at 5:00 p.m. I arrived in Lublin on Wednesday at 9:00 a.m. I visited there with my in-law [37] until 10:00 p.m. From there I traveled to Kiev. I left Kiev on Thursday at midnight, and on Friday (9 Iyar) at 11:00 a.m. I arrived in Kharal. I cannot describe my great joy upon seeing my children and their family, may they live, as well as my in-law the rabbi and Gaon, may he live long, and all of those who are near to me, as well all made the "shehechayanu" [38] blessing with tears of joy. On the first Sabbath, we observed the yahrzeit (anniversary of death) of the Tolner Rebbe, may his merit protect us [39].

Even as I was dwelling in peace in Kharal with my beloved son David Yonah, with protection to insure that nobody should trouble me, the work and tribulations that I had gone through on a daily basis broke my body, and all of my limbs were weakened. The good G-d should send me a complete recovery, so that I will recover my health and be able to draw more strength to be able to study and pray with honor and well being, for many years to come. As well, I pray and hope for G-d's assistance, so that there will be good news in all areas that affect the situation of the Jewish people, both in a spiritual and physical respect. Amen, and may it be G-d's will.

TRANSLATOR'S FOOTNOTES:

1. These dates in the secular calendar are from Friday July 31, 1914 to Tuesday April 20, 1915 (according to the Gregorian calendar – a later footnote indicates that any secular dates provided in this article use the old Julian calendar, whose dates are 13 days earlier than the Julian calendar). The Hebrew month of Av is often termed 'Menachem Av' – the comforting Av, on account of the traditional day of Jewish calamity, Tisha Beov, which occurs in that month – expressing the hope that the month will turn to a time of comfort. Incidentally, the day of the outbreak of World War I, Saturday August 1, 1914, was Tisha Beov (although the observance of the fast day is postponed one day when it falls on the Sabbath). Jewish weeks are often referred to by the Torah portion of the upcoming Sabbath. Acharei Mot-Kedoshim is a Sabbath upon which two Torah portions are read. The Torah portion preceding Tisha Beov is always Devarim, and the Torah portion following Tisha Beov is always Vaetchanan.
2. This entire document follows a cycle of Torah portions to designate weeks. For those interested in following along chronologically, the Torah portion sequence is as follows: Devarim (prior to Tisha Beov), Vaetchanan, Ekev, Reeh, Shoftim, Ki Tetzeh, Ki Tavoh, Nitzavim (sometimes combined with Vayelech – and always preceding Rosh Hashanah), Vayelech, Haazinu (always preceding Sukkot), Vezot Habracha (the last portion of the Torah, always read on Simchat Torah), Breishit, Noach, Lech Lecha, Vayera, Chayey Sarah, Toldot, Vayetze, Vayishlach, Vayeshev, Miketz (at Chanuka time), Vayigash, Vayechi, Shmot, Vaera, Bo, Beshalach, Yitro, Mishpatim, Teruma, Tetzaveh, Ki Tissa, Vayakhel (often combined with the following portion) Pekudey, Vaykra, Tzav (always before Passover,

except during a Jewish leap year, when Passover is a few weeks later), Shmini, Tazria, Metzora (sometimes combined with Tazria), Acharai Mot, Kedoshim (sometimes combined with Acharei Mot), Emor, Bahar, Bechukotai (sometimes combined with Bahar). I have omitted the following portions of the book of Numbers, as they do not appear in this narrative.

3. Seemingly an expression indicating that they could not have even imagined what this was going to lead to.
4. Jewish court of law – here meaning members of an informal Jewish court who were seemingly on a delegation to a different location.
5. At times of war, a conditional bill of divorce is often drawn up for soldiers, which would take effect retroactively if he does not return from battle after a set period of time. This allows the wife to remarry in cases where the husband is presumed, but not proven, to have died.
6. A footnote in the text here indicates that this date, and all further dates in this diary use the old Russian calendar (The Julian Calendar).
7. There is some error in the dates here, as Ki Tavoh is always two Torah portions prior to Rosh Hashanah, and therefore must fall in the latter half of Elul. The Torah portion here would have been Shoftim.
8. The Sabbath between Rosh Hashanah and Yom Kippur is known as Shabbat Shuva (The Sabbath or Return), or less commonly but the term used here, Shabbat Teshuva (The Sabbath of Repentance).
9. A mikva is a ritual bath, used by women once a month at the conclusion of the menstrual cycle. It is also used by men on various occasions, depending on custom, but it is a universal custom among observant men to immerse in the mikva on the eve of Yom Kippur.
10. The Avoda is the central part of the Yom Kippur Mussaf service, which recalls the details of the Temple service on Yom Kippur. The counting of "Achat"… (Literally One, One and One, One and Two, …) is recited communally, and commemorates the counting that was done by the High Priest as he performed the ritual sprinkling of blood in the Holy of Holies.
11. Neila is the concluding prayer service of Yom Kippur.
12. The date is obviously wrong here. This would be the 11th of Tishrei, the day after Yom Kippur.
13. Personal safety is the assumed meaning here.
14. There are 4 days between Yom Kippur and Sukkot. Often, one of these days is a Sabbath. In the current case, Sukkot would start on Sunday night.
15. A barber-surgeon, considered an important professional at that time.
16. Autopsies are prohibited by Jewish Law, except in cases of great need.
17. The durations mentioned in this sentence were unclear. I added in the word 'particular' to clarify somewhat.
18. The meaning of the word 'converted' 'farvanderenten' is unclear here. It does not seem to have any religious connotations.
19. Evidently, Astrian was from Radom.
20. Referring here to the Jewish deathbed confessional rather than to a legal procedure.
21. A Yiddish expression of woe.
22. "Hear Oh Israel, the L-rd our G-d, the L-rd is one", the main Jewish doxology, recited thrice daily, and also, if possible, to be recited prior to death.
23. I am not sure what this means, but from the context it is apparently some type of infirmary.
24. I am not sure of the identity of this town. It is spelled as 'Kharal' in the Yiddish, but there is no town in Poland or Ukraine by exactly that name. Could be Khorol, Ukraine, in Poltava gubernia.
25. I am not sure of the meaning of this – perhaps an ox drawn carriage was the only means of transportation at that time.
26. Referring to the study of Torah.
27. Above, it is Tuesday, 21st of Cheshvan.
28. Given that this was the Sabbath, he would not have accepted a ride in an automobile or wagon.
29. A city in Siberia.
30. I am not sure what this means – perhaps civic defense committees.
31. The word used here is 'verst', which is a unit of distance.
32. Something seems incorrect here, as this is a large amount of matzo. Perhaps it refers to the entire food ration per soldier for the entire Passover festival.
33. Passover begins on the night of the 15th of Nissan. The evening before, on the night of the 14th of Nissan, the search for chometz (leaven) is conducted in the house. Remnants of bread and leavened products are burnt the next morning.

34. The term here is in Hebrew, perhaps a Hebrew term for a Russian city.
35. The Yiddish word here is equivalent with "Kaiser", but from the context, it refers to Czar and not Kaiser. Both words come from the same Germanic root (originating from the Latin Caesar), and would often be rendered equivalently in Yiddish (unless the Yiddish is simply transliterating the word).
36. In the book of Jeremiah, the Jewish exiles in Babylon ask the prophet how one should act under the conditions of exile. Among other things, Jeremiah advises them to pray for the well-being of the country in which they find themselves. This is the source of the tradition to pray for the well-being of one's country.
37. The date of May 28 cannot be correct here. I believe it is the 28th of March from the context. (Note, according to the Gregorian calendar, Passover cannot conclude by March 28th, but it can according to the Julian calendar.)
38. The word "mechutan" means the parent's of one's child's spouse.
39. A blessing, thanking G-d for keeping us alive, which is made upon hearing of good tidings, as well as at certain set festive times of the year (such as upon lighting the Chanuka candles, hearing the Megilla, hearing the Shofar, and at the beginning of each festival).
40. The Tolner Hassidic dynasty is still present today. The family name is Twersky (a name which is mentioned previously in this section as well).

[Page-297]

Kielcer Organizations in Israel and the Diaspora

Translated by Judy Montel

Organization of Immigrants from Kielce in Israel

There are roughly 600 families from Kielce in Israel and most are members of the Organization of Immigrants from Kielce.

This organization was founded before World War II by the early immigrants from Kielce with the goal of aiding and supporting immigrants from Kielce when they first arrived in the country.

After the war, and especially after the Kielce Pogrom in 1946, when the stream of immigrants to Israel grew stronger, the activities of the organization broadened and grew more numerous both in the area of social help that was given to immigrants to help in their initial settling in period in the country, as well as in other areas of housing, employment placement, constructive loans for obtaining manufacturing workshops, work tools, materials, employment opportunities, an apartment, etc. The organization was continually headed by the active members, Mosze Rotenberg, Z"L, Szmuel Kligman, Z"L, Aharon Grandapel Z"L and, may they live long lives, Zalman Kalichsztajn, Zew Kluska, Elazar Arten, Baruch Ajzenberg, Icak Pieskogorski, Mosze Kaminer, Dawid Lewartowski, Szlomo Binoszewicz, Bernard Staszewski, Dr. Icak Kajzer and others.

Among the important activities that the organization succeeded in carrying out were: the writing of a Sefer Torah dedicated to the martyrs of Kielce who perished during the Shoah and the Pogrom in 1946, the founding of a charitable loan association that until now has given out loans to over 130 families from Kielce amounting to 250 Israeli lira apiece, and the publication of this book, which will constitute a monument and memorial for the Kielce community which was destroyed by the Nazi minions may their names be erased, and to the holy Jews of Kielce who perished in this Holocaust.

In addition to this, the organization arranges a memorial mourning service every year on the 9th of Elul, the anniversary of the destruction of the Jews of Kielce, to commemorate the martyrs. Most of the Kielcers who are in Israel participate in this service; many hundreds take this day to commune with the souls of their parents and siblings who perished in the Shoah.

The current members of the organization's committee are: Elazar Arten, Chair, Zalman Kalichsztajn and Zew Kluska, Assistant Chairs, Baruch Ajzenberg, Treasurer, Dawid Lewartowski, Secretary, Sara Lewkowicz, Chana Lifszicz, Ben-Cion Albirt, Szymon Bornsztajn, Chaim Posloszni and Cwi Rozenberg.

The members of the editorial board of the "Kielce" book are: Awraham Goldrat, Elazar Arten, Awraham Kirszenbaum and Zalman Kalichsztajn.

[Page-298]

הנשיאות והועד של ארגון עולי קילץ בישראל

The Leadership and committee of the Organization
of Immigrants from Kielce in Israel
Sitting (left to right): Baruch Ajzenberg, Treasurer, Zalman Kalichsztajn, Assistant Chair, Elazar Arten, Chair,
Pinchas Cytron (author of the book), Zew Kluska, Assistant Chair, Dawid Lewartowski, Secretary.
Standing: Ben-Cion Albirt, Cwi Rozenberg, Chana Lifszicz, Chaim Posloszni, Sara Lewkowicz, Awraham Kirszenbaum, Szymon Bornsztajn

[Page-299]

The celebration of the completion of the writing
of the Sefer Torah by the Organization of Immigrants from Kielce in Israel
in memory of the martyrs who perished in the Shoah

[Page-300]

New York Delegates 2nd Conference of the Kielcer Landsleit for Resettlement of Kielcer Jews – Dec. 27-28 1947 Chicago, Ill

[Page-301]

Organization of Kielcers in New York
(Kielcer Society in New York)

The Kielcer Society in New York has been in existence for over 50 years. In 1954 it celebrated it's 50 year Jubilee:

Heading the Society are Messrs.: I. Pienkowicz, Z. Sztajnhauer, M. Machtynger, W. Adler, S. Majerson, J. Minc, H. Dam, H. Moskowicz, Rabbi Mejer Blumenfeld, M. Zylbersztajn, R. Romberg, A. Rozencwajg, S. Wigan, M. Dziadek, R. Szugierman, P. Adler, J. Altman, Dr. A. Mantel, Dr. Rajzman and the honorary president, founder of the Society 50 years ago, H. S. Markowicz. Aside from these names the following participate in the Society's activities: Messrs. M. Heller, M. Cytryn, H. Goldlust, S. Hejd, M. Fajgen, A. Cytryn, D. Herszkowicz, S. Hendler, S. Ezryng, S. Cwajgenbaum, J. Slimowicz, D. Moskowicz, F. Bimko, Professor A. Lewi and others.

The Society also has an aid committee of ladies from Kielce headed by: P. Rotkowski, R. Sejnes, H. Rozencwajg, D. Moskowicz, G. Goldsztajn, H. Cytryn, J. Dam, S. Pienkowicz, E. Machtynger, M. Heller, M. Majerson, R. Dziadek, S. Szugierman, L. Kirszenbaum and Goldlust.

The Society was very active after the world war in granting aid to refugees and survivors from Kielce in the displaced persons camps in Germany, Sweden and other places and also aided Kielcers who immigrated to Israel with significant sums.

Rabbi Mejer Blumenfeld,
the rabbi of Newark, New Jersey
grandson of Rabbi Izrael Sofer from Kielce

[Page-302]

The Committee of the Society of Kielcers in Los Angeles

Key to photo on Page 302: Sitting from right to left: Mosze Jakob Gold, Assistant Chair, Anna Blak, Assistant Chair, Jona Szapiro, Chair, Philip Golombek, Assistant Chair. Second Row: Sane Cooper (Kupczik), the oldest Kielcer in the world (aged 94), Mrs. Gold, Mryam Braza, Toli Szapiro, Mrs. Golombek, Harry Jura, Treasurer. Third Row: Lea Ross (Rozenszafir), Awraham Ross (Rozenszafir), Lea Jura Fourth Row: Mrs. Garfinkel from Edmonton, Mrs. Manela, Zalman Manela, Financial Secretary, Fanny Agranow, Max (Motke) Agranow (Agranowicz), General Manager.

[Page-303]

Organization of Kielcers in Los Angeles
(Kielcer Society in Los Angeles)

This organization is the most active in the United States. Thanks to its massive support the charitable fund for immigrants from Kielce in Israel was established, which thrives and develops thanks to the continual help of this Society. The enlivening spirit of the Society is Mr. Max Agranow, a dear Jew, faithful public activist, devoted heart and soul to the needs and works of the public.

At the head of this active Society are the following: J. Szapiro, Chair, M. J. Gold, Assistant Chair, Anna Blak, Assistant Chair, Philip Golombek, Assistant Chair, H. Jura, Treasurer, Lea Ross (Rozenszafir), Secretary, L. Wiggins, A. Rozenszafir, Zalman Manela, Financial Secretary, Max Agranow, General and Financial Manager and Sane Cooper (Kupczik).

Among the Kielcers in other cities in the United States, the following are outstanding in their public activity: Mr. Wiliam Agranow in Miami, Izrael Garfin in Edmonton and Mrs. Beker in Chicago.

[Page-304]

Jona Szapira
president of the Kielcers
in Los Angeles

Max Agranow (Motke Agranowicz)
the founder and driving spirit in the Society
of Kielcers in Los Angeles

[Page 305]

Organization of Kielcers in Toronto (Canada)
(Kielcer Society in Toronto)

The Kielce organization in Toronto is very active in extending aid to needy Kielcers around the world and especially in Israel. Its continual aid to the charitable fund of the Kielcers in Israel contributed immensely to the development and thriving of this fund. Among those who stand at the head of the organization and who are especially devoted to this work are the members Akiwa Ladowski and Aharon Ladowski, who faithfully work for the public good and especially the Kielcer public in Israel.

The members of the Society leadership are: Cz. Garden, C. Abela, C. Szprechman, N. Jasne, A. Czenrendorf, Aharon Ladowski, Akiwa Ladowski and others.

עקיבא לאדאווסקי

Akiwa Ladowski
member of the leadership of the Kielcer Society in Toronto

[Page-306]

Organization of Kielcers in Argentina

This organization was founded in its day by Mr. Lichtensztajn, Z"L, and provides services and aid for Kielcers in Buenos Aires and participates in the cultural work of the organizations of Polish Jews in Argentina, which has a broad range of activity. For a variety of reasons, mainly difficulty in transferring funds and a low exchange rate, this organization has not participated in aid to Jews of Kielce around the world except in Argentina, and also did not participate in financial aid to Kielcers in Israel.

Organization of Kielcers in Paris (France)

There is an organization of people from Kielce in Paris as well, which is active among the Kielcers there mainly in extending legal aid vis a vis the authorities in getting work permits and trade licenses and obtaining French citizenship.

Besides this, the organization is active in obtaining reparations from Germany for those who were tortured in the Nazi concentration camps during the war.

Among the founders and leaders of the organization are: Mosze Zajfman, Z"L, Jehuda Zajde, Dr. Wajnberger, Majer Zajde, Jonatan Grinszpan and others.

[Page-307]

Appendix
For technical reasons this description was not printed in the chapter that dealt with the political parties in Kielce.

A History of the Poalei Zion Movement (left) in Kielce

by Chaim Posloszni and Szaul Goldman

The history of the Poalei Zion Movement in Kielce actually begins back in 1904/5. Kielce was one of the first cities in Poland in which groups of "Poalei Zion" started.

As an active party, the movement arose in Kielce only at the end of the Austrian occupation during world War I and with the establishment of the state of Poland.

1918 was the inaugural year of the labor movement in Poland, which at the time emerged from underground to a public life.

Poalei Zion was then the only labor party on the Jewish streets of Kielce. At its head then stood Lazar Szulman, Zalewski, Rochale Machtynger, Berl Praposzinski, Izrael Apel and Izrael Wajnsztok (they all perished in the Nazi Shoah) and youth activists Mosze Kornfeld and Jehuda Zajde. To aid them, the center in Warsaw sent them Baruch Szapiro and Eliasz, the organizers.

All of the Jewish professional associations in the city were led by the party. In order to help the unemployed, the party opened a cooperative kitchen and a childcare crèche at which the poor of the population received food for a small sum.

In 1919 the first democratic municipal elections were held. The party participated in these elections and in spite of the persecutions and pressure by the government institutions, its representative Awraham Wajncwajg was elected as a member of the municipality.

At the first meeting of the municipality, when Wajncwajg read his party's platform (in Yiddish), the Endeks assaulted him with cries of scorn and threats, and from then on looked for opportunities to take their revenge upon him. They found such an opportunity with the outbreak of the Polish-Bolshevik war. Even beforehand, the party suffered from government persecution for its enthusiasm for the Russian October Revolution.

Using the excuse that the party building was used to hold anti-Polish meetings, the police attacked the building and arrested its members Wajncwajg and Szulman. A trial was staged against Wajncwajg and he was sentenced to a year in prison.

The police persecutions against the leaders forced these people to leave the city, and a few of them even emigrated. The party's activity was severely weakened.

[Page-308]

The central committee sent member Awraham Wengrad to revive activities, but he became ill and died in the Kielce hospital (and several thousand people from all ranks participated in his funeral).

Only in 1926 did the party recover and renew its activities. In this year there were new municipal elections. The party established an active election committee and from that point on the party's work was renewed and spread to numerous areas. The party also conquered most of the professional associations in the city, which had been under the influence of the "Reds" (the communists), like the Needle Workers, the Woodworkers, the Leather Workers and others.

The most active members in these associations were Mosze Kornfeld and Menachem Zylbersztajn, who was an exceptional speaker of enormous talent. As the secretary of the Leather Workers' Association Menachem Zylbersztajn devoted much of his energies to popularize the ideals of proletarian Zionism among the workers and to battle the demagoguery of the "Reds". In his appearances he succeeded in persuading many of the youth divisions of this association, among them Chaim Posloszni (who is in Israel) and Mordechai Wajsbrot, Mosze Josef Szenker and Jechiel Zylbersztajn (who perished in the Shoah).

This group, which he converted to the party, was the founding group of the youth association of Poalei Zion called "Jugend" as well as the Union of Working Children "Jung-bor".

In 1928 the party organized the sport club "Gwiazda Stern"; the club was headed by Mosze Kornfeld, Zelig Garfinkel (perished in the Shoah) Hersz Strawczinski (now in Israel) and Jehuda Zajde (in Paris). They had divisions for football, boxing, ping-pong and light athletics. The club also served as a place for social and cultural activities.

The most active members of the club were Jerachmiel Rabinowicz, Izrael Winogrodzki, Izrael Pinkusowicz, Lajb-Ber Rzyto, Icak Dziwicki, Jakob Gotowizna (all perished in the Shoah) and Dawid Choderland, Lajbel Kuperberg, and Icza Chornzawski (who are in Israel), Awraham Rembiszewski and Icza Oszerowicz (in America).

The party also established a society for evening classes for laborers, at which they learned languages, History (General and Jewish) and other subjects and at which there were also cultural and literary lectures.

The party was affiliated with a dramatic circle called "Yiddishe Arbeiter Bine", which became well known in the area.

Among the party youth "Jugend" especially outstanding were Szaul Goldman (in Israel), Mosze Kirszencwajg, Perl Strawczinska and Lajbel Kochen (perished in the Shoah).

Between 1934-1936, when the "Senacia" authorities became more and more Hitlerian and the persecutions against the Jewish population of Poland grew worse, especially against the Jewish labor movements, the evening class society was closed to laborers and its property was confiscated.

[Page-309]

After the general strike of the Jewish professional association on March 17, 1936, which was declared throughout Poland by the "Land-Rat" (The National Council) of the professional associations, as a protest against the anti-Semitic riots, Hersz Strawczinski, the party secretary, was arrested and tried.

On May 1st, 1936, a giant demonstration was held jointly by the Poalei Zion C.S. and P.P.S., which made a tremendous impression upon the entire population of the city. As a result of this, the Endeks and their newsletter "Orndovnik" began a venomous anti-Semitic campaign against the Jews that caused frequent assaults on the streets upon the Jewish population in Kielce. At the initiative of Poalei Zion (Left), Jewish patrols were set up in the streets of the city. The groups of the meat workers excelled at these patrols especially, as well as those of the sports clubs "Stern" and "HaPoel".

"The Association of Friends of the Laborers of the Land of Israel" had a special place in party activities. Besides its propaganda value it was very effective at gathering contributions for laborers in the Land of Israel.

A turning point in the development of the party was the decision, taken by the convention of 1938, to participate in all the activities of the Zionist movement, Congress, funds, etc. A new realm of action opened to the members of the party, who participated with enthusiasm in all the tasks of gathering contributions for the funds, distributing "shekels" and especially activities for the League of Laborers of the Land of Israel, while simultaneously, not neglecting the daily tasks of the political and economic struggle to improve the lot of the workers and the professional associations.

This change had no small influence on creating closer ties with Poalei Zion (C.S.) and "HaShomer Hatza'ir". This was after the dispersal of the cmmunist party in Poland by the Comintern. The "Bund" was also trying to establish itself in Kielce at the time using the Communists. This situation caused stronger connections between the Zionist-Socialist movements and to joint public appearances.

A fine example of such joint activities were the performances on the first of May of the last few years before the war and especially the great demonstration in 1938, in which the performance of Kibbutz Borochov (under the influence of Poalei Zion – C.S.) was especially notable.

One of the best chapters of the struggle of the Jewish laborers in Kielce were the municipal elections in 1938.

In order to minimize the representation of the laborers and progressives in the municipalities, the authorities passed a new law of personal-district elections. The government divided the city into electoral districts in such a way that the laborers would not be able to elect their representatives. Under the agreement of the party with Poalei Zion (C.S.) and other non-party members, a joint list of candidates was presented at the elections. As a result, the Endek authorities lost in a landslide. In all the districts representatives of the P.P.S. (the Polish Socialist Party) were elected with the help of the Jews and the party's candidate Mosze Solrz was elected by a large majority.

This victory was the swan song of the party and of the entire Jewish population in Kielce.

1939 arrived and together with it a world war and great Shoah, which wiped out the Jews in the state of Poland, among them the Jews of Kielce in all their political parties and public life.

[Page-310]

List of Activists in the Professional Movements in Kielce During the last years before the Nazi Shoah

Leather Workers Association:

Poalei Zion (Left) – Jechiel Zylbersztajn, Szaul Goldman, Mosze Kirszencwajg and Chaim Posloszni.
Poalei Zion (C.S.) – Wolf Kalichsztajn, Lisman, Goldlust.
Bund – Berisz Wajnsztok.
Communist Practice ("Reds") – Mosze Zlotnik, Dawid Kirszencwajg, Jona Rozmajti.
Poalei Agudat Yisrael – Dawid Golinski.

Needle Workers Association:

Poalei Zion (Left) – Pinchas Kirszencwajg, Mejer Dawid Grynberg.
The Communist Practice – Flomenbaum, Jehoszua Szternfeld, Mosze Josef Laks.

Meat Workers Association:

Herszkowicz, Jeszaja Cuker, Mosze Godel Bukszpan, Dawid Oszerowicz.

Bakers Association:

Henich Pinkusowicz.

Clerks Association:

Kuba Chwat.

Szymon Strawczinski functioned as the organizer of the Food Association (representing Poalei Zion C.S.)

[Page-311]

Memorial to Natives of Kielce Who Fell Defending the Land and the State

Jerachmiel Solnik, member of the Hagana,
Fell at Ramat HaKovesh in 1937.

Jakob Berger, commander of the Hagana in Jerusalem
Fell on the day Hanita was established in 1938.

Szaul Korman, born in 1912, moved to the land of Israel in 1938,
Fell defending Jerusalem in February 1948.

Szmuel Strawczinski, member of the Palmach,
Fell in battle with the Ka'ukji Gangs defending Mishmar HaEmek in April 1948.

Izrael Korngold
Fell defending Ramat HaShofet.

Mordechai Goldrat, son of Mejer, born in 1907, moved to the land of Israel in 1929,
Fell defending the Quarry of Migdal-Tzedek during the War of Independence in 1948.

Natan Hocherman, born in 1935, officer in the IDF,
Fell in the battle at Kalkilya in 5717 (1956).

Izrael-Izak Machtinger, son of Mordechai, born in 1918,
Fell in the Sinai Campaign in the battle for Gaza on the 1st of Kislev, 5717

(November-December 1956).

[Page-312]

Four generations of the Jews of Kielce:
Izrael Kochen, his son Chaim Kochen, the son-in-law
of Chaim Kochen – Pinchas Cytron (author of the book) and his son, Arye Cytron

[Page 313-327]

Index of Names

Arranged by El. Arten

Please note: The pages numbers in this table refer to the page numbers in the original book.

Family name	First name	Page Number
ABELA	C.	305
ABELE	Rabbi Awraham	154
ABELE	Rabbi Awraham HaKohen (Rapaport)	94, 165, 166, 197, 242
ABRAMOWICH	Cwi Jehuda	163
ABRAMOWICZ	Abisz	35
ABRAMOWICZ	Hirsz Lejb	35
ABRAMOWICZ	Izrael Icza	35
ABRAMOWICZ	Simcha	153
ADLER	Chaim Szloma Kohen	163
ADLER	Mosze Kohen	163
ADLER	P.	301
ADLER	W.	301
AGRANOW (AGRANOWICZ)	Fanny	303
AGRANOW (AGRANOWICZ)	Max (Motke)	303, 304
AGRANOW (AGRANOWICZ)	William	303
AHARONOWICZ	Luba	128
AJLBIRT	Izrael Mosze	255
AJLBIRT	Mosze	32, 228
AJLENBERG	A.	138
AJLENBERG	Jehoszua Heszel	187
AJLENBERG	Simcha Bunem	187

AJZENBERG		23, 35, 246
AJZENBERG	Awraham Ber	23, 94, 95, 110, 163
AJZENBERG	Baruch	137, 297, 298, 299
AJZENBERG	Chaim Judel	32, 152, 163
AJZENBERG	Elija Naftali	28, 29, 91, 148, 164, 198
AJZENBERG	Hirszel	25
AJZENBERG	Josel (Kaczka)	27, 28, 30, 196
AJZENBERG	Lulek	245
AJZENBERG	Magister**(Master)	249
AJZENBERG	Manja	123
AJZENBERG	Mejer	30, 97, 136, 148, 163, 196, 209
AJZENBERG	Mendel	30, 162, 211
AJZENBERG	Mosze Dawid (Elija Naftali's)	23. 27, 91, 97, 134, 135, 136, 148, 163, 197, 209
AJZENBERG	Naftali	164
AJZENBERG	Pinchas	254
AJZENBERG	Sara Frajda	28
AJZENBERG	Sz.	163
AJZENBERG	Szlomo	163
AJZENBERG	Szmelke	25
ALBERT		254
ALBERT	Alter	138
ALBERT	Cwi Arje	163
ALBIRT	Ben-Cion	297, 298
ALBIRT	Icak	130
ALBIRT	Mosze	163
ALEKS	Leah	245
ALMER	Mosze Josef	163

ALPERT	Izrael Szmul	163
ALPERT	Jechiel	128, 253-257
ALPERT	Jehuda Lajb	163
ALTER	Mina	130
ALTMAN	J.	301
AMI'EL	Rabbi	110, 111, 166
ANDERS	General	247
ANSZER		44, 63
ANSZER	(lawyer)	45
APEL	Izrael	307
ARTEN	Elazar	8, 69, 86, 137, 150, 151, 153, 297, 298
ARTEN	Fajga	68, 98, 99, 130
ARTWINSKI		191
ASZKENAZI	Rabbi Majer	154
AUERBACH	Baruch	164
AUERBACH	J.	43
BAJRZECINER	Mejer'l	89
BALICKI	Icak Icza	163
BALICKI	Szmul (Szmuel) Aba	163, 198
BALMONT		63
BARUCH	Dr.	85
BEJN		256
BEKER	Berisz	164
BEKER	Mrs.	303
BEKERMAN	Awraham	163
BEKERMAN	Awraham Chaim	163
BELFER (CHROBERSKI) DAWID		89
BELS		132

BEN-GURION	David	124
BEN-TZVI	Itzchak	124
BERGER	Jakob	311
BERKOWICZ	Manos	245
BERKOWICZ	Rywka	15
BERLINSKI	Szlomo	215, 216
BERMAN	Adolf	248, 256, 259
BESER	Icak Mejer	163
BESER	Szlomo	163
BESERGLIK	Icak Mejer	163
BESTER	Awraham Josef	163
BESTER	Mosze Jechiel	163
BIALOBRODA		38, 240
BIDERMAN	Zisza	164
BIMKA	Doberisz	164
BIMKA	Echezkel	29, 163
BIMKA	Motel	163
BIMKO	Fiszel	214, 215, 301
BINENTAL	Szlomo Icak	180
BINOSZEWICZ	Szlomo	297
BIRENBAUM	Natan	131
BIRENCWAJG		121
BISKOPSKA	Antonina	260
BISTRICINI		131
BLACHAROWICZ	Frajda	14
BLACHAROWICZ	Lajbusz	163
BLACHARZ	Josef (Cyna)	36
BLACHATOWSKI	Fejwel	45
BLACHOT	Wladislaw	258
BLAK	Anna	303

BLASZCZAK	Henryk	258, 261
BLEJCHER	Fiszel	291
BLICKI AND SONS		35
BLICKI	Icak Icza	163
BLICKI	Jakob	28
BLICKI	M.B.	28
BLICKI	Szmul Abesz	28, 163, 198
BLUMENFELD	Berza (Isachar Berisz)	150, 204
BLUMENFELD	Izrael Sofer	186
BLUMENFELD	Mejer	301
BLUMENFELD	Rabbi Josef Baruch	186
BLUMENFELD	Szlomo	186
BLUMENFELD	Szmul	186
BODENHEIMER		279
BORKOWSKI		35
BORKOWSKI	Jochewed	126
BORKOWSKI	Szmuel	126
BORNSZTAJN	Chana	245
BORNSZTAJN	Dow Berisz	30, 163
BORNSZTAJN	Lula	123
BORNSZTAJN	Menachem Mendel	164, 245
BORNSZTAJN	Mendel (Paczanower)	89
BORNSZTAJN	Mordechai	163
BORNSZTAJN	Motel	89
BORNSZTAJN	Szymon	297, 298, 299
BOROCHOW	Dow	124
BORSZTAJN	Aharon	126
BORUCHOWICZ	Izrael Icak	165
BOSTERLENKA	Chaim Tykociner	163
BRAK	Szlomo Zalman	163

BRAUN	Dr. Noach	85, 86
BRAZA	Mirjam	303
BRONROT	Rabbi	114
BROT	Rabbi Sz.	113
BRUNER		25
BUCHBINDER	Dawid	267
BUGAJER		23
BUGAJER	Fred	245
BUKOWSKI		32, 201
BUKSZPAN	Mosze Godel	310
BURSZTIN	Aharon	126
CANIN	M.	264
CEL-CION	Dr.	41
CELCER	Szymon	239
CETEL	Mejer	230-232
CHARENDORF	Aba	89
CHARENDORF	Mordechai	164
CHARSON	Miatek	245
CHAZAN		85
CHELMNER		22
CHELMNER	Jose'le	186, 187
CHELMNER	Mosze'le	187
CHERNIAKOW	Engineer	208
CHMELOSZ	Eli Mejer	164
CHMIELARZ		30
CHMIELEWSKI		267
CHMIELNICKI	Izrael	245
CHMIELNICKI	Josef Szymon	100
CHMIELNICKI	Rozia	245
CHMIELNICKI	Sz. Z.	92

CHODERLAND	Dawid	308
CHORNZAWSKI	Icza	308
CHROBERSKI	Dawid (Belfer)	89
CHROBERSKI	Jechiel Dawid	164
CHWAT		79, 80, 160
CHWAT	Kuba	310
COOPER (KUPCZIK)	Sane	301, 302
CUKER	Jeszaja	310
CUKERMAN	Antek	255
CUKERMAN	Elazar	163
CUKERMAN	Jakob	163, 164
CUKERMAN	Pesach	35
CWAJGEL	Family	32, 37
CWAJGEL	Izrael	15, 37
CWAJGEL	Jehoszua Heszel	163
CWAJGEL	Nachum	15
CWAJGENBAUM	S.	301
CYMERMAN	Szlomo	163
CYNA	Chaim Jeszaja	36
CYNA	Josef (Blacharz)	36
CYNA	Lemel	36
CYPROS	Bronek	245
CYTRON	A.	299
CYTRON	Aharon HaLevi	187
CYTRON	Arje	312
CYTRON	Pinchas	3, 8, 83, 88, 114, 128, 142, 159, 297, 298, 312
CYTRYN		24
CYTRYN	A.	301
CYTRYN	H.	301

CYTRYN	Izrael Mejer	163
CYTRYN	M.	301
CYTRYN	Mejer	26
CZERENDORF	A.	305
CZERNIAKOW		208
DAJBUCH	Fajvel	122
DAJBUCH	Jakob	60, 71
DAJTELCWAJG	Alter	163
DAM	H.	301
DAM	J.	301
DAMOWSKI	Roman	48
DANOSZEWSKI	Rabbi Mosze	270
DEUCZER	Mosze	111
DIAMEND	Family	38
DIAMEND	Nachman	32
DIAMENT	Mrs.	99
DIGASZINSKI	Adolf	13
DOBRZANSKI	(lawyer)	48
DOIDISLAW	Jakob Josef	163
DONIN	(lawyer)	48
DORARZ		260
DYZENHAUS	Dawid	59
DZIADEK	Duba Rajzel	14
DZIADEK	M.	301
DZIADEK	R.	301
DZIALOWSKI	Izrael	128
DZIWICKI	Icak	308
DZJURA	Jochewed	126
DZJURA	Menachem	126
EDELSZTAJN	Ajgnasz (Ignasz)	69, 99, 121

EDELSZTAJN	Reuwen	164
EHRLICH	Alter	105, 106, 142, 197
EHRLICH	Brothers	59
EHRLICH	Jehuda	21
EHRLICHMAN		32
EJDELS	R.	137
EL-ROI	Elimelech J. (lawyer)	45, 120
ELBAUM		66
ELBAUM	Najcze (Kino)	123
ELENCWAJG		121
ELENCWAJG	Baruch Josef HaKohen	163
ELENCWAJG	Berl	163
ELENCWAJG	Mendel	38, 59, 63, 66
ELENCWAJG	Naftali HaKohen	163
ELIASZ		307
ELIAZER	Efraim	286
ELKMAN	J.	299
EMBERG		35
ENACH	Josef	97, 136
ENGELRAD	Melech	150
ENOCH	Josef	97, 136
EPSZTAJN	Rabbi Josef "Der Guter Jud"	167
EPSZTAJN	Rabbi Kalonymus Kalman	167
ERLICH (EHRLICH)	Sara	99, 130
EZRYNG	S.	301
FAJGEN	M.	301
FAJGENBLAT	Chanoch	32
FAJNGOLD	Fajga	130, 198
FAJNKOCHEN		255
FAJNMESER	Ceszja	245

FAJNSZTAT		241
FEDERMAN		32
FEFER (PFFEFER)	Berisz	194
FEFER (PFFEFER)	Mosze (Menachem Menli) HaKohen	17, 91, 163-4, 188-195, 209, 211
FEFER	(Pffefer) Ester'l	189
FEFER	(Pffefer) Jeszaja	194
FEFERMAN	Rabbi Izrael	199
FELC (PELC)	Dr. Mosze	41, 87, 92, 97, 98, 208, 213, 240, 266
FELDMAN	Dawid	163
FELDMAN	Motel	163
FERSZTER	M.	288
FEUER	Dr.	87
FEUER	Dr.	45, 69, 85
FINKELSZTAJN		99
FINKELSZTAJN	Awraham	198
FINKELSZTAJN	Chana	130
FINKELSZTAJN	Fejwel	163
FINKELSZTAJN	Leon	216, 217
FINKELSZTAJN	N.	60
FINKELSZTAJN	R.	211
FINKLER	Icak	83, 87, 88, 89, 94, 95, 174
FINKLER	Pinchas (Pinja)	173-175
FINKLER	Rabbi Chaim Mejer (The Admo"r of Pinczow)	88, 173
FINKLER	Rabbi Eliezer	174
FINKLER	Rabbi Gaon Icak	173
FINKLER	Rabbi Hilel of Radoszyce	173
FIRSTENBERG	Dr.	41, 196

FIRSTENBERG	Paltiel	196
å		91
FISZ	Regina	256, 260
FISZER		43, 240
FISZMAN	Joske	32, 144, 163, 209
FISZMAN	Lajzer	249
FLESZLER	Dr.	94
FLOMENBAUM		310
FRAJMAN		99
FRAJMAN	Szymon	121
FRAJTAG	Anszel	163
FRAJZYNGER		45
FRANCEK		245
FRIDENZON	Szaul Eliezer	71
FRIDMAN		60
FRIDMAN	Icak	245
FRIDMAN	Jakob	150, 153
FRIDMAN	Josef	196
FRIDMAN	Sela	123
FRISZMAN	Artek	122, 123
FRISZMAN	Aszer	229, 230
FRISZMAN	Dawid	230
FRISZMAN	Dr. A.	230
FROHMAN	Mosze Mordechai	163
FRYDLAND		63
FUKS	Zew (Wawe)	71, 164
FUKSZIWINSKI	Julian	260
GAJER		29
GARDEN	Cz.	305
GARFIN	Izrael	303

GARFINKEL	Dawid	29, 164
GARFINKEL	Isocher	163
GARFINKEL	Mordechai	122
GARFINKEL	Mrs.	303
GARFINKEL	Szmuel Aharon	163
GARFINKEL	Zelig	308
GAT	Szmul	163
GEJST	Kalman	232
GEPNER	Mordechai Menachem	164
GERTLER	Awraham	29
GERTLER	Brothers	83
GERTLER	Josef	93
GERTLER	Michl	137
GERTLER	Mordechai	256
GERTLER	Zecharja	29
GERTNER	Lajbel	164
GIEFILHAUZ	J.M.	136
GINCBERG	Awraham	291
GINZBURG	Chana	126
GINZBURG	Dow	125
GINZBURG	Jehudit	126
GINZBURG	Jochewed	126
GINZBURG	Sisters	125
GINZBURG	Towa	126
GISER	Bajla	14
GISER	Dawid	14
GLIKMAN		122
GNAT	Jedidja	164
GODFRID	Elazar	165
GOLD	Mosze Jakob	303, 304

GOLD	Mrs.	303
GOLD	Rabbi Zew	22, 112, 113
GOLDBERG	A.	95
GOLDBERG	Abram Mosze	14
GOLDBERG	B.	38
GOLDBERG	Ela	245
GOLDBERG	Emanuel	163
GOLDBERG	Heszel	97, 163, 197, 209
GOLDBERG	Icak Majer	122, 163
GOLDBERG	Lajbel	30, 93
GOLDBERG	Michl	14
GOLDBERG	Mosze	210
GOLDBERG	Zew	30
GOLDBERG	Zola	245
GOLDBLUM		122
GOLDBLUM	Aharon	245
GOLDBLUM	D.	60
GOLDBLUM	Family	38
GOLDBLUM	Joszijahu	245
GOLDBLUM	Mosze	165
GOLDFARB FAMILY		22
GOLDFARB	Ben-Cion	122
GOLDFARB	Sender	37
GOLDFARB	Simcha	37
GOLDLUST		301
GOLDLUST	H.	301
GOLDMAN	Mendel	175, 207
GOLDMAN	Rabbi Dawid (The Admor of Chmielnik)	175, 207
GOLDMAN	Rabbi Jeszaja'le	175

GOLDMAN	Simcha Bunem	148, 175, 205, 207, 213
GOLDMAN	Szaul	307, 308, 310
GOLDRAT	Awraham	137, 138, 185, 297
GOLDRAT	Isachar [szochet ubodek (ritual slaughterer)]	185
GOLDRAT	Mejer	311
GOLDRAT	Mordechai	311
GOLDSZAJDER	Abram Dawid	14
GOLDSZAJDER	Hynda	14
GOLDSZAJDER	Josef	37, 61, 143-146
GOLDSZMID	Lajbel	198
GOLDSZMID	Malka Lea	198
GOLDSZMID	Mordechai	164
GOLDSZTAJN	G.	301
GOLEMBIOSKI	Family	23
GOLEMBIOWSKI	Jehuda Lajbusz	163
GOLINSKI	Dawid	310
GOLOMBEK	Mrs.	303
GOLOMBEK	Philip	303
GORDON	Rabbi Eliezer	270
GOTFRAJD	(Gutfrajd) M.	137
GOTFRID	Mejer Jechiel	180
GOTLIB		243
GOTMAN	Nota	163
GOTOWIZNA	Jakob	308
GRANDAPEL	Aharon	196, 297
GRANEK		35
GRANEK	Hersz Mordechai	163
GRINBAUM	Icak	165
GRINGRAS	Kopel	25, 26

GRINGRAS	Leopold	26
GRINSZPAN		34
GRINSZPAN	Cwi Hersz	163
GRINSZPAN	Jonatan	306
GRINSZPAN	Rabbi Cwi	187, 197
GRINSZPAN	Rabbi Herszel	166
GRINSZPAN	Rabbi I.	163
GRINSZPAN	Zelig	164
GROJBRAD		87
GROJBRAD	Rabbi Mahari"l	289
GROJBRAD	Sara'nke	245
GROJSEM	Brothers	44
GROS	J.	129
GROSBERG	Pola	245
GROSFELD	Zelig (Paczke)	62
GROSMAN FAMILY		38
GROSMAN	Aharon	38
GROSZ	Wiktor General	262
GRUSI		129
GRYNBAUM	Icak	52, 175, 207
GRYNBAUM	Szarceh	14
GRYNBERG		32, 86
GRYNBERG	Baruch	122
GRYNBERG	Jakob Icak	163
GRYNBERG	Josef	163, 245
GRYNBERG	Mejer Dawid	310
GRYNBERG	Zew	245
GRYNSZPAN	M.	211, 212
GRYNSZPAN	Rabbi Cwi	187, 197
GUREWICZ	Zygmunt	245

GUT	Icak Mosze	164
GUTFRAJD	(Gotfrajd) Mosze [szochet ubodek (ritual slaughterer)	187
GUTHART	Fiszel	89, 114, 118, 119
GUTMAN	Judel	37, 61, 94, 142, 145, 148
GUTMAN	Rabbi Dawid	154
GUTMAN	Rabbi Tuwia Gutman HaKohen	17, 154, 202
HAGERMAN	Szmuel (Hakatan - the small)	163, 180
HAJT	Frajda	15
HAJT	Hersz	15
HAKOHEN	Chaim	162, 163
HAKOHEN	Jechiel Michl	163
HAKOHEN	Rabbi Dawid Gutman	154
HAKOHEN	Rabbi Israel Mejer of Radin	270
HAKOHEN	Rabbi Izrael	154
HAKOHEN	Rabbi Mosze	154
HAKOHEN	Rabbi Tuwia Gutman	17, 154, 202
HAKOHEN	Rabbi Zew	154
HALLER	Chaim	128
HALOND	Cardinal	260, 261, 268
HASMAN	Dawid	163
HASSENBAJN		32, 91, 193
HASSENBAJN	(lawyer)	45, 193
HAUS	Ester	14
HEJD	S.	301
HEJN	Josef Szymon	163
HELLER	M.	301
HELLER	Yom-Tow Lipman	198
HENDLER	S.	301

HERCL	Dr.	63
HERMAN	Dr. Awraham	41, 198
HERMAN	Dr. Jakob	41, 198
HERMAN	Jechiel, Lawyer	45, 198
HERMAN	Szewa	198
HERMAN	Zyskind	110, 198
HERMANSZTAT		241
HERSZBERG	Jeszaja	163
HERSZKOWICZ		24, 310
HERSZKOWICZ	C.	301
HERSZKOWICZ	D.	97, 301
HERSZKOWICZ	Dora	128
HERSZKOWICZ	Todros	32
HERSZOWICZ	H.	66
HERTGLAS	A., Lawyer	52
HIRSZZON	Chaim Dow	163
HITLER		53, 55
HOCHERMAN	Icak	281, 283
HOCHERMAN	Jakob	282
HOCHERMAN	Natan	311
HOFMAN	Anja	245
HOLC	Icak Pinchas (Icza Pinja)	137
HOLEJNER	Zew Wolf	163
HORBERG	Michl	94, 136, 148
HORBERG	Rabbi Alter Josef Baruch	94, 166, 186
HORBERG	Rabbi Icak Becalel	164, 186
HOROWICZ	Rabbi Chaim Szmuel HaLevi (the Admo"r of Checiny)	167-169
HOROWICZ	Rabbi Cwi Hersz	167
HOROWICZ	Rabbi Elazar	167

HOROWICZ	Rabbi Eliezer	170
HOROWICZ	Rabbi Heszel	170
HOROWICZ	Rabbi Icak Szlomo	171
HOROWICZ	Rabbi Jakob Icak HaLevi (The Seer of Lublin)	167
HOROWICZ	Rabbi Szalom	171
HORWICZ	Mejer	163
HORWICZ	Wolf	89, 164
ICKOWICZ		35
IGELBERG	Chawa	15
ISACHAR BER	Rabbi (The Admo"r of Radoszyce)	173
IZRAEL	Majer	163
IZRAELSKI	Simcha Bunem	24, 162, 211, 241
JABOTINSKI	Ze'ev	127, 129, 130, 207
JAGELO	Wladislaw	157
JAKIL'S	Szmuel	209
JAKUBOWICZ	Jakob	66
JAKUBOWICZ	Mosze	89
JAKUBOWICZ	Mosze Chaim	184
JANAI	Alexander	128
JANKIELEWSKI	Brothers	22
JASNY	N.	305
JEGIER		32, 123
JEGIER	Szmuel	163
JERONSKI	(lawyer)	48
JERUSALIMSKI (JERUSZALMI)	Szymszon Dow	273
JERUSALIMSKI	Rabbi Mosze Nachum	17, 155-165, 270-293
JERUZALIMSKI	Benjamin	278

JERUZALIMSKI	Chana Roszja	273
JERUZALIMSKI	Dawid Jena	273, 298
JEZWICKI	Chana	245
JEZWICKI	Ester	245
JEZWICKI	Szmuel	245
JIKIL'S	Szmuel	209
JOSKOWICZ	Brothers	74
JOSKOWICZ	Izrael	74
JURA		30
JURA	Harry	303
JURA	Lea	303
JURA	Szmuel	128
JURKOWSKI		32
JURKOWSKI	Eduard	260
JUSTMAN	Elija	136, 148
KAC	Rabbi Dow Berisz	154
KAC	Rabbi Icak (Ba'al "Gevurot Anashim")	154
KAC	Rabbi Icak (Charif)	154
KACZOROWSKI	Minister	250, 259
KAHAN	Josef	44
KAHANA	Dawid	256-257
KAHANA	Dr.	253-255
KAHANA	Lemel	22, 91
KAJZER	Brothers	104, 105
KAJZER	Chawa	99
KAJZER	Ester	105, 130
KAJZER	Icak, Dr.	41, 105, 297
KAJZER	Lea	123
KAJZER	Nechemja	29, 60, 105

KAJZER	Szlomo	60, 122
KAJZER	Szymon	60, 104, 115
KALICHSZTAJN	Awraham	122
KALICHSZTAJN	Mosze	29, 63, 106
KALICHSZTAJN	P.	60
KALICHSZTAJN	Szamaj HaKohen	163
KALICHSZTAJN	Szaul	122
KALICHSZTAJN	Wolf	310
KALICHSZTAJN	Zalman	51, 60, 297, 298
KALISZ	Rabbi Icak (The Admo"r of Worka)	175
KALUMEL	Dr.	152
KAMINER	B.	136
KAMINER	Benjamin Mejer	94
KAMINER	Brajndl	132
KAMINER	Chanoch Henich	163
KAMINER	Cwi	164
KAMINER	Icak	38, 142, 162, 210
KAMINER	Icak Cwi	163
KAMINER	J.	136, 138
KAMINER	Jakob	136
KAMINER	Jom Tow Lipa Cwi	163
KAMINER	Judel	132, 133, 136, 148, 150, 179, 202
KAMINER	Meszulam	132
KAMINER	Mordechai Fiszel	28, 29, 97, 132, 136, 144, 148, 150
KAMINER	Mosze	297
KAMINER	Mosze Chaim	23, 132, 164, 194, 202, 203, 290
KAMINER	Sz.	94

KAMINER	Szamaj	299
KANER	Chaim	163, 176
KANER	Family	38, 201
KANER	Icak Mejer	163
KARBEL	Gisela (Girza)	244-5
KARBEL	Irwin	244
KARBEL	Sara	243-4
KARPOSZINSKI	Berl	307
KASPI	lawyer	45
KASRIELEWICZ	Riszja	245
KASZANSKI	Dawid	90
KASZANSKI	Josef	114-117
KASZANSKI	Nachman Dawid	71, 90
KAUFMAN		279
KAUFMAN	Awraham Icak	14
KAUFMAN	C.	99
KAUFMAN	Guta	121
KAUFMAN	M.	99
KAUFMAN	Mosze (Haim)	14, 69, 86, 148, 149, 197
KAUFMAN	Pola	121
KAZLOWSKI	Fiszel Aszer	93, 148, 163
KIND	Izrael Ajzik	164
KINIGSBERG	Mosze	35, 59
KINO		63, 64
KINO	Izrael	123, 124
KINO	Najcze (Elbaum)	123, 124
KIPER		42
KIRSZENBAUM	Arje	120
KIRSZENBAUM	Awraham	120, 125, 126, 297, 298

KIRSZENBAUM	Cipa'le (Lewartowski	119
KIRSZENBAUM	Elimelech (El-Roi) Lawyer	45, 120
KIRSZENBAUM	Icak	110, 119-120, 196, 197, 211
KIRSZENBAUM	L.	301
KIRSZENBAUM	Mosze	120
KIRSZENBAUM	Sima	120
KIRSZENCWAJG	Dawid	310
KIRSZENCWAJG	Mosze	308, 310
KIRSZENCWAJG	Pinchas	310
KLAJNMAN	Icak	23, 196, 197
KLAJNMAN	Joel	23, 94, 196
KLAJNSZTAJN	Anna	15
KLAJNSZTAJN	Awigdor Mendl	15
KLAJNSZTAJN	Josef	15
KLIGMAN	Mosze	123
KLIGMAN	Sela (Sara)	68
KLIGMAN	Szmuel	63, 92, 95, 97, 297
KLINBERG	Chana	245
KLINBERG	Dawid	245
KLINGBAJL	Mosze	128
KLOMEL	Dr.	152
KLUSKA	Kalman	152, 153
KLUSKA	Zew	92, 94, 95, 110, 197, 205, 206, 207, 297, 298
KNOBEL	Eliahu	253
KOCHEN		153
KOCHEN	Ch.	22
KOCHEN	Chaim	35, 59, 312
KOCHEN	Dawid	30

KOCHEN	Family	32
KOCHEN	Fiszel	90, 148
KOCHEN	Hanna	13
KOCHEN	Izrael	35, 312
KOCHEN	Lajbel	308
KOHEN		122
KOHEN (KOCHEN)	Fiszel	90
KOHEN	Awraham	32
KOHEN	Dow Berisz	154
KOHEN	Elazar	163, 283
KOHEN	Fiszel	90
KOHEN	Isidor	267
KOHEN	J.	94
KOHEN	Jakob	238
KOHEN	Josef	148
KOHEN	Josel	94
KOHEN	Mane	163
KOHEN	Mosze	150, 283
KOPEL	Icak	32, 210
KOPEL	Tula	68
KOPEL	Wolf	32
KOPF	Dora	128
KOPF	Jehuda	199
KOPF	Rabbi Awraham Aba	199
KORMAN	Szaul	123, 311
KORNFELD	Mosze	307, 308
KORNGOLD	Aharon	163
KORNGOLD	Izrael	123, 311
KORNGOLD	Josef	163
KORZMINSKI	Lieutenant Colonel	259

KOSWICKI	M.	256, 259
KOWALSKI	(lawyer)	45
KOWALSKI	Rabbi	111, 112
KOZOWSKI		71, 81
KRAKAUER	Mendl	60, 220
KRAUZE		43
KRAUZE	Dr.	41, 94, 99
KRENSKI	Minister	72
KRYSTAL		22, 122
KRYSTAL	Mordechai Dawid	196
KRYSTAL	Wolf	196
KUPEF	Awraham Aba	199
KUPEF	Dora	128
KUPEF	Jehuda	127, 199
KUPERBERG		153
KUPERBERG (NECHUSTAI)	Rafael	123
KUPERBERG	Barukh	36
KUPERBERG	Lajbel	308
KUPERBERG	Mosze	95
KUPERBERG	Sora	14
KUPERBERG	Yek'l	36
KWEKZYLBER	Hanna	14
LADOWSKI	Aharon	305
LADOWSKI	Akiwa	305
LADOWSKI	Awraham	163
LADOWSKI	Icak Icza	163
LADOWSKI	Szmuel Fejwel	163
LAJCHTER	Szmuel	61, 93, 143
LAKS	Mosze Josef	310

LAKS	Sara'nke	245
LANDAU	Rabbi Jechezkel, "Noda Beyehuda"	119
LANMAN	L.	261
LAPA	Hersz	14
LAPA	Szejndl-Ita	14
LEDERMAN	Sara'nke	245
LEMBERG	Jechezkel	238
LEMELS	Kalman	29
LENDER	Mina	245
LERER	Chana	126
LERER	J.	126
LESZEC	Cwi	128
LESZEC	Jehoszua Szlomo	164
LEW	Benjamin	97, 134, 136, 148, 197, 213
LEW	L.	136
LEW	Mosze	136
LEWARTOWSKA	E.	128
LEWARTOWSKI	Chana-Sara	196
LEWARTOWSKI	Cipa'le (Kirszenbaum)	119
LEWARTOWSKI	Cwia	108
LEWARTOWSKI	Dawid	119, 129, 196, 297, 298
LEWARTOWSKI	Guta	108
LEWARTOWSKI	Rachel (nee Szofman)	108
LEWARTOWSKI	Szmuel	62, 107, 108, 152, 196
LEWENSZTAJN	Brothers	24
LEWENSZTAJN	Chaim Jehoszua	227, 228
LEWENSZTAJN	Josef	126

LEWENSZTAJN	Mosze	69, 70
LEWI	Adolf	130
LEWI	B.	32
LEWI	Brothers	37
LEWI	Dr.	278
LEWI	Fejwel-Artur, Professor	217-219, 301
LEWI	Fiszel	63
LEWI	Herman	23, 148, 240, 243, 246, 266
LEWIN	Dr. Gerszon	64
LEWINZON		32
LEWINZON	Dr.	40, 290
LEWKOWICZ	Gerszon	267
LEWKOWICZ	Henich	163
LEWKOWICZ	Lejbusz	201
LEWKOWICZ	Mosze	163
LEWKOWICZ	Sara	297, 298
LIBERMAN	Lejbusz	164
LICHT	Reuwen Szlomo	287
LICHTENSZTAJN		306
LICHTENSZTAJN	Chaim Szalom	94, 95
LIFSZICZ	Chana	297, 298
LIFSZICZ	Lula	153
LIFSZICZ	Mosze	153
LIFSZYCZ	Mendel	22, 93, 196
LIGIN	Governor	274
LIPKO	Mosze Zew	163
LIS		13
LIS	Anszel	14
LIS	Josef	14

LISMAN		310
LITAUER	Awigdor	163
LITTAUER		62
LUBLINER		121
LUDWIG		121
LUFT	Lajbusz Mendel	164
LUSINSKI	Bishop Augustin	157, 159
MACHTYNGER		126
MACHTYNGER	E.	301
MACHTYNGER	Family	23
MACHTYNGER	Izrael Ajzik	198, 311
MACHTYNGER	M.	301
MACHTYNGER	Mordechai	198, 311
MACHTYNGER	Rochale	307
MACHTYNGER	Szmarja	198
MAJERCZIK		178
MAJERSON	M.	301
MAJERSON	S.	301
MAJEWSKI		85
MAJFELD	(lawyer)	45
MAJTLES	Helena	256
MAJZEL	Lawyer	45, 191, 193
MALIANSKI	Mordechai	164
MALINIAK	Jakob	163
MANELA	Dawid	32, 238
MANELA	Elazar	90
MANELA	J. (lawyer)	45
MANELA	Jakob	164, 238
MANELA	Mosze	219, 220
MANELA	Mrs.	303

MANELA	Szlomo	32
MANELA	Zalman	303
MANTEL	Dr. A.	301
MARBERG	Ch. Alter	163
MARGALIOT	Rabbi Menachem Mendel	154
MARKOWICZ		30, 246
MARKOWICZ	H.S.	301
MARKOWICZ	Szmuel	153
MARMONT	Pesil	14
MARYNKA	Josel	94
MAUERBERGER	S.	99
MAURBERGER		41
MAURBERGER	Alter	288
MAZUPE	Hersz	163
MAZUR	Stefan	260
MEJER JECHIEL	Rabbi (The Admo"r of Ostrowiec)	178
MENDEL	Mordechai	164
MENDEL	Rabbi (The Admo"r of Kock)	26, 196
MENDELBAUM	Chawa	245
MENDELEWICZ		24
MENGEL	Sz.	129
MERBER		99, 121, 142, 179
MICKIWICZ		127
MICNMACHER		35
MICNMACHER	J.L.	88
MICNMACHER	Mejer	165
MIKOLAJCZIK		260
MINC		38
MINC	Alter	138

MINC	J.	301
MINC	Lily	245
MINC	Menasze	138
MINC	Michael Mejer	163
MINC	Myrjam	77
MINC	Sisters	77, 78
MINCBERG	Hena	99, 196
MIODOWICZ	Szlomo Jakob	163
MISZPIENKI	G.	162
MITELMAN		43
MITELMAN	Jechiel	38
MORA		253
MORDKOWICZ	Natan	30
MORDOKOWICZ	Kalman	126
MORGENSZTERN		30
MOSKOWICZ (MOSZKOWICZ)	Aharon Josef	86, 150, 153, 196, 197
MOSKOWICZ (MOSZKOWICZ)	Mordechai-Gimpel	163, 196
MOSKOWICZ	D.	301
MOSKOWICZ	H.	301
MOSKOWICZ	P.	301
MOSZCZICKI	Professor	218
MOSZENBERG	and Sons	35
MOSZENBERG	Baruch	163, 211
MOSZENBERG	Berel	56, 59
MOSZENBERG	Brothers	38
MOSZENBERG	Jakob-Lewek	15
MOSZENBERG	Josef	15
MOSZKOWICZ (MOSKOWICZ)	Aharon Josef	86, 150, 153, 196, 197

MOSZKOWICZ (MOSKOWICZ)	Mordechai-Gimpel	163, 196
MOSZKOWICZ	Dora	153
MOSZKOWICZ	Family	32
MOSZKOWICZ	Jakob Szlomo	163
MOSZKOWICZ	Lena	68, 153
MOSZKOWICZ	Mordechai Gimpel	163, 196
MOSZKOWSKI	Hinda-Fajga	15
MOSZKOWSKI	Izrael	14
MOSZKOWSKI	Josef	15
MOSZKOWSKI	Kalman Bunem	14
MUSZKAT	Rabbi Awraham	175
MUSZKAT	Rabbi Jeszaja (of Prague)	175
NAROTOWICZ	Professor	111
NECHUSTAJ	Rafael	123
NIBILSKI	Cwi	70, 114-116
NOWAK	Brothers	59, 60, 62
NOWAK	Henryk	204, 288
NOWAK	Jakob	204
NOWAK	Szlomo	204
NOWAKOWSKI	Karzomirz	260
OBERMAN	Hilel	82, 110, 164
OBERZANSKI		26
OPATOWSKI	Ch.	129
OPPENHAJMER	Prof.	279
ORBAJTL-ROZENBERG	Lea	130
ORBAJTL	Awraham (Gerber)	23
ORBAJTL	Josef	22, 211
ORBAJTL	Szmul	23
OSTROWICZ	Nechemia	62, 98, 197

OSZEROWICZ	Dawid	310
OSZEROWICZ	Icza	308
PACHEL	Ester	126
PACZANOWER	Mendel Bornsztajn	89
PAPARSZTAK	Jechezkel	163
PAPIWSKI		191
PARADYSTAL		59, 61, 75, 140-143
PARTINSKI	Jechezkel	163
PASERMAN	Family	201
PASERMAN	J.	197
PASERMAN	Jakob Hilel	32, 163
PELC	(Felc) Dr. Mosze	41, 87, 92, 97, 98, 208, 213, 240, 266
PERELMAN	Dr.	40, 59, 62, 140
PFFEFER (FEFER)	Berisz	194
PFFEFER (FEFER)	Ester'l	189
PFFEFER (FEFER)	Jeszaja	194
PFFEFER (FEFER)	Mosze (Menachem Menli) HaKohen	17, 91, 163-4, 188-195, 209, 211
PIASECKI	Brothers	24
PIEKARSKI	Cwi	60, 66
PIEKARSKI	Engineer	99
PIEKARSKI	Menachem Dow	163
PIEKARSKI	Mosze	62, 105
PIENKOWICZ	Izrael	301
PIENKOWICZ	S.	301
PIESKOGORSKI	Icak	297
PIETROWSKI	Szmuel	162
PILSUDSKI	Jozef	53, 54, 149, 159, 231
PINIES	Motel	168

PINKUSOWICZ	Henich	310
PINKUSOWICZ	Izrael	308
PIOTRKOWSKI	Awraham	92
PIOTRKOWSKI	Mosze	163
PIOTROWSKI	A.	148
PIOTROWSKI	Beril	29
PIWKO	Awraham	126
POLAK		121
POLAK	Dr.	41
POMERANC	Perel	14
PORISZKWICZ		283
POSLOSZNI	Chaim	297, 298, 307, 308, 310
POTASZNIK	Cwi	123
POTASZNIK	Pnina	123
POZNANSKI		29, 251
PRAJS	Herszel	276
PRAJS	Icak	256
PRAJS	J.	136
PRAPOSZINSKI	Berl	307
PRASZOWSKI	Judel	43
PRASZOWSKI	Welwel	43
PRIWLAN	Dow	164
PRIWLAN	Szachna	164
PROSZKOWSKI	Antoni	260
PROSZOWSKI		240
PROSZOWSKI	Irena	245
PRYBULSKI	Menachem	80, 120
PRYLUCKI	Noach	145, 195, 217
PUKACZ		35

PUKACZ	Azriel	163
RABINOWICZ	Jerachmiel	308
RABINOWICZ	Rabbi Cemach (The Admo"r of Rakow)	177
RABINOWICZ	Rabbi Cwi Hersz	270
RABINOWICZ	Rabbi Elimelech (The Admo"r of Suchedniow)	176, 198
RABINOWICZ	Rabbi Jakob Icak (The Holy Jew of Przysucha)	176
RABINOWICZ	Rabbi Natan	176
RABINOWICZ	Rabbi Natan Dawid (The Admo"r of Szydlowiec)	176
RABINOWICZ	Rabbi Ozer Awraham Josef (The Admo"r of Rakow)	177
RACHUM	Josef	130
RACZKIEWICZ	Minister	256, 259
RAFALOWICZ	Rafael	95, 136, 148
RAFELKES		124
RAJTER	Zuszja	245
RAJZLER	Josef (Josele Badchan [The Joker])	66, 224, 225
RAJZMAN	Awigdor	91, 162, 205
RAJZMAN	Dr.	301
RAJZMAN	Eliezer	23
RAJZMAN	Herszl	23
RAJZMAN	Icza Mejer	76, 94, 142, 143, 150, 205, 206
RAJZMAN	L.	98
RAJZMAN	Leon	196
RAJZMAN	Simcha	204, 205
RAJZMAN	Sloma	76
RAJZMAN	Szlomo	205
RAJZMAN	Szmulik	163

RAPAPORT	Baruch	137, 138
RAPAPORT	Icak	136, 148, 196, 209
RAPAPORT	Icak Majer	29
RAPAPORT	Rabbi Awraham Abele HaKohen	94, 165, 166, 197, 242
RAPAPORT	Rabbi of Andrzejewo	109
RAPAPORT	Rabbi Tuwia Gutman	17, 154, 155
RAWICKI		140, 141, 142
REBBE'LE	Eli	182, 183
RECHCMAN		32, 38
RECHT	Menachem	245
RECHT	Mosze Cwi (Szochet uBodek - Ritual Slaughterer)	163
RECHTSMAN		245
REMBISZEWSKI		68
REMBISZEWSKI	Awraham	308
REMBISZEWSKI	Dawid	24, 123
REMBISZEWSKI	Gerszon	29, 66
REMBISZEWSKI	Henik	121
RENKOSZYNSKI	Alter	130
RIGER		191
RIMONT		127
ROMBERG	R.	301
RONDBERG		35
ROSS (ROZENSZAFIR)	Awraham	303
ROSS (ROZENSZAFIR)	Lea	303
ROTBRAD		68
ROTENBERG	A.	30, 99
ROTENBERG	Bela	99, 130

ROTENBERG	Eliahu (Nachum's)	180
ROTENBERG	Family	32
ROTENBERG	Hela	68
ROTENBERG	Jakob Josef (Joszke)	163, 196
ROTENBERG	Jehuda	196
ROTENBERG	Mosze	85, 107, 196, 213, 297
ROTENBERG	N.	60
ROTENSZTRAJCH	Fiszel	151
ROTERBAND	Baruch Szaul	164
ROTKOWSKI	P.	301
ROTMAN		30, 41, 44
ROTMAN	Ch. B.	24
ROTMAN	Dr.	85
ROTMAN	Jona	94
ROTMAN	Szlomo	24
ROTSZILD	Jehuda (Judel)	89, 163, 164
ROZEN	J.	66
ROZENBERG-ORBAJTL	Lea	130
ROZENBERG	Cwi	24, 297, 298
ROZENBERG	Dawid	60, 63, 130, 143, 150, 152, 205, 206
ROZENBERG	Hela	130
ROZENBERG	Izrael	187
ROZENBERG	Josel (Sara Chana's)	29
ROZENBERG	L.	24
ROZENBERG	Mordechai Motel (Nachum's)	163, 187
ROZENBERG	Zecharja	163
ROZENBLUM	Elijahu (Ely) Iser	95, 114, 117, 118
ROZENBLUM	Mosze	92, 153

ROZENCWAJG	A.	301
ROZENCWAJG	Gisela	245
ROZENCWAJG	H.	301
ROZENCWAJG	Januszek	245
ROZENHOLC	Family	22
ROZENKRANC	Pinek	122
ROZENSZTRICH	Rabbi Menachem Mendel	157
ROZENWALD	Dawid	100
ROZENWALD	Jehudit	126
ROZENWALD	Josef	126
ROZMAJTI	Jona	310
ROZMARIN	Dr. Henryk	151
RUBINEK	Brothers	25
RUBINSZTAJN	Josef Icak	163
RUBINSZTAJN	Szlomo	163
RUDEL	Lajbl	70, 128, 130, 220
RUDEL	Pinchas	32
RURZANSKI	Jan	249
RUSEK		86
RZELINSKI	Icak	86, 87
RZENDOWSKI	Brothers	38
RZEROMSKI		127
RZETELNI	B.	138
RZETELNY	S.	137
RZOK		22
RZYLONY	Chaim	70, 221
RZYMNOWODA	W.	69, 239, 240
RZYTO	Lajb-Ber	308
SAPIR	Mercel	245
SASKI		48

SEJNES	R.	301
SERCARZ		238
SERCARZ	Herszel	85, 150
SERWETNIK		44
SFAT EMET	The (The Admo"r of Gur)	132, 202
SIENKOWICZ		127
SIRKIS	Daniel	132
SKORECKI	Dolek	123
SKURA	Eliezer	38
SLAWATYCKI	Mosze	163
SLAWATYCKI	Rabbi J.	163
SLIMOWICZ	J.	301
SMULKA		158
SOCZINSKI	Major	259
SOFER	Izrael	301
SOKOLOWSKI	Baruch	94, 197, 242
SOLNIK	Jerachmiel	311
SOLRZ	Mosze	309
SOSNOWSKI	Szymon	163
SOWCZINSKI		248, 255
SOWKOWER	Rabbi Emanuel	179
STASZEWSKI	Bernard	297
STASZEWSKI	J.	137
STERNZYS	Baruch	165
STRAWCZINSKI		240
STRAWCZINSKI	Brothers	61, 146
STRAWCZINSKI	Hersz	308, 309
STRAWCZINSKI	Perl	308
STRAWCZINSKI	Szmuel	311

STRAWCZINSKI	Szymon	70, 90, 126, 146, 310
SUKENIK		91
SZA"CH (SIFTAJ KOHEN)		154
SZAC	Dr. Jakob	41, 130
SZAFIR	Dawid Gedalja	163, 209
SZAFIR	Izrael Majer	163, 209
SZAFIR	Motel	163
SZAJBLER		29
SZAJNFELD		32
SZAJNFELD	Aharon	196
SZAJNFELD	Icak Mejer	163
SZAJNFELD	J.	136
SZAJNFELD	Jakob	196
SZAJNFELD	Jechiel	29, 163, 179, 196
SZAJNFELD	Szalom	196
SZALIT	Daniel	92, 97
SZAPIRO		24
SZAPIRO	Baruch	307
SZAPIRO	Jona	303, 304
SZAPIRO	Jona HaKohen	163
SZAPIRO	Malka	15
SZAPIRO	Toli	303
SZCEDROWICKI	Rabbi	299
SZEFTEL		43
SZENKER	Mosze Josef	308
SZIF	Mosze	176
SZINDLER		239, 240
SZLAMOWICZ	Josef	163
SZLIWA	Jozef	260

SZMULEWICZ	B.	24
SZMULEWICZ	M.L.	38
SZOFMAN	Rachel (Lewartowski)	108
SZOR	Professor	117
SZORER	Chaim	120
SZPIGIEL	Johan	240, 267
SZPILMAN	Anszel (Ansze'le Klezmer)	222, 223
SZPILMAN	Szlomo	122
SZPRECHMAN	C.	305
SZRAJBER	H.	72
SZROGRODER (LAWYER)		45
SZTAJNHAUER	Z.	301
SZTARK	Rabbi Icak Natan	157
SZTARKE		25
SZTERN	Ben-Cion	29
SZTERNFELD	Jehoszua	310
SZTERNSZOS	Motel	164
SZTROSBERG	Brothers	32
SZTROZBERG		94
SZTROZBERG	Berl	163
SZTROZBERG	J.	137
SZTROZBERG	Szymszon	32
SZTUNKE	Dow Berl	202
SZTUNKE	Mejer	201, 202, 209
SZUGIERMAN	R.	301
SZUGIERMAN	S.	301
SZULMAN	Lajzar	307
SZWIANSKI		25
SZWICER	Josef	209

SZYDLOWSKI	Chaim	163
SZYMSZON	Rabbi of Ostropoli	119
TABENKIN	Itzchak	124
TAUBER	Fela	153
TAUMAN	Eliezer	28, 198
TAUMAN	Icak Mejer	186, 187
TAUMAN	Josef	198
TAUMAN	Szeftel	197
TENCER	Chaim	163
TENCER	Lajb	126
TENENBAUM		28, 30
TENENBAUM	Eliezer	162
TENENBAUM	Family	23
TENENBAUM	Rozszka	128
TENENBAUM	Szymon	181
TENENWURCEL	Aleksander	126
TENENWURCEL	Cwi	163
TEOMIM	Rabbi Jehoszua Fejwel	154
TEOMIM	Rabbi Jona	154
TRAGER		243
TRAJMAN	Mosze (Aharondl's)	187, 230
TWERSKI	Mahari"l	289
TWERSKI	Rabbi Awraham (The Magid of Trisk)	171
TWERSKI	Rabbi Cwi Hersz	171
TWERSKI	Rabbi Lajbeniew	176, 197
TWERSKI	Rabbi Mordechai (The Magid of Czernobyl)	171
TWERSKI	Rabbi Motele (The Admo"r of Kuzmir)	171-173, 176
TWERSKI	Rabbi Nachum	171, 176

TYKOCINER	Chaim	163
UBSZANI		50
WAGMAJSTER	Joel	158
WAJCMAN		24
WAJCMAN	Mordechai Josef	163
WAJNBERG	Dr.	304
WAJNBERG	Plejusz	245
WAJNBERGER	Dr.	306
WAJNCWAJG	Awraham	307
WAJNRYB	Baruch	38
WAJNRYB	Chaim	86, 92, 150
WAJNRYB	Herszke	254
WAJNRYB	W.	197
WAJNSZTOK	Berisz	310
WAJNSZTOK	Brothers	128
WAJNSZTOK	Izrael	307
WAJNSZTOK	Mendel	129
WAJNTRAUB		30
WAJNTRAUB	Chaim	163
WAJS	Mosze	15
WAJS	Szlomo	15
WAJSBAUM	Nete Zew	164
WAJSBROT	Mordechai	308
WAJSBROT	Myrjam	15
WAJSBROT	R.B.	137
WAJSMAN	Jona	163
WAKSBERG		286
WAKSBERG	A.	276, 287
WAKSBERG	C.	60
WAKSBERG	Ch.	60

WAKSBERG	Herszel	143
WAKSBERG	Jeszaja	23
WAKSBERG	N.	276, 279
WAKSMAN	M.Ch.	137
WALD-LIPRENT	Karol	245
WALDBERG		197
WALDEN	Aharon	226, 227
WALDEN	Mosze Mendel	226
WALDEN	Sara	227
WARGON	A.	66
WASSER	Josef	165
WASSERMAN	Hersz	15
WASSERMAN	Icak	15
WELISZ		148
WENGRAD	Awraham	308
WERMAN	Dr.	40
WESTERMAN	Awraham	291
WIGAN	S.	301
WIGGINS	L.	301
WIKINSKI		32
WILK		13
WILNER		153, 242
WILNER	A.J.	66
WILNER	C.	99
WINOGRAD	Awraham	308
WINOGRODZKI	Izrael	308
WIRZEWA	Simcha Bunem	82, 90, 164
WISZLIC	Major	249, 250, 257
WISZNICKI		254
WITLIN	Master M.	128, 129, 130

WLODLIPRANT	Karol	245
WLODWER	Efrajm	29
WLOSZCZOWSKI		35
WOLMAN		22, 59, 61
WOLMAN	Stefanja	22, 69, 74, 98, 115, 121, 132, 241
WULF	Gerszon Zew	187
ZAGAJSKI	Awraham	22
ZAGAJSKI	Brothers	210
ZAGAJSKI	Chaim	96, 97, 197
ZAGAJSKI	Cwi	22, 96, 97, 106, 197, 205, 206, 242
ZAGAJSKI	Elimelech (Miczislaw)	22
ZAGAJSKI	Family	22, 91, 96, 98, 195, 197, 264
ZAGAJSKI	Jakob	22, 96, 196, 206
ZAGAJSKI	Jechiel	97, 197, 255
ZAGAJSKI	Lea	99
ZAGORSKI		259
ZAHERMAN	Pinchas Hakohen	163
ZAJDE	Fajga	99
ZAJDE	Jehuda	198, 306, 307, 308
ZAJDE	M.	60
ZAJDE	Majer	198, 306
ZAJDE	Manja	198
ZAJDE	Pinchas	198
ZAJFMAN	Brothers	121-2
ZAJFMAN	Jakob (Jakusz)	123, 200
ZAJFMAN	Kalmen	200
ZAJFMAN	Mosze	200, 306
ZAJFMAN	Natan Dawid	199, 200

ZAKAJ	Ada	120
ZALCBERG		243
ZALCBERG	Anszel	37
ZALCER	Fajga	15
ZALCER	Heszel	89
ZALCMAN	B.	129
ZALEWSKI		307
ZAUBERMAN	Fajbusz	245
ZAUERMAN	Josef	163
ZAUERMAN	P.	32
ZELICKI		256
ZELINGER	Szlomo	130
ZERUBAVEL		124
ZILBER-EWEN	Casza	198
ZILBERBERG		94
ZILBERSZAC	Frajdl	15
ZINGER	Josef	125, 126
ZIUNCZKOWSKI	Josef	211
ZIUNCZKOWSKI	R.	29
ZLOTNIK	Mosze	310
ZLOTNIK	Rabbi J.L.	110
ZLOTO	Hilel	199
ZLOTO	Jakob	128
ZLOTO	Jechiel	122
ZLOTO	Mejer	32, 95, 130, 150, 199, 211
ZLOTO	Natan	199
ZLOTO	Pinchas	198, 199
ZYLBERMAN		38
ZYLBERSZLAG	Dr.	40

ZYLBERSZPIC	Dawid	28, 35, 163
ZYLBERSZTAJN		38
ZYLBERSZTAJN	Ajzik	59
ZYLBERSZTAJN	Awraham Icak	163
ZYLBERSZTAJN	Cila	120
ZYLBERSZTAJN	Dora	245
ZYLBERSZTAJN	Elimelech	163
ZYLBERSZTAJN	Family	32, 38
ZYLBERSZTAJN	Icak	153
ZYLBERSZTAJN	Izrael	45, 110
ZYLBERSZTAJN	Jakob	14
ZYLBERSZTAJN	Jakob Szlomo	110, 163
ZYLBERSZTAJN	Jechiel	308, 310
ZYLBERSZTAJN	Jojzef	153
ZYLBERSZTAJN	Josef-Lajb	14
ZYLBERSZTAJN	Josef	163
ZYLBERSZTAJN	M.	301
ZYLBERSZTAJN	Menachem	307, 308
ZYLBERSZTAJN	Miljusza	245
ZYNGERMAN		42
ZYNGERMAN	Ch.	279
ZYSMAN	Herszel	122

LAST NAME INDEX

Please note: The page numbers in the Last Name Index refer to the page numbers of this English translation

A

Abela, 274, 282
Abele, 144, 154, 155, 156, 282
Abramowich, 282
Abramowicz, 29, 152, 282
Adler, 152, 270, 282
Agranow, 272, 273, 282
Agranowicz, 272, 273, 282
Aharondl, 176
Aharonowicz, 118, 282
Ajlbirt, 27, 217, 242, 282
Ajlenberg, 128, 176, 283
Ajzenberg, 18, 19, 20, 22, 23, 24, 25, 27, 29, 82, 85, 86, 88, 100, 113, 124, 126, 138, 142, 152, 153, 185, 186, 187, 198, 199, 201, 230, 233, 236, 241, 267, 268, 283
Albert, 128, 153, 236, 241, 283
Albirt, 119, 152, 267, 268, 283, 284
Aleks, 230, 284
Almer, 153, 284
Alpert, 117, 152, 240, 243, 284
Alter, 120, 284
Altman, 270, 284
Ami'el, 284
Anders, 234, 284
Anszer, 37, 54, 284
Apel, 276, 284
Arindel, 219
Arten, 4, 6, 59, 76, 77, 89, 90, 120, 127, 140, 141, 267, 268, 282, 284
Artwinski, 180, 284
Astrian, 258, 265
Aszkenazi, 144, 284
Auerbach, 36, 153, 284

B

Bachwiener, 251
Badchan, 58, 212, 213, 214
Bajrzeciner, 80, 284
Balfour, 73, 74, 95, 100, 113, 195
Balicki, 152, 186, 284
Balmont, 54, 284
Baruch, 75, 284
Batszewa, 187
Becalel, 153, 175
Beck, 46
Bejn, 242, 284
Beker, 153, 273, 284
Bekerman, 153, 284
Belfer, 80, 285
Bels, 122, 285
Ben-Gurion, 113, 285
Ben-Tzvi, 113, 285
Berger, 280, 285
Berisz, 144, 153
Berkowicz, 12, 231, 285
Berlinski, 204, 285
Berman, 235, 242, 245, 285
Beser, 152, 285
Beserglik, 152, 285
Bester, 152, 285
Bialik, 119
Bialobroda, 32, 225, 285
Biderman, 153, 285
Bimka, 24, 152, 285
Bimko, 203, 204, 270, 285
Binental, 170, 285
Binoszewicz, 267, 285
Birenbaum, 285
Birencwajg, 110, 285
Birnbaum, 121
Birnzweig, 255
Biskopska, 246, 285
Bistricini, 285
Bistricki, 120
Blacharowicz, 12, 152, 285
Blacharz, 30, 285
Blachatowski, 37, 286
Blachot, 244, 286

Blak, 272, 273, 286
Blaszczak, 244, 286
Blaszczik, 247
Blatt, 1, 2, 17, 39, 49, 62, 82, 92, 130, 144
Bleicher, 262
Blejcher, 286
Blicki, 23, 29, 286
Blumenfeld, 140, 175, 194, 270, 271, 286
Bodenheimer, 257, 286
Borkowski, 29, 115, 286
Bornsztajn, 25, 80, 113, 152, 153, 230, 231, 267, 268, 286
Borochov, 113, 115
Borochow, 286
Borsztajn, 115, 286
Boruchowicz, 154, 287
Bosterlenka, 152, 287
Brak, 116, 153, 287
Braun, 75, 77, 287
Braza, 272, 287
Bronrot, 103, 287
Brot, 103, 287
Bruner, 20, 287
Buchbinder, 287
Bugajer, 18, 230, 287
Bukowski, 27, 191, 287
Bukszpan, 279, 287
Bursztin, 287
Buzek, 170

C

Canin, 287
Celcer, 225, 287
Cel-cion, 287
Cel-Cion, 34
Cetel, 219, 220, 221, 287
Charendorf, 80, 153, 287
Charif, 144
Charson, 232, 287
Chazan, 287
Chelmner, 18, 176, 287
Chenciner, 176
Cherniakow, 287
Chmelosz, 153, 287
Chmielarz, 25, 287
Chmielevski, 251
Chmielewski, 287
Chmielnicki, 83, 90, 231, 287, 288

Choderland, 277, 288
Chornzawski, 277, 288
Chroberski, 80, 153, 285, 288
Chwat, 70, 71, 150, 279, 288
Cimbalist, 211
Cohen, 144, 208, 252
Cooper, 272, 273, 288
Cuker, 279, 288
Cukerman, 29, 153, 242, 288
Cwajgel, 12, 27, 31, 152, 288
Cwajgenbaum, 270, 288
Cymerman, 152, 288
Cyna, 30, 288
Cypros, 231, 288
Cytron, 1, 2, 3, 4, 6, 79, 268, 281, 288
Cytryn, 21, 152, 270, 271, 289
Czenrendorf, 274
Czerendorf, 289
Czerniakow, 197, 289

D

Dajbuch, 52, 62, 111, 289
Dajtelcwajg, 153, 289
Dam, 270, 271, 289
Damowski, 40, 289
Danoszewski, 253, 289
Dawid, 166, 243
Deuczer, 101, 289
Diamend, 27, 32, 289
Diament, 90, 289
Digaszinski, 289
Dobrzanski, 40, 289
Doidislaw, 153, 289
Donin, 40, 289
Dorarz, 246, 289
Dow, 115, 176
Dugszinski, 10
Dyzenhaus, 51, 289
Dziadek, 12, 270, 271, 289
Dzialowski, 117, 289
Dziwicki, 277, 289
Dzjura, 115, 290

E

Edelsztajn, 59, 90, 110, 153, 290
Ehrlich, 17, 51, 95, 96, 120, 133, 186, 290
Ehrlichman, 27, 290
Ejdels, 127, 290

Elbaum, 57, 113, 290
Elencwajg, 32, 51, 55, 57, 110, 152, 290
Eliasz, 290
Eliazer, 290
Elkman, 290
El-Roi, 290
Emberg, 29, 290
Enach, 88, 126, 290
Engelrad, 140, 290
Enoch, 290
Epsztajn, 33, 157, 290
Erlich, 290
Ezryng, 270, 290

F

Fajgen, 270, 290
Fajgenblat, 27, 290
Fajngold, 120, 186, 291
Fajnkochen, 242
Fajnmeser, 231, 291
Fajnsztat, 227, 291
Federman, 27, 291
Fefer, 14, 82, 153, 291, 312
Feferman, 188, 291
Felc, 34, 291
Feldman, 153, 291
Ferszter, 291
Feuer, 37, 60, 78, 191, 291
Finkelsztajn, 52, 90, 120, 152, 186, 201, 205, 291
Finkler, 74, 78, 85, 86, 162, 163, 164, 291, 292
Firstenberg, 34, 185, 292
Firster, 82, 292
Fisz, 242, 246, 292
Fiszel, 122, 140, 170
Fiszer, 35, 226, 292
Fiszman, 27, 134, 152, 199, 236, 292
Fleszler, 85, 292
Flomenbaum, 279, 292
Frajman, 90, 110, 292
Frajtag, 152, 292
Frajzynger, 37, 292
Francek, 231, 292
Fridenzon, 62, 292
Fridman, 52, 112, 140, 185, 231, 292
Friszman, 112, 218, 219, 292
Frohman, 153, 292
Frydland, 54, 292
Fuerster, 261

Fuks, 62, 153, 292
Fuksziwinski, 292

G

Gajer, 24, 293
Garden, 274, 293
Garfin, 273, 293
Garfinkel, 24, 111, 152, 272, 277, 293
Gat, 153, 293
Gejst, 221, 293
Gepner, 153, 293
Gerber, 19
Gertler, 24, 73, 84, 127, 242, 293
Gertner, 153, 293
Giefilhauz, 126, 293
Gincberg, 262, 293
Ginsburg, 102
Ginzburg, 115, 293
Giser, 12, 293
Glikman, 112, 293
Gnat, 153, 294
Godfrid, 154, 294
Gold, 18, 102, 103, 272, 273, 294
Goldberg, 11, 25, 32, 84, 86, 88, 112, 152, 186, 199, 231, 294
Goldblum, 32, 52, 111, 154, 231, 294
Goldfarb, 18, 31, 111, 294
Goldlust, 270, 271, 279, 294
Goldman, 138, 165, 195, 197, 202, 276, 277, 279, 294, 295
Goldrat, 4, 127, 128, 174, 175, 267, 280, 295
Goldszajder, 11, 31, 53, 133, 134, 135, 136, 295
Goldszmid, 153, 187, 295
Goldsztajn, 271, 295
Golembioski, 295
Golembiowski, 18, 153, 295
Golinski, 279, 295
Golombek, 272, 273, 295
Gorcki, 245
Gordon, 253, 295
Gotfrajd, 127, 295
Gotfrid, 170, 295
Gotlib, 229, 295
Gotman, 153, 295
Gotowizna, 277, 295
Grandapel, 185, 267, 295
Granek, 29, 153, 295, 296
Graubard, 261

Grinbaum, 155, 164, 296
Gringras, 20, 21, 296
Grinszpan, 153, 156, 176, 186, 275, 296
Grojbrad, 78, 231, 296
Grojsem, 37, 296
Gros, 118, 296
Grosberg, 231, 296
Grosfeld, 53, 296
Grosman, 32, 296
Grosz, 248, 296
Grusi, 296
Grynbaum, 11, 44, 197, 296
Grynberg, 27, 76, 112, 152, 231, 279, 296
Grynszpan, 201, 297
Gurewicz, 231, 297
Gut, 153, 297
Gutfrajd, 176, 297
Guthart, 79, 104, 108, 297
Gutman, 31, 53, 85, 133, 134, 135, 138, 144, 192, 297

H

Hagerman, 152, 169, 297
Hajt, 12, 297
HaKatan, 169
HaKohen, 14, 144, 145, 152, 154, 156, 253, 297
Haler, 45
HaLevi, 104, 176
Haller, 117, 297
Halond, 246, 297
Hasman, 152, 297
Hassenbajn, 27, 37, 82, 182, 297
Haus, 12, 297
Hecherman, 258, 259
Hegel, 102
Hejd, 270, 297
Hejn, 152, 297
Heller, 187, 270, 271, 298
Hendler, 270, 298
Hercl, 298
Herman, 18, 34, 37, 100, 138, 187, 298
Hermansztat, 227, 298
Herszberg, 153, 298
Herszkowicz, 20, 27, 88, 117, 270, 279, 298
Herszowicz, 57, 298
Hertglas, 44, 298
Herzl, 53, 54, 92, 99
Hirszzon, 152, 298

Hitler, 46, 98, 113, 125, 223, 235, 244, 298
Hlond, 252
Hocherman, 280, 298
Hofman, 231, 298
Holc, 127, 298
Holejner, 153, 298
Horberg, 85, 126, 138, 156, 175, 298
Horowicz, 156, 157, 299
Horwicz, 80, 152, 153, 299

I

Ickowicz, 29, 299
Igelberg, 12, 299
Isachar Ber, 299
Izrael, 299
Izraelski, 20, 152, 201, 299

J

Jabotinski, 299
Jabotinsky, 117, 118, 119, 196, 197, 221
Jagelo, 147, 299
Jakil's, 198
Jakil's, 299
Jakubowicz, 57, 80, 173, 299
Janai, 299
Jankielewski, 18, 299
Jasne, 274
Jasny, 299
Jegier, 27, 112, 153, 299
Jekil's, 65
Jeronski, 40, 299
Jerusalimski, 145, 146, 147, 148, 151, 152, 153, 154, 253, 254, 300
Jeruszalmi, 300
Jeruzalimski, 14, 254, 300
Jezwicki, 230, 300
Jikil's, 300
Jorkowski, 246
Joskowicz, 64, 65, 300
Jura, 25, 117, 272, 273, 300
Jurkowski, 27, 300
Justman, 126, 138, 300

K

Kac, 300
Kaczka, 22, 185
Kaczorowski, 245, 300

Kahan, 300
Kahana, 18, 82, 240, 241, 242, 300
Kahn, 259
Kajzer, 24, 34, 52, 90, 94, 95, 111, 112, 120, 267, 300, 301
Kalichsztajn, 24, 43, 52, 55, 96, 111, 112, 152, 267, 268, 279, 301
Kalisz, 301
Kalumel, 141, 301
Kalwaria, 25
Kaminer, 19, 23, 24, 32, 85, 88, 121, 122, 126, 128, 133, 134, 138, 140, 152, 153, 168, 182, 183, 192, 193, 199, 262, 267, 301, 302
Kaner, 32, 152, 167, 191, 302
Kant, 102, 205
Karbel, 229, 231, 302
Karposzinski, 302
Kaspi, 302
Kasrielewicz, 230, 302
Kaszanski, 62, 81, 104, 105, 106, 302
Katczrowski, 237
Kaufman, 12, 60, 76, 90, 110, 138, 139, 186, 257, 302
Kazlowski, 84, 138, 153, 302
Kind, 153, 302
Kinigsberg, 29, 51, 302
Kino, 54, 113, 302
Kiper, 34, 303
Kirszenbaum, 4, 37, 100, 109, 110, 114, 116, 185, 186, 201, 267, 268, 271, 303
Kirszencwajg, 277, 279, 303
Klajnman, 18, 85, 185, 186, 303
Klajnsztajn, 12, 303
Klezmer, 211, 212
Kligman, 54, 83, 86, 88, 113, 267, 303
Klinberg, 231, 303
Klingbajl, 118, 303
Klomel, 303
Kluska, 83, 85, 86, 100, 142, 186, 195, 196, 267, 268, 303
Knobel, 240, 303
Kochen, 11, 18, 25, 27, 29, 51, 138, 277, 281, 304
Kohen, 27, 80, 85, 112, 138, 140, 144, 224, 304, 319
Kopel, 20, 27, 59, 199, 304
Kopf, 4, 117, 118, 188, 304
Korman, 113, 280, 304
Kornfeld, 276, 277, 304
Korngold, 113, 152, 280, 305

Korzminski, 305
Koswicki, 305
Koussevitsky, 242, 245
Kowalski, 37, 101, 305
Kozowski, 62, 72, 73, 305
Krakauer, 52, 209, 305
Krauze, 34, 35, 85, 90, 305
Kreczmark, 240
Krenski, 63, 305
Krochmal, 102
Krystal, 18, 111, 185, 305
Kupczik, 272, 273, 288
Kupef, 305
Kuperberg, 11, 30, 113, 277, 305
Kuzminski, 245
Kwekzylber, 11, 305

L

Ladowski, 153, 274, 275, 305, 306
Lajbeniew, 167
Lajchter, 53, 84, 133, 306
Laks, 231, 279, 306
Landau, 109, 254, 306
Lanman, 306
Lapa, 11, 306
Lederman, 231, 306
Leftkowich, 251
Lemberg, 224, 306
Lemels, 24, 306
Lender, 231, 306
Lenman, 247
Lerer, 115, 306
Leszec, 118, 153, 306
Levi, 251
Lew, 88, 123, 126, 138, 186, 202, 306
Lewartowska, 117, 306
Lewartowski, 53, 97, 98, 109, 118, 142, 185, 267, 268, 306, 307
Lewensohn, 262
Lewensztajn, 20, 60, 61, 116, 216, 307
Lewi, 18, 27, 31, 55, 119, 138, 206, 207, 226, 229, 232, 256, 270, 307
Lewin, 56, 307
Lewinzon, 27, 33, 307
Lewkowicz, 152, 191, 267, 268, 307
Liberman, 153, 307
Licht, 261, 307
Lichtensztajn, 85, 86, 275, 307

Lifszicz, 267, 268, 307
Lifszycz, 18, 84, 185, 307
Ligin, 254, 307
Lipko, 153, 308
Lis, 10, 11, 308
Lisman, 279, 308
Litauer, 152, 308
Littauer, 54, 308
Lodzki, 24, 25, 34, 144
Lubliner, 110, 308
Ludwig, 110, 308
Luft, 153, 308
Lusinski, 147, 148, 149, 308

M

Machtinger, 280
Machtynger, 18, 116, 186, 270, 271, 276, 308
Majerczik, 308
Majerson, 270, 271, 308
Majewski, 308
Majfeld, 37, 308
Majtles, 242, 308
Majzel, 37, 180, 181, 182, 308
Malianski, 153, 308
Maliniak, 152, 308
Manela, 4, 27, 37, 81, 153, 207, 208, 224, 272, 273, 308, 309
Mantel, 270, 309
Marberg, 152, 309
Margaliot, 144, 309
Markowicz, 25, 233, 270, 309
Marmont, 11, 309
Marszilik, 213
Marynka, 85, 309
Mauerberger, 309
Maurberger, 34, 90, 261, 309
Mazor, 246
Mazupe, 153, 309
Mazur, 309
Mejer Jechiel, 309
Mejerczik, 167
Mendel, 153, 309
Mendelbaum, 231, 309
Mendelewicz, 20, 309
Mengel, 118, 309
Merber, 90, 110, 133, 169, 309
Mickiewicz, 116
Mickiwicz, 309

Micnmacher, 29, 79, 154, 309, 310
Mieckiewicz, 248
Mieckowicz, 211
Mikolaiczik, 246
Mikolajczik, 310
Minc, 32, 68, 69, 128, 153, 231, 270, 310
Mincberg, 90, 185, 310
Miodowicz, 152, 310
Miszpienki, 152, 310
Mitelman, 32, 35, 310
Mora, 240, 310
Mordkowicz, 25, 310
Mordokowicz, 116, 310
Morgensztern, 25, 310
Moskowicz, 153, 186, 270, 271, 310, 311
Moszczicki, 207, 310
Moszenberg, 12, 29, 32, 48, 51, 152, 201, 310, 311
Moszkowicz, 27, 76, 140, 153, 184, 310, 311
Moszkowski, 11, 12, 311
Muszkat, 311

N

Naftali, 124, 198
Narotowicz, 101, 311
Nechustai, 305
Nechustaj, 4, 311
Nechusztai, 113
Nibilski, 61, 104, 105, 106, 311
Nicolai I, 13
Nicolas I, 9
Nietzsche, 205
Nikolewicz, 194
Nowak, 51, 53, 193, 194, 261, 311
Nowakowski, 311

O

Oberman, 72, 100, 153, 311
Oberzanski, 21, 311
Opatowski, 118, 311
Oppenhajmer, 311
Oppenheimer, 257
Orbajtl, 18, 19, 201, 312
Orbajtl-Rozenberg, 120, 311
Orzszkowa, 249
Ostrowicz, 53, 89, 186, 312
Oszerowicz, 277, 279, 312

P

Pachel, 116, 312
Paczanower, 80, 312
Paczke, 53
Paparsztak, 152, 312
Papiwski, 312
Paradystal, 51, 53, 65, 131, 132, 133, 312
Partinski, 152, 312
Paserman, 27, 152, 186, 191, 312
Pelc, 78, 83, 87, 88, 89, 197, 202, 226, 291, 312
Peled, 1
Pelwa, 50, 53
Pelz, 251
Penkalla, 41
Perelman, 33, 51, 53, 131, 312
Peretz, 203
Perl, 251, 319
Pffefer, 177, 178, 179, 180, 181, 182, 183, 184, 198, 200, 291, 312
Piasecki, 20, 312
Piekarski, 52, 53, 57, 90, 95, 152, 312
Pienkowicz, 270, 271, 312
Pieskogorski, 267, 312
Pietrowski, 152, 313
Pilsudski, 45, 46, 139, 149, 220, 313
Pinies, 157, 313
Pinkusowicz, 277, 279, 313
Piotrkowski, 83, 152, 313
Piotrowski, 24, 138, 313
Piwko, 116, 313
Poksziwinski, 246
Polak, 34, 110, 313
Pomeranc, 11, 313
Poriszkwicz, 313
Posloszni, 267, 268, 276, 277, 279, 313
Potasznik, 112, 113, 313
Poznanski, 24, 168, 238, 313
Prajs, 126, 242, 313
Praposzinski, 276, 313
Praszowski, 35, 313
Preis, 255
Prince Joachim, 257
Priwlan, 153, 313
Proszkowski, 246, 313
Proszowski, 225, 231, 313
Prybulski, 71, 109, 314
Prylucki, 136, 183, 205, 314
Pucacz, 314
Pukacz, 29, 152
Puriszkewicz, 259

R

Rabinowicz, 166, 167, 187, 253, 277, 314
Rachum, 120, 314
Rackiewicz, 242
Raczkiewicz, 314
Radkiewicz, 245
Rafalowicz, 86, 126, 138, 314
Rafelkes, 113, 314
Rajter, 231, 314
Rajzler, 58, 212, 314
Rajzman, 18, 67, 68, 82, 85, 89, 133, 140, 152, 185, 194, 195, 270, 314, 315
Rapaport, 24, 85, 99, 126, 127, 128, 138, 154, 155, 186, 199, 315
Rapoport, 228
Rappaport, 261
Rawicki, 131, 132, 133, 315
Rebbe'le, 171, 172, 173, 315
Rechcman, 27, 32, 315
Recht, 153, 231, 315
Rechtsman, 232, 315
Rembiszewski, 20, 24, 57, 110, 113, 277, 315
Renkoszynski, 119, 315
Riger, 180, 181, 315
Rimont, 315
Romberg, 270, 315
Rondberg, 29, 315
Ross, 272, 273, 315
Rotbrad, 316
Rotenberg, 25, 27, 52, 59, 90, 96, 97, 120, 169, 185, 202, 267, 316
Rotensztrajch, 141, 316
Roterband, 153, 316
Rotkowski, 271, 316
Rotman, 20, 25, 34, 75, 85, 316
Rotszild, 80, 152, 153, 316
Rozanski, 236
Rozen, 57, 316
Rozenberg, 20, 24, 52, 55, 119, 120, 133, 140, 142, 152, 176, 195, 196, 267, 268, 316, 317
Rozenberg-Orbajtl, 316
Rozenblum, 83, 86, 104, 107, 108, 317
Rozencwajg, 231, 270, 271, 317
Rozenholc, 18, 317
Rozenkranc, 112, 317

Rozenman, 237
Rozenszafir, 272, 273, 315
Rozensztrich, 148, 317
Rozenwald, 90, 115, 317
Rozmajti, 279, 317
Rozmarin, 141, 317
Rubinek, 20, 317
Rubinsztajn, 153, 317
Rudel, 27, 61, 118, 120, 209, 317
Rurzanski, 317
Rusek, 77, 317
Rymont, 116
Rzelinski, 78, 317
Rzendowski, 32, 317
Rzeromski, 317
Rzetelni, 128, 317
Rzetelny, 127, 317
Rzok, 18, 317
Rzromski, 249
Rzylony, 61, 209, 317
Rzymnowoda, 60, 225, 226, 317
Rzyto, 277, 318

S

Sapir, 231, 318
Sara Chana, 24
Saski, 40, 217, 318
Sejnes, 271, 318
Sercarz, 140, 224, 318
Serwetnik, 37, 318
Sforim, 203, 215
Shabtai Tzvi, 51
Shalom Aleichem, 58, 172, 213
Shneiur, 119
Sienkiewicz, 116
Sienkowicz, 318
Sifraj Kohen, 319
Sigmund I, 9
Singerman, 257
Sirkis, 122, 318
Skorecki, 113, 318
Skura, 32, 318
Slawatycki, 152, 318
Slimowicz, 270, 318
Sliwa, 246
Slonimsky, 157
Slowcki, 248
Smulka, 148, 318

Sobczinski, 242, 245, 247
Soczinski, 318
Sofer, 318
Sokolow, 100, 157
Sokolowski, 85, 186, 228, 318
Solnik, 280, 318
Solrz, 278, 318
Sosnowski, 152, 318
Sowczinski, 318
Sowkower, 168, 318
Spiegel, 251
Spinoza, 205
Staszewski, 127, 267, 318
Sternzys, 154, 318
Stoliapin, 146
Strawczinska, 277
Strawczinski, 53, 61, 116, 137, 225, 277, 278, 279, 280, 318, 319
Strozberg, 127
Subcinski, 235
Sukenik, 82, 319
Szac, 34, 119, 319
Szafir, 152, 198, 319
Szajbler, 24, 319
Szajnfeld, 24, 27, 126, 152, 168, 169, 185, 319
Szalit, 83, 88, 319
Szapira, 273
Szapiro, 12, 20, 153, 272, 273, 276, 319
Szaragder, 259
Szcedrowicki, 319
Szefer, 70
Szeftel, 35, 319
Szenker, 277, 319
Szif, 166, 319
Szindler, 225, 226, 319
Szlamowicz, 152, 320
Szliwa, 320
Szmulewicz, 20, 32, 320
Sznidski, 110
Szofman, 98, 306, 320
Szor, 106, 320
Szorer, 110, 320
Szpigiel, 225, 320
Szpilman, 111, 112, 211, 320
Szprechman, 274, 320
Szrajber, 63, 320
Szrogroder, 37, 320
Sztajnhauer, 270, 320

Sztark, 147, 320
Sztarke, 20, 320
Sztern, 24, 320
Szternfeld, 279, 320
Szternszos, 153, 320
Sztrosberg, 27, 320
Sztrozberg, 75, 85, 153, 320
Sztunke, 191, 192, 198, 320
Szugierman, 270, 271, 320
Szulman, 276, 277, 320
Szwianski, 20, 321
Szwiantoslawski, 208
Szwicer, 198, 321
Szydlowski, 153, 321
Szymszon, 109, 321

T

Tabenkin, 113, 321
Tauber, 321
Tauman, 23, 176, 185, 187, 321
Tencer, 116, 152, 321
Tenenbaum, 19, 23, 25, 118, 152, 170, 321
Tenenwurcel, 116, 321
Tenwurcel, 153
Teomim, 144, 321
Trager, 229, 321
Trajman, 176, 321
Twerski, 161, 186, 321, 322
Twersky, 167, 261, 266
Tykociner, 322

U

Ubszani, 42, 322

V

von Hecht, 232

W

Wachsberg, 255, 257, 258, 260, 261
Wagmajster, 148, 322
Wajcman, 20, 153, 322
Wajnberg, 231, 322
Wajnberger, 275, 322
Wajncwajg, 276, 277, 322
Wajnryb, 32, 76, 83, 140, 186, 241, 322
Wajnsztok, 118, 276, 279, 322
Wajntraub, 25, 152, 322

Wajs, 12, 322
Wajsbaum, 153, 322
Wajsbrot, 12, 127, 277, 322
Wajsman, 153, 322
Waksberg, 19, 52, 133, 322, 323
Waksman, 127, 323
Waldberg, 186, 323
Walden, 215, 323
Wald-Liprent, 231, 323
Wargon, 57, 323
Wasser, 154, 323
Wasserman, 12, 323
Welisz, 138, 323
Wengrad, 277, 323
Werman, 33, 323
Westerman, 323
Wigan, 270, 323
Wiggins, 273, 323
Wikinski, 27, 323
Wilk, 323
Wilner, 57, 90, 228, 323
Winograd, 323
Winogrodzki, 277, 323
Wirzewa, 72, 81, 153, 323
Wiszlic, 236, 243, 324
Wisznicki, 241, 324
Witlin, 118, 120, 324
Wlodliprant, 324
Wlodwer, 24, 324
Wloszczowski, 29, 324
Wolman, 18, 51, 53, 59, 65, 66, 68, 71, 89, 105, 110, 122, 227, 324
Wulf, 176, 324

Y

Yannai, 117

Z

Zagajski, 18, 82, 86, 87, 88, 89, 90, 95, 184, 185, 186, 195, 199, 228, 242, 324
Zageiski, 260
Zagiski, 250, 252
Zagorski, 245, 324
Zaherman, 153, 324
Zajde, 52, 90, 186, 275, 276, 277, 324
Zajfman, 111, 113, 189, 190, 275, 324, 325
Zakaj, 325
Zalcberg, 31, 228, 325

Zalcer, 12, 80, 325
Zalcman, 118, 325
Zalewski, 276, 325
Zauberman, 231, 325
Zauerman, 27, 153, 325
Zelicki, 242, 325
Zelinger, 119, 325
Zerubavel, 113, 325
Zilberberg, 85, 325
Zilber-Ewen, 186, 325
Zilberszac, 12, 325
Zinger, 114, 115, 325
Ziunczkowski, 24, 201, 325

Zlotnik, 100, 279, 325
Zloto, 27, 86, 112, 117, 120, 140, 187, 188, 201, 325, 326
Zylberman, 32, 326
Zylberspic, 29
Zylberszlag, 33, 326
Zylberszpic, 23, 152
Zylbersztajn, 12, 27, 32, 37, 51, 100, 110, 152, 231, 270, 277, 279, 326
Zylerszpic, 326
Zyngerman, 34, 326
Zyromski, 116
Zysman, 111, 326

Appendix

This appendix is not part of the original Yizkor Book

The Painter Gershon Iskowitz

A Kielce Native

By: Irv Osterer

Gershon Iskowitz, Painter of Light book cover. Book by: Adele Freedman; Public domain.

Online images were used to guide drawings. Original compositions by Irv Osterer

Iskowitz portrait collage
Iskowitz, 1982
Gershon Iskowitz: A Retrospective • January 23-March 7, 1982. Poster printed by the Art Gallery of Ontario.
Collection: Irv Osterer
Gershon Iskowitz Foundation logo
Gershon Iskowitz tombstone, Mount Sinai Cemetery, Toronto, ON. Photo: Lauren Robilliard

GERSHON ISKOWITZ RCA (1919–1988), one of Canada's most venerated artists, was born in Kielce.

His parents hoped he would become a rabbi but recognized after several unhappy years in *yeshiva* that his passion was art. His father encouraged this talent by creating a studio space in the family home where he could draw and paint. At a young age he was creating posters for Kielce theaters in exchange for movie tickets. He also gained some recognition for fine portraits and caricatures of family and friends.

He was accepted into the Academy of Fine Arts in Warsaw and arrived there in August 1939, only to return to Kielce when the Nazis invaded the city. Seven months later he and his family joined the city's Jewish community, as well as many Jews from surrounding towns and villages in a ghetto. Some 25,000 people were forced to live in a few dense city blocks surrounded by barbed wires and locked gates. Hunger and typhoid were rampant, leading to many deaths. In several post war watercolour, gouache, and ink pieces now in the National Galley of Canada, Iskowitz recorded several incidents that bore witness to these terrible events.

When the Nazis liquidated the Kielce ghetto in August 1942, many sick, elderly and disabled Jews were murdered. Others were sent by train to concentration camps. Iskowitz's parents, brother Itchen, and sister Devorah perished at Treblinka. Gershon and a surviving brother Yosl were sent to the Henryków labour camp and, in then in early fall 1943, to Monowitz-Buna, one of the three main sites of the Auschwitz complex. There, Iskowitz's left arm was tattooed with the prisoner number B-3124.

He recalled his experiences in Auschwitz in detail to author Adele Freedman (*Gershon Iskowitz:Painter of Light*). In spite of his hunger and pain, he scavenged art materials. German guards were impressed with his skill and paid him for drawings with scraps of food. At night, he sketched the horrors he witnessed and hid these drawings under loose boards in the barracks. Sadly, these works are lost. In 1944, he survived the 250 km death march to Buchenwald but brother Yosl was not among the marchers and probably perished in Auschwitz.

Iskowitz continued to draw in Buchenwald, but only two sketches have survived – *Condemned*, c.1944–46 (National Gallery of Art, Ottawa) and *Buchenwald,* c.1944–45 (McMaster Museum of Art). Towards the end of the war, Iskowitz made a desperate attempt to escape but was shot and left for dead by Nazi pursuers. Friends brought him back to the barracks, where he remained until American troops liberated the camp. The injury left Iskowitz with a pronounced limp for the rest of his life.

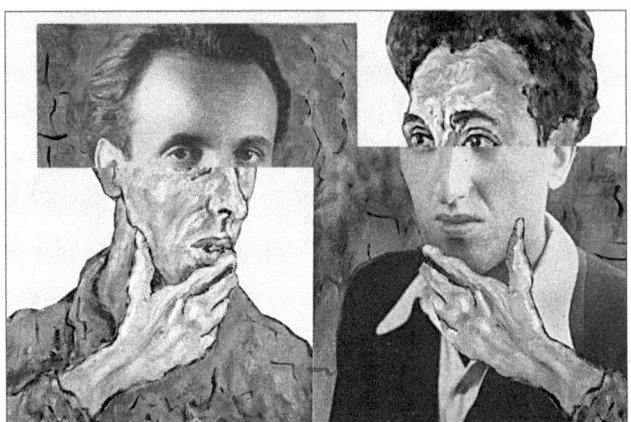

Collage of Iskowitz with self portrait

After being liberated, he spent time at the Feldafing Displaced Persons Camp and resumed painting. There is unconfirmed anecdotal evidence that he may have audited courses at the Academy of Fine Arts in Munich.

Iskowitz had no home or family to return to and would have no doubt heard about the terrible post-war pogrom in Kielce in 1946. Understandably, he decided to leave Europe and build a new life in North America. After many immigration hurdles, he was met by a maternal uncle and other members of his extended family in Toronto. An aunt invited him to stay with her until he got settled. Over the next few years, Iskowitz moved from one boarding house to another. He did casual jobs and visited the local galleries.

Iskowitz' early post-war drawings and canvases leaned heavily on memories of his camp experiences and of Kielce before the Nazis. This was followed by a period during which he painted portraits and still lifes. To support his artistic practice, Iskowitz taught evening art classes at Holy Blossom Temple and did some commissioned works.

Toronto's Jewish community followed Iskowitz's career, and his exhibitions were reviewed in the *Canadian Jewish News*. He was not openly observant, but maintained social connections with his Jewish contemporaries. Iskowitz became friends with watercolourist Eric Freifeld and painted his portrait in 1955. He was acquainted with Abba Bayefsky who was a distinguished Canadian war artist.

Iskowitz was impressed and inspired by the Canadian landscape and soon began attending a series of painting summer schools in McKellar, Ontario. Here, artists mentored students in exchange for food and lodgings. He attended life drawing classes at the *Artist's Workshop* in

Toronto and had his first exhibition with the *Canadian Society of Graphic Art* (CSGA) in 1954, selling two ink and watercolour pieces for $300 each — the highest price paid for any work at this show. Through his affiliation with the CSGA, Iskowitz met many of the most influential artists in Metro Toronto and had his first solo exhibition at the Hayter Gallery in 1957. Iskowitz felt that Canada was now his home and became a citizen in 1959.

By 1964, Iskowitz could afford to rent studio space — a two room apartment along Spadina Avenue, then the centre of the Jewish garment district. He could easily walk to Gwartzman's Art Supplies at 448 Spadina, where he purchased his paint and canvas.

With the opening of new avant-garde spaces such as the Isaacs Gallery in the early 1960s and the emergence of *Painters Eleven*, art and artists became very fashionable in Toronto. Gallery openings were highly publicized events. Iskowitz was introduced to Walter Moos (1926–2013), a well-connected and influential German-born Jewish émigré who had opened a gallery in trendy Yorkville. Moos developed an active professional relationship with Iskowitz that lasted for well over two decades, managing all aspects of the artist's career and finances. Iskowitz's first of many exhibitions at Gallery Moos was held in October 1964.

A 1967 trip to Churchill, Manitoba, became a turning point in the artist's mature period. Iskowitz' interest in aerial perspective prompted him to charter an aircraft for a bird's eye view of the Hudson Bay coastline. He repeated this exercise at different locations in Canada's north. in Art historian Ihor Holubizky's (*Gershon Izkowitz Life& Work*, Art Canada Institute, 2019) extraordinary definitive study about the artist and his work, the author identifies and articulates why the Iskowitz changed direction from representational to abstract art. He contends that Iskowitz was simply fascinated and amazed by the vast spaces and brilliant crystal-clear colours seen through the scattered cloud cover during his aerial adventures. Iskowitz had experienced Auschwitz and the loss of everything dear to him. He endured unimaginable cruelty at the hands of the supposedly sophisticated people of Germany, Austria and Poland. The beauty of the vast, unspoiled Canadian landscape must have been truly inspiring. This revelation was as Barry Lord so perfectly said in a 1970 review for the *Toronto Star* — "Color as Proof of Survival."

On his return to Toronto, he painted much larger works. He produced a series of *Seasons* canvases — *No. 1* and *No. 2* whose titles were inspired by Vivaldi's violin concertos — music Iskowitz loved and often listened to as he worked. Both were included in his solo exhibition at the Moos in 1970. *Seasons No. 1* was subsequently purchased by the National Gallery of Canada. That year *Seasons No. 2* was selected for the exhibition *Eight Artists from Canada* organized by the National Gallery for the Tel-Aviv Art Museum in Israel.

A very active market had developed for Iskowitz's luminous abstract landscapes. His regular exhibitions at Gallery Moos garnered critical acclaim and impressive sales. Iskowitz was selected for travelling exhibitions across Canada, including to the Art Gallery of Nova Scotia and the Glenbow Museum.

In 1972, he and sculptor Walter Redinger represented Canada at the very prestigious *Venice Biennale.* Iskowitz's selection affirmed that he was considered an artist of considerable stature in his new homeland.

He was elected a member of the *Royal Canadian Academy of Arts* in 1974. Several important group and solo exhibitions in New York followed, with a *New York Times* review calling him an artist that is "extremely gifted in selecting and arranging lyrically beautiful colours that coalesce into a radiant composition." (David L. Shirley review, *New York Times,* May 1980)

In 1977, he received the *Queen's Silver Jubilee Medal* and was one of the artists featured in the *Seven Canadian Painters* show that toured Australia and New Zealand.

Iskowitz with one of his luminous canvases in 1982

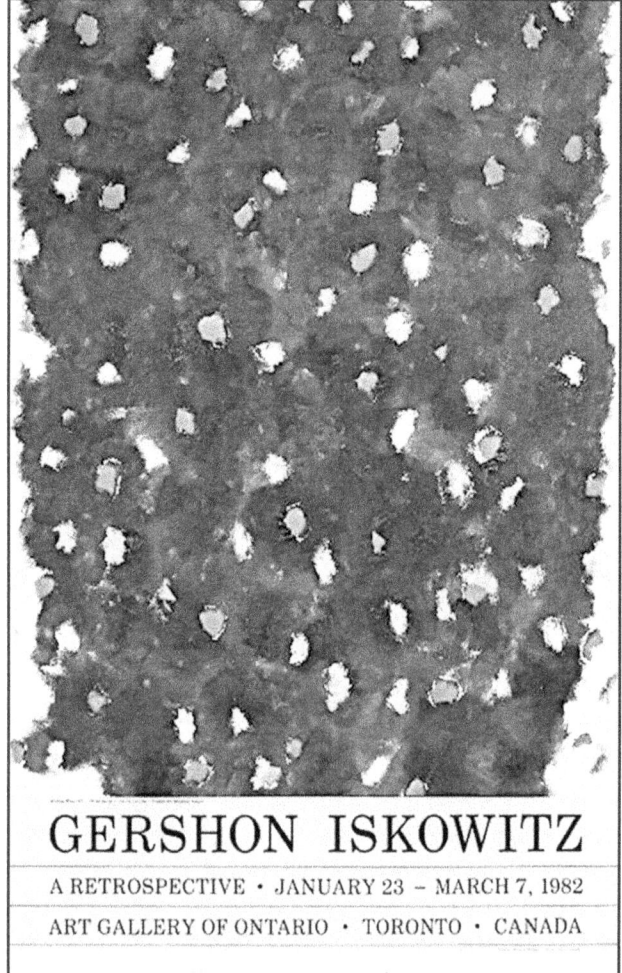

Poster printed by the Art Gallery of Ontario for Iskowitz's 1982 Retrospective in Toronto.

In 1982, Gershon was honoured by the Art Gallery of Ontario with a 40-year retrospective of his work.
In gratitude for the Canada Council grants he had received,

GERSHON ISKOWITZ FOUNDATION

he established the *Gershon Iskowitz Foundation* in 1985. Iskowitz wanted his estate to provide financial support to artists through an annual $25,000 prize. He stated:

> **It's very important to give something so the next generation can really believe in something.** I think the artist works for himself for the most part. Every artist goes through stages of fear and love or whatever it is and has to fight day after day to survive like everyone else. Art is a form of satisfying yourself and satisfying others. We want to be good and belong. That goes through history; we're striving for it.
>
> *Gershon Iskowitz Foundation*

On January 26, 1988, Gershon Iskowitz passed away. He was only 68 years old. His death was due to his deteriorating physical and medical condition. Sadly, he has no close family. A memorial service was held at Benjamin's Park Memorial Chapel in Toronto, where the attending rabbi and Walter Moos spoke at the service.

Gershon Iskowitz is buried at the Mount Sinai Memorial Park, in Toronto. On his *matzevah,* is inscribed the simple but most appropriate epitaph — *Painter of Light.*

Irv Osterer
Ottawa, Canada

Irv is a graduate of the Ontario College of Art and has had a life long interest in Jewish artists and their work. He was a contributing editor to *Arts and Activities Magazine* and retired in 2020 after a forty year career as a fine arts administrator and teacher of applied design and visual art.

Art historian Ihor Holubizky, a Trustee of the Gershon Iskowitz Foundation, explores the artist's career in *Gershon Iskowitz: His Life & Work,* a superb book published in print and virtually in 2019, under the auspices of *The Canadian Online Art Book Project,* a digital library commissioned by the Art Canada Institute.

For those wishing to gain a deeper appreciation of Iskowitz's work, it must be seen in colour. Holubizky's efforts can be downloaded free of charge in English or French in PDF format from the Art Canada Institute website —

https://www.aci-iac.ca/art-books/gershon-iskowitz/sources-and-resources/#selected-reviews

---

Freedman, Adele. *Gershon Iskowitz: Painter of Light.* Merritt Publishing Company Limited, 1982.

Lord, Barry. "Color as Proof of Survival" in the *Toronto Daily Star,* February 20, 1970.

"Gershon Iskowitz" www.gallery.ca
https://iskowitzfoundation.ca/
https://en.wikipedia.org/wiki/Gershon_Iskowitz

www.ingramcontent.com/pod-product-compliance
Lightning Source LLC
Chambersburg PA
CBHW082004150426
42814CB00005BA/226

9781962054041